# JOSEF VON STERNBERG

# ASPECTS OF FILM

*Advisory Editor*
Garth S. Jowett

# Josef von Sternberg

## Herman G. Weinberg

**ARNO PRESS**
A New York Times Company
New York ● 1978

Editorial Supervision: **MARIA CASALE**

———◆———

Reprint Edition 1978 by Arno Press Inc.

Copyright © 1966 by Editions Seghers

Reprinted by permission of Herman G. Weinberg

ASPECTS OF FILM
ISBN for complete set: 0-405-11125-8
See last pages of this volume for titles.

Manufactured in the United States of America

———◆———

**Library of Congress Cataloging in Publication Data**

Weinberg, Herman G
    Josef von Sternberg.

    (Aspects of film)
    Reprint of the 1967 ed. published by  Dutton,
New York.
    Filmography:  p.
    Bibliography:  p.
    1.  Von Sternberg, Josef, 1894-1969.  I.  Series.
[PN1998.A3V618 1978]    791.43'0233'0924    77-11388
ISBN 0-405-11137-1

# JOSEF VON STERNBERG

PYGMALION AND GALATEA
Sternberg and Dietrich on the set
of *The Scarlet Empress* (1934)

# Josef von Sternberg

A Critical Study by

## Herman G. Weinberg

*A Dutton*  *Paperback*

New York
E. P. DUTTON & CO., INC.
1967

To my daughter, Gretchen,
faithful companion of my "thousand and one nights" of filmgoing.

H.G.W.

## ACKNOWLEDGMENTS

The author would like to thank the following for their collabora-
tion on this book: Mlle. Michèle Firk and the Messrs. Henri Agel,
Michel Aubriant, Peter Balbusch, Kirk Bond, Jean de Baroncelli,
Michel Cournot, Philippe Demonsablon, Philippe Esnault, Charles
Ford, Robert Florey, Charles Graves, René Jeanne, Ado Kyrou,
Andrew Sarris, and Jack Smith. Also, the publishing houses of Édi-
tions du Terrain Vague, Éditions Robert Laffont, and Éditions
Universitaires, and the publications *The Bystander, Film Courier,
Film Culture, Positif, Cahiers du Cinéma, France-Soir, Paris-Presse,
Le Monde, Le Nouvel Observateur*, and the Museum of Modern
Art for certain stills from their collection. Also, the Institut des
Hautes Études Cinématographiques.

The author wishes particularly to thank Mr. Pierre Lherminier,
who supervised the original French edition of this book for Éditions
Seghers and for selecting the French critical reviews. Also, Mr.
Herbert G. Luft for his help in establishing certain historical facts
in connection with Sternberg's Berlin period.

Finally, the author wishes to thank Mr. Josef von Sternberg, himself, for putting numerous documents from his personal archives at
my disposal and for checking the factual aspects of the manuscript.

H. G. W.

All notes and translations from the French by Herman G.
Weinberg.

# TABLE OF CONTENTS

## LIST OF ILLUSTRATIONS

# PROLOGUE

Everything is in the human face—all mysteries, all dreams and desires. The character behind the right face for the role reaches you with the speed of light. Compare Gerard van Honthorst's *Dionysus* with Caravaggio's *Bacchus*. It isn't necessary for Caravaggio to depict Bacchus in action doing "a Bacchic thing," as Honthorst is impelled to do by showing Dionysus pressing wine from grapes, to get the point across. Caravaggio does it simply in his portrayal of Bacchus's face. So expressive of the subject is it that he could even have omitted the vine leaves in his hair.

. . .

"In old Canton there once abounded a type of magician called 'bewitchers of the night,' who, with the help of lanterns and Bengal lights, cymbal music, burning incense, sweet nectars and balls of jade, which spectators were asked to rub between their fingers, played on the five human senses until they succeeded in casting their audience into a dream world that turned an ordinary evening into a night of fantasy and revelry."

—DR. FELIX MARTI-IBAÑEZ

"Only one kind of director is dangerous to an actor—the timid guy, the kind guy, the guy who is unsure. A tough guy who knows what he wants is no problem for a pro—you give him what he wants, and that's the end of it."

—PETER USTINOV

"There are no facts, only interpretations of facts."

—NIETZSCHE

"You use 7 people to paint a crowd—not 700."

—DEGAS

JOSEF VON STERNBERG

# I

Josef von Sternberg was born in Vienna (at Blumauer-
gasse 25—the house is still standing) on May 29, 1894,
of Austrian parents. At seven he was brought to the United
States, but subsequently returned to Vienna to attend
school. It was there, from Arthur Schnitzler, that he received
his first encouragement. He returned to the United States
where he eventually found work in the motion picture industry in Fort Lee, New Jersey, as a film-patcher for the
old World Film Company, gradually working himself up
to cutter, writer, assistant director and, finally, personal
advisor to William A. Brady, then general manager of the
World Film Company. When the United States entered
the First World War in 1917, Sternberg joined the Army
Signal Corps and was stationed at G.H.Q. in Washington,
D.C., where he made training and indoctrination films for
recruits. For his exemplary work he was cited by the War
College. Following the Armistice, he embarked on his *Wan-
derjahre*—a period he terms his apprenticeship—spent in
New York, England, and Hollywood, during which he
worked with such early directors as Hugo Ballin, Wallace
Worsley, Lawrence C. Windom, Roy William Neill, and
Émile Chautard.

It was Émile Chautard, the French director, who in 1921
first stimulated the young Sternberg during the filming by
Chautard of *The Mystery of the Yellow Room* from the
famous mystery novel by Gaston Leroux. Chautard, who
had previously won renown as a stage actor (he had appeared with Sarah Bernhardt in Paris), invited Sternberg
to watch the players through the camera's view-finder.
Chautard showed him how to put objects in front of the
camera in their proper perspective, thereby giving every
angle a perfect balance. "A long journey begins with a single

step," said Lao Tse (echoed many years later by Sternberg in his narration for *Anatahan*). This introduction to "framing the shot" was to become for Sternberg a very long and memorable journey, indeed, as he explored its possibilities, ultimately to become one of the screen's greatest masters of pictorial composition. Sternberg feels that the encouragement given him by Chautard (who was later to appear as an actor in two of Sternberg's films, as the French officer who speaks at the engagement reception of Amy Jolly and LeBessière in *Morocco* and as the dishonored French officer, Major Lenard, in *Shanghai Express*) helped him to a great degree in his determination to pursue his creative aspirations via the cinema.

In 1922 Sternberg found himself in England at the Twickenham Studios with the Alliance Film Company, working with Harold Shaw.

It was in this early formative period that a popular matinée idol of the day, Elliott Dexter, who was the star of a film, *By Divine Right* (1924), on which Sternberg was scenarist and assistant to director Roy Neill, suggested that a "von" be added to Sternberg's name, not only to enhance his screen credit but also to enhance the "artistic prestige" of the picture. "I was ennobled by Elliott Dexter," said Sternberg wryly years later. But the "von" stuck and few aristocrats have carried the noble prefix to their family name with the grace and patrician achievement of Sternberg. (By 1924 the antipathy to Germanic names and titles, so rife during and immediately after the war years in the United States [as Stroheim found out], had abated. Quite incidentally, there *is* an ancient noble family of von Sternbergs in Vienna.)

The *Wanderjahre* continued and now included Paris, Prague, Naples, Berlin, with intermittent forays of film work in London, Hollywood, and New York. On one such he was assistant to William Neill, in 1924, at the F.B.O. studios on Neill's production of *Vanity's Price*, starring Anna Q. Nilsson, adapted from a best-selling novel of the day, *Black Oxen*, by Gertrude Atherton, a story of synthetically preserved youth. The vogue of "rejuvenation" was all the rage. (Dr. Serge Voronoff and his grafting of young monkey glands on old people was as popular in the public fancy as any movie star!) The last scene of the film, given to Sternberg to direct after the director became unavailable, took place in the penumbral chiaroscuro of the operating amphitheatre of a hospital during a "rejuvenation" operation on a woman. Medical students are watching the operation under the glare of the surgical lamp from their gallery seats. Sternberg cross-cut the operation with close-ups of their reactions: one showed disgust, another leaned toward his colleague and leered, a third looked faintly amused. Long after this tawdry film was forgotten, this final scene was remembered. And with it came the first recognition of Sternberg as a director.

The idea of cutting away from an action to show reaction was to become a favorite device of directors, but seldom has it been used meaningfully, to *add* to the action or to comment on it. Years later, Sternberg was to repeat the device in the stunning scene of the reaction of the crowd in the Moroccan café at the initial entrance of Amy Jolly (Marlene Dietrich) in her man's formal evening dress . . . top hat, white tie, and tails . . . notably the marvelous mixed reaction of Legionnaire Tom Brown (Gary Cooper), perhaps the most memorable introduction of a new actress in the annals of the screen.*

In 1924, Sternberg was returning from one of his periodic European junkets on a cattle boat from London to New York, from which he was to continue by bus to Hollywood to start work for the F.B.O. (Film Booking Office) studios. It was on this return to Hollywood that he met George K. Arthur, a young British actor who was trying to break into the movies as a comedian and who had some $4800 to invest in a modest production venture he had in mind, something called *Just Plain Buggs*. Sternberg showed Arthur a scenario he himself had written, *The Salvation Hunters*.

*The Salvation Hunters* marked the debut of Sternberg as a director, as well as George K. Arthur as an actor, though

---

* One is reminded of Franz Farga's description (in *Violins and Violinists*, London, 1940) of a Paganini concert: "The spell ended and the applause began—with a vehemence never before heard in the Imperial ballroom. People shouted and yelled madly. The magician was still standing on the platform, his face unmoved. His mouth twisted into a wry smile and the glittering eyes, wearing a cunning look, seemed to be mocking the crowd of admirers for behaving so foolishly."

Budget—$4800. The project—*The Salvation Hunters*. What would the future hold? The young Sternberg flanked by his two players, George K. Arthur and Georgia Hale. The lonely beginning. (1924)

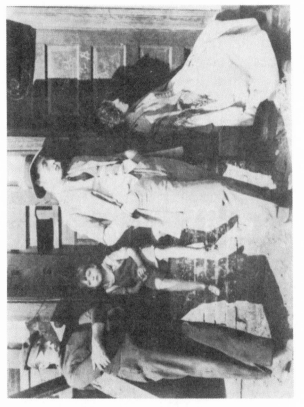

The dregs of the earth . . . the coward, the procurer, and the girl. One of the early scenes of *The Salvation Hunters*. (1924)

not as a comedian. Filmed in and around the mud-flats of San Pedro, south of the Los Angeles dockside wharves, the *leitmotif* was a dredge in San Pedro Bay, scooping up mud into a barge from the bay bottom, which haunted the lives of the film's three characters, a trio of derelicts. Doubtlessly influenced by *Greed* in its sordid realism, it split its viewers into two violently opposed camps—those who loathed it and those who were ecstatic. In the latter camp was Max Reinhardt, who declared, "It is inconceivable that such cinematic greatness could have come from America." Both Chaplin and Douglas Fairbanks also were enthusiastic, and Fairbanks bought it for their company, United Artists. Said Chaplin: "It gives me pleasure to recommend *The Salvation Hunters.* To me it revealed a spontaneous and admirable film technique, combined with artistic composition and rhythm of presentation. It is a great picture—and different." The English pianist, Elly Ney, and the Dutch conductor, Willem van Hoogstraten, said it was the best film they had ever seen. "The handling of the theme is almost symphonic, its simplicity puts it on a plane rarely attained in the motion pictures." "Wonderful!" exclaimed Morris Gest, the theatrical impresario. "I'm wiring Douglas Fairbanks and Mary Pickford tonight that I think *The Salvation Hunters* is the greatest compliment to the American movie public ever paid them by an American director. I was reminded of Gorky's *The Lower Depths* and felt that at last we had a Eugene O'Neill of the screen." It made several of the "Ten Best" lists of 1925. Some time afterwards, Chaplin, being asked to name the best films he had ever seen, replied, *"The Birth of a Nation, Intolerance, Hearts of the World,* and *The Salvation Hunters."* Chaplin not only took Sternberg's discovery, Georgia Hale, who played the girl in *The Salvation Hunters,* for the feminine lead in *The Gold Rush* but two years later paid him the compliment of entrusting the direction of one of his own productions, *The Sea Gull,* starring Edna Purviance, to Sternberg. Years later, after *The Blue Angel, Morocco, Dishonored,* Sternberg continued to announce himself in the full-page trade ads directors customarily inserted annually in the *Film Daily Year Book:* "Josef von Sternberg—Director of *The Salvation Hunters."* He never forgot his experiences in the mud-flats of San Pedro and what they meant to him. One does not forget one's first love. (In

Success . . . United Artists, represented here by Douglas Fairbanks, buys *The Salvation Hunters*. George K. Arthur smiles but the dour Sternberg still tries to peer into the future.

the 1950's he designed for himself and his family a luxurious bungalow on the cliffs of the New Jersey palisades overlooking the Hudson River, directly above a dredge like the one in *The Salvation Hunters.*)

Now launched as a full-fledged director, Sternberg was asked by Mary Pickford to guide her in her next picture. It was Ernst Lubitsch who had guided Miss Pickford the year before in *Rosita,* a "Spanish romance" upon which they compromised after she rejected his wish to do *Marguerite and Faust* and he rejected her wish to do *Dorothy Vernon of Haddon Hall.* The result was neither "*echt*-Lubitsch," nor even "*echt*-Pickford," but she determined to try again with another brilliant new "foreign" director. Sternberg's first idea for her had marvelous pictorial possibilities—the world as seen in the imagination of a blind girl who has never seen it. But Miss Pickford did not like the idea of playing a blind girl. So Sternberg left for Pittsburgh to elaborate a story for her against the industrial background of that city. On his return, she asked him to wait before proceeding with the film and Sternberg refused. The project was abandoned. Obviously, the problems of the mechanical age did not interest Miss Pickford, nor did they suit her romantic style. Marshal Neilan replaced Sternberg.

Since MGM had the next option on his services, Sternberg went there to develop Alden Brooks's novel *Escape,* and to write the screenplay with Alice Deuer Miller. Starring Conrad Nagel, Renée Adoree, and Paulette Duval, and titled *The Exquisite Sinner,* the movie was completed in the Spring of 1926. It told the story of a rich young man's running away from a stifling home to live with the gypsies and of his family and fiancée's trying unsuccessfully to induce him to return. The setting is Brittany. It is described by Robert Florey (Sternberg's assistant on the film, and one of the few people who saw it) as "a high comedy almost too subtle for the screen." MGM did not like it and ordered it remade by one Phil Rosen, who managed what Sternberg had done (including his screenplay) beyond recognition. "The result," commented Sternberg years later, "was that they now had two ineffective films instead of one." The remake was called *Heaven on Earth,* today mercifully forgotten.

In the same year, Sternberg began a second film for MGM (under his eight-picture contract), *The Masked Bride,* star-

A contract with MGM follows, the result is *The Exquisite Sinner*—
"too exquisite" for L. B. Mayer, and they remake it. A scene from
the original version. (1925)

Pacific Coast Beach near Santa Monica, on location for *The Exquisite Sinner*. L. to R.—Robert Florey (special French assistant), Max Fabian (cameraman), Nick Grinde (assistant), Paulette Duval (actress), Sternberg, and the ubiquitous musicians to inspire the players with "mood" music, a charming Hollywood fixture of the Twenties.

ring Mae Murray. Florey, who again assisted on the production, says: "He shot only two reels before he became disgusted with his assignment, turned the camera to the ceiling and shot the studio rafters as his departing gesture to the film. But *what* two reels they were! No one saw them except L. B. Mayer and the gang, Sam Winston (Sternberg's cutter), Bill Levanway (MGM's head editor), Sternberg, and myself. Just as in the case of the marvelous first version of *The Exquisite Sinner*, if this one had been finished and kept intact at MGM, it would still be showing today in the ciné-clubs and film societies everywhere; it was a masterpiece. Sternberg never shot a foot of film indifferently. . . ." The contract was broken by mutual consent and the project turned over to Christy Cabanne. Rumors now flew about that the brooding young director with the Oriental mustache and ubiquitous cane was hard to handle and that he objected temperamentally to studio supervision of any kind. At any rate, Sternberg left for a European vacation, to allow Hollywood's attitude toward him to "cool off."

On his return, Chaplin asked him to direct a film intended to bring Chaplin's erstwhile leading lady, Edna Purviance, out of retirement. It was to have been her first serious film since the memorable *A Woman of Paris*, and it was the only occasion when Chaplin entrusted another director with one of his own productions. Titled *The Sea Gull* (no relation to the Chekov play), later titled *A Woman of the Sea*, the film, from an original tale by Sternberg, was a simple love story set against the background of the changing patterns of the sea, which were themselves used for psychological as well as atmospheric underscoring of the action. It was photographed largely on the seacoast of Monterey, California. When it was finished, Chaplin's reaction was that it was too sophisticated for general audiences, that they would not understand it. John Grierson, the eminent Scottish critic, said: "Even a masterful intuition cannot take a man everywhere, and Chaplin has, though I hate to say this, his blind spots. It is my guess, for example, that he is completely blind to the visual beauties of Von Sternberg's *Woman of the Sea*. This picture was made for him and Chaplin failed to release it. I think I know the reason, because I heard Chaplin go over his own version of it two nights before Sternberg showed it to me. Here was Chaplin concentrating on the human drama of the picture—

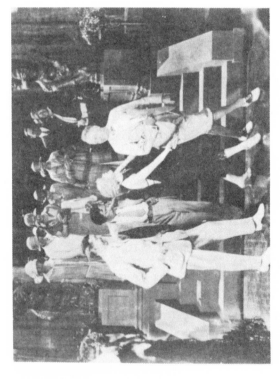

The second film for MGM is *The Masked Bride*, on a set of which Will Hays (first movie czar), Mae Murray, and Robert Z. Leonard disport themselves as the still dour Sternberg looks on. After several days he quit. *Where was the future?* (1925)

Chaplin, impressed with *The Salvation Hunters*, confides the direction of *The Sea Gull*, from another Sternberg story, to its author in a film designed as a starring vehicle for his loyal leading lady, Edna Purviance (second from right). (1926)

and on nothing else; here was Von Sternberg concentrating on the visual beauty of the picture—and on scarcely anything else! Chaplin's version was magnificent from a humanist point of view: it had feeling in it, emotion, movement: and I can still see him picture the scene in the fishing boat with the men sweating at the nets and the wind-blown hair and the wriggling fish. But beyond that Chaplin was not concerned and is, I believe, never concerned. The visual pattern of the masts and rigging, the pattern of sunlight on the drying nets, the sculpturesque pattern of the human figures were nothing to him. They were everything to Von Sternberg—too much everything! The irony of *Woman of the Sea* is that it is the most beautiful picture ever produced in Hollywood, and the least human. . . . If Chaplin had done it himself it would have been the most human, and, from a visual point of view, one of the least beautiful. There is the issue! Von Sternberg needs a great deal of what Chaplin has: Chaplin needs something of what Von Sternberg has."

"Two versions were made," says Florey. "Chaplin suggested changes for the second version to which Sternberg agreed, without compromising his original idea. The story was over the heads of the audience at the single preview it had in Beverly Hills. However, it would have pleased the movie elite, the 'Boeuf-sur-le-Toit' boys, Cocteau, Picabia, Buñuel, Dali, etc. It was extremely interesting and not as static as *The Salvation Hunters*. The photography was extremely good and Edna Purviance looked much better than in *A Woman of Paris*."

"The final version satisfied neither Chaplin nor Sternberg," commented Grierson. "It was still extraordinarily beautiful—but empty—possibly the most beautiful film I had ever seen." Three versions of the conflict were bruited about: (a) Chaplin didn't understand the film; (b) Eve Sothern outshone Edna Purviance as an actress; (c) Chaplin was upset because Sternberg had arranged the Beverly Hills preview on his own initiative.

Whatever the reasons were, Chaplin decided not to release it. Curiously, Chaplin makes no reference to this film in his autobiography.

Again Sternberg departed for Europe and on his return was approached by Paramount, to be an assistant director again. He accepted. His acceptance was to have notable results, for it led to an association with Paramount that was to last for eight years (1927–1935), during which he did most of his best work, including the discovery of Marlene Dietrich; work that was to make him world famous. When the studio had editing problems with Frank Lloyd's *Children of Divorce*, starring Gary Cooper, Clara Bow, and Einar Hanson, Paramount's production head, B.P. Schulberg, asked Sternberg to look at the picture and make suggestions for recutting. Sternberg saw the footage and declared it didn't just need recutting or even retakes but a completely new story approach. He agreed to do the rewriting, direct the additional scenes, and do the final editing. Half the original footage was discarded and the new half shot by Sternberg in three days of 20-hours-a-day shifts. Since most of the actors were busy on other assignments, he could work with them only when they were free—mostly at night. When the press saw *Children of Divorce* they picked out Sternberg's scenes to comment upon, particularly a sequence showing London's glittering Covent Garden conjured up almost overnight by Sternberg on the studio's back lot. *Children of Divorce* did much to dissipate the myth of Sternberg's intractability. He had salvaged a picture that had been condemned as worthless. The film went on to become a critical and box-office success. He had proved himself a director who could work swiftly and effectively and Schulberg now considered him for a major film, *Underworld*, from a screen original by Ben Hecht about Chicago gangsters and the quasi-Nietzschean world they inhabited. Erich Pommer, then also at Paramount, says that producers then under contract to Paramount were asked by Schulberg to give their opinions of Sternberg's qualifications for this assignment. Unanimously they recommended him for the job.

Early in 1927 Sternberg embarked on the filming of *Underworld* from a scenario written by himself, based on Hecht's 18-page story, which Hecht says he wrote in the form of a film-treatment with Arthur Rosson. Wrote Hecht in his autobiography, *A Child of the Century*: "I made up a movie about a Chicago gunman and his moll, called Feathers McCoy. As a newspaperman I had learned that nice people— the audience—loved criminals, doted on reading about their love problems as well as their sadism. My movie, grounded on this simple truth, was produced with the title, *Under-*

The future has arrived, in just one year . . . *Underworld*, with its swift, laconic style. The pattern for the gangster film is set. George Bancroft, Clive Brook, Evelyn Brent. (1927)

Just as Stroheim had rescued Zasu Pitts from slapstick comedies for *Greed*, Sternberg gave the genial Larry Semon his one chance in a straight role in *Underworld*. Here he is with Evelyn Brent at a gangster's ball.

*world.* It was the first gangster movie to bedazzle the movie fans and there were no lies in it—except for a half-dozen sentimental touches introduced by its director, Jo von Sternberg." Sternberg admits Hecht was not pleased with the picture and asked that his name be taken off the screen. Yet when the first Academy Awards presentations were made for 1927–28, it was Ben Hecht who won the writing "Oscar" for the "Best Original Screen Story." The film went on to become an enormous box-office success, for which Paramount gave Sternberg a $10,000 bonus. For the first time in film history, a theatre (the big new Paramount palace in New York) had to give midnight showings to accommodate the crowds. *Underworld* was a potent mixture of realism and poetry done in the vernacular of the period, and was to set the pattern for the whole cycle of American gangster films to come, though Fritz Lang may have anticipated this *genre* in his *Dr. Mabuse der Spieler* in 1922, with gangsters firing from escaping automobiles, and so on. At any rate, the *genre* it so eloquently established started a vogue that lasted an entire generation until the outbreak of the Second World War when gangsterism on a much bigger scale made the little criminals of *Underworld* seem petty indeed. But for the cinema, *Underworld* was a milestone in its progress toward maturity. Years later René Clair said in "Reflections on the Cinema" (London, 1953): "When the producers imposed on Sternberg the 'news-item' plot of *Underworld*, or on Feyder the *feuilleton* yarn of *Thérèse Raquin*, they did not suspect that these poor stories would give birth to the poignant screen tragedies we know."

Now the pet of Paramount, Sternberg undertook to fulfill a promise made to Erich von Stroheim to re-edit the latter's *The Wedding March*, which Paramount was releasing and which had been taken away from its director when his own edited version ran to what they regarded as an impossible length. Here, in Sternberg's own words, is what happened: "As I recall, both of us, von Stroheim and I, were under contract to Paramount, though he had finished *The Wedding March* and edited it long before I was assigned to cut it down to releasable length. We were friendly, he had repeatedly expressed admiration for my work. The company had told him to cut it down so that it could be released, and he said he could not. Thereupon it was suggested that others handle it, and, until my name was mentioned, he objected strenuously. He, himself, showed me the film (to my recollection it included everything he intended to show). He asked me personally to take over the assignment, and I did so without any protest on his part. I told him precisely what I would shorten; we were friendly before, during, and afterwards. . . . I showed him the shortened version and he thanked me. Had he objected to anything, I would not only have restored the film to its original length but would have refused to have anything more to do with it. I am explicit about this for it seems to be generally thought that I edited his work without his O.K., which is something I would not have done under any circumstances. . . . I had been strongly impressed with his earlier *Greed* . . . I know nothing about the division of the film into two parts. I never saw the film again and how it was finally shown is unknown to me."

Sternberg next turned to the writing of an original story for Emil Jannings, who, after his international successes in *The Last Laugh, Tartuffe, Faust,* and *Variety* (especially the latter, which Paramount released in the United States), was brought to Hollywood, where he made his debut in the maudlin *The Way of All Flesh,* a misbegotten attempt to combine his roles as the old porter in *The Last Laugh* with the virile robustness of his trapeze artist in *Variety.* Sternberg's story, *The Street of Sin,* was a Salvation Army tale set in the slums of London's Soho, and featured Fay Wray and Olga Baclanova. Jannings was cast as a Soho bully in .it and the direction was turned over to Mauritz Stiller, who had recently arrived from Sweden as the mentor of Greta Garbo, and who was out of a job after he and MGM broke up during the filming of her second American film, *The Temptress.*

The genesis of Sternberg's next directorial effort for Paramount was an anecdote casually told him by Lubitsch (who was also working at Paramount). It was the true story of an ex-Czarist general who, after the Revolution, drifted to Hollywood, like so many others, and found himself playing his own life role on a movie set. Contrary to the screen credits of the film, says Sternberg, Lajos Biro, John S. Goodrich, and Herman J. Mankiewicz had nothing to do with the story treatment or final screenplay of *The Last Command.* Characteristically, it was written by the director himself. The film gave Sternberg an opportunity to castigate the superficiality

The fall from power . . . The Grand Duke Sergius Alexander lords it over the Russian troops at the front. Emil Jannings in *The Last Command*, that bitter and ironic paragraph from World War I. (1928)

of Hollywood movie making, while initiating what was to become for him a favorite theme, the fall from power of a once formidable being. With the camera flexibility of G. W. Pabst's *Jeanne Ney*, *The Last Command* was a story within a story, told in flashback, exploiting the milieu of Hollywood itself, and great care was taken to separate the two layers of consciousness. It also provided Emil Jannings with his best American role as the proud Russian general who falls from power and grace through circumstances beyond his control.

The critical reception of *The Last Command* was delirious, each reviewer seemed to vie with the others in finding superlatives that would do ample justice to the film's dramatic power. Clearly Sternberg had captivated the popular imagination more completely and overwhelmingly than ever before. Among the first to congratulate him was Douglas Fairbanks: "A psychoanalyst would probably say that my deep enjoyment of *The Last Command* had its foundation in selfishness. And I can't deny that it was soul-warming to have the faith I've always had in you so beautifully justified—feeling, as I do, that I am, in a sense, your *pater in industria*. Can't tell you how fine I think the picture is with its movement, power, and depth of feeling. I know nothing finer in art or literature. Sincerest congratulations!" From Feodor Chaliapin came a telegram: "Saw *Last Command* yesterday. Have rarely experienced such artistic pleasure. Cannot refrain from congratulating you on your admirable work in this splendid production." "The Russian Revolution was not altogether in vain," said the London *Sunday Graphic*, "It has produced *The Last Command*, one of the greatest pictures ever screened." "It is the greatest film in the world. There is no qualifying sentence to that praise of *The Last Command*," wrote the London *Daily Sketch*. The Paramount Office in Berlin received the following wire from Warsaw: "The première of *The Last Command* was sold out to capacity. Screening attended by ministers and members of diplomatic corps. Jannings's work claimed to be better than anything seen before. For the first time in the history of Warsaw, speculators were selling tickets in front of the theatre at higher prices than box office. Many hundreds of people turned away because of lack of seats." In *Theatre Arts* magazine, New York, the "certain, structural touch of Sternberg" was analyzed. "Movement under his hand is not unrelated and

A refugee reduced to playing his former role in a film studio, with its lacerating comments on Hollywood superficialities. The fall from grace was to become a favorite theme of Sternberg. (Emil Jannings in *The Last Command*.)

haphazard, but is built up, tier upon tier, until the peak is attained in some dramatic climax. . . . And once again, as in *Underworld*, Sternberg shows himself a master of suggestion, which implies a willingness to concede the presence of constructive intelligence in his audience." So knowing a director as the late Preston Sturges called *The Last Command* perhaps the only perfect picture he had ever seen.

His favorite "femme fatale" of the period, Evelyn Brent (who was in both *Underworld* and *The Last Command*), was to serve again as the "fatal woman" of Sternberg's next film, *The Dragnet*, another gangster film. For the second time, Sternberg inserted a ballroom scene frenetic with flying confetti and paper streamers (previously seen in *Underworld*), which was to become a favorite pictorial element with him, subsequently demonstrated in *Dishonored* and *The Devil Is a Woman*.

That same year, 1928, Sternberg turned out the pictorially remarkable *Docks of New York*, which earned the praise of George Bernard Shaw. In it George Bancroft (who had become a favorite actor of Sternberg since *Underworld*, appearing in four of his films) moved with the grace of a ballet dancer, despite his heavy bulk, so integrated were his movements. Out of an imagination and sense of fantasy as vivid and evocative as Thomas Burke's evocations of London's Soho and Whitechapel in *Limehouse Nights* (and in an instinctive echo of the ancient Greeks who ordained that "every man owes five days a year to Dionysus"?), Sternberg conjured up a section of the Hoboken waterfront in the studio, complete with a dirty tramp steamer tied up to the dock, its smoke-filled saloons with their wooden staircases outside leading to the upstairs rooms of the cheap prostitutes, the steaming boiler-room in the ship's hold with the glistening bodies of the stokers manning the fire-ovens, the sweating faces of those laboring in front of red-hot coal and looking forward to shore leave, which meant cold beer and the soft, yielding arms of the saloon girls . . . all rendered in photography of the richest chiaroscuro. Except for a fleeting glimpse of the New York skyline and oil slicks on the lapping waters of the bay, *The Docks of New York* was wholly studio-made. The director felt that only on the studio stages could he control the infinite shades of black-and-white photography, which he had developed by this time to an art in

The juxtaposition of serpentine and confetti with characters who live dangerously has become a "high tessitura" of Sternberg's style. ( See *Underworld, Dishonored, The Devil Is a Woman*.) William Powell and Evelyn Brent in *The Dragnet*. (1928)

itself. With some of the scenes veiled in artificial mist or harbor fog, the pictorial composition had a dreamlike quality that could not have been obtained in a natural setting under the conditions imposed by the director. (The case of Tissé successfully photographing the harbor fog of Odessa for *Potemkin* was something else—it just happened, and Eisenstein said, "Shoot it!" It was a chance thing, like Eisenstein's chance coming upon the steps of Odessa and suddenly deciding to stage his massacre scene on them. Poetic license takes many forms.) "Half Hogarth, half Mack Sennett," wrote Thomas Quinn Curtiss of it in the Paris *Tribune* many years afterwards, after a showing at the Cinémathèque Française. "A film of pictorial brilliance, telling atmosphere, and some wonderful low humor." He compares it with another waterfront screen drama, *On the Waterfront*, Elia Kazan's film with Marlon Brando, and finds the latter dismally lacking in any unity or conviction in comparison. "From the humanistic standpoint," Curtiss wrote, "the performances are so incredibly good that players and characters seem one." The London *Daily Telegraph* went on to say, "It conveys, quite unobtrusively, a great moral lesson. By a hundred deft touches, Sternberg makes us poignantly aware of some vague, inarticulate longings for something better that may haunt human souls seemingly depraved beyond redemption." As for its technique, a critic of the time wrote: "Let us not forget that the silent film is actually being stifled by its own perfection. Carl Dreyer's *La Passion de Jeanne d'Arc* and Sternberg's *Docks of New York* prove this indubitably. What remains to be done? Repeat the technical triumphs, the wonderful lighting, the overwhelming settings, with actors denuded of staginess as were those who took part in it? No, we have demonstrably reached the culmination of one form of cinematic expression and if the sound film had not been invented, producers the world over would have been looking for something else. . . ."

The Dies Irae of the silent film was already tolling fitfully though its full clangor was not to drown out all else for another year. Made in the transition period from silence to sound, *The Case of Lena Smith*, like some other notable "last minute" silent films of the period, was obscured in the furore attendant upon the debut of the first sound films. It was Sternberg's first film with a Viennese setting, this time

"His world was a battlefield of light and dark," said Goethe of
Beethoven. The stoke-hold of a tramp steamer. Clyde Cook and
George Bancroft in *The Docks of New York.* (1928)

Sternberg with megaphone, directing a scene from *The Docks of New York*, that ciné-flower plucked from the grime of the lower depths. "The finest film I've ever seen," said Bernard Shaw. (1928)

Dante consigned carnal sinners only to the second circle of hell of the nine. Sternberg isn't even sure they belong to the first. Betty Compson was extraordinarily touching in *The Docks of New York*. Above all, Sternberg was a director of women. (George Bancroft as the stevedore on a spree.) (1928)

the *fin du siècle* Vienna (1894–1914), the severe caste-rid-
den citadel of anti-Semitism and reaction in Europe, which
despite its intoxication with Lehar's *The Merry Widow* and
its great annual Spring Flower Parade of the "upper ten
thousand" rolling in their fancy carriages through the Prater,
was termed by one of its most distinguished citizens, Sig-
mund Freud, "disgusting in the highest degree." So much for
"alt Wien," gay old Vienna and the already rotting Hapsburg
dynasty and its glittering panoply during its long, protracted
sunset. Fair it may have been to see from the outside (as
Winston Churchill remarked, looking back, in his *The
World Crisis*), but all its culture could not save it from the
Junkerism that held it in thrall until the incident at Sarajevo
and that fatal day in August, 1914 when the guns "gloriously" boomed. Against this bittersweet background, Sternberg told the pitiful story of a peasant girl who secretly
marries a profligate army officer, bears him a child, and becomes a servant in his father's house. When the father
attempts to take her child, she rails against him as a tyrant.
The callousness and prejudice of the officer class was limned
with unrelenting harshness, but with incisive psychological
insight, too, for the weak but well-meaning seducer of the
girl, helpless to help her when her child is placed in an
orphanage by his father, shoots himself. And the desperate
terror of Lena's flight from the orphanage with her child—
dirty, torn, and bloody, a fugitive from the law, making her
way back to her village in the country—is one of the great
searing passages in the cinema. "Lena's flight," wrote Dwight
Macdonald in the March, 1931, *Miscellany*, "is expressed by
the camera following her like a watchful eye as she moves
along a wall, hiding behind water pipes and shrinking into
dark corners. . . . Von Sternberg does not use his skill in
handling the camera to avoid coming to grips with his story.
His attack is direct, aggressive, bringing out all the power of
his theme, the love, nay, urge, of a mother for her child. . . .
'Note that most good films are characterized by very simple
themes and relatively uncomplicated action,' is a remark by
Pudovkin that applies well to *The Case of Lena Smith*. . . .
I regard it as the most completely satisfying American film
I have seen."

It was Sternberg's last silent film.

How would he make the transition to the sound film? Let

Finally Sternberg evokes the "Old Vienna" of his youth, but the rake-hell lieutenant-seducer and the pretty servant girl are no longer stock characters but creatures who suffer under Junker tyranny. His last silent film, *The Case of Lena Smith*. (1928—what a year for him!)

"*Wien, Wien, nur du allein . . . !*" Vienna, Vienna, only you . . . !
The paroxysmic escape of the young mother from a reformatory, in
search of her child. Dwight Macdonald has written lyrically of this
sequence. Esther Ralston in *The Case of Lena Smith*. (1928)

a telegram to Sternberg from the German director of *A Waltz Dream* fame, Ludwig Berger, one of the shining lights of Ufa, then also in Hollywood, answer: "I saw your film *Thunderbolt* and congratulate you with my heart. It is the first fully realized and artistically accomplished sound film ... Bravo!" *Thunderbolt* was a return by Sternberg to the milieu of the gangster film that he had made so uniquely his own. This time he told a prison story that was startling even for him in its brutality of theme and its all but unbearable suspense in the film's second half; it is set in the death house of a federal penitentiary where the merciless account of crime, revenge, and punishment grinds to a terrible halt when the gangster boss, "Thunderbolt," is led to the electric chair. There was no background music. The photography was cold and gray. It was a work of realism, unprettified in the slightest degree. *The Salvation Hunters* had been such a work. But *The Salvation Hunters* ended on a note of hope. *Thunderbolt* ends hopelessly. Had success made of the artist a pessimist? End of the first phase ...

The advent of the sound film and the resultant return to Germany from Hollywood of Emil Jannings (because of his bad English) and Erich Pommer (ordered to return by Ufa, to which he was still under contract) was to mark a turning point in Sternberg's career. Among Pommer's first tasks, as production head of Ufa, was to launch Jannings's return to the German screen in 1929 in the latter's first talking film.

Sternberg was sent for at the request of Jannings and on his arrival in Berlin was shown by Jannings a novel, *Professor Unrat*, a violent attack on Imperial Germany, written in 1905 by Heinrich Mann (brother of Thomas Mann), who had remained on the political left after the 1918 revolution. The book was a dissimulated attack on bureaucracy, symbolized by Professor Rat,* a model of bourgeois virtue and discipline with "feet of clay," who succumbs to the tempta-

---

* In German the name "Rat" has the connotation of "counsellor" but the Professor's students nickname him "unrat"—"unclean" (or even *merde*)—a classification for the stuffy bureaucrat, also. (Originally, G.W. Pabst had planned to film *Professor Unrat* but this didn't materialize. Jannings' first suggestion to Sternberg was a film on Rasputin, which Sternberg rejected.)

With his first sound film, Sternberg returns again to the *milieu* of *Underworld* and the gangster prototype set by George Bancroft. There was no background music, only source music, another innovation that was to become characteristic of him. *Thunderbolt.* (1929)

tions of a sluttish cabaret singer, for all his middle-class façade of respectability, and then goes on to become an important social figure. Pommer and Sternberg agreed that here were the possibilities for a strong human characterization by Jannings but the story itself would have to be rewritten. In the adaptation by Sternberg, the Professor Rat of the film is not the character in the book—Sternberg created a new character, a new "psychology," that was appropriate to the art of the film. What was good as literature would be lost in a literal interpretation and transposition to the screen. The last third of the novel was dispensed with altogether. Sternberg says that Robert Liebmann helped him with the German dialogue. Pommer says Carl Zuckmayer contributed some details. Karl Vollmoeller, who had previously accompanied Sternberg on a world tour, did some minor revisions on the script at Sternberg's request. Sternberg says he directed the picture from his own notes; there wasn't any "screenplay." Henry F. Pringle in his "Profile" of Sternberg in *The New Yorker* magazine of March 28, 1931, affirmed: "He interferes with his writers so much that scenarists avoid working with him when they can." Many things in the film were inserted by Sternberg that are not to be found in the book, such as the leitmotif of the apostle-clock admonishing the listener to practice "virtue and sincerity until the grave," the Professor's pet bird (to illustrate his loneliness), the silent clown who presages the Professor's becoming a clown himself, the wedding celebration, the jilted Professor, now a clown, imitating a rooster, the Professor's frenzied insanity when he sees Lola with her new lover, and his dazed return to his old classroom where he embraces his desk (symbol of his former dignity) in the grip of death. Characteristic of Sternberg was his reply to an interpretation by film students giving the Professor's loss of mind as being due to his humiliation rather than to his infatuation with Lola-Lola. "The loss of his mind was an invention of mine. It was to show his incapacity to deal with reality. I would not wish to defend this, as the pathology of insanity is not easily traced, nor does it necessarily follow an indulgence in foolish behavior. Insanity is due to many causes over which the victim has little control and it has afflicted many great men whose lives were exemplary. The study of insanity belongs to the specialist in psychiatry and not to the student of motion pictures."

Pommer wanted Lucie Mannheim for the role of the siren, Lola-Lola, and Jannings agreed, but Sternberg refused to accept the unglamorous Miss Mannheim for a picture that was costing Ufa a half-million dollars, for Germany a very high budget at that time. Heinrich Mann suggested his girl friend, the actress Trude Hesterberg, while Sternberg, meanwhile, was trying to sign Brigitte Helm, who wasn't available.

By chance, Sternberg saw Marlene Dietrich in a play, *Zwei Kravatten*, by Georg Kaiser, where he was supposed to watch Hans Albers, who had been suggested for the minor role of Mazeppa, the circus artist who steals Lola away from the Professor.

From the moment Sternberg noticed Dietrich on the stage he knew he had found his Lola, but neither she nor the heads of Ufa were sure she could do it. It took a lot of persuasion before she agreed to a screen test. Sternberg was pleased with it and Pommer, who always protected the artistic choice of his directors, approved the signing of Miss Dietrich.

Since the accent of the story was now changed from the Professor to Lola-Lola, the title of the film was changed from *Professor Unrat* to *The Blue Angel*, the name of the cabaret where she sang. Heinrich Mann realized that his literary contribution to the future success of this film would be insignificant compared to Sternberg's vision. Sternberg made it clear that the film would not be based on but only stimulated by the novel. When the film was finished, Jannings asked Mann what he thought of his performance, to which the author replied brusquely, "The success of the film will rely in a great measure on the naked thighs of Miss Dietrich!"

Alfred Hugenberg, the industrialist head of Ufa and an old Junker, found a disconcerting resemblance, physically, between himself and the jilted Professor Rat portrayed by Jannings. He also objected to any association of Heinrich Mann with the film, since the novel had been written to discredit Prussian authority, and he refused to endorse the release of the film for its première scheduled for April 1, 1930, at Ufa's flagship theatre, the Palast am Zoo. Sternberg had already left for the United States, without waiting for the opening. Pommer, desperate, asked Mann for a statement confirming that the meaning of his novel had been reversed in the film. Mann's reply was: "Had I been more mature

And then it happened—the epochal discovery of Marlene Dietrich for the Lola-Lola role in *The Blue Angel*. "Not your acting," said Heinrich Mann to its star, Jannings, "will determine the success of this film but her thighs!" The most celebrated of all German sound films. (1930)

"The shot heard 'round the world"—the most famous of all Sternberg scenes—Dietrich about to sing "Ich bin von Kopf bis Fuss auf Liebe eingestellt" ("Falling in love again") in *The Blue Angel*.

(when I wrote it), I would have developed the character of Professor Unrat more humanly, as in the film."

But Hugenberg was not appeased by Mann's implied withdrawal from the authorship of *The Blue Angel*. Already under the spell of the growing Nazi movement, Hugenberg adamantly refused to allow the film to open, inspiring one of the reactionary Berlin newspapers to publish an attack on Heinrich Mann and his whole literary output. This was answered by an article by Pommer in the *Berliner Tageblatt* stating that Ufa was proud of the film. The struggle within the hierarchy of Ufa went on till the very eve of the première when Hugenberg, to protect his investment, finally relented. Instinctively, Hugenberg, the real power behind the forces of German reaction, had sensed that, within the framework of an entertainment film, Sternberg had subtly mirrored the paranoiac tendencies of the Prussian bourgeoisie. But Sternberg has denied any political intent. "I went to Germany to make *The Blue Angel* without any knowledge of the conditions there—mine was an artist's pilgrimage, and no more. I would like to caution against the reading of too much into it unless the film itself clearly articulates its meaning. I am not partial to mystification."

The première of *The Blue Angel* was, of course, a great success * but Dietrich left Berlin that same night for Bremerhaven to depart for America. At Sternberg's recommendation, Paramount had offered her a contract and she accepted. She followed her director to Hollywood,† where he was already engaged in looking for a story for her next film, which was, in fact, to introduce her to American audiences, even before the release of *The Blue Angel* in the United States by Paramount, which had already acquired the rights. (So real were the scenes in the film that the eminent violinist, Josef Szigeti, in his autobiography, *With Strings Attached*, compared a café-cabaret he had visited in Hamburg during a tour to the sleazy joint in *The Blue Angel*.)

Back in California in the San Fernando valley, in a steel house designed by himself like a small castle, complete with

---

* Some time later, James Joyce told Dietrich that he had seen her in *The Blue Angel*, to which she replied, "Then, monsieur, you have seen the best of me."

† I met her at the pier in New York.

a moat surrounding it,* Sternberg housed a magnificent collection of modern art, one of the most notable private collections in the United States. He was himself a not untalented painter and sculptor, as attested by some landscapes, some incisive portraits, and a virile bronze torso. He also became the subject of sculptures by Rudolf Belling, David Edstrom, and Peter Balbusch and of paintings by Boris Deutsch and David Siqueiros.

It was Dietrich who suggested to Sternberg an obscure novel, *Amy Jolly* (subtitled *The Woman of Marrakech*), by Benno Vigny, which was to serve as the inspiration for their first American film together, *Morocco*,† in which she received second billing to Gary Cooper, just as in Berlin she received second billing to Jannings in *The Blue Angel*. After those two films she received star billing. She had scored a personal triumph unmatched by any actress on the screen since the florescence of Garbo. (Incidentally, the two have never met, although Dietrich always wanted to. What a confrontation of *monstres sacrés* that would be!).

"I have nothing to learn from Europe," Sternberg had said before departing for Germany and *The Blue Angel*. ‡ On his return to Hollywood he proved it by developing and elaborating his own highly personal style, which was to become increasingly more baroque, obsessed as he became with the succession of films he was forced by Paramount and Dietrich to make for her after *Morocco*, a kind of theme and variations on the subject of the love goddess, the twentieth-century Venus in the new mythology of the screen. The screen Dietrich was solely Sternberg's invention, though rooted in an old image of the movies, the mysterious *femme fatale*.

---

* The moat was very characteristic of Von Sternberg, for even those who thought they were closest to him felt an intellectual "moat" around him that was impossible to cross unless he "let the drawbridge down." The inscrutable Buddhalike mask of his visage was always a formidable warning of this.

† One has only to read the novel *Amy Jolly* to see how different and how much better the film is. Again, as in the case of *Professor Unrat* vs. *The Blue Angel*, the film version amounted to a completely original work. In both cases, the original acted only as a "stimulus" (Sternberg's word) for the new work.

‡ So much has been written about *The Blue Angel* that its stunning world success needs no detailing here.

Here was the old Greek legend (that had served Shaw so well) of Pygmalion and Galatea being enacted all over again, between the artist and his creation, and even the story of Svengali and Trilby, if you will, though when an interviewer for the London *Daily Sketch* in 1936 asked Dietrich if she felt Sternberg had been her Svengali, she replied with a mischievous smile, savoring the words deliciously, "I only wish he had been!"

*Morocco* premièred December 6, 1930. From Sergei Eisenstein (then in Hollywood) came a telegram: "Of all your great works, *Morocco* is the most beautiful. Admiration and love to you and Marlene." Robert E. Sherwood, then a film critic but soon to become one of America's most distinguished playwrights, said: "*Morocco* should come as a message of reassurance for those who have lately been depressed by the justifiable conviction that imagination is dead in Hollywood. It is a real film, taking advantage of the extraordinary opportunities for dramatic expression that the camera affords, making full and appropriate usage of sound, and placing a negligible emphasis on spoken words." Then he goes on to describe the wonderful scene of the dinner party celebration of the engagement of LeBessière and Amy Jolly, when the conversation falters as the distant drums and bugles of the returning Legionnaires are heard. "There is hardly a single scene in *Morocco* which is not equally artful in its capitalization of the advantages of sound. It never is allowed to interfere with the film's essential pictorial qualities, but it amplifies and enriches them to an incalculable extent. One must congratulate Josef von Sternberg on the best job of direction—of imaginative conception—that has been performed since the screen found its voice. It is incredible to me that anyone can see the results he has achieved in *Morocco* and still say that the old spell of the movies has been broken."

Georgia Hale, in a letter to Sternberg, quotes Chaplin as saying after attending the première with her, "Yes, he is an artist . . . it's his best film." Chaplin felt he took something away with him after seeing it, she said, because it was so beautiful.

*Morocco* was done with a supple sense of rhythmic phrase. The rhythm is never four-square; the action flows through, to use a musical equivalent, the bar-line from scene to scene.

It is the ultimate meaning of each scene, not the bar-lines, that condition this cinematographic flow and it is a lesson in cinema metrics. Sternberg, here, effaced the last vestiges of demarcation between the silent and the sound film and even the dialogue seems almost incidental in its reticence.

(In *Morocco* also appears the first of the black cats that are to silently stalk through subsequent Sternberg films, as in *Dishonored* and *Macao*.)

Chaplin had ridiculed the coming of sound in the opening scene of *City Lights* and resisted it longer than anyone else; René Clair was desolate over it and said it marked the end of the cinema's florescence—then went on to make three brilliant sound films in a row, *Sous les Toits de Paris*, *Le Million*, *À Nous la Liberté*; in the U.S.S.R., Eisenstein, Pudovkin, and Alexandrov heralded it as the dawn of a new era and issued their famous manifesto on the sound film—which, alas, was never to be realized. Sternberg welcomed sound heartily. Demanding and getting control over every aspect of his films, he was no longer at the mercy of movie house pianists or organists for the music. Now he could control even that by putting such music as he wished on the sound track of the films themselves. The strange thing is that he really, at least in the beginning, did not wish any "background music" for his films. There is not a note of such "atmospheric" music in *Thunderbolt*, *The Blue Angel*, *Morocco*, and *Dishonored*— what music is in them comes from natural sources as integral parts of the action. It takes assurance and courage to do that; few directors then or even now would risk it. Most of the time, music is used as a kind of dubious crutch on which the director leans, hoping the "surge" of the music will "fill in" and make up for any deficiencies his films might otherwise have. However, when background music is used properly, to heighten the intensity (or contrapuntally, though this use is very rarely found), it can be very effective, as music is a legitimate corollary to film and, indeed, in the silent days all films were shown with musical accompaniment. The background music Sternberg used for *The Scarlet Empress* was a notable example of how effective this device can be when controlled by a master, as in the last scene, the triumph of Catherine as Empress against the pealing bells and cannonade of the closing peroration of Tchaikovsky's thunderous *1812 Overture*, with the smiling and breathless Catherine in the white uniform of a hussar standing by her magnificent white stallion (almost as handsome as she was) and doves, harbinger of a new 'era of peace for Holy Russia, fluttering about her ... Pabst told me it was for him one of the peaks of cinema achievement. Another instance of Sternberg's felicitous use of background music was the surprise entrance of Don Pasquale during the carnival ball at the rendezvous of Don Antonio and Concha in their box in *The Devil Is a Woman*. The double doors swing open to the passionate Spanish chant of *Venga Jaleo*, with its flamenco wail, already old when the Moors were in Andalusia, and there stands the jealous Don Pasquale against a huge mural of a *corrida*—the matador about to close in for the kill. . . .

*Morocco*, like *The Blue Angel*, swept the world. When Sternberg found himself in Cannes some time afterwards, he met the Pasha of Marrakech who asked him why he had not visited him while in his domain. "I told him," says Sternberg in his autobiography, "I would have paid my respects had I ever been in Morocco, whereupon he said he had seen a film of mine and that it contained scenes photographed on streets that he recognized. He smiled when I told him that this was no more than an accidental resemblance, a flaw due to my lack of talent to avoid such similarity." "Two Orientals" jousting with each other. Saladin couldn't have said it better. It is one of Sternberg's favorite anecdotes because it reinforces his belief that it is not necessary to go to the actual locales to achieve realism if you understand the essence of the reality you're after. An edge of the Sahara Desert was recreated on the Paramount studio's back lot for *Morocco*, just as years later he was to reconstruct a South Pacific jungle island in a Japanese studio for *Anatahan*.*

Hardly had Sternberg said that he now wanted to go his

* What the layman or average observer fails to comprehend is that the creative process makes its own demands and that the greatest of these demands is upon the work itself. Joyce Cary, that modern renaissance man of arts and letters, said that audiences had an obligation to educate themselves so that they could comprehend the artist's form of communication. On the relationship of art and fact, he said: "Only art can convey both the fact and the feeling about the fact, for it works in the medium of common sympathies, common feeling, universal reaction to color, sound, form. It is the bridge between souls, meaning by that not only men's minds but their character and feeling."

separate way when he found himself working on a third picture with Dietrich. This time he devised a story for her loosely based on the exploits of a notorious World War I woman spy working for the Central Powers. The setting was again the harsh pre-World War I Vienna of *The Case of Lena Smith*, a somber film, fitfully lit with a kind of desperate gaiety, flecked with glints of sardonic dialogue, darkly whirling around its black theme of death in war with something of love and decency straining hopelessly to survive the senseless carnage—the whole made fluid and malleable in the creative imagination of the artist. *Dishonored* is to the cinema what Ravel's *La Valse* is to music—the Viennese waltz disintegrating into the First World War.

Sternberg next turned to *An American Tragedy*, from the novel by Theodore Dreiser, which Paramount wished him to make after they rejected Eisenstein's scenario on the same story. Although Sternberg and Eisenstein were friends (Sternberg was the only one in Hollywood who signed an affidavit permitting Eisenstein's re-entry into the United States on the latter's way back from Mexico to the U.S.S.R. after Eisenstein's abortive Mexican film venture), Sternberg never saw Eisenstein's script nor did he ever discuss it with him. (Eisenstein was already in Mexico when Sternberg began work on the film.) Although Samuel Hoffenstein was credited for the scenario, Sternberg says Hoffenstein collaborated with him only on the treatment and that the final scenario was by himself (Sternberg). The dialogue used was Dreiser's own. Every bit of conversation in the film came directly from the novel. But Dreiser felt the film had betrayed his book, which indicted society for Clyde Griffiths's murder of his inamorata so he could marry a rich girl. Dreiser claimed that Clyde Griffiths's sense of values was corrupted by society and his religious background (his parents were missionaries) and that the social implications of his novel were bypassed by the film. He sued Paramount and lost. Two of the foremost critics of the time defended Sternberg's film. Pare Lorentz said: "It is an important picture, not because of the novel but in spite of it." And Benjamin De Casseres said, "It is far superior to the book, which is tripe. The film has raised this tripe to the dignity of good hokum." Although the film was not a popular success in the United States, it was a big success in Europe.

By this time, Sternberg was one of the few American directors whose name appeared on theatre marquees along with the stars, both in the United States and abroad, and sometimes even without the stars.

*Vanity Fair*, then America's most distinguished magazine of the arts, placed him on a par with Eisenstein (issue of January, 1932) and the brilliant Berlin monthly, *Der Querschnitt*, that same year ran a symposium on "American Titans" in which he was included along with Sinclair Lewis, Andrew Mellon, and Theodore Dreiser.

Dietrich recalls that "In those days of block-booking, Paramount would offer exhibitors 'two Marlene Dietrichs' per year, before we had any idea of what they would be about, but we had to produce them on schedule just the same. More than once we were told in the middle of one picture that we must begin the next immediately after finishing the current one. In those circumstances he [Sternberg] had no choice but to make up his own stories."

And so Dietrich appeared as Shanghai Lily in her next picture with Sternberg, *Shanghai Express*, one of their greatest successes. Just as Sternberg had never been to Morocco before making *Morocco*, he had never been to China before making *Shanghai Express*. He said he was not interested in a "realistic China"—he wanted only to *evoke* China on the screen as an impressionist painter might. It was one of his most characteristic attitudes and was to be carried even further by him in *The Scarlet Empress* and *The Devil Is a Woman*, where he similarly evoked the Byzantine Russia of Catherine the Great and the rococo Spain of Pierre Louys in a style of "high cinema baroque" unprecedented up to that time and, indeed, never repeated by him or anyone else since. Following a private showing, Mary Pickford wrote Sternberg: "Douglas and I saw *Shanghai Express* at the house the other night and we loved it. I think it's your best picture. . . . Sorry I missed seeing *Dishonored*, as everyone speaks so enthusiastically of it. Am looking forward to catching up with it. Douglas joins me in best wishes and congratulations." And Robert E. Sherwood wrote: "*Shanghai Express* is a technological triumph . . . for the principal protagonist of this drama is a railroad train, a perfect vehicle for the expression of von Sternberg's peculiar intelligence. He has recorded the progress of this vehicle with such remarkable expertness that one is given no opportunity to worry about the insufficiency of its mortal cargo. . . . Indeed, I was sorry to leave the train at its final destination. . . . He knows more than anyone else how to use the marvelous mechanical equipment at his disposal. He can make his camera talk and his microphone listen in a positively human manner. Thus, he establishes communion with the physical senses of his audience and he exploits this communion with remarkable skill. . . . Beautiful shot follows beautiful shot but no matter what Clive Brook is saying to Marlene Dietrich the Shanghai Express is speeding on." Everyone was enthralled, especially, with the color, atmosphere, and plangency of the opening scenes preparatory to the Shanghai Express's leaving for its trip. The late Leslie Howard remarked on this, "There you have a definite feeling of reality conveyed in the movement and sound of the train and of the people on the platform and the crowded village."

*Shanghai Express* was followed by *Blonde Venus*, a sentimental story in which Dietrich, looking more beautiful in each new film made by Sternberg with her, was now more beautiful than ever. Perhaps it was to make up for a lack of a real story. In any case, it had its share of Sternbergian *bizarrerie*, such as the "Hot Voodoo" number that Dietrich sang in a fantastic blonde "fuzzy-wuzzy" wig after emerging startlingly in all her lissomeness from the hairy ugliness of an ape-skin. Its vivid evocation of the American South was particularly striking, utilizing the full range of black-and-white chiaroscuro with dazzling effect.

In August of 1932 Sternberg received a moving letter from the Mexican painter, Siqueiros: "Once more I ask for your help, but it is your own fault, because you're the only one in Los Angeles that has a conscience about art and who understands the lives of those dedicated to this activity. I am locked in Los Angeles and cannot get out of it for lack of money. I have to be in New York for my exhibition in two weeks and you are the only one who can help me. . . . I want you to buy the painting of the enclosed photograph. I want the money to buy an old car to make the trip to New York with my family and my paintings. Thank you." Needless to add, Sternberg bought the painting.

In November 1932 Sternberg left for the West Indies with his cameraman of *The Sea Gull*, Paul Ivano, to shoot backgrounds for a circus story he planned to do next with Miss Dietrich. He was primarily in search of a hurricane, which obstinately refused to materialize, so he abandoned the project and left for another extended holiday in Europe.

On his return he started work on his next film with Dietrich, *The Scarlet Empress*, episodes in the life of Catherine the Great based on her private diaries. Meanwhile, Paramount believed a change of director for her would be in everyone's interest and suggested that she might like to make *The Song of Songs*, from the Sudermann novel, for Rouben Mamoulian. Von Sternberg advised her to accept. He felt it would be good for her to experience a change in director.

Sternberg evoked for *The Scarlet Empress* a Peterhof Palace such as never was and yet was never anything else but Russian, eighteenth-century Byzantine Russian. The twisted, anguished sculptures of saints and martyrs were gargoyles sprung, like Athena from the head of Zeus, from the unendingly fecund imagination of the director and masterfully executed under his supervision by the Swiss sculptor, Peter Balbusch, a long-time Sternberg devotee. Similarly, Richard Kollorsz, a German painter, executed ikons and portraits more Byzantine than any real ikons of the Russian Orthodox Church. Just as Eisenstein a decade later was to heighten the Kremlin palace of Ivan the Terrible with a poetic realism, Sternberg heightened the Peterhof Palace the same way—and not only the décor but the very characters themselves—but Sternberg did it first. In the same way, the elaborate ritual of the wedding of Catherine and Peter in the Cathedral of Kazan in Sternberg's film antedates the elaborate ritual of the coronation of Ivan IV in the Ouspensky cathedral in Eisenstein's. It was this that caused Henri Langlois, curator of the Cinémathèque Française (and an avowed admirer of Eisenstein), to cable Sternberg, after he had belatedly seen *The Scarlet Empress* in March, 1964: "Have just seen marvelous *Scarlet Empress*. Stop. What grand film. Stop. All *Ivan Grozny* comes from your film. Stop. All my respect and admiration." After World War II, when Pabst came to America to try to persuade Garbo to play the dual roles of Penelope and Circe in his project to film Homer's *Odyssey*, I discussed Sternberg with him. He confessed that whenever he heard that *The Scarlet Empress* was being shown anywhere in Europe, he would drop whatever he was doing and rush to see it. "I look at the screen," he said in awe, "I don't believe I see what I am seeing, but there it is! I think I am losing my mind, it is so incredible!" It was Pabst's way of saying it was the most eye-smiting film he had ever seen. A popular critic of the period when *The Scarlet Empress* first appeared (her name was Elsie Finn) began her review: "Has Josef von Sternberg gone mad? Has the cinema turned like Frankenstein's monster on the director who came closer to giving it life than most others within its shadow?"

"It is not reality that matters in a film," says Chaplin in his autobiography, "but what the imagination can make of it. . . . When I realize how distorted even recent events have become, history as such only arouses my skepticism—whereas a poetic interpretation achieves a general effect of the period. After all, there are more valid facts and details in works of art than there are in history books." In short, in the creative process, art is often anti-fact and fact anti-art.

Following the release of *The Scarlet Empress* to a "mixed" reception, B.P. Schulberg, production chief of Paramount, left that studio for Columbia. He was succeeded at Paramount by Ernst Lubitsch, who not only agreed to let Sternberg make still another film with Dietrich—the last he was due to direct for the studio under his contract—but also persuaded Dietrich to sign a new long-term contract.

Paramount had long owned the rights to Pierre Louys's novel *Woman and Puppet,* filmed by them in 1920 with Geraldine Farrar as the ruthless Spanish sorceress, Conchita Perez, who seduces, ridicules, and finally destroys a middle-aged officer of the Civil Guard. Sternberg wanted to call his version *Caprice Espagnole* but Lubitsch decided on *The Devil Is a Woman.* It went into production early in 1935, ironically enough at the moment Elisabeth Bergner, Dietrich's idol of her Berlin days, had finished in England Alexander Korda's version of *Catherine the Great.*

During the shooting, Von Sternberg stated that *The Devil Is a Woman* would be his last picture with Dietrich. "Miss Dietrich and I," he said, "have progressed as far as possible together. My being with her any further will not help her or me. If we continued we would get into a pattern which would be harmful to both of us." "As far as possible" resulted in the most bewitchingly beautiful photography (Sternberg took screen credit for the photography of this one himself, although he had always supervised the photography of his films), a now ravishingly beautiful Dietrich as Sternberg's camera witchery caught her, the most fantastically impressionistic sets of a dream Spain, and the most audacious gowns with which the director costumed his star.

Louys's title for *Woman and Puppet* was derived from Goya's *Tapices, XLII:* "In the meadow of Manzanares four young Spanish women toss a male puppet in a blanket." Goya's small painting of this scene is in the Prado. The novel is a study in sado-masochism and a minor masterpiece of its *genre*. (It will be recalled that Louys was Oscar Wilde's favorite French novelist.) Its heroine is the *femme fatale* carried to the *n*th degree: *"Elle se faisait mal non pour le plaisir de pécher mais pour la joie de faire mal à quelqu'un."* (*Vide* Stroheim's heroine in his novel, *Paprika.*) But, as Richard Griffith (ex-curator of the Film Library of the Museum of Modern Art in New York) pointed out, "Such a literal devil could no longer be brought to the American screen intact and the Concha Perez of this film emerged as a coquette." But if she was a coquette, she was that *genre* raised to its ultimate power, also, and the difference for most of her victims was academic. Concha no longer danced naked but sang a risqué song. The end result for her victims was the same.

"This is the masterpiece of Josef von Sternberg," wrote the Uruguayan critic, Emil Rodriguez Monegal, "directed with the greatest freedom. It offers in all its glory the absurd Spain of the foreigner—Spanish music *à la* Rimsky-Korsakov in the background, the German Marlene as an improbable Andalusian enchantress, and Goya and Spanish baroque as seen through the eyes of a German expressionist. Yet it is a film of enormous stylistic persuasion and sophisticated grace. The director has made luminous in this extreme achievement that woman of such presence and seductive sexuality that must have been (and still is?) Marlene Dietrich."

There were other things, too, to smite the eye, like the incredible shot of the snowbound train, unwittingly carrying Concha and the officer she will bedevil. It is all but covered with snow, as if an avalanche had descended upon it and engulfed it. Only the very tops of the train windows are still visible. It is absolutely the *ne plus ultra* of being snowbound—it is, as I said, incredible—and it is magnificent. There is the bewitching opening, of the pre-Lenten carnival and its frenzy of serpentine, with its stunningly beautiful serpent in the person of Concha in her carriage threading her way through the maze of merrymakers and, always and unceasingly, there are those grotesque masks, dwarfs and satyrs darting through the whirling lights and shadows, and a puppet with which the puppet himself (the bedeviled officer) toys. There is even a golliwog jack-in-the-box who delivers a note of assignation from Concha to her newest victim—echoes of all the gargoyles of *The Scarlet Empress*. There is the duel in the rain which is like a shower of diamonds on the glistening participants and Concha, herself, already swathed in black for whichever of her dueling lovers will not emerge from the fray over her. There is, in short, scarcely a moment in this extraordinary work without its own wonder.

Then a curious thing happened. The Republican government of Spain objected officially to the film for its portrayal of an officer of the Civil Guard being made ridiculous by a (shall we say?) loose woman. On October 31, 1935, the Spanish Minister of War, Gil Robles, announced that all Paramount films would be barred in Spain unless *The Devil Is a Woman* was immediately withdrawn from world circulation and the negative burned. A commercial treaty being planned at that time between the United States and Spain was rumored as the reason for the quick capitulation to this arrogant ultimatum, which was little less than blackmail. Entitled "Susceptibilité Excessif," an article in *Intercine*, official film publication of the League of Nations in Rome, commented: "*L'Espagne de von Sternberg n'était et n'a jamais été l'Espagne: c' était un pays imaginaire, un pays de conte, une espèce de paradis artificiel et romantique peuplé des fantasmes carnavalesques et d'amours impossibles. . . . Pourquoi ce féroce autodafé?*" Clearly the Spanish Republican government lacked a sense of humor. It has since been learned that Paramount did *not* burn the negative and that the real reason for the Spanish government's attitude was that a wealthy Spanish industrialist promised to build a complex of modern studios in Madrid if he could be guaranteed a minimum of competition from foreign films. Whatever the reasons, *The Devil Is a Woman* had a limited circulation. It remains the favorite of all the films they did together, of both the director and star. The Dietrich "episode" in the career of Sternberg was over. End of the second phase . . .

Sternberg then rejoined Schulberg at Columbia where he made two films, *Crime and Punishment*, after Dostoievski, and *The King Steps Out*, from the operetta, *Cissy*, by Herbert and Ernst Marischka, with music drawn from Fritz Kreisler. Only a nimble mind could jump from Louys to Dostoievski and then to a Kreisler operetta. The true artist encompasses the whole world. From the Kreisler trifle Sternberg was soon to make another spectacular jump, to the decadent world of the Roman Emperor Claudius. The break with Paramount had freed him from his tie with Dietrich and its countless variations on a single theme. His brief experience at Columbia was not a felicitous one for him, lacking as he did the freedom and the largesse he enjoyed at Paramount.

He decided he needed a respite from films and took off on a leisurely trip around the world. On the return leg of the long journey he became ill and entered a London nursing home. Upon his recovery, Alexander Korda proposed a partnership with him in London Films, which Sternberg rejected, but when Korda then asked him to salvage a project he (Korda) had initiated, the filming of *I, Claudius*, from the historical novel by Robert Graves, Sternberg accepted the directorial reins. The year was now 1936. Korda had been having difficulties with Charles Laughton in the title role, despite the great success these two had with *The Private Life of Henry VIII*. Merle Oberon was to play Messalina and others in the cast were Flora Robson, Robert Newton, and Emlyn Williams.

Sets were designed by Vincent Korda, and Georges Périnal was the cameraman. Having already played Nero in De Mille's *Sign of the Cross* (1933), Laughton was thought to be a "natural" for Tiberius Claudius Drusus, the driveling imbecile successor to Caligula. But Laughton developed some odd quirks during the early stages of filming. "I had great difficulty managing Laughton," said Sternberg afterwards. "So did Korda; and when Merle Oberon sustained a bad concussion in an automobile accident, which meant so much delay that all our preparations and contracts were invalidated, it was decided to halt the film. It might have been my most successful work. There was no other reason." A comment echoed by Lotte Eisner who, referring to the two reels of *I, Claudius* now reposing in the vaults of the National Film Archives in

London, said it might indeed have become Sternberg's greatest film. Korda, himself, said of this preliminary footage that it was as beautiful as anything he had ever seen on the screen. (It should be noted here that all the stories about Sternberg being a "difficult" and "arrogant" director, like most such stories, were untrue. After the debacle of *I, Claudius,* Korda wrote Sternberg: "If it is any consolation to you to know, you have left behind you the most loyal and devoted production unit that I have known in connection with any director working for our company [London Films] and should you ever be persuaded to come back and try your hand with us again I know very well that everybody here will be heart and soul with you.")

That same year, Aeneas Mackenzie, writing in *Life and Letters Today* (London, 1936), in an article titled, "The Leonardo of the Lenses," said, "[His shots], each of which is developed internally . . . detonate into shock, surprise, or startling beauty. And it is by means of this Ford-like internal combustion that a Von Sternberg film progresses in audience interest: before the effect of one emotional percussion has subsided, the next is under way. Consequently, the story does not move his pictures; it is his pictures which move the story."

Recently the British Broadcasting Corporation put together a most unusual film, *The Epic That Never Was,* a 75-minute documentary on Sternberg's unfinished *"cinéma maudit"* detailing the contretemps in filming *I, Claudius.* Filmed in 35mm but primarily for television showing, it is made up in part of interviews with Sternberg, Robert Graves, the costume designer, Merle Oberon, Emlyn Williams (who played Caligula), and Flora Robson (who played the empress-dowager mother of Claudius). Each gives his version of why the film was never completed. The remaining part consists of rushes, as they came from Périnal's camera, of the principal footage shot. It is to be hoped that this film will be made available to television stations and ciné-clubs universally so that audiences may get at least some idea of what this extraordinary project was like.

What was it like?

In some respects it was like the best work of the director, with its ravishing lighting, its silken chiaroscuro, the incandescent softness of the photography in general, especially in the close-ups of faces; also excellence in the acting, especially of Laughton, magnificent as the pitiful Claudius in a long and moving tirade he delivers in the Roman senate defending his right of ascension to the throne. But Emlyn Williams, too, the incarnation of evil as Caligula (there is a single close-up of him worth a hundred lines of the most telling description by the most vivid writer), and the enchanting Merle Oberon in diaphanous veils and bewitching smile that could unnerve a saint, giving youthful promise of the harlot-Messalina she was to become. In short, the complete control over camerawork and direction that we have always known as the hallmark of the director. These images are signed "Sternberg"—you would recognize them as his work even if you did not know beforehand where they came from.

But hold, there is something else—something we have not seen before in Sternberg's films. Or is it the Roman setting, so unusual for Sternberg, that is responsible for our feeling that we have not seen anything like this before from him? In the Temple of Dionysus under a high, vaulted ceiling, pierced by shafts of light from the mid-day sun bathing the enormous enclave in an effulgent luminosity, move worshippers, slowly move the worshippers, their arms outstretched in prayer (shades of Satie's *Gymnopediés*!). The camera, equidistant from the floor of the temple and the ceiling, takes all of this stupendous shot in on one frame, in a single image—and it is breathtaking, *literally* (not figuratively, this time) breathtaking. Nor is a single dimension enough for the director, it never was enough, there always was an overtone to the physical image, a second dimension, a corollary or additional meaning vibrating after the initial "tone" was struck, like "sympathetic harmonies" in music. What Sternberg himself refers to as *"Nachklange."* In this case, it was the awesome sense of the mysticism of the Roman religion. Sternberg has been called everything but never before a mystic. Mysticism is supposed to be the special province of Dreyer, or perhaps Bresson. In this incredible shot, Sternberg is a mystic.

What do the personages interviewed say? Sternberg says least of all. In a few slowly measured words, speaking like a High Lama (so characteristic of him), he dismisses the project philosophically. For him it seemed to be a subject that could not be discussed because it was never completed. Merle Oberon and Flora Robson are voluble, however, especially

Miss Oberon. "Sternberg was chosen because he was considered to be a woman's director," she says. She has much else to say and even jokes about the automobile accident that brought a final halt to the production. Best of all, this Eurasian beauty looks as beautiful as ever, and that's more important than her jocular remarks about "what happened." Flora Robson is still haunted by Sternberg's appearance on the set. "He was the only director I ever saw who really looked like a director," she says. "He would come on the set in riding boots and turban, or even in a silk dressing gown. He was always a little frightening. . . ." She speaks about the miracle of makeup performed on her, transforming her then youthfulness into doddering old age; about the weight of the costumes she had to wear. . . . At one point Emlyn Williams is cut in right after Sternberg has commented wryly that the automobile accident of Merle Oberon "truncated my film." Says Williams, "Truncated his film? It almost truncated poor Merle!" Referring to Sternberg's difficulties with Laughton, Williams facetiously hazards the guess that the film's producer, Alexander Korda, was himself the chauffeur of the car in which Miss Oberon had the accident, "purposely engineered, probably, to bring an end to the hopeless impasse." The costume designer remarks that he was asked to costume not just six vestal virgins (the number prescribed by Roman ritual as priestesses of the goddess Vesta to tend the sacred fire in her temple), but many times that number because it looked more impressive. Also, that they were to be robed in transparent white tulle revealing their nudity underneath. "Since they were sworn to chastity, it is unlikely," said the costumer, "that they would have been so accoutered. It was all very impressive," he admits (and we see the scene on the screen), "but it had nothing to do with the Roman religion." Robert Graves, author of the book adapted for the film, mutters genially, but has nothing actually to contribute to this "symposium." Only Laughton might have explained, in the face of the reticence of Sternberg to speak, and, alas, this explanation Providence did not vouchsafe us.

The English actor Dirk Bogarde acts as "master of ceremonies" of the BBC film and attempts to fill in the gaps with rumors and hearsay and what sketchy facts have survived the years. So, in the final analysis, only the fragments of the film itself remain, *multum in parvo*, to bear witness to a "beautiful impossibility" that could not for some strange reason be realized, by its very nature, and to remind us in Bacon's words that "there is no excellent beauty that has not some strangeness in the proportion."

While in England, Sternberg planned two other projects, *The Forty Days of Musa Dagh* by Franz Werfel (documenting the grisly Turkish-Armenian aftermath of the First World War) and Zola's *Germinal* (which Pudovkin also once wanted to make). But a recurrence of his illness forced him to abandon both projects and he returned to California.

In January, 1938 he was honored by the Austrian government for furthering Austrian culture and offered the post of director of fine arts in the Austrian ministry, a post he politely declined when it became evident that Hitler was about to annex that country.

In October of that year, MGM offered him a one-picture contract to direct Hedy Lamarr in her second American film, her first, *Algiers*, the remake of *Pepe le Moko*, having been such a success. Although his previous experience with MGM twelve years earlier had been disastrous, he accepted. What was more natural than to think he might do for Hedy Lamarr, certainly the most beautiful screen personality since Dietrich, what he had done for Dietrich? The story, *New York Cinderella*, was by Charles MacArthur and the co-stars were Spencer Tracy and Walter Pidgeon. Harold Rosson was the cameraman. After eight days of shooting, Sternberg and MGM called it quits, again over the issue of the director's freedom, and Frank Borzage was called in to replace him. Borzage's version displeased MGM so much that it was scrapped and entirely reshot by a third director, William S. Van Dyke. Under the title of *I Take This Woman* it was released and went immediately into oblivion. In truth, MGM was a jinx company for Sternberg. He fulfilled his contract for them with another project of their own, *Sergeant Madden*, a tentative return to the *roman policier* type of film with which he had so distinguished himself at Paramount a decade earlier. But his heart wasn't in it—and that always shows.

For two years he was inactive. Then in 1941 the producer Arnold Pressburger decided to revive the idea of filming a sensational play that had resisted all attempts to tame it for the screen—John Colton's *The Shanghai Gesture*, whose setting was a swank Chinese brothel. A violent attack on moral hypocrisy (like Maugham's "Sadie Thompson," which Colton had dramatized as *Rain*), it was an incisive dissection of that tribute (in the irony of La Rochefoucauld) which vice pays to virtue. Sternberg made an adaptation that was both faithful in spirit to the original and could still placate the moral guardians of the American screen.

Sternberg was back in his *milieu* again, with a sympathetic producer, his former directorial freedom, and absolute authority over every department, including the casting. When he offered to send Albert Basserman the script (Sternberg wanted him to play the Police Commissioner), the great German actor replied that he was honored to play in a Sternberg film and it would not be necessary for him to see the script first. For the role of "Mother" Gin Sling (changed from Mother Goddam), Sternberg transformed Ona Munson into a "Chinese Dietrich." The setting, too, was changed, from a brothel, which was then tabu on the sancrosanct American screen, to a high-class gambling house, and several characters were added, including that of Dr. Omar (played by Victor Mature), the Levantine sensualist of shady origins and occupations. Sternberg was fascinated by the many facets of evil displayed by the characters in the Colton melodrama in which the sinners pay their debts, as is the ancient Chinese custom, on the eve of the New Year. The constant return to the huge roulette table in the center of the circular casino, giving the effect of a descent into a maelstrom of iniquity, served as a suggestive pictorial leitmotif throughout the film. And Gene Tierney never looked more beautiful. Originally the film opened with a bearded Sikh policeman directing traffic on a busy intersection of the Shanghai bund, like the conductor of an orchestra. It was, inexplicably, later cut from the film. In any case, the master of *chinoiserie* had done it again. "His strangest and most fascinating work," said *Cahiers du Cinéma*. "I speak in behalf of a whole group of young admirers of your work in Paris," wrote Ado Kyrou to Sternberg, "who consider you as one of the greatest directors that ever lived. We have a huge admiration for your work from *The Salvation Hunters* to the admirable *Shanghai Gesture*. This latest masterpiece of yours is now regularly programmed at the best Parisian ciné-clubs and is passionately discussed at each showing. . . . These audiences are not only sensitive to the magic and metaphysics of the moods so characteristically Sternbergian, but eagerly willing to know analytically of your projects, your plans, and your views about the present cinema."

Whatever the art of the cinema was, it wasn't the "international language of goodwill," nor the ambassador of goodwill," nor the force by which "barriers to mutual understanding" would be overcome, and all the other high-sounding things claimed for it as the cementer of peace between nations. For all the smiles and hand-shaking and bowing at international film festivals, the brotherhood of the cinema was impotent to delay the start of World War II by one second. Refugees began to flee in the wake of the holocaust that was soon to engulf Europe. Among them was the painter, Oskar Kokoschka, whom Sternberg provided with the necessary affidavit to be admitted to the United States with his wife. A touching letter of gratitude from Kokoschka to Sternberg attests to how precious such a document was to the hunted when often it meant the difference between life and death.

When Pearl Harbor was attacked, Sternberg offered his services to the government; later he joined the newly formed OWI (Office of War Information), for which he made a short documentary, *The Town*, on the people in a small Middlewestern community—Madison, Wisconsin. The film was part of a series, "The American Scene." Unlike anything he had ever done before, it showed a great warmth and love for the United States, a film that, during the hysteria of war, eschewed flag-waving patriotism for the positive values of the melting-pot that was the United States. Focusing his camera like a microscope on a tiny segment of this country, he revealed the various foreign elements that went into making the "American way of life." The film (ten minutes long) ended with columns of young soldiers marching out to fight for the security of such an average town and the serenity of its life.

In 1945, Sternberg joined the newly formed Vanguard Films and became consultant to the company's head, David O. Selznick. A year later, while he was serving in an advisory capacity on Selznick's *Duel in the Sun*, he replaced King Vidor briefly, during the latter's illness, as director of the film. (It is an interesting "game" to pick out the scenes that are "*echt*-Sternberg" in this film.)

In 1947, he accepted an appointment at the University of Southern California to teach a class in film direction. The following year he moved to New York.

In 1950 a book appeared in Switzerland, *L'Histoire Universelle*, by Jean Apothéloz, detailing the principal historic events from prehistoric times to that year. Among the historic contributions to the arts was included that of Sternberg.

The year before, Sternberg's former scenarist, Jules Furthman, suggested him for the directorial assignment on Howard Hughes's contemplated aviation epic, *Jet Pilot*. The producer of such box-office successes as *Hell's Angels*, *Two Arabian Knights*, and *The Outlaw* had dabbled in the movies as a rich man's plaything. But his chief business interests involved the manufacture of machine-tools and airplanes. He was himself a considerable flier. Now, for his aviation film, he would consider Sternberg, if the latter shot some "test footage" for him, as if Hughes was interviewing a novice. As if again to disprove the stories of his "arrogance," Sternberg agreed to make a test; which agreement so pleased Hughes that Sternberg was given the assignment. It was to be his first color film. Shooting started in 1950. On its completion, Mr. Hughes decided to cut the film himself. Then he added more flying scenes and recut it. Then still more flying scenes (since flying was *his* obsession, not films), which necessitated still more cutting and rearranging of scenes. Being not only rich but very rich, Mr. Hughes could afford to indulge himself and, because he was young, time didn't matter either. (*Jet Pilot* was not released till 1957.)

While waiting for Hughes to make up his mind about the form in which he would release *Jet Pilot*, Sternberg embarked on the second film of his two-picture contract with Hughes, *Macao*. Despite considerable studio interference, *Macao* was completed by Sternberg in a form that satisfied him. But his satisfaction was to be short-lived. Nicholas Ray was called in to re-shoot the film. The resulting abortion pleased no one, least of all the critics. The film was a critical and box-office fiasco.

"*De l'audace! toujours de l'audace!*" cried Danton. An apt Sternbergian maxim.

No work or project of Sternberg's was ever more audacious

than the book on which he took an option to film next—
Shelby Foote's *Follow Me Down*, a violent tale of a sexual
crime (set in the deep American South) as it is reconstructed
in the bewilderingly conflicting testimony of the witnesses
called on to testify in court . . . a sort of American *Rashomon*.
How Sternberg would have overcome the explicitness of the
sexual details of this cauterizing story will, *hélas*, never be
known. Failing to interest financial backers for the project,
he abandoned it. End of the third phase . . .

We are now in 1952. Sternberg receives an offer to make
a film in Japan, with the guarantee of complete freedom
to make whatever he wishes. (He has always been very popular there. An entire issue of the Japanese magazine *The
Film Critic* [108 pp.] was once devoted to him.) He chooses
a factual incident of the war in the South Pacific concerning a group of Japanese sailors shipwrecked in June 1944 on
the island of Anatahan near Saipan in the Mariana archipelago, who held out there for seven years, refusing to believe
that the war was long since ended and that Japan had been
defeated. Eventually they are convinced, and the survivors
of their intramural fighting over the lone young woman they
found there are returned to the mother country: finally, the
war is over for them. This bizarre incident was turned into
*The Saga of Anatahan*, for which the director both wrote and
spoke a narration in English over the Japanese dialogue—a
narration that is one of the most searching probes into human
behavior and the mysteries of the human heart that exists
in our time.

The Parisian press was ecstatic. "He has summed up the
vision of the world and the philosophy of existence in it. . . .
From the first image we are again plunged into that famous
enchanted world of Sternberg. It is not only his crowning
achievement but at the same time the best Japanese film,"
wrote *Arts-Spectacles*.

"We are happy to find in this work a Sternberg true to
himself, true to his vision of the world, and true to his old
sorcery," wrote *Le Monde*. "He is behind every image, every
word. A signed film is rare—a film marked by the indelible
print of its author."

"The screen is fairly torn apart and ignited by the fulminations flung upon it, which Von Sternberg, we are sure, drew

from the very depths of his heart. He has won for himself the greatest possible freedom to express a poetic truth and this heightened plane of presentation enhances the radiance of the matter treated. . . . In sum, it is a realization of that kind of work of art considered impossible to accomplish." (*Cahiers du Cinéma*)

In London, Berlin, Switzerland, Australia, and New York the reviews were equally rapturous. And the American Ambassador to Japan, Robert Murphy, congratulated Sternberg on the film.

With *The Saga of Anatahan*, Sternberg had now entered the fourth and final phase of his career—a return to the young artist who had made *The Salvation Hunters*; that is to say, he had regained the complete freedom of expression of his first film, a work of evangelism, a purity of statement without guile, an enunciation of eternal verities. . . . *The Saga of Anatahan*, for all its violence, ends quietly on a brooding note, with just a momentary "flashback" on the sound track of a wisp of remembered passions before the final renunciation of passion is uttered, lowly and wistful, before the Kabuki woodblocks herald the end of the drama . . . "And· if I know anything at all about Keiko," concludes the narrator, "she, too, must have been there."

. . .

In 1957 Sternberg is awarded the George Eastman House medal of honor for distinguished contribution to the art of the motion pictures.

In 1960 he is given an "homage" and retrospective showing of his principal films by the Cinémathèque Française.

. . . He is elected an honorary member of the Akademie der Kunst in Berlin, the German counterpart of the Académie Française.

In 1961 he begins a round of the international film festivals, heading the juries at San Francisco, Acapulco, Mar del Plata, Cartagena, Locarno, Cannes, Venice, Vienna, and Berlin. He lectures at universities in Colombia and Argentina.

1962 . . . He is cited by the Museum of Performing Arts of San Francisco for his "consistently significant and artistic contributions rendered to the world of the performing arts and for enriching the culture of our time."

. . . *Show* magazine in New York runs a symposium of

distinguished foreigners who have contributed to American culture: "To make progress," said the introduction, "every culture must periodically recapture the exhilaration of danger, what Kierkegaard called 'the passionate expectancy' of the committed man." The list included Dali, Adler, Gropius, Breuer, Mann, Teller, Fermi, Einstein, Ernst, Neutra, Nabokov, Mies van der Rohe, and two film names—Stroheim and Sternberg.

1963 . . . Jorge Luis Borges, the greatest living Spanish writer, mentions the influence of Sternberg's films on his work in the foreword to his novel *La Muerta y la Brujula*.

. . . He is honored by the West German government for "his services to the German film industry" (for *The Blue Angel*, made 34 years before).

. . . He is honored by the Mexican government for his artistic and humanist contributions to the cinema.

1964 . . . Retrospective showings of his films and tributes are given him by the University of California and Dartmouth College.

. . . He lectures at universities in Minnesota, California, Illinois, Iowa, and at Notre Dame College.

. . . Walter Starkie, professor of Spanish, Irish, and Italian literature and former director of the Abbey Theatre in Dublin, testifies in a tribute given Sternberg at the University of California in Los Angeles that Shaw, Pirandello, Joyce, and Lorca admired and often discussed his films.

1965 . . . He teaches a film directing course at U.C.L.A. in California.

. . . He begins the revision of an autobiography on which he has been working for several years. Originally called *Guide to a Labyrinth*, it appears in 1965 as *Fun in a Chinese Laundry*.

Just as in the first part of *Faust*, the protagonist has not yet found, in the world of desire and passion, that wonderful moment of existence to which he could really wish to cling, but finds it in the second part when, after tasting every form of intellectual and worldly power, he turns to good works, taking an interest in a project to reclaim land from the sea, a project which will mean little to him, personally, but which will bring untold good to countless others, so did Sternberg turn from the clamorous world of Hollywood and its glitter to a threnody that is at the same time an affirmation of life,

*The Saga of Anatahan,* for which his only reward has been the elation it has given others *sans* any material reward to himself.

1966 . . . Retrospective showing of his films at Mannheim, Germany, at which is issued a 200-page "documentation" of his complete work.

1967 . . . Retrospective showing of his films in Stockholm and Sydney.

.   .   .

In a *milieu* with its easy contempt for aesthetic values, the hieratic disdain of his style—which ranks with the most patrician filmmaking in the world—is a thrilling thing to see, as it always is wherever work is touched, "beyond the call of duty," with the vital grace of art.

# II

*"To know what to reveal and what to conceal
is the secret of art."*

*"Everything I have to say about Miss
Dietrich I have said with the camera."*
                                        —Josef von Sternberg

A discussion of "Sternberg and Marlene" has its origins in the mists of antiquity, its roots in Hellenic culture, "the Greek miracle," before Pan disappeared into the forests, never to be seen again. The great poets that followed Homer invented a mythology based on the ancient Greek religion that illumined what the early Greeks were like, a matter of importance to us, who are their descendants intellectually and artistically. Nothing we learn about them is alien to ourselves. The whole of Western civilization owes its genesis to the ancient Greeks, and Herodotus limns them succinctly when he says, "Of old the Hellenic race was marked off from the barbarian as more keen-witted and more free from nonsense." Whereas the Egyptians represented their goddesses in unhuman form, a woman with a cat's head or a monstrous, mysterious sphinx, Greek mythology humanized the world, freeing men from the paralyzing fear of an omnipotent Unknown. The men who made the myths disliked the irrational and had a love for facts, no matter how wildly fantastic some of the stories are. They occur in a world that is essentially rational and matter-of-fact. Although the ethical background of these tales is religious, many are nonreligious and have to do with explaining natural phenomena, thus becoming a kind of early science. Better than that, they were highly poetic. Some explained nothing at all, being tales of pure entertainment, springing solely from the human heart and its limitless fantasies, such as the tale Ovid tells of Pygmalion and Galatea. Like the legend of Orpheus and Eurydice, it has no conceivable connection with nature or religion. Such tales were written as pure entertainment, becoming at the same time the first literature.

Pygmalion and Galatea.* . . . Perhaps in no artist–creation relationship of the twentieth century is the spirit of this immortal tale more vividly exemplified than in the Sternberg–Marlene relationship in the seven (ah, seven, that old mystical number!) films he made of her. I purposely do not say "with her"—but "of her"—because seven times he, too, "sculpted" her—as did Pygmalion sculpt Galatea, making seven versions of an ideal, each time refining the vision he had of her, adding a detail here, subtracting one there, revealing a facet of her "eternal mystery" here, concealing one there, until the sum total, which is to say, the final creation, was exquisite. Both Pygmalion and Sternberg labored long and devotedly on their creation but did not rest content. Under their skilled fingers it grew more and more beautiful. No woman ever born, no representation of a woman ever made, could approach it. Ovid does not tell us how long Pygmalion worked on his Galatea. Sternberg worked five years on his. Only in one way did they differ: The well-spring of Pygmalion's art was his hatred of women: "Detesting the faults beyond measure which nature has given to women," in the words of Ovid. Thus, resolving never to marry, Pygmalion embarked on the sculpture of a woman, the perfect woman, to show men the deficiencies of the kind they had to put up with. With Sternberg it was different. He may not have

---

* Sternberg's first Galatea was a wax mannikin in a short story published by him in 1924, *The Waxen Galatea*, that was to presage things to come. A shy man falls desperately in love with a mannikin in the window of a women's fashion shop. Day after day he gazes with adoration on this inert figure of wax, wrapt in silent rapture at her indefatigable grace of gesture, marveling at the gown which draped her nudity. One day the unhappy man sees passing in the street the living image of his goddess. He follows her but she has a rendezvous with another man who, at the woman's request, humiliates her adorer who has become an irksome intruder on her rendezvous. Dismayed, he removes himself, deciding never again to take the risk, in the future, of loving anyone more than the mannikin.

thought much of them as actresses (nor of men as actors) without a sensitive director's guiding hand, but for women as women he had the highest respect. This is borne out by the films of his pre-Dietrich period, long before he met her, in his treatment of Georgia Hale, Edna Purviance, Evelyn Brent, Betty Compson, and Esther Ralston—every one of them portrayed sympathetically, as loyal companions of their men. Even in his own A.D. period, "After Dietrich," his attitude remained constant in his equally sympathetic handling of Marian Marsh, Ona Munson, Gene Tierney, Janet Leigh, Jane Russell, and Akemi Negishi. There are no villainesses in the films of Von Sternberg, not even Lola-Lola of *The Blue Angel*, who describes her problem in the song she sings the night the Professor visits her cabaret:

*"Men flutter round me like moths around a flame,*
*And if they get burned then, well, I am not to blame."*

But the Professor does not heed the warning. His head is turned by the odor of musk and civet she exudes for him. He is consumed in the flame, being unable to cope with this reality, victim of a sexual drive he never faced before, and run over by it.

And, as Edith Hamilton, that great Greek scholar, goes on to say, in retelling the story of Pygmalion, "When nothing could be added to the statue's perfection, a strange fate befell its creator: he had fallen in love, deeply, passionately in love, with the thing he had made. It must be said in explanation that the statue did not look like a statue; no one would have thought it was ivory or stone, but warm human flesh, motionless for a moment only. Such was the wondrous power of this disdainful young man. *The supreme achievement of art was his, the art of concealing art.*" (Italics mine.) Does Sternberg depart again from Pygmalion in this respect? We are free to believe it or not. The truth is beside the point; such is the nature of art that it transcends homely truths. The things great or beautiful done by men are greater or more beautiful than they are. They would not be *great* artists or scientists or whatever if their work did not transcend themselves. That goes for Nietzsche, himself, who said just the opposite, that nothing in itself is beautiful: man, alone, is beautiful. It is beautiful only because *he* is there to admire it. Which only goes to show that opposites can be one, for this statement is not so opposite after all.

*The Blue Angel* posed its own problems for Sternberg, a whoop-dee-do which had to be set within the limitations of the characters of the impudent Lola-Lola and the fool Professor. Sternberg etches his *dramatis personae* swiftly, like a newspaper or magazine caricaturist doing his regular stint for, let us say, *Simplicissimus*, the acidly brilliant satirical weekly that flourished in Germany up to the advent of Hitler. He is *engagé* by the erotic appeal of the plump, pretty dumpling he finds in Dietrich, as perfectly suited in his mind for the cantharidic lubricity of this brazen Berlin tart, baiting the customers of a third-rate dive—we can almost smell the stale beer, tobacco smoke, and sweat of this sleazy cabaret. *The Blue Angel* was the most realistic German film since *Variety* with hymeneal hymns to priapic exploits (as in the coarse ditty, "Tonight, Fellows, I'm Looking for a Real Man"). He senses the animal breath of her sensual person but no one but he does. Until then she was a minor actress in some minor films and stage revues. And even after he introduces her to Pommer and Jannings at Ufa as a *fait accompli*, the Lola-Lola to-be of *The Blue Angel*, no one but he can smell this animal breath. Of course, by the time he finished the picture, and it knocked a gala opening night audience into stupefaction, they smelled it too. But Sternberg didn't wait to see the effect of the film on audiences; he returned to Hollywood, knowing full well the havoc he had done, and determined to consolidate this accomplishment with Dietrich's first American film. It was she who gave him the romantic novel to read on the boat returning to New York, *Amy Jolly*, by an obscure writer, Benno Vigny. It was this that Sternberg decided had the germ of an idea for her American debut, which he would call *Morocco*.

The sleek and mysterious Amy Jolly of *Morocco* was a far cry from the buxom trollop of *The Blue Angel*, as different as the two stories themselves were. For *Morocco*, Sternberg abandoned the realistic style of *The Blue Angel* for the "glamorous style" of Hollywood. Marlene had been signed by Paramount to a long-term contract, she had to be groomed to the American taste and the American taste called for glamour—not realism. (For a realistic picture of the

Foreign Legion, see Feyder's *Le Grande Jeu* or Duvivier's *La Bandera*.) Sternberg saw to this. Master of many styles, he set a tone for Marlene's American debut that suited her so well that he was unable to free himself from involvement in it. "After my second picture with Marlene," he said, "I did not want to make any more films with her. But Miss Dietrich said to me, 'You want to show the world you're a great director and that I am a bad actress. Isn't that what you want to do? You want me to go to another director.' Being a gentleman, I continued."

It is very disconcerting to interview Sternberg. He pretends you know the right questions to ask, the pertinent ones, and it's almost impossible to think of a right question when you consider the answers you get to those you do ask. When Stephen Watts in London in the late Thirties interviewed him in an article captioned: "The Truth About Dietrich and von Sternberg," the director was quoted: "If I had not brought out Miss Dietrich's qualities [he always refers to her, with the barest exceptions, as "Miss Dietrich"], somebody else would have done so six months later. I played the part of an abstract destiny, rather than a discoverer. She was grateful—not sentimentally, but with an intellectual gratitude. . . ."

Then: "We went on making films together because we were forced to. I did it reluctantly. From my own point of view as a director, I was through with Miss Dietrich after *Morocco*. I had made *The Blue Angel* in Germany showing her in one mood, and in Hollywood I tried the experiment of showing her in a lazier, more exotic style. I had no more experiments in mind and she had no need of me. . . ."

Finally: "But we were made to go on, protesting, until at last I refused to plagiarize myself anymore."

*Selah!* These are the facts and facts are stubborn things, you cannot argue with them. But what do they tell us of the "mysterious" *rapport* in this unique example of director and star, absolutely unique in the annals of the screen? Of the influence they had on each other? There are aesthetic truths that are truer than facts. "Art is a lie," said Picasso, "that helps us see the truth." Then we must go back to the films, themselves, for the answer. Or, before doing so, we can recall some of Dietrich's own statements on the subject of her mentor: After completing their last film together, *The Devil Is a Woman*, she was quoted by a London interviewer

(Charles Graves, in *The Daily Sketch*) as saying: "He is by far the greatest director in the world. I would love to be in one of his pictures again—even in a small part." On another occasion: "If anyone says anything against him, I have nothing to say to such a person, I don't even see this person, I look right through him."

Let's try going back to the films for a clue ...

The Czech novelist, Max Brod, in *Die Frau nach der man sich sehnt* (*The Woman You Are Yearning For*)—in which Dietrich co-starred with Fritz Kortner and Uno Henning in Germany a year before *The Blue Angel* (a 1929 silent film directed by Kurt Bernhardt)—has for its theme the "ideal" woman of a man's dreams. Dietrich prophetically played this role, for she was to become the consummation of a dream long held some 6000 miles from Berlin by a young director in Hollywood in whom, in the women he chose for his films, there seemed to be a groping for some quality he wanted but only fitfully obtained and that never fully. Study the sullen face of Georgia Hale in *The Salvation Hunters*, with its weary glances, and see how it is repeated in the faces of Evelyn Brent in *Underworld*, *The Dragnet*, and *The Last Command*, and again by Betty Compson in *Docks of New York*. These are all world-weary women, searching, themselves, for something they want. Never once does a nimbus shine from them, never once do they light up the screen with a radiance —why? Because the director has not yet been inspired by them. They are all very attractive and play their parts well, but you feel that the director is not inspired by them. They don't catch fire because the director hasn't caught fire. He is doing magnificent jobs on the pictures, but his women stars don't "send" him, as the saying goes. But you sense that he is feeling his way and you hope with him that some day he will find her. He seemingly abandons the search in his choice of the very sympathetic Esther Ralston for *The Case of Lena Smith* ... and a thoroughly colorless Fay Wray in *Thunderbolt*, both in 1929, bridging the transition from the silent film to sound with the latter ...

And then came the invitation from Erich Pommer, of Ufa, via Emil Jannings's recommendation, to come to Berlin.

Sternberg has said that the image he had in mind for Lola-Lola had already been drawn by the acidulous French artist, Félicien Rops. When he found her that night at a performance of Georg Kaiser's play, *Zwei Krawatten* (*Two Neck-ties*), she "was not only a model who had been designed by Rops, but Toulouse-Lautrec would have turned a couple of handsprings had he laid eyes on her." Obviously, with two such mordant artist-*flâneurs* as her spiritual "godfathers" in the mind of the director, two such acrid observer-denizens of the *demi-monde*, she would be ideal as the tawdry saloon singer of Heinrich Mann's story, capable of leading that "pillar of respectability," Professor Immanuel Rat, by the nose. But what initially attracted the director to her was the "cold disdain" that emanated from her presence on the stage that night, her "impressive poise." He had not only found his Lola-Lola, he had found something more, much more, as it turned out to be. Was he aware of that at the time? Again, we can believe it or not. Sternberg had already changed the name of the heroine, if that's the word for her, from the novel's Rosa Froehlich to Lola-Lola, inspired by Wedekind's Lulu in *Pandora's Box*. If it was just a ques-tion of settling for the right Lola-Lola, well, that wouldn't necessarily have taken too long—Berlin had many attractive young actresses who could have been manipulated by a clever director every-which-way. Hadn't Pabst imported Louise Brooks from Hollywood for his film of *Pandora's Box*. And, after an immediate follow-up second picture with her, hadn't he sent her back to Hollywood? He saw only Lulu in her, no-thing else. (Even in *Diary of a Lost One* she still was Lulu.) But Sternberg did see something else in Dietrich, something that was to change both their lives and careers for the next five years. *Morocco*, the second film he made with her, was utterly different from *The Blue Angel*, as was Amy Jolly from Lola-Lola. Now he refined her screen image and now a nimbus radiated from her and she shined on the screen with a radiant light. The old sullenness was back, the weary glance, the world-weariness of his first screen women—only now he *was* inspired, now he painted her with soft lights and shadows, now he had a star on whose face he could lavish his treasure, the limitless knowledge he had of light-ing and photography. If ever the camera caressed the face of a star, it did so in the films they made together. Erwin, the hero of Brod's novel, had found his Stasha, the woman he was yearning for, Pygmalion had found his Galatea. Of course, he wanted to leave her after *Morocco*; of course, she refused. The gods who attend these things smile at human bickerings and give them just enough leeway to let them think they are creatures of free will. Paramount was appointed by them the *deus ex machina* of this *comédie humaine*. A poet a thousand years ago wrote, "On the first day of creation was set down what the last day of reckoning will read." There is no such thing as chance, then; it is fate, misnamed . . . so they say.

Now this is all terribly romantic, I know, but how else do you write on the subject of "Sternberg and Marlene"? Good films, like all other good art, are not made in a vacuum. They spring from real thoughts, real feelings. You can be as objective as you like, but you cannot hide it, though you may disguise it. At the risk of compounding one error into two, I repeat: "There are aesthetic truths that are truer than the facts."

We have remarked on the uniqueness of this director–star relationship. It was in truth unique. You cannot compare the Czinner–Bergner director–star relationship with it for, though for a long while Paul Czinner directed only Elisabeth Bergner, there were two differences: (a) she was his wife; (b) she always played the same part, at least for a long time she did; the child–woman. The same goes for Godard and Anna Karina. Stiller–Garbo? One picture together, though it meant something more to him than that. Who else? Antonioni–Vitti? Romantic only to themselves. . . .

Another point. In connection with my earlier musings on the women in Sternberg's first films, it is interesting to note that, when being interviewed by him for *The Blue Angel*, Dietrich informed the director that she had seen some of his previous work, and, though she reluctantly conceded that he knew how to handle men, she doubted that he could do as well with women. When Merle Oberon was interviewed by the BBC in London for *The Epic That Never Was*, you will recall that Miss Oberon volunteered the information that Sternberg was chosen by Alexander Korda to direct *I, Claudius* because he had become famous as a "woman's director." (Miss Oberon was married to Mr. Korda at the time.) This was, of course, *after* the Dietrich films. Richard Griffith, former curator of the Museum of Modern Art Film Library, quotes "a not entirely bemused observer," C. H. Rand: "I know well enough, of course, that the enchantment is not Marlene alone. I see her through the eyes of Josef von Sternberg, Like all the great screen characters, Marlene is a myth, a symbol, an idea. And it is because she is the perfect embodiment of that idea that she has this fascination for me. As with all men, a fair part of my subconscious life spends itself in a dream of a perfect vamp. I want a woman whose passion is not a blind rage of the body or the soul, but a recognition of mutual attraction in which reason or humor will play their part, as far as love permits. But vamps with brains are far to seek. And vamps with humor even further. I find all my requisites in the screen character of Marlene Dietrich. She has beauty in abundance. She has a rich, sensuous allure. And you have only to look at her eyes to see that she has brains, and at her mouth to see that she has humor."

*Bien sur*, it is exactly these qualities which she has in her Sternberg films, and in no other, in absolutely no other. Most of the characters in the films of Von Sternberg are mouthpieces for the director—they say what he would say in their places, male or female, it makes no difference. He wrote all their dialogue, anyway. Often, they speak like he does, in slow, measured cadences, or with dry, deadpan wit. Sometimes they even look like him, as Lionel Atwill did as Don Pasquale in *The Devil Is a Woman*.

"Out of this matrix of legend," continues Richard Griffith, "sprang two mutually contradictory ones, each in its own way, like Freudian dreamwork, trying to account for the provenance of the screen Marlene. Because she would work with no other director, it was for a long time almost universally believed that Marlene Dietrich and Josef von Sternberg constituted a Trilby and Svengali of the studios, with the star under the hypnotic domination of the director, much to her own detriment: this legend held that Von Sternberg was merely using Dietrich and her great popularity as a prop to enable him to indulge his taste for pictorial extravagance, Dietrich being to him no more than a red thread in the elaborate visual pattern of his films. The opposing legend, subscribed to by the much smaller number of the director's admirers, was that his obsession with Marlene was destroying him as an artist. How else to account for his exclusive concentration on her, at the expense of the narrative and dramatic aspects of their films? Here was a superb director, potentially second to none, enslaved to an image! To no one—including this writer—does it seem to have occurred at the time that it is not only the business but the golden privilege of a film director to create great images, and that in Marlene Dietrich Von Sternberg knew that he had made the discovery of a lifetime."

Have we said that Dietrich took a real interest in the techniques of filmmaking, of the lighting and photography in particular? Being intelligent and having, herself, artistic sensibility, she was frequently helpful. "She was a good assistant," said Sternberg. They worked, as the saying goes, "hand in glove." There was never a better fit,

Between *The Blonde Venus* and *The Scarlet Empress*, which is to say, after five pictures in a row with Sternberg, she made *The Song of Songs* with Rouben Mamoulian at Sternberg's suggestion. "It will do you good to work with another director, for a change," he said. As the heroine of Hermann Sudermann's novel she played an innocent peasant girl who meets a famous sculptor who asks her to model a nude statue of the ideal of feminine loveliness. She does and he falls in love with her. Pygmalion and Galatea again? Let us not make too much of this analogy despite its persistence, though why shouldn't we note here that Sternberg was a sculptor, too, not just metaphorically, but actually? One of his works is a striking nude female torso—with a rosary.

Finally, who had the greater influence on whom? Sternberg would have been Sternberg and everything that that connotes even without Dietrich. He was that long before he met her, and in the fragments of *I, Claudius*, in *The Shanghai Gesture* and *Anatahan*, he was still that even without her. She was nothing before she met him and only occasionally interesting after the two broke up, very occasionally, and even then almost completely without the humor and *panache* with which she played under Sternberg. For instance, her Concha in *The Devil Is a Woman* is played on the highest level of wit, a devastating parody of the whole idea of the *femme fatale*, a type of role she and Sternberg raised to the highest comic (but most telling) degree, the apogee of what Renoir strove for in Catherine Hessling's stylized playing of the title role in his *Nana*. (As a contrast of how you do this when you're in dead earnest, one could cite the way the vamp is portrayed in Renoir's *La Chienne*.)

And apropos *The Devil Is a Woman*, this sado-masochistic story, played in that vein to the *n*th power, do we not find in this extraordinary swan-song of its director–star collaboration a clue to the fire that activated their seven films together? It is their favorite film. It is a summing up of everything they went through together, in and out of the studio. Both knew it was to be their last together and they made their ultimate statements on this relationship in it. This was more than a Svengali–Trilby affair, if it ever was that, for it was bruited that this Trilby also had a hypnotic effect on her Svengali. If so, this paradox would fit in with the characteristically perverse humor with which the Sternberg–Dietrich films are rife. (Like the lesbian joke in *Morocco*, for instance, or the delicate goddess emerging from the horrendous gorilla costume in *The Blonde Venus*.) A psychoanalyst might flippantly hazard the guess that it was Trilby who hypnotized Svengali, rather than the other way around, though, of course, Svengali never realized that. He could make quite a case for it, *after the fact*, of course, since you can rationalize almost anything, given the smallest "fulcrum and a place to stand" to paraphrase Archimedes.

But enough of this game. Let the marvelous epiphanies these two created together for whatever reason (the elements that go into the making of a work of art must always, in the last analysis, remain a mystery) suffice us.

"Dietrich never influenced me," says Sternberg. "I influenced her. Her stature absorbed what I had to offer. In that respect she was good."

And Pygmalion, in the legend as Ovid tells it, what happened to him? Oh, it all ended banally enough. Venus took pity on his pinings over the statue and brought it to life. With unutterable gratitude and joy he put his arms around his love and saw her smile into his eyes and blush. Venus herself graced their marriage with her presence. They had a son and lived happily ever after, *pardee*!

But that has nothing to do with the cinema.

# III

The Salvation Hunters opens with a sea gull perched on
a piece of flotsam floating in Los Angeles bay and Anatahan
ends on a Japanese airfield. Between these two far-flung
images is a span of 28 years, during which Sternberg completed 22 films (John Ford made 129), of which 18 are
still available for re-viewing and re-evaluation today. Woman
of the Sea is owned by Chaplin, who has made no copy
available to any cinémathèque. The Dragnet and The Case
of Lena Smith are similarly not to be found in any cinémathèque. Jet Pilot, even in its mutilated released form, is also
unavailable for re-viewing, being owned by the elusive Howard
Hughes, who has apparently withdrawn it from circulation.
And of these 18, three may be dismissed as having been made
under unfelicitous conditions—Crime and Punishment, The
King Steps Out, and Sergeant Madden. Remains 15 . . .
What do these 15 films say to us today that is still cogent? Certainly, the world of 1967 is different from the
one a generation ago—1925—that witnessed the birth of
Sternberg's art. Seeing them today, in the midst of all the
new films, they look so different as to seem to have been
made on another planet. (Or maybe it is the new films
that look so different that they seem to have been made on
another planet—anyway, both do not come from the same
world.) And not only Sternberg's films but those of all that
hallowed company of his colleagues in the cinema pantheon
as well. And why is this? Because there has been no transition. Here we have the one serious lack in the cinema as a
continuing art that is present in all the other arts, e.g., the
continuity of tradition through the flowering of disciples. This
is present not only in all other creative arts but in the performing arts as well. Only the cinema has no traditions that
are maintained, and its "old masters," the first ones, the

Giottos of the film, have no disciples. Some of them exerted a brief influence, chiefly because those influences were a vogue of the moment, but when that vogue was over these influences disappeared. Most of them had no influence at all. The stronger the individuality of the artist in the cinema, the less influence he usually exerts, because the idea of disciples is not natural to the cinema. On the rare occasions when it happened, it was self-willed and this will had to be imposed on the film industry, for it never meant to be an art but an industry. It became an art despite itself by stubborn self-willed artists who imposed themselves on this industry. This is the only salutary tradition of the cinema—the will of the artist. The "Western" flowered in America because individuality of statement did not matter in this *genre*. Bad "Westerns" were as rare as good "Westerns," the general level of acceptable competence being on such a low plane. The triumph of this *genre* is the triumph of mediocrity—always the safest and surest level on which to work. In the very beginning, Griffith, Mack Sennett, Chaplin, Stroheim, Murnau, and Lubitsch (in his early American films) can be said to have had some disciples for a while during the formative years of the motion pictures. But this did not last or develop except sporadically and with increasingly less frequency. Who were the disciples of the apocalyptic visions of the Lang of the *Nibelungen* and *Metropolis*, the Gance of *J'Accuse* and *Napoleon*, of that most cerebral of film poets, Eisenstein? Who was the disciple of the Dreyer of *La Passion de Jeanne d'Arc*? Of course it was perfectly natural that new talents would develop over the years in a new medium that was "catching on" so popularly. But if we are mindful that the word, disciple, comes from discipline, which is to say, the training that develops self-control, character, orderliness, and efficiency, even those new talents (when they *were* talented) who wanted to go their own way could not bypass the rules of film grammar and syntax with which the film language had been initially formed. And style, too, if it was to be followed, or copied, or to serve as an inspiration, it, too, had its rules of weights and balances, its limits of interplay beyond which the interplay would lose itself in irrelevancies; most of all it had its celebration of indigenously cinematic epiphanies, *vide*, Renoir's *Nana* or Ford's *My Darling Clementine*, to take two disparate examples. Would there have been the Soviet *New Babylon* without this *Nana* to show it the way? Yesterday, Renoir was idolized by the French New Wave but no one is following in his footsteps. There are many roads to Parnassus but you have to at least be *on* the road, if that's where you're headed for. Who makes those roads? Every new creative artist with a vision of his own who does not see his personal vision on the horizon of an already existing path. He uses the same tools to climb that path but he carries his own banner, his style. And he is subject to the laws of artistic gravity and aesthetic equilibrium once he is on that path (e.g., discipline) and must beware the pitfalls of imbalance or he will fall. The eclectics, like Orson Welles, are bound by the same unity and harmony of purpose that binds them all, all those who would reach Parnassus, where Apollo and the Muses dwell. The poets, like Vigo, Clair, and Cocteau, do not even have to climb, they are winged . . . But every true artist is a poet or he would not even be looking toward Parnassus but at the box office.

All of which is by way of introduction to the fact that Sternberg's films, like those of all the "old masters," do not exist in a vacuum, nor are they today like hot-house flowers that must be artificially nurtured to retain their bloom. The bloom will forever be on them. What made them exceptional in their time is what gives them their staying power today, and those qualities are still, and always will be, exceptional. The cogency of those films for us today is in their validity of statement and the technique with which that statement was made, the formal discipline that guided that technique, and its obeisance to the immutable laws of aesthetics, for this is a part of the statement, just like the editing of a film is a part of the direction. In short—the way a story is told is part of that story. You can tell the same story badly or well; you can also tell it well enough or magnificently. It depends on who is telling the story. That is perhaps why form is, in the last analysis, as Freud pointed out, of more decisive importance than content, though under ideal conditions the latter dictates the style of the former. There is always one best way to tell a story and that way has to be found. "The difference between the right word and the almost-right word," said Mark Twain, "is the difference between lightning and a fire-fly."

Let us begin our critical "re-evaluation" of Sternberg today by briefly examining first his influence. *Underworld*, as we have noted, had a decided influence in catapulting a new *genre*—the gangster film—in America. Not only did he introduce a new theme (always a rarity) to the American screen but even something of his laconic style seeped into the plethora of gangster films that followed (*Quick Millions, Scarface, Doorway to Hell, The Public Enemy, Little Caesar*). But having said that, it is difficult to find further influences save in single occasional works here and there. If Mamoulian owed *Love Me Tonight* to Lubitsch, he certainly owed *The Song of Songs* to Sternberg, but only pictorially—the harshness and sardonic edge of Sternberg, which was his strength beyond his exotic pictorialism, was missing. Nicholas Farkas's *La Bataille*, especially in its English version (*Thunder in the East*, with Boyer, Inkijinoff, Merle Oberon, and John Loder) is a "Sternbergian" film, and certainly Ozep's *Der Moerder Karamazov* is almost *echt*-Sternberg throughout—the only film I know from another director that I would not have been surprised to see signed by him. I mean this as a compliment to Ozep. I cannot think of another, offhand, until Welles's *Lady from Shanghai*, especially for its elliptical style, so characteristic of the director of *Underworld* and *Morocco*, and its penchant for *bizarrerie*. Although Sternberg did not attach much importance to the dialogue in his sound films, regarding it chiefly as intonations, as part of the sound, like the individual notes of a music score have importance not singly but only as part of an orchestration, it is interesting to notice that the dialogue in his films, for all that, is invariably highly literate and sophisticated. This quality is to be found also in the Farkas, Ozep, and Welles illustrations above cited. Since then there has been nothing I know of traceable to Sternberg's work, although I have heard that Jacques Demy (in *Lola* and *The Bay of Angels*) is regarded as fitfully reflecting Sternberg's influence, an observation I reject without prejudice to Demy. So much for Sternberg's influence . . .

One of the reasons for the lack of films influenced by his work is their daring, both technical and ideological. He took risks, not out of bravado (the plane of his intelligence was always too high for that) but because his *daemon* impelled him toward it; it was as if it were *inevitable* that he do

it. The inexorable logic of *Morocco*, since it is a true love story, is that, if it has to come to that, one risks all for love. And just as Amy Jolly leaves the rich LeBessière to follow her Legionnaire into the desert,* at which bourgeois audiences laugh because they would never do such a foolish thing, least of all for love, Sternberg, too, hazards the same risk his heroine does because he, too, has done it for the same reason. Both have been true to themselves—hence their actions were inevitable. Proust, in his preface to Paul Morand's *Green Shoots*, admires his stylistic brilliance but finds one fault—that Morand's imagery is *not always inevitable*. This is the heart of the matter. One does not cavil with the first rule of human conduct—"Know thyself." And just as most audiences would not have followed Amy Jolly's action, most directors would not be apt to follow Sternberg's. Maybe they knew themselves, also, and their selves were different. But note that the three illustrations cited as possibly being influenced by Sternberg carry the same convictions. In *Thunder in the East*, the Japanese naval commander commits *hara kiri* because he feels he has dishonored himself through his wife, although he dearly loves her. In *Der Moerder Karamazov*, Grushinka willingly follows Dmitri on a prison train to Siberia for ten years because, as she says, "People love in Siberia, too." In *Lady from Shanghai*, the hero allows himself to become involved with a sinister character in a plot that, if successful, might make it possible for him to run off with the young woman he's in love with. He knows he is playing with fire but is willing to risk it. Audiences in their snug seats and directors in their snug berths are disturbed by such seeming self-sacrifices and laugh them off in self-protection. But Sternberg could well say with Gide, "To disturb, that is my role."

Who would dare to follow the director of such paroxysmic explosions of the baroque as *The Scarlet Empress* and *The Devil Is a Woman*? (You can only make such films—and get away with them—once.) Who would become a disciple of a director who follows a film in which the action pivots around a dredge scooping up mud from a river bottom (*The*

* Much has been made of the "absurdity" of this scene where Amy Jolly goes into the desert on high heels. Unperceptive critics as well as audiences failed to notice that after a few impulsive steps she kicks her heels off.

*Salvation Hunters*), and whose characters are the dregs of the earth, with one that was so physically beautiful (*Woman of the Sea*) that its producer was bewildered by it and refused to release it? How do you follow a director who then makes six harsh films in a row, each getting progressively harsher and more bitter, from *Underworld* to *The Blue Angel*, among them the unforgettable *Docks of New York*, which rivals *Woman of the Sea* in beauty of photography and poetry of motion, although half the action takes place either in the stoke-hole of a dirty tramp steamer or a sordid waterfront saloon, and then follows this with a romantic film so unique in its use of sound against image (*Morocco*) as to still be, thirty-seven years later, one of the supreme examples of utilizing the best elements of both the silent and the sound film? Not only would the prospective disciple be bewildered by such versatility but to follow in the footsteps of Sternberg he would have to come up with something original and unprecedented of his own, too, all the while. It is not just a matter of copying Sternberg's glistening photography. The usually perceptive John Grierson made one of the silliest statements in film history when, after praising the photography of *Woman of the Sea*, he concluded wistfully, "When a director dies he becomes a photographer." The very next film Sternberg made was *Underworld*, which catapulted him into overnight fame as a director. The disciple would also have to have such control over every element of his film as has been vouchsafed few directors in what has become increasingly a producer's medium, rather than the director's. Who would dare such a shot as the train getting under way in the beginning of *Shanghai Express*, slowly chugging its way through a narrow Chinese street so crowded with people as to make one wonder if such a thing were possible? Directors more timid and more discreet would not hazard such an "unrealistic" scene—with their usual banal results, *bien entendu.* Sternberg throws discretion to the winds where it serves his artistic purpose. He reserves discretion for where it belongs—in the relations between his characters. How better to get across the idea of a "China teeming with people" than the way he does it? The essence of reality is better than reality, where art is concerned. Both Goethe and Picasso have attested to this as an aesthetic principle. Renoir's Nana was not like Zola's, and neither was like the real Nana, for

there was a real Nana. But what does it matter? Only the idea matters and that is. the function of art. In the words of Klee, "Art does not reproduce the visible, it *makes* visible." When the chant from the muezzin calls the faithful to prayer in *Morocco*, the Arabs under the *soukh* fall to their knees and bend down, but not all of them (though any other director would have had all of them)—two Arabs walk away from the camera and the shadows of the overhanging trellises that form the *soukh* glide with delicate tracery across their white robes. Sternberg gives us something to enchant the eye while the song of prayer is going on, but even this isn't done gratuitously, for the moment of prayer serves to introduce the leading character, Gary Cooper, as the Legionnaire, who uses the preoccupation of the Arabs to make an assignation in pantomime with a native girl eyeing him from a doorway. And even this isn't all; the handsome Cooper's devastating effect on women is laconically stated a moment before when a young Arab woman from a low rooftop lets down her veil for a second to reveal her prettiness to him. All of this rich detail while the muezzin chant is going on takes less than half a minute of screen time. This is how you direct, this is how you avoid soul-destroying waits between things happening (for screen-time is highly concentrated and fifteen seconds of watching someone read a letter on the screen can make a misanthrope out of an angel), this is how you employ cinematic polyphony, as a composer does in musical composition. The inter-cutting of several images and sounds to orchestrate a scene to its fullest plangency, all contributing to the story, plot-wise or nuance-wise (no nuance is so delicate that it cannot enrich a scene), is one of Sternberg's most characteristic effects (*vide* his "reaction" scenes in *Vanity's Price* mentioned earlier). *Morocco*, that endlessly fascinating source of felicitous screen direction, opens polyphonically with two opposing actions—a column of Legionnaires marching from the far distance into a town to the arrogant beat of their drums—and, as they approach nearer and nearer, an Arab in the foreground struggling frantically to get his donkey off the road, cursing the stubborn animal and his forebears. The Arab's exasperated fulminations are like a farrago of crazy arpeggios over the inexorably approaching drum beats, getting louder and louder. Humor and suspense from the first frame. Just in time, the Arab manages

The die is cast. Dietrich prepares to go on for her American début in the memorable café scene of *Morocco*. Paul Porcasi as the Levantine impresario. The havoc wrought by this unprecedented cinema odalisque was incalculable. (1930)

Playing together like the meshed gears of a Rolls Royce, Dietrich and Gary Cooper gave the film what we call "pizzazz" and the French call *panache* under the mordant humor and exquisite sensibility of Sternberg's direction. (*Morocco*)

to push the donkey to one side of the road as the Legionnaires thud past—but not before the Colonel, marching at
their head, gives the donkey a final push to get the animal
out of the way, for the Arab didn't quite make it completely.
And here, momentarily, the two opposing actions join (as in
music two opposing rhythms finally cross and meet; a moment
that gives the two their relation and the passage its meaning).
It's a nuance, the smallest possible, but the scene is richer
for it. Later in *Morocco*, during the famous scene of the
engagement dinner of Amy Jolly (Dietrich) and LeBessière
(Menjou), which begins gaily and suddenly starts to lose
momentum and languish when the faint drum beats from
the outside distance (this time laced with bugle flourishes)
herald the approach of the Legionnaires returning from a
skirmish with the Arabs, the single strand of action and
sound (of the guests at the dinner party) becomes two
strands at the moment when Dietrich, realizing her Legionnaire lover may be back, gets up in panic, breaking her
necklace of pearls (her engagement gift from LeBessière),
which she caught on the back of a chair in her haste (the
rupture that suddenly makes of the one strand of the action
two). She rushes out to join the column of troops outside,
searching for her Legionnaire (Cooper), while back at the
dinner party the conversation has slowed almost to a full
stop and desperate but futile attempts are made to revive it.
As the guests speak, LeBessière looks blankly at whomever is
talking, but he hears nothing and, indeed, there is nothing
to hear. The conversation is inane, turns on the weather, it
is not worth hearing, ultimately it crumbles. All the life has
gone out of the dinner party . . . just as years later Sternberg
was to note in *Anatahan*, in his brooding commentary, that
despite the violent fighting over the lone girl the shipwrecked
sailors found on the island, when she left the island ". . . there
was no more fighting . . . there was also no more life." The
vital force of woman as the life-giver is one of the beautiful
overtones of both films.

One could write a book on the subtleties of *Morocco* alone
and its audio-visuals, which are as rich in their polyphonies
as a score by Brahms or Ravel.

This kind of incandescent filmmaking, which illumines
everything (in contrast to the present vogue for mystification
and opaqueness), has naturally attracted no disciples. Most

films today are apotheoses of the single-entendre, when they are not being "mystical" or "profound."

Literal expositions and redundancies have no place in Sternberg's art and those who say that *Anatahan* contradicts this have failed to feel the virtue of its simplicity. Here the "left hand," as in a piano score by Brahms or Ravel, for instance, is more important than the "right hand"—the former being, in this case, the eloquent commentary (mentioned earlier) spoken by the narrator, the latter being the images. Critics of *Anatahan* don't realize you could turn the images off and just listen to the sound track (or vice-versa, turn the sound track off and just watch the sequence of images) and the story of *Anatahan* would unfold itself with equal clarity. And, since both are so right for each other, they complement each other. The narrator of the commentary is supposed to be one of the survivors of this island incident and, indeed, there *was* one such who wrote a book about this from which Sternberg adapted his film. The book is written in the first person, as is the commentary. The technical fact that this method obviates the necessity for sub-titles to translate the Japanese dialogue seems to have been overlooked by its critics. They have curiously also overlooked the fact that the presence of Sternberg's voice is in itself a rare asset to the film, for he not only wrote the narration but speaks it himself. How many film records do we have of great directors' voices, in which we can study their personalities through their voices? Why are not *Anatahan*'s critics grateful for this? Anyway, why must every film be made like every other film so·that it is easily recognized as such and hence does not disturb but falls into a convenient category for the critic? Many critics were upset by the polyphonic *Mr. Arkadin*, but praised the decidedly nonpolyphonic *The Umbrellas of Cherbourg* (which leans with all its weight on one song by Michel Legrand) without apparently having even heard the wonderfully vertiginous music score by Paul Misraki in the former and being totally ignorant of the best of the *genre* of the sung-film, *Amphitryon*, by Reinhold Schuenzel and Franz Doelle, made in Germany in 1933. I am inclined to think that many film critics are tone-deaf or they would have remarked on the impeccably modulated timbre of Sternberg's voice uttering its glinting drops of sorrow, its evocations of eternal truths, which form the core

of this remarkable outpouring of the human heart, which blends so beautifully in *Anatahan* with Ifukube's lovely music score. Besides being tone-deaf, I think many are blind, too. They look but they do not see. One of the most poetic moments in *Anatahan* has never to my knowledge been commented upon. It is possible it wasn't even understood. Several journalists asked me how the girl ever got off the island since this was never shown, they claimed. Keiko, the lone female on the island in *Anatahan*, is tired of being fought over and accepts the offer from an American warship waiting offshore to be returned to Japan, an offer made by leaflets dropped to all the shipwrecked Japanese sailors, an offer which they reject as an absurd enemy trick, not knowing the war is over and Japan was defeated. She stands on a promontory waving one of the leaflets to attract the attention of the ship while the narrator says, "A long time ago, Keiko said that if she had the wings of a bird she'd fly home." And at that moment her waving arms are like the flapping wings of a bird—and it is this motion which gets her off the island and back home. How simple and beautiful this is! But how unsensational! How invisible to the literal-minded. How unlike the palpable mystifications and symbolisms so portentously commented upon today. The corruption of the eye has never been more rampant. A distinguished psychiatrist told me the pseudo-Freudian symbolisms of $8\frac{1}{2}$ were as phony as a three-dollar bill.

This brings us inexorably to the matter of sex, since Sternberg's work has been so often equated with eroticism, especially in his films with Dietrich.

Ironically, it is just here that Sternberg has been at his most discreet. In a medium that has become, as Edmond Greville put it, one in which "voyeurism and cinema are synonymous," the films of Sternberg are by comparison anti-erotic. The director's mind is so involved with the refinements of his technique that there is no impulse to wallow in erotic swamps. Like Stroheim and Pabst and all the great directors from Griffith and Chaplin to Renoir and Bresson, sex is implicit, not explicit in his films. Only once, and that only in a five-second shot, did he ever make an explicit erotic comment, in *The Blue Angel*, the brief shot following the first time we see Dietrich (on the stage of the cabaret).

She is singing "Ich bin die fesche Lola" and Sternberg cuts from a long shot to a medium close-up of her magnificent legs from the midriff down to accent not who is singing but *what* is singing. The shot is witty and laconically makes its point, after which it isn't necessary to belabor it.

After that, the director follows the dictum of Polonius, "by indirection find direction out," and proves that literalness in sex is not only unnecessary but ultimately inhibiting because a clever director can always imply more than a less imaginative director can show, with all his explicitness. (*Vide* the complete work of Lubitsch from *The Marriage Circle* to *Trouble in Paradise*.) Besides, literalness in sex is a redundancy, and redundancy is a bore. (*Vide* Bergman's *The Silence*.) There are no scabrous passages ever in Sternberg, not because he is a moralist—although he is that, in its most salutary sense, without any *a priori* moral judgments, like a psychologist or psychoanalyst—but because it would be a waste of film footage, every foot of which is precious to a director with so much to say, with so many comments to make. His characters hardly ever even kiss and on the rare occasions when they do it is usually hidden behind a fan, a cloak, a back, or in a half-light. He has better ways of indicating romantic feeling or, when he wants to, purely sexual ones, by innuendo in his incisive dialogue and telling imagery. So sure is he of what he is doing that he doesn't need to pander to his audiences. His is a cinematic language of the utmost circumspection. The salacious nature of so many of today's films results from their directors' inability to resist their own stimuli, their contempt for their audiences, or, at best (or is it worst?), the demands of their financial backers. Audiences flock to these pictures as to a trough. Catch-penny lubricity for the "vulgar herd" of Baudelaire . . . When Gauguin stated, "I wanted to make it possible for the artist to dare anything," he did not mean that the artist could even become a pornographer as long as he remained an artist. Such a thing is a contradiction in terms. Art, like morality, consists in knowing where to draw the line. Gauguin meant: to dare anything *stylistically*. There is not a single erotic canvas by him. There are erotic drawings by Utamaro, Beardsley, and Picasso, but it is not their best work. There are none, *mirabile dictu*, by Toulouse-Lautrec, for all the low-

life of much of his subject matter. The really great artists don't succumb to their own stimuli . . . at least not in their art.

Let us consider another criticism leveled against Sternberg in the past—his "mannerisms," i.e., his cinema calligraphy. Now, mannerism is a way of doing things and that is what style is. And if that style is different from the usual way of doing things it becomes a "mannerism." Such criticism is never leveled against directors without any recognizable style—thus, they have no mannerisms. Is this a good thing? All the great directors have had highly individual styles (and even certain lesser ones whose work has somewhat more than routine interest)—so they, too, have their mannerisms by this definition. Today, Godard and Antonioni may be said to have their mannerisms. Buñuel's shock-therapy via his surrealist inserts is a form of mannerism. Orson Welles, of course, is a striking example. In short, it is just those elements in their work that set them apart from others that could be (and often are) held against them. This kind of glib criticism, which appears on the surface to make sense but which actually makes no sense at all, is unfortunately epidemic in the cinema. Sternberg without his "mannerisms" would not be Sternberg, just as Stroheim without his and Griffith without his and Orson Welles and even Chaplin without theirs would not be what they are. Even if by mannerisms these critics mean "excesses" they are still wrong because they don't understand that even excess has its function in art, for through excess ultimate expressiveness is reached, ultimate statements are made. "Were it not for his excesses," said Romain Rolland, "Beethoven would not have been Beethoven." Art is not a cup of tisane or camomile tea, it is not polite for the sake of being polite, it is not a warm bath, it is not necessarily a comfortable or even a comforting experience. It is in constant ferment, it breaks barriers and defies accepted canons of conventions, it is by its very nature anarchistic, in the sense that Saint-Just was anarchistic. If Stroheim felt he needed 40 reels to properly present *Greed*, who understood better than he what he was talking about? When a conductor to whom Beethoven had presented a new score looked incredulously at it and said he (Beethoven) was crazy if he thought the violin section of the orchestra could play such a difficult work, Beethoven replied

angrily, "What do I care about your lousy violins when the spirit moves me?"

Every artist of any distinction (distinction not only of merit but those characteristics which make him distinct from others) has his mannerisms. Dietrich and Garbo had theirs, Bardot with her monotone *moue* like a sulky Pekinese has hers, El Greco and Debussy had theirs, Maurice Chevalier and John Barrymore, Josephine Baker and Jascha Heifetz, Catherine Hessling, Paganini and Mistinguette, W. C. Fields and Picasso, Harpo Marx and Eisenstein, Frederick Lowe, the *douanier* Rousseau, Paul Klee, De Pachmann, Semmelweiss and Lenin, Brigitte Helm as the robot girl of *Metropolis*, Charles-Henri Alkan, *Hallelujah* and *Hallelujah the Hills*, Cocteau, Oscar Wilde, Harry Langdon, Norman McLaren, Satie . . . wherever you turn you find highly mannered artists, queer fish all. Their mannerisms are the stuff of their originality, to whatever degree, but even professional critics are not always capable of appreciating originality for what it is, and if they personally don't like it they call it a "mannerism" as if it were a tic. By and large, people don't want the *status quo* of their opinions and attitudes disturbed and have little capacity to make distinctions to the fullest degree, though they may make approximate distinctions. Pascal in his *Pensées* may have had this in mind when he said, "The greater intellect one has, the more originality one finds in men. Ordinary people find no difference between men." They may regard one film (since we are dealing with films) as better than another, but that the difference between the two may be that one is not just better but is as far above the other as the distance between the earth and the moon doesn't occur to them. Their horizon has not that wide a latitude.

There used to be a facetious axiom that everyone had two businesses, his own and the movies. Since the movies are a popular art, it is easy to give opinions on them and enlist solemn approval or equally solemn disapproval from others without necessarily anyone involved having any critical basis (i.e., an aesthetic formulated from the entire history of the films) for his opinions. This dilettantism spills over into much writing by professional film critics also. In no other art could a professional critic get away with as much ignorance about the art he is writing about than in that of the motion pictures. But in the comparatively short span of the cinema as

an art, the 52 years from *The Birth of a Nation* till today,
enough cogent and sober writing has taken place to have built
up a solid basis for a real aesthetic from which students can
learn, for the cinema is an art also to be studied, like any
other, from books and other writings as well as from the
works themselves. It is up to the teacher to guide the student
through the maze of these writings, however, as more than
in any other body of critical writing are there writings that
obfuscate rather than clarify. Mis-statements of facts alone
are particularly endemic to this field, being based on that
old bawd, Dame Hearsay (so many films having disappeared
or are not easily accessible), the repetition of facile shib-
boleths and half-truths, hoary canards that once made "good
copy" and which die hard, lies told from ignorance and kept
up for the royalties ... *Sic semper cinema!*

Mis-statements of evaluations are something else. Usually
history rights these in time, *de gustibus non disputandum* not-
withstanding, as it does where such mis-statements occur in
the other arts. One need only accept the fact that there
exist objective standards in all the arts by which their excellence is measured and that the works themselves fall into
their rightful places apart from personal likes and dislikes
(rationalizations of prejudices) as if governed by a higher
power than the animadversions of critics, for far more harm
has been done by not praising good work than by praising
bad work. Thus, when Sternberg's first film, *The Salvation
Hunters*, that highly poetic affirmation of life, was first
screened, a Hollywood trade-paper of unlamented memory
called *Harrison's Reports* said of it, "We cannot decide
which of the two films, *Greed* or *The Salvation Hunters*, is
the filthier piece of work. ... Thinking it over, we have
decided that perhaps the more loathsome of the two is *The
Salvation Hunters.*" It is obviously not enough just to have
an opinion—beyond the "I-know-what-I-like" school of criticism, you have to be qualified to have an opinion. There goes
your *de gustibus*. . . .

No, Sternberg's "mannerisms" do not exist in a vacuum
and alone anymore than his art does. It is part of the whole
clamorous and exultant world wherever interesting people
are to be found in and out of the arts, in science and sociol-
ogy too, wherever dedicated men and women with a salutary

purpose are even "going against the grain" to accomplish their work.

Seen today, Sternberg's films remind us of all this, they are a reminder of the richness that has all but disappeared from the screens of the world, and of how beautiful it was to see the continuity of an intensely personal style maintained from film to film in a medium so frequently composed of anonymous works. Sex and violence are brazenly rampant on our liberated screens today but this liberation has only meant that those who exploit it have become slaves of their passions. Censorship at least enforced subtlety on the screen artist. Today you don't need to be subtle, you can be "frank," if that's the world for today's effusions. *Yesterday, Today, and Tomorrow* and *Night Games* have supplanted Lubitsch's *Kiss Me Again* and *So This Is Paris*. Is this really progress?

By richness I don't just mean striking pictorial composition but something even better—an attitude. At the end of a Sternberg film you know the director's attitude on a hundred things or more. Most modern films have no more attitude than a picture calendar (with someone's advertisement). They are impersonal works, carrying no personal statement. The picture is one thing—its director another; there is not necessarily any bond between them. That's never so in the work of a true artist. He makes a personal statement by everything, even the slightest and most casual thing, he does. Nothing happens by chance in such films—and that is their worth because everything in them has been inserted because it has value. This makes a rich film. It is also possible to become so mesmerized by the witchery of a Sternberg film that only when it is over (I'm thinking particularly of *The Docks of New York*) do you realize it has been a silent film. This also makes a rich film.

Best of all that make films rich are the human touches that make us smile inside before the smile is reflected on our faces or that tug even faintly at the heart in their brief passing, to remind us that we are still human beings for all our much vaunted cynicism in a cynical age and that it is an endearing thing to be in the presence of a work of art by another human being like ourselves, because it is sometimes possible to feel in the world that, in the final analysis, in the last reckoning, one is alone in those deepest recesses of the

heart where it counts most. The brief shot of the tear-stained sleeping faces of the Sieppe children, after their spanking, on the bed during the wedding party in *Greed*; the Tahitian natives draped over the masts and rigging of the visiting schooner in the bay in *Tabu*, as if the boat had suddenly sprouted blossoms; after the saloon fight in *The Docks of New York*, when the husky stevedore (George Bancroft) accidentally breaks a chair over the head of one of his adversaries and, being sorry, lifts the man up and rubs his head like a mother would, "to make the ache go away," without even looking at him but surveying the havoc around him with faint amusement; Dietrich as the condemned spy in *Dishonored* taking the blindfold offered her by the young officer commanding the execution squad and with it wiping a tear away on the young man's cheek; the final shot of the humiliated Professor Rat in *The Blue Angel* back at his old school desk, the symbol of his former dignity as a man, grasping the desk with a grip of passion so strong that the nightwatchman who discovers him there cannot pry the dead man's hands loose from it—one of the all-time great moments of the cinema (not in Heinrich Mann's book but inserted by Sternberg); the *mea culpa* of the mother at the end of *An American Tragedy* when she knows her son will be executed; the basic fraternity of decency that should exist even among political or social antagonists that results in the rebel Chang's (in *Shanghai Express*) permitting the French officer to go freely, although his army passport says he was dishonorably discharged and he is illegally still wearing his army uniform, because he is visiting his sister and doesn't want her to know of his disgrace; Walter Huston's sudden realization of his defection as a father when he learns the truth about his daughter, Poppy, in *The Shanghai Gesture* and wryly remarks, "The sins of the fathers..." leaving the rest unspoken but completed in the hearts of the spectators; the return of the defeated Japanese soldiers, those who survived the war, back home, in *Anatahan*—selected by Sternberg from Japanese newsreel footage but so trenchantly chosen as to overwhelm the viewer; the marvelous ending of that same film with the return of the smiling survivors from the island on an airfield in Japan, then the unsmiling ghosts of those slain on the island over the girl—the background is a shadowy and amorphous wing of a huge plane on the airfield with

the vague forms of a guard or two standing at attention as if in a dream—and finally the girl herself, watching the ghosts of those who did not return, as the narrator concludes, " . . . and if I know anything at all about Keiko, she, too, must have been there."

Once again, and for the last time, Sternberg has echoed the theme that has haunted all his films . . . that waste of life of which Rimbaud speaks in his *"Par delicatesse j'ai perdu ma vie . . ."*

Much is made of the film spectacle today—big sets, hordes of extras, astronomical budgets, all of which are milked to the *n*th degree until we are surfeited with just the idea of bigness for its own sake. But to film a fairly elaborate scene just for the sake of a nuance is far more spectacular and I ask you to recall one in *The Devil Is a Woman*: The morning after Concha has been beaten by Don Pasquale for tantalizing him, when she visits him out of pique. "I came to see if you had killed yourself, after last night," she pouts. "If you had really loved me, you would have killed yourself." She tastes his breakfast cocoa. "Terrible," she says. "I can make much better cocoa." He pays no attention to her, out on a balcony where he stands with his back to her. And while she chatters away the marvel occurs, for rising up from the early morning mist of the harbor below Don Pasquale's rooms are, barely discernible, the tops of the masts of sailing vessels tied up at the quai, gently swaying, bobbing slowly from side to side. Thus Sternberg evokes a small seaport on the Spanish coast (as deftly and as impressionistically as he evoked the fog-shrouded Mediterranean crossing in *Morocco*) and we can feel the cool morning air which contrasts so blessedly with the sultry events of the night before. And we are as grateful for it as Don Pasquale must be. It is one of the most ravishing shots in all cinema and yet it wasn't necessary, the scene would have played without it, but the fact that it was there enriched the scene and was yet another indication of that urge "beyond the call of duty" that is always a jubilant thing to see. The wedding feast in *The Scarlet Empress* with death also sitting at the table in the person of a skeleton who needs no invitation . . . This is the fourth dimension in filmmaking. *This* is spectacular filmmaking . . .

And finally—the audience . . .

What the late Hungarian composer Zoltan Kodaly said of music applies most acutely to the film also. "For most people," he said, "music is a kind of bath to wash in. They react with their nerves, not with their minds." Sometimes this reaction coincides with the work, more often it does not. A thing is to be fully understood, after all, only with the mind. Such cinema lapidary works as *Shanghai Express* and *The Devil Is a Woman*, done with the aloof reserve of a Degas and the all but numbing perfection of an Ingres, limned with that grave ecstasy a seventeenth-century Dutch painter could divine in painting the transparency of glass or the yellow curve of a lemon peel—how much of this color that Sternberg applied in his details, without revealing any sign of a "brush stroke" with his lens, did the audience see?

They looked for a *chahut* in his films, as they do in all films, and he gave them the formal cadences of a pavane.

. . .

There were no turd-kickers in his films, no false coyness, empty in the middle and leering at the edges. Neither were there fools in his films, for he confessed he encompassed all his characters, their weaknesses as well as their strengths. But he never had any truck with fools. As any artist does, he interpreted the world as he saw it, and like all true artists his was an integrity that was inauctionable.

What remains to be said? We could sum up his work by saying that the iridescent flame of his technique, unique in the cinema, has been put to the service of what the Slavs call *zoll* and the Germans, *Weltschmerz*, that world pain, that life-hurt, for it is a sad, guilty world, and his sad, misanthropic films reflect this. "All noble things are touched with melancholy," remarked Melville. There are few resolutions in his films, although there is sometimes a gallant sort of hope. Shall we say something before concluding about the man behind the artist? His fastidiousness, his intransigence, his implacability where his art is concerned? But that brings us to the artist again. Let us just say that those who truly know him would agree that the frost of knighthood is in his manner, this mandarin among Hollywood directors. There is a considerable name in the history of the cinema—Josef von Sternberg—and he has earned it.

Somewhere in the Old Testament is recounted the fable of the burning bush . . . something to the effect that "the

bush burned and it was not consumed." It was a testament of faith in the glory of God, in Jehovah the beneficent. Good was the positive force on earth and evil the negative. The Judaeo-Christian religion has always needed miracles to impress its constituents, though that need does not militate in the least against its precepts, which are fine, if people would only practice them.

What is the history of art but a succession of fables? "Art is a lie which helps us to see the truth," said Picasso. "For the sake of truthfulness, one can even deny truth," said Goethe.

Art implies artifice, something artificial, but it also stems from the Latin, *ars* or *artis*, meaning skill in putting together. This is what the artist does in his creative imagination. "But he finds a way of return from his world of fantasy," said Freud, "back to reality. With his special gifts he molds his fantasies into new kinds of reality and men concede them a justification as valuable reflections of actual life."

Art is a constant miracle.

# A personal note

Some reminiscences recalled from over the years...

We'd meet for lunch, which I welcomed, for it was then that he was at his most expansive, discussing the events of the day, a conversation invariably spiced with his acerbic wit. I had mentioned a light scandal currently peppering the gossip columns about an American heiress allegedly involved in an affair with her colored chauffeur, whom she was now suing for defamation of character or some such thing. A trial was in the offing. "Oh," he said, "she'll settle it out of court." "How do you know?" I asked. "Why should she go to court?" he replied, not missing a forkful in the steady rhythm of eating. "She'll say she didn't and he'll say she did."

As it turned out, it was settled out of court.

Shortly after that he departed for Japan to make *Anatahan*.

He came back like a real sailor with a duffle-bag containing a print of the film. It proved you could do everything with grace, especially if that quality was second-nature to you, as they say. He had a special white canvas duffle-bag constructed for him in Japan to contain the nine reels of the film, a handsome and jaunty thing drawn together with white rope, and it was certainly more sensible, since it made the print so much lighter to carry, than when encased in the conventional metal boxes.

Of course we talked over old times, such as when he informed Paramount that he wanted Adolphe Menjou for the third angle of the triangle in *Morocco*, the role of the suave LeBessière, and they objected. Menjou was through, finished, they said, a "has-been," in that sort of role, played by him principally in silent films under Chaplin, Lubitsch, d'Arrast, Mal St. Clair, and others. Sternberg insisted and had his way. "But I said to him (Menjou)," he told me, "before we began, that ideally I'd prefer to cast him as a shady

Levantine selling fake Turkish rugs from table to table on the terrace of a Paris café."

Menjou didn't exactly like that but he played well for Sternberg in *Morocco* and his stock rose considerably afterward, taking him out of obscurity into the second phase of his career, which was to last a long time. Just as *Morocco* rescued Gary Cooper from vapid Westerns and the movie equivalent of pulp-fiction and started him on a bright career almost equally as long. As for *Dietrich*, it made her—it was only afterwards that *The Blue Angel* was shown here. To make three careers in one picture is not only not bad it is spectacular. Add what it did for its director, himself, and you have a fourth.

He wasn't always as prescient as in the matter of the heiress and her chauffeur. In 1937 he was in London, just returned from a world tour. In an interview he stated this fact, adding, "I have talked to people high and low; there will be no war." Two years later, of course, World War II began.

Sometimes I would steer the conversation gingerly toward other directors. He liked Clouzot and René Clair, Chaplin, of course, and Stroheim's *Greed*. He couldn't stand Griffith. He liked Zoltan Korda's *Cry, the Beloved Country*. Eisenstein, with whom he was very friendly. Most of all, as I recall, he liked the work of Buñuel. Sternberg wasn't anymore superficial than was Oscar Wilde, both of whom were frequently thus labeled. (Wasn't it Eisenstein who said that if it hadn't been for his discovery of Karl Marx—Eisenstein had already discovered, that is, for himself, Leonardo da Vinci and Freud —he might have become "a cinema Oscar Wilde"?) Where Sternberg's own work was concerned, as well as the work of others, he was absolutely objective, despite all reports to the contrary. No one could sort the chaff from the wheat of his own films better than he, himself, could.

"Though my films have been, and still are, studied by other directors, here and abroad," he once said, "I regard them only as reasonably arrogant gestures of mine. They were often only protests against other films of the time.* Frequently they were attempts to investigate techniques

---

* Like Stravinsky's idea for a little travelling theatre, for which he composed his "L'Histoire du Soldat", as a protest against the orchestral mammothism of Mahler and Richard Strauss.

which might broaden their appeal. They don't carry my endorsement, they only carry my name."

Surely an apostolic utterance by a devoted disciple of Saint Cinema . . .

As I write these notes in the Spring of this year, I think of the note I recently sent him upon his return from Stockholm, where he attended yet another retrospective of his work. "I thought I was finished with the book," I wrote, "but they've asked for a personal note on you. Got any suggestions? It's not easy to do . . . I quake at the thought!" To which he replied laconically, "Don't quake."

So I'm on my own . . .

To him the highest callings are those of the creative artist and the dedicated teacher, though he has a healthy respect for science used to better the lot of man, which is to say, when it is not manifesting the destructive side of its schizophrenic nature.

He has taught film direction, e.g., film aesthetics ("since you cannot teach film direction—it requires an attitude"), at the University of Southern California and lectured at the University of California in Los Angeles. He has also lectured on this subject in many American universities and most recently at the hallowed Uppsala University and at the University of Lund in Sweden. This year he will also go to Sydney, Australia, at the invitation of the Sydney Film Festival, which this Spring had their own first retrospective showing of his films.

They say Kant never left Koenigsberg—but become a great film director and see the world. Or a great violinist, like Heifetz or Kreisler, both of whom Sternberg numbered among his many friends among the world's ornaments of the twentieth century.

Speaking of Kreisler, he had, of course, a broad Viennese accent straight out of the Wurstelprater, but not any broader than the Viennese accent of Sternberg when speaking German, thick enough so you could skate on it (it's slippery enough, heaven knows!) throughout the four seasons. I was present at a two-hour interview with the late Manfred Georg, editor of *Aufbau*, and not a word of English was exchanged between the two of them throughout the luncheon-interview. Sternberg's impeccable English, however, has not even the faintest trace of this Austrian accent and is, if anything,

slightly clipped and Oxfordian, with an amusing admixture of pure Americanese. In Hamburg he addressed the large student body of a university in their own language.

But he is as circumspect in his speech as he is in his films. I have never heard him swear. Indeed, he is so meticulous not only in his writings but in his speech that sometimes he will disconcert his *vis-à-vis* (usually an interviewer, whose studied aplomb he likes to frustrate) by employing circumlocutions like "His name is not unknown to me" for "Yes, I know him." This usually stops you in your tracks. But you must hold on or you're lost beyond retrieving . . .

He is both a painter and sculptor, or at least he was, and several moody heads of Dietrich and a striking nude female torso (with an actual rosary draped around the neck) attest to this. He has himself been painted and sculpted (not to mention caricatured) all over the world and these portraits form part of the art collection (what's left of it, anyway, it once having been one of the most important private collections of modern art in America) that now adorns his home in Los Angeles. The rest is composed of books and more books, African and Oceanic masks, and exotic souvenirs of his many travels, interests, and, perhaps, fetishes.

Before that, he lived in a house he himself designed and had built on the Palisades overlooking the Hudson River in Weehawken. He carved the baroque wooden entrance door himself. The second floor consisted of one enormous room the size of the house itself with almost a floor to ceiling and wall to wall window so vast that it encompassed nearly the entire Manhattan skyline from the Battery to the George Washington Bridge. Talk about a room with a view! On the window ledge was nothing to obstruct the view, that is, nothing but a small figure of a saucy nude dancer looking out at the spectacular sight.

Several light wood-and-canvas director's chairs around a folding table served as a relaxed spot before the window where the gracious Mrs. Von Sternberg, as pretty as any of the heroines of his films, would serve drinks, liqueurs, or wild strawberries dusted with powdered sugar.

And before that, his "ivory tower" was a modernistic construction of steel, concrete, and glass surrounded by a foot-deep moat in which swam goldfish, a house also designed by

him and set among the hills of San Fernando Valley, California.

Among the photos in his own collection I found one of him accoutered in ceremonial Korean robes (he even looked Korean with his then droopy, Charlie Chan moustache)—a souvenir of a temporary elevation to some Oriental deity by his idolators there.

Thirty years after sporting a trim Van Dyke beard in the Orient, behind which he embarked on the direction of *I, Claudius* in London on his return, he is sporting one anew, white this time, above which the ever youthful mischievous eyes still twinkle.

I played a record for him that I had run across once. It was called "A Hollywood Party" and consisted of parodies by the English night-club star, Florence Desmond, of various Hollywood celebrity guests at a birthday party given by Tallulah Bankhead. The guests included Zasu Pitts, Jimmy Durante, Garbo, and, *bien entendu*, Dietrich, who was riding the crest of the wave at that time, having just finished *Dishonored*, her third film with Sternberg. "I'm afraid I can't stay very long," the ebullient Miss Desmond has her say in a devastating voice imitation, low and somewhat breathless, "I have to be up at dawn to be shot—no, not another spy picture. Von Sternberg doesn't like me staying late at parties. When I tell him the truth, he doesn't believe me; when I tell him a lie, he does. So like a man. Goodbye!"

His only reaction to this was, "What people will do."

The English journalist Kevin Brownlow has reported the first meeting between Sternberg and Clive Brook, who was later to star in the director's *Underworld* and *Shanghai Express*. "I first met Jo when he was an assistant director on a picture in England," recalled Clive Brook. "He was Jo Sternberg then. On location in Wales, we slept in the same bedroom and I remember seeing him one morning staring into the mirror."

"Which is more horrible?" he asked. "With or without a moustache?"

"What do you want to look horrible for?" I asked.

"The only way to succeed," he said, "is to make people hate you. That way they remember you."

Some forty years later, Brownlow quotes Sternberg echo-

ing that corrosive exchange with Clive Brook: "When I teach at universities on how to direct, I propose some absolutely horrible qualifications. I say a director must know languages, he must know the history of the theatre from the beginning of time. He must be an expert at psychoanalysis and must have some psychiatric training. He must know every emotion. And they say, 'Did you know all that?' And I say, 'No, but then I never asked anyone how to become a director.'"

On another occasion, in 1954, he was invited to introduce *The Salvation Hunters* at a film society showing at The New School in New York, to which he had just returned after spending many months in Japan on *Anatahan*. He likes to accept as many invitations as he can, especially if they are from young people. But once on the podium, he began: "I don't know why I should introduce this film since I made it to introduce me ..." Then he proceeded to tear it apart, noting only occasionally what was good in it.

A typical corrective, reflected in the filmography at the end of this book, is supplied by Sternberg in, say, the matter of Dietrich's costumes in her films with him, which played so important a part in delineating these roles. "Although ideas were sometimes submitted by the wardrobe people," he once wrote me, "I must say that everything essential was handled directly by me. I usually based the costume conceptions on some prior fantasies by painters and illustrators of long ago. . . . I do not wish to appear immodest but, with the exception of *Sergeant Madden*, *Jet Pilot*, and *Macao*, nothing in any of my films should be attributed to others save where I used the basic ideas of Hecht, Dreiser, Pierre Louys, Heinrich Mann, etc., to reorganize into my filmic conceptions. This is easily checked if you look at another director's handling of the same subject—say, *The Blue Angel* [the Edward Dmytrik remake with Mai Britt]. A director *writes* with his camera, whether or not it be his intention."

Apropos writing, Sternberg's handwriting might be described as "elegant rococo," with its small calligraphy punctuated by sweeping flourishes. He even had a typewriter whose type-face could also be described as "elegant rococo." At any rate, it was so elegant and so rococo that the publisher of his autobiography had to have the entire manuscript retyped so the typesetters could read it.

Today, between flying trips hither and yon, to this retrospective or that film festival, he lives serenely in California with Mrs. von Sternberg and their two handsome children, Nicky and Cathy.

"As I get older," he says, "I become more demanding of my own work. I have been busy with many things and I have not applied myself to the making of films. . . . Unless I can find a perfect vehicle, I will not direct another film. Another thing has interrupted my desire to make films. We live in a very disturbed world. I would like, if I make a film, not to disturb it more. I read a lot of literature, but I do not believe it is right for the screen. *The Blue Angel* was not based on the novel by Mann, it was merely stimulated by it. The motion picture is a unique art form and writers should write exclusively for it. So, while I am not working in the cinema, I take my car apart, play chess, study the evolution of the mail system in early China, and I also study anthropology and psychiatry . . . and somehow or other the time passes."

In a letter to me discussing *Anatahan*, sent from Japan, while still working on the film, he wrote, "I intend to set a standard of visual excellence with this picture." But he had crossed out the word "picture" and written above it "film." There is a difference. In that difference lies the history of the art of the motion pictures.

# An Interview

In Nicole Vedrès's *Life Starts Tomorrow*, a film of interviews with notable men, the interviewer says to André Gide, "May I ask you an indiscreet question?" To which Gide replies, "There are no indiscreet questions, there are only indiscreet answers." It was enough to inhibit the interviewer from pursuing this course, not being the *bravo* that another interviewer was on a different occasion when the latter made so bold as to ask the great French writer, "Is it true, *cher maître*, that you are a homosexual?" To which Gide replied testily, with that refined distinction so characteristic of him, "No monsieur, I am *not* a homosexual, I am a pederast!"

Sternberg draws lines just as fine in his own interviews, while disconcerting his interviewers from behind his inscrutable Buddhalike mask, with what are often curt, acrid answers. He will sit, like the Grand High Lama, before his interviewer, speaking in a low, well-modulated and cultured voice, criticizing the questions when he finds them unworthy, or blunting what the interviewer might regard as a sharp question by answering it with such simplicity, with such forthrightness and directness in lieu of the "profound" or "epochally revelatory" statement the interviewer had expected, that the latter is nonplussed. In the ensuing havoc, his next question, in a desperate attempt to make up for his loss of ground (for it has already become a battle of wits, willy-nilly), is invariably sure to be both "safe" and, as a pitiful by-product of that "safety," asinine.

It is not that Sternberg doesn't like to be interviewed; he can be very voluble about his work when the questions are intelligently posed. It is just that he resents being put on trial, as if his interviewer was a self-appointed (as was usually the case) inquisitioner, and made to defend himself,

i.e., his work, for no one would ever dare ask him any other kind of question. It is his work that matters, as far as the world outside him is concerned, and nothing else.

Interviews have been published (that's the amazing part of it) in verbal duels with him that were harrowing in the amount of "blood" they drew from the interviewer at the hands of Sternberg's sardonic rapier. They must be masochists to submit to such hazardous forays, but getting an interview from Sternberg at all is an heroic feat and a good journalist will not be intimidated by this "dragon."

What sets many of his interviewers on edge is that they feel they are in the presence of an egocentric celebrity. This unconsciously puts them on the defensive and in the course of the interview the process of transference takes place, all but invisibly, and suddenly an innocent question may, in the subtle change of ambiance, take on the tone of an impertinent one and the sparks start flying. The interviewer has unconsciously transferred his defensiveness to the subject of his "torment." And yet it is common for world celebrities to be egocentrics—a notable example in our time being Igor Stravinsky. And why shouldn't such men be? You will notice that mediocrities are never accused of that fault. But is it a fault? Not when thought out, for its basis is as it is used in philosophy, e.g., the world existing only as conceived in the individual mind. Great religious leaders, who certainly have never been accused of being egocentrics, have been directly or indirectly responsible for endless bloodletting in the cause of "holy wars" and other such genocidal massacres in the name of one god or another, but no artist, no matter how "egocentric" or "eccentric" or whatever, has ever harmed anyone. This goes for all artists in all fields and in all times. The real egocentrics, in the popular sense of the word, which occasioned these animadversions, are the villains of this world . . . from Holofernes to Hitler, and the like.

All of which is by way of lengthy introduction to the sample interview that follows, not one of the more harrowing ones, to be sure, but one of the gentler ones, so that it may be witnessed that the right questions fuse illuminating answers. For his usual prodigality of sarcastic energy when faced with stupid or banal questions, Sternberg here substitutes glints of his dry wit, such as his reply to the ques-

tion, "When you directed *The Blue Angel*, were you conscious that you were transforming the actress you discovered into a myth?"

Sternberg: "I am always conscious when I direct."

Admittedly, it isn't much of a question because it should have been obvious to his for-the-most-part intelligent interviewers that Sternberg could then have had no idea of the plangent effect his star would have on the world in the context in which he put her. He knew what he was doing, but not that he was creating a *myth*.

Nor is his answer the *non sequitur* it appears to be because the question was a foolish one, spoken without thinking, to which he could not resist the facetious (but true) reply he gave. But it had the *wish* to be an intelligent question and this counts for something, too. Sternberg felt this and bypassed it gracefully and even with humor. Good will engenders good will.

—*Under whose influence were you at the time of* The Salvation Hunters?

—That's a difficult question. Everyone is influenced by his environment without realizing it. What has to be added in my case is that in the beginning I was influenced not by cinéastes but by writers and painters.

—*Your first film*, The Salvation Hunters, *could make one believe in the influence of Chaplin or even Griffith?*

—Only the titles are in the tone of Griffith. I detested Griffith's films. But I was bound to be influenced by Chaplin, whom I admired very much. I also admired *Greed* very much.

—*What is your judgment today of this first work?*

—*The Salvation Hunters* is not a good film but I couldn't prevent its showing as it belongs to the history of the cinema. First of all, we had many difficulties during the shooting. It is one of the least expensive films I know but the expenses were covered at the first showing. Then you must know that I did it as a reaction against the cinema of that era, in reaction mainly against stars and their gesticulations. The purposely slow action seems excessive to me now and I would do the opposite today. Finally, the meaning of

the film seems naive to me. At that time I was young,
which means terribly serious!

—*And now?*

—No longer at all!

—*Do you think that* Underworld *was your first important
film?*

—I don't understand you. It is difficult for me to talk
about my films, to say that this one or that one is better
or worse. And above all, I don't think that any of my films
are important.

—*You have just seen again* Docks of New York, *which is
supposedly one of the last masterworks of the silent era.
What was your impression?*

—It's the first time I saw this picture in a theatre since
it was edited. Let me remind you of what I said before the
showing: my first pictures seem stupid to me today, but
stupidity is an ingredient of success. One has to be stupid
to become a film director.

—*How did you react to the exploitation of the talkies?*

—There never were silent movies. The actors spoke and
the titles reproduced their lines. There also was the ac-
companying music, which I preferred to choose myself.
Thus, far from being opposed to the talkies, I made sound
films myself right away. I even made one before *The Blue
Angel.*

—*When you were directing this film, were you conscious
of transforming the actress you had discovered into a myth?*

—When I'm directing I am always conscious. I don't
work with my feelings but with my ideas, my brain.

—*Can you say a few words about* Shanghai Express?

—It is not a German film, as is sometimes stated, but an
American one. I took great pleasure in recreating China in
Hollywood, according to my imagination. Later on I went
there. I took the Shanghai Express and it was quite different.
This is why I'm glad I made this film before, following my
fancy. I'm sort of a poet.

—*Certain historians and critics say that your work faltered
during the later years. Do you think so too? For which
reasons?*

—I stopped making films in 1935.

—*How do you explain this break-off?*

—My ideas about the cinema became more precise in the

light of my experiences. I was tired of seeing studio opposition to any creative ideas of the cinéaste at the different stages of its expression. Whereas a painter uses his brushes, canvas and colors, following only the bent of his imagination, the film director has to consider other men and human material.

After a trip around the world, I wanted to work according to certain principles; for instance, that we should be concerned to create expressive effects achieved in literature—and I hoped to work with more freedom. A lot of unhappy events prevented me from this, such as the tragic events of those years.

—*When you were shooting* Anatahan, *why did you choose to work in a studio in Japan?*

—Look at a map: Anatahan is an island located two thousand kilometers from Japan, halfway from the Philippines. Anyway, it was impossible to shoot a picture there: it's a jungle. But if I did not work on location, it was on purpose. I prefer to work in a studio. Outside, the tourists get in my way. I like to be comfortable; too bad if the actors are not. You have seen *Docks of New York*; well, that film was made in a studio. I recreated China in a studio for *Shanghai Express*, for *The Shanghai Gesture*, for *Macao.* . . . Everything is "artificial" in *Anatahan*, even the clouds are painted and the plane is a toy. This film is my own creation.

To reality, one should prefer the *illusion of reality*. Otherwise, you do what Jean Rouch did in *Jaguar*, which we just saw: you film everything that happens in front of the camera. This is documentary, it is not art.

—*Let us get to the more general questions. You seem to be disillusioned, disappointed in your career to such an extent that you minimize it. Still, you have known glory and your work is marked indelibly in the history of the cinema.*

—In 1930, as the result of a vote among professionals, I was named the American cinéaste whose influence had been the strongest. At that time, posters would advertise "Josef von Sternberg's new picture." It is my privilege to be dissatisfied with my films.

—*Did you not have a lasting influence upon certain cinéastes?*

—I cannot answer this question. I told you: it is very difficult to know by whom or what one is influenced. We are influenced by everything: these walls, this room ... A cinéaste may be influenced by a writer—Zola, for instance, in my case—or by a painter, as well as by another cinéaste. All these influences and all experiences combine themselves. Being influenced is nothing to blush about. Imitation is not embarrassing, as long as from this imitation one creates something personal. To imitate does not necessarily mean to copy.

—*Perhaps you suffered from not being able to express yourself freely?*

—I'm responsible for my films. I did what I wanted!

—*Not always! Will you say a few words about the troubles you had with the censors?*

—Little, in truth, with my finished films. *The Blue Angel*, for example, which they did not want to export, "as giving an unfavorable picture of Germany." On the other hand, there were films which I would have preferred not to be shown ...

—*Didn't you have to make personal concessions, sometimes, with regard to your plans? One gets the impression, when seeing certain of your films whose scripts are not on as high a level as the intentions, that you found it necessary to vulgarize your subjects for commercial reasons.*

—I don't understand what you mean when you speak of "the necessity to vulgarize my scripts for commercial reasons." As far as I know, I have never been vulgar.

—*It also seems that certain of your films have been "watered down" during the process of shooting or editing. Were you free in your work?*

—Of course there were certain limitations. For example, because of the actors. I had to compose with stars like Bancroft and Marlene Dietrich, so as to model their parts after themselves. I made seven films with Marlene Dietrich; in reality I wanted to make only two: *The Blue Angel* and *Morocco*. But she was bound by contract to a studio. In America, one can say that a cinéaste is free within the limits of commercial success.

—*Then you are concerned with the financial success of your films? What do you think of the audience?*

—One is bound to worry about the receipts but I don't

Dietrich sets a new pattern for the *femme fatale*. Here as an Austrian spy, X-27, trapping the traitor (Warner Oland)—the *milieu* is again World War I—in another "valse triste" by Sternberg to the memory of the last days of "alt Wien." (*Dishonored—* 1931)

worry about the audience. What is the audience? How can you mingle the people of Tokyo, Berlin, Paris, and New York who will see the same film?

Whatever it is, in my eyes the public is stupid. The crowd is always stupid. Individually, men may have qualities; in a crowd they become stupid. I prefer to please myself.

—*Once more, you seem pessimistic . . .*

—Why should I be pessimistic? You are the ones who think I am. Facing the same reality, two contrary reactions are possible: looking at a half-empty theater, the pessimist will say: "It's half empty," and the optimist: "It's half filled." I don't believe I'm a pessimist. Look at *Docks of New York*; it's an optimistic film.

—*You are supposed to have made the following disillusioned statement: "The cinema is an industry which could have been an art." Do you confirm it?*

—I don't think I said that. I don't think it's bad that the cinema is an industry.

—*But commercialism and industrial methods can obstruct and restrain personal expression.*

—There is nothing perfect in this world. It is normal for people to try to make money out of films. The problem of creation is an interior one.

—*But without money, a cinéaste cannot express himself, can he?*

—Sometimes it is preferable not to have money. Painters too—Van Gogh, Modigliani, Utrillo—worked in order to eat.

—*All they needed was a canvas and a few tubes of paint to create something. A cinéaste needs millions, which he receives only under certain conditions.*

—One must fight, fight, always fight!

—*You were nine years without making a film, from 1941 to 1950; and since* Anatahan *(1953) you have not made a single picture. One cannot interpret these long silences as simple failures of creativeness, can one?*

—I have mentioned to you all my difficulties—with producers, actors, distributors, managers, audiences. To me the important thing is to express myself as I can, as much as I can. Too many people have the power to deform and

A rare scene of a deglamorized Dietrich (with Lew Cody in *Dishonored*) in which she parodied a peasant wench with delicious humor, manipulated by the unerring strings held by the director.

mutilate our films. We wish there would be institutions to protect our creations, from their conceptions.

I tried progressively to secure more and more control of the animate and inanimate material through which I was to express myself. I wanted to *master* the cinema. Since 1924, for thirty-six years, I have been wanting to make my work easier, to change the conditions which gradually turned the cinema into this complicated machine, and to adapt it to creative work. It was a ticklish enterprise. I am sure that when I made a successful picture, its success was due only to stupid things. Film directors could do much better if they did not have to clash with futile absurdities and ignorance, and if they were *encouraged* by the financiers and the public.

—*A certain number of ideas, feelings, and themes reappear frequently in your films. Do you think your work has a general significance?*

—That's too broad a question. "It's not up to the chicken to speak about its own soup," the Russians say. I don't want to be enclosed in formulas. I like variety. I'm glad to have had an irregular career.

—*In several of your films, love triumphs over duty. Do you believe that love is the supreme value of life, the only one, perhaps?*

—"No, I don't believe that. Love is a driving element of life, but the supreme value to me is justice. Like for Zola!

—*You have, no doubt, a personal ideal?*

—I don't consider myself important in my own eyes. What is important to me is to behave like a human being, to know the joys of family life, and to educate people.

—*What has been your essential preoccupation as a cinéaste?*

—To find the means of expressiveness, to discover its possibilities. What interests me is expressiveness achieved by means of technical investigation.

—*Do you prepare your films minutely or do you believe in improvisation?*

—I love to improvise.

—*What do you think about the direction of actors?*

—Actors are material with which one works.

—*Which function do you assign to the décor?*

Again, as in the case of *The Wedding March*, Sternberg solves a problem for Paramount by filming *An American Tragedy* after the studio's rejection of Eisenstein's screen play. Phillips Holmes as Clyde Griffiths and Sylvia Sidney as Roberta Alden. (1931)

—I control the décor just as I control each element of the work I create.

—*Your films have a photographic style, homogeneous lighting. What importance do you give to lighting?*

—I am responsible for the lighting in my films. It is an element inseparable from photography.

—*You have made interesting experiments with color. Seeing Jet Pilot one gets the impression that your ideal would be to use color for personal, not realistic, ends. Do you think this purpose is still valid?*

—The ideal, indeed, is to use color in a personal and unreal way. I was limited in the total application of this principle for *Jet Pilot*, in which many scenes seem not to be my own.

—*You have kept a liking for symbols though they become more and more integrated into your films . . .*

—I have never deliberately introduced symbolism of any sort into my films though the composition of certain images one finds in them may appear as purposeful symbols to those who have decided to find one at every opportunity.

—*Have you edited all your films?*

—Yes, all of them. The changes were made later.

—*I will ask you another question which is too broad: what is your definition of the cinema?*

—That's a *very* broad and very difficult question. I would *like* to answer it because I have many ideas which I have never expressed. But I cannot do it in a few words; besides which, the translation could modify the meaning of my words. The next best thing is to refer you to my writings. I have published several texts on the cinema and I taught aesthetics of the cinema seven or eight years ago at the University of California.

The ideal is to experiment in films. I would especially like to study movement and sound. One cannot talk about the cinema with words alone. We are three persons here. Let one of us tell about a film he would like to make and the result will be three different films in our minds. We cannot understand each other in this way.

Finally, I must say that I am pliable and changeable. I don't know what I will think tomorrow.

—*What do you think succinctly today of the cinema's future?*

—It is unforeseeable. Oscar Wilde said: "What a pity that progress should go toward the future instead of going toward the past!"

—*Do you think that the cinema may still experience further decisive transformations such as sound, color, and wide-screen?*

—Why not? Anything is possible. And anything that is possible is worth trying. In my next film, I would like to try something new.

—*Do you believe, for instance, in the possibilities of the variable screen and polyvision?*

—Oh, yes, Abel Gance! Why not? It's the result that counts. If it works out, all the better!

—*Is television, in your opinion, a threat to the cinema?*

—Not at all. They are two completely different techniques. Television can do good things, but not the same things as the cinema.

—Recorded by Philippe Esnault
and Michèle Firk and published
in *Positif* (Paris) Nos. 37–38,
January and March 1961.

# Excerpts from Correspondence

The virtue of interviews is that they are—both questions and answers—spontaneous things. Letters, however, tend to be more studied and reflective. Both have their place in the task of presenting "the total man." So many interviews with Sternberg have appeared and he has been quoted so often that I decided to present, as personal statements by him on the art of the film in general and his own art in particular, completely new and unknown material. These half-dozen excerpts from letters, covering a span of 15 years from 1949 to 1964, present in highly concentrated form some of the attitudes that resulted in the films by him that we know.

*To Curtis Harrington,*
*June 15, 1949*

Poetry is not exclusive to any single medium of expression, and you will find a clue to much of my work, if not to all of it, in noting that I use images and sound like others have used words. It is difficult to take issue with a poet, except on the point of merit, since he is primarily concerned in ordering apparent chaos or, paradoxically enough, presenting chaos as an orderly phenomenon. I have always avoided emotionalizing my films, choosing rather to present emotion as a casual component of other elements. The world is avid for easily digestible formulas, and in exploiting film to carry no such apparent solutions, I could not escape severe criticism. But I also did not escape praise, though it was not always correctly applied. I only sought to find a way to sound out cinematic power, leaving it to others to

employ it in selling emotions. Analyzing the laws of film is the job of a scientist who, too, must leave his emotions out of the result. At the core of science is the poetry of the universe—and ably or not I set out to investigate this, whenever I could do so without hurting others. The scientist is privileged to withhold his findings, not so the film director. Now I am not too sure that I always did this with full knowledge, but I am reasonably certain in the light of later developments that such were my drives and inclinations. I would like to close by encouraging you to pursue your studies in criticism and not be tempted to give reasons for the behavior of others solely because the questions have not yet been clearly articulated.

*To Richard Griffith,*
　*January 16, 1959*

The artist who selects the size and shape of his canvas is usually influenced by what he intends to paint. But here, in our medium, where the artist as yet is as rare as a hen's square egg, the size and shape is predetermined. Gulliver pegged to the ground by the Lilliputians is just right for the present rectangular area, but Gulliver on his feet extinguishing the tiny Queen's palace fire by the most instantly available method becomes a problem. In my work I use the camera to include only that which the viewer is to see, and to exclude what is pictorial wasteland; I control the time of the visual impact and establish a tempo. That is no longer easy, there is now spiritual space on both sides, and the force, the flow, and the impulse is hampered by the spectre of a gaping void. But this is not the worst, the circular screen will come, the screen all around us will bring revolving chairs into use, the ceiling projection, currently in beautiful use at the Planetarium will compel us to lie down. But the ultimate hazard is not the shape of the screen, large or small, it is the audience that supports piffle and junk with enthusiasm. There will come all sorts of innovations to appeal to that audience, though ultimately, I wish I could foresee the joyous day when the text and the skill with which it is told will dominate this great art form.

You will recall that Oscar Wilde put it very nicely: "The only trouble with progress is that it goes forward and not backwards."

ON INFLUENCES

*To W. G. Simpson,*
*December 26, 1959*

On the general subject contained in your letter I would like to mention that there is little work on earth, if any, that is entirely without influence. Such influence is at times difficult to trace for it may be inspired by abstractions from an entirely unrelated field. Where influence is obvious it becomes imitation.

It is possible that some of my work has been imitated, as in many parts of the world I have been told that it has not been ignored. I have only seen one of Bergman's films, and that recently in Venice, and I perceived nothing that I could label an imitation of my work. I might add, rather lightly, that I do not think it too easy to imitate my work in films, as it might require so much skill in avoiding pitfalls, that such technical skill could more easily be applied to something less obvious. If, however, my work has served to subtly influence others in films or in any other territories, it would please me and not be contrary to my hopes. On the other hand I might add that I have had scenes taken from my work, or copied so bluntly, that this did not afford me any satisfaction, nor did such unimaginative use of the camera escape the disapproval of others who love the film as I do.

ON RESONANCE

*To Rafael Bosch,*
*October 3, 1960*

There is a Russian saying: "A chicken does not discuss its own broth," and it might help to explain my reluctance to indulge in articulating my ideas in any other medium than my chosen work. Much of what you said in your Caracas lecture may be pertinent, particularly the application of your quotation by Eisenstein. Amusingly enough, though Eisenstein wrote about horizontal and vertical montage, he never made use of it. I attempt to make my work completely homogeneous. Image, sound, abstraction, and the effect of these on the beholder are interlaced and must follow an inner rhythm and an orchestration which, though it vanishes with the film, remains as a *"Nachklang."* It is this "after-timbre," this ghost-resonance, this lasting vibration that I seek—though I may not achieve it. And it has no possible connection with whatever may be inherent in any German influence. I am not German, I was born in Vienna and came to the United States at the age of seven. This, I can assure you, is no clue to my work. Nor do I assume that you seek such clues. In your analysis you enter a labyrinth, the labyrinth of influences. That is not unambitious. For an observing and sensitive person it is almost impossible to escape the influence of even the most trivial experience, nor do I mean to infer that influence always comes from without. The human, being with his complicated heritage, is influenced in the main by as yet unlisted factors.

ON STYLE

*To Tom Foral,*
  *May 2, 1962*

Generally speaking, all art is an exploration of an unreal world. Style is the inevitable result of imposing control on the elements with which creative work concerns itself. It is not necessarily a confining of form, but it results from a search for abstraction not normally contained in presenting things as they are.


ON SURREALISM

*To Yves Kovacs,*
  *May 25, 1964*

Thanks for your letter of April 24 in which you ask me to comment on the subject of surrealism. I have been familiar with it since its modern beginning. I assume that you are not attempting to trace it back to Hieronymus Bosch and to those who influenced him. I have not been consciously influenced by this phase of the arts, though I must concede that nothing I have ever seen has not somehow been absorbed by me. As for direct influences on my work, this is dealt with at length in my book which is now being published. The title of my book is *A Guide to a Labyrinth,* which title might indicate to you the large scope of the questions that might be asked about all creative stimulants.*

---

* Although this book, when published the following year, was titled *Fun in a Chinese Laundry,* no change in the text was made to "fit" the new title, save for a fleeting reference to it.

# Extracts from Scenarios

### SHANGHAI EXPRESS
Opening Sequence

The following is from the preliminary script as written by Sternberg. As he edited the film himself, eliminating certain scenes and details, modifying others during the actual shooting, frequently adding different details (like the sudden startling close-up of a recumbent camel attended by a coolie, seen against the huge glistening wheels of the train getting under way, which was not in the original script), the released version of the film was often different. The determining factor of the ultimate visuals and sound track were the nuances sought by the director to give the work a "symphonic curve," as a composer orchestrates a score. When a director exercises the fullest autonomy over his work, as Sternberg did, he becomes both conductor and composer. The result is an authoritative performance of an original work.

FADE IN:

EXTERIOR: PEKING CITY CANAL—DAY—
CLOSE SHOT—

of a dozen half-naked coolies running abreast on native treadmill which pumps water into a large pipe.

DISSOLVE TO:

FOLLOW SHOT—

of pipe to show destination of water. The pipe rises on supports which overhang railroad track and tender of the

great American engine of the Shanghai Express, the side
of which should be marked with the proper Chinese characters.

DISSOLVE TO:
FULL SHOT—

of coolie cleaning window of second-class coach. Information board fastened to car beside window reads down:

> Peking,
> Tientsin, Tsinan,
> Yenchow, Sutsien,
> Chinkiang, Pukow,
> Shanghai.

As window-cleaner rubs window we see faces of Chinese
passengers gradually appearing behind cleaned glass.

DISSOLVE TO:
ANOTHER FOLLOW SHOT—

of train, showing a gang of coolies loading baggage into
baggage car; another gang loading sacks of mail and express into next car; while still another gang is filling
storage tanks of dining car with ice and provisions. We
pass an armored car in front of which a Chinese officer
is inspecting a company of soldiers which is to guard the
train on its journey to Shanghai.

DISSOLVE TO:

FULL SHOT—

of station filled with Chinese pedestrians and European
stragglers. A native produce market is in operation on station platform. A company of Chinese soldiers, carrying
rifles, is waiting for its train to embark.

EXTERIOR AND INTERIOR: PEKING RAILROAD
STATION—FOLLOW SHOT—

of large poster on wall of station advertising in Chinese
and English that the Shanghai Express is the fastest train-

de-luxe in China and showing its route from Peking to Shanghai, etc. In foreground we see a small crowd surrounding public water-heater, drawing hot water to make tea. All races are represented—Chinese, Manchus, Tartars, Russians, Mongolian lamas, and the air is filled with the racket of a dozen tongues. CAMERA GOES INTO STATION and shows Mrs. Haggerty, a boarding-house keeper, entering from the street door. She carries a small grip in one hand and in the other she carries a large closed lunch-basket. She is breathless with haste and goes to ticket window. She carefully sets down basket and addresses the ticket agent, who is an elderly Englishman.

MRS. HAGGERTY (in Cockney dialect and all in one breath): *The Shanghai Express ain't gone yet, has it? I wants a ticket to Shanghai—first-class, please.*

Rev. Carmichael, carrying a grip, has entered behind her and is waiting his turn with more or less impatience. At the next window a long queue of Chinese farmers and coolies are waiting to purchase second-class and third-class tickets.

TICKET AGENT (answering Mrs. Haggerty with a precise, cultured accent): *Thirty-five dollars and twenty-five cents Mex, Madame.*
MRS. HAGGERTY (counting out money): *Is there a dining car this time?*

Rev. Carmichael listens with increasing impatience and indignantly consults his watch.

TICKET AGENT (briskly—as he takes money): *Yes, Madame—everything but a Turkish bath!* (Then giving her ticket in exchange.) *Here you are—*
MRS. HAGGERTY (giving him a card): *I keeps a boarding-house in Shanghai—and very respectable it is—Yorkshire pudding a specialty—and if you're ever down that way—*

The rest is drowned out by an angry snort of impatience from Rev. Carmichael. Mrs. Haggerty, startled, backs

away from the ticket window, gives Rev. Carmichael an indignant sniff as she picks up grip and lunch-basket and exits toward train.

MOVING SHOT—

of Mrs. Haggerty as she goes to gate of ticket inspector, a young Englishman. She gives him her ticket and as he punches it he glances at lunch-basket she is carrying.

TICKET INSPECTOR: *What's in that basket?*
MRS. HAGGERTY: *Just a little snack of lunch my niece put up for me—*
TICKET INSPECTOR (sharply): *No animals?*
MRS. HAGGERTY (haughtily): I hopes not!

She steps back as four coolies enter carrying a luxurious curtained palanquin. The jeweled hand of a Chinese woman is extended through curtains. The long-nailed fingers are holding railroad ticket. Ticket Inspector takes it, pushes aside curtains, glances at occupant, nods recognition, punches ticket, and hands it back to owner. Hand disappears inside curtains and coolies carry palanquin out toward train, followed by CAMERA.

EXTERIOR: PEKING STATION—MOVING SHOT—

of coolies as they carry palanquin through throng jabbering in tongues of all nations to track where Shanghai Express is waiting. It passes observation car, third-class and second-class car, decorated with proper Chinese characters, jammed with coolies and farmers who are leaning out sides, saying goodbye to relatives and friends, buying food from hucksters, chatting with a group of soldiers. The palanquin pauses in front of open doorway of first-class car.

Sam Salt, the bookmaker, is standing here comparing watches with the British Station Master. He glances at palanquin as curtains are drawn aside and Hui Fei, a Chinese courtesan, gets out. She speaks in Chinese to coolies, who take baggage out of palanquin and follow

her as she exits into train. Sam Salt, turning a sage and wordly eye on the Station Master, resumes serious business of setting watch.

SAM SALT: *Twelve forty-three—you say?*
STATION MASTER (putting his watch away): *Exactly.*
SAM SALT: *How soon do we leave?*
STATION MASTER: *On time—in seven minutes—*
SAM SALT (with a grin): *It'll be the first train in China that ever left on time!* (He snaps a card out of his vest pocket and hands it to Station Master, adding affably.) *I run a little book down Shanghai way, and if you ever want to lay a bet on anything that's going anywhere—barring twins and foot races—just drop me a line—Sam Salt's the name—*
STATION MASTER: *Thanks.*

Dispatcher's clerk has entered with sheaf of train orders. He gives them to Station Master, who takes them, nods to Sam Salt and starts up toward engine, glancing at orders. CAMERA, following him, shows groups of people saying goodbye to passengers leaning out doorways and windows of armored first-class cars.

Chinese officer of train guard chatting with native girl who leans out window. His soldiers standing at ease. Car inspectors testing the air brakes and tapping wheels. Coolies still loading ice and provisions .into dining car—mail and express and baggage in other cars—speeding up to the last-minute rush. Station Master pauses by engine, where a Chinese conductor is chatting with a Chinese engineer. He hands each a copy of orders, saying:

*Here you are, lads—all clear till you meet* No. 2 *outside Tientsin—*

DISSOLVE TO:

INTERIOR: PEKING RAILROAD STATION—FULL SHOT—

of Rolls limousine stopping outside street door. A young

woman, wearing a heavy dark veil, alights and comes into station, followed by Chinese chauffeur, who carries her hand baggage. CAMERA follows her as she goes with quiet certainty across station to gate of ticket inspector, who is just punching ticket of Henry Chang, an Eurasian merchant. Latter is glancing at headline of newspaper—*The North China Star.* (NOTE: Please get copies of Anglo-Chinese newspapers.)

The young woman produces her ticket and Chang, taking his ticket from inspector, looks her over with an eager, appraising eye, gazing at Lily over his shoulder with increasing interest as he starts off toward train, followed by CAMERA.

EXTERIOR: PEKING RAILROAD STATION—
MOVING SHOT—

of Chang as he walks out toward train. He is furtively accosted by a shabby young Chinaman who has evidently been on the lookout for Chang. Latter does not stop and young Chinaman, walking at his side, speaks rapidly in Chinese to Chang, who meanwhile is looking around to see if they are being observed. Then, making a curt, silencing gesture, Chang walks on, allowing the young Chinaman to drop behind. He pauses by platform of second-class coach, looking after Chang, who is encountering the Station Master, a weather-beaten Britisher in a neat uniform, who greets him with a smile of recognition and strolls along train with Chang.

(As he does this.) *Glad to have you with us again, Mr. Chang—you haven't patronized us for several months—*

Chang nods, looking back over his shoulder in Lily's direction, while the Station Master, walking along train with him, continues without pause.

*—I suppose you've been concerned about the rebellion— but there's really nothing to worry about—the Shanghai Express always gets through on time—*

At this moment a window in first-class car is jerked open and Rev. Carmichael sticks out his head.

CARMICHAEL (angrily): *Guard!*
GUARD (entering and touching cap): *Yes, sir?*
CARMICHAEL: *Come in here—*

Guard obeys and exits into car, followed by CAMERA.

INTERIOR: VESTIBULE ARMORED CAR—
FOLLOW SHOT—

of guard going to door of compartment where Rev. Carmichael stands beside small pile of luggage. Inside we see Hui Fei, the Chinese courtesan, smoking and playing solitaire.

(To guard.) *I won't share a compartment with this woman!*
GUARD: *Change tonight.*
CARMICHAEL (angrily): *You'll change me now! I haven't lived in this country ten years not to know a woman like that when I see one!*

Hui Fei looks up at him—then resumes game. Guard picks up his bags as another guard enters with luggage belonging to Shanghai Lily. She follows guard, who exchanges short conversation in Chinese with other guard. Result is that Lily is given share in Hui Fei's compartment while Rev. Carmichael is led away to more respectable precincts. As he goes he says to Lily:

CARMICHAEL: *You may not find this compartment entirely to your liking—*

He glances significantly at Hui Fei. Lily's glance follows his. She comprehends Hui Fei's profession.

LILY: *Why not?*

Hui Fei looks up at them—and then goes on with her

game. Lily jerks off hat and veil, throws it up into rack and motions guard to put bags under the seat. Rev. Carmichael, staring at her, says half-apologetically:

CARMICHAEL: *I didn't mean to offend.*
LILY (glancing at Hui Fei): *Probably not—me.*

With that rebuff Rev. Carmichael makes his exit, following guard down vestibule to door of another compartment. Chang has been an interested spectator of this scene, and smiles at Hui Fei, who glances at him, rises, and closes the door.

INTERIOR: MRS. HAGGERTY'S COMPARTMENT —FULL SHOT—

of guard opening door and depositing Rev. Carmichael's luggage on floor of empty compartment which also shows signs of occupancy. He exits and Rev. Carmichael enters, staring suspiciously at Mrs. Haggerty's grip, which rests on best seat, and lunch-basket, which has been shoved under other seat.

EXTERIOR: ARMORED CAR—STATION PLATFORM—FULL SHOT—

of Mrs. Haggerty leaning out vestibule window and buying *Saturday Evening Post* from Chinese huckster.

MRS. HAGGERTY (looking at magazine): *Here—wait a bit —this says August 15th—1927—*
HUCKSTER: *Latest number, Madame.*
MRS. HAGGERTY: *But I tell you it's four years old—*
HUCKSTER: *Latest number, Madame.*

Mrs. Haggerty turns helplessly to Colonel Lenard, a grizzled old French veteran who is leaning out adjoining window.

MRS. HAGGERTY: *Is this 1931 or am I out of me mind?*
LENARD (with a polite smile—in broken English): *Madame,*

*I'm sorry, but I don't speak English enough to answer you
—je ne parle pas anglais, parlez-vous—français?*

FULL SHOT—

of Captain Harvey, a British army officer, leaning out window of compartment and chatting with a fellow officer who
stands on platform. Latter is joined by a young subaltern
who has been roaming along train.

SUBALTERN (to Captain Harvey): *I say, Harvey, you're in
   for a good time! D'you know who's on this train?*
HARVEY: *Who?*
SUBALTERN: *Shanghai Lily!*
HARVEY: *Who's Shanghai Lily?*
OTHER BRITISH OFFICER: *Don't tell me you haven't
   heard of Shanghai Lily! Everybody in China knows her!
   She's a notorious Coaster—*
HARVEY (puzzled): *What in the name of Confucius is a
   Coaster?*
SUBALTERN: *You're hopeless, sir! A Coaster's a woman who
   lives by her wits along the China Coast—*
HARVEY (drily): *I dare say I shan't be able to avoid her—
   on a three-day journey—*

INTERIOR: HARVEY'S COMPARTMENT—FULL
SHOT—

of guard entering with heavy load of hand-baggage belonging to Eric Baum, a German invalid. Latter follows guard
into compartment, muffled up in a heavy overcoat, with a
coolie bringing up rear with another load of hand-baggage.
Baum, opening a heavy grip, which contains about fifty
pounds of Chinese cash, takes out a string, gives coolie and
guard the proper tip, and as they exit Baum goes over and
gently taps Captain Harvey, who is leaning out window,
on the arm.

BAUM (in German—as Captain Harvey draws in his head):
   *Sir, I am an invalid, and it is very dangerous for me to
   travel in a compartment where the window is open—*
HARVEY: *Sorry—*(Then, closing window, he starts toward

door, asking Baum in a sympathetic tone.) *Anything I can do for you?*
BAUM (in broken English): *I can look after myself, thank you—*

He sneezes violently and glares at open door, which Captain Harvey hastily closes behind him. Baum, buttoning up his overcoat, proceeds to make himself comfortable, removing a small bag, which belongs to the other occupant (Colonel Lenard) from the best seat and covering his knees with a rug. Then door is slid back and Colonel Lenard enters.

LENARD (in French): *Whew! It's hot in here! D'you mind if I—?* (He starts to open window, but Baum stops him with a gesture of formal protest.)
BAUM (beginning in German): Sir, I am an invalid—

CUT TO:

INTERIOR: MRS. HAGGERTY'S COMPARTMENT —FULL SHOT—

of Rev. Carmichael stretched out in best seat reading a book. Mrs. Haggerty enters and sees him. He looks up at her, realizes she is owner of luggage in other seat and rises with a snort of disgust.

MRS. HAGGERTY (coquettishly): *You don't mind?*
CARMICHAEL (angrily gathering up his things): *It just means I'll have to move again!*
MRS. HAGGERTY (in surprise): *Why?*
CARMICHAEL (disdaining to explain, sticks head out window): *Guard!*
GUARD (entering outside): *Yes, sir?*
CARMICHAEL: *Put me in another compartment—and if there's anybody in it—be sure it's a man!*
GUARD (outside): *Yes, sir—*

He exists and Rev. Carmichael pulls in his head.

CLOSEUP—

of lunch-basket under seat. Top is open and Mrs. Haggerty's dog (which she has concealed in lunch-basket so she could smuggle her pet aboard train) sticks out head and is stepped on by Carmichael. Dogs lets out a yelp of pain.

FULL SHOT—

of Rev. Carmichael uttering an exclamation of alarm. He jumps away and looks down under seat.

CARMICHAEL (seeing dog): *What's that animal doing in here?*

MRS. HAGGERTY (in alarm—as guard enters outside in vestibule): *In Heaven's name—hush—they'll take him away from me—*

GUARD (entering and seeing dog): *No dogs allowed—*(He picks up dog by scruff of neck and starts out, saying.)—*belong in baggage car—*

MRS. HAGGERTY (following him in alarm): *He won't do harm—let me have him—*

INTERIOR: VESTIBULE ARMORED CAR—FOL-LOW SHOT—

of guard making off with dog with Mrs. Haggerty following him in alarm.

EXTERIOR: TRAIN—STATION PLATFORM—FOL-LOW SHOT—

of guard alighting with dog and starting up toward baggage car with Mrs. Haggerty threatening at his heels.

*I'll have the law on you—if you harm a single bone in his head—he's got to have his biscuit twice a day—and nothing but boiled water—*

CONDUCTOR'S VOICE: *All aboard!*

Mrs. Haggerty hears the cry taken up along the train.

She stops, torn between conflicting emotions. There is a

chorus of shouts and last goodbyes. Mrs. Haggerty yells after dog.

MRS. HAGGERTY: *Don't worry, Waffles—I'll look after you*—(Then she turns and runs back toward car.)
VOICES OF TRAINMEN: *All aboard!*

CLOSEUP—STATION CLOCK

It is exactly one o'clock.

INTERIOR: PEKING RAILROAD STATION—CLOSE SHOT—

of British ticket-seller pulling down window and shade.

FULL SHOT—

of ticket inspector closing and locking gate.

EXTERIOR: ENGINE SHANGHAI EXPRESS—CLOSE SHOT—

of bell starting to ring.

CLOSE SHOT—

of native engineer in cab of engine. He is looking back along train for signal to start.

CLOSE SHOT—

of native conductor waiting for coolies to toss last sack into mail car. He turns and makes hand-signal out of scene as coolies exit with empty truck.

CLOSE SHOT—

of engineer answering with a toot-toot of whistle and slowly pulling open throttle.

CLOSE SHOT ENGINE WHEEL

of giant piston as it starts to move and great jet of steam escapes with a hissing roar.

FOLLOW SHOT—

along train as it starts, with conductor and brakeman climbing aboard and guards closing doors.

INTERIOR: CHANG'S COMPARTMENT—MOVING TRAIN—FULL SHOT—

of Henry Chang, the Eurasian merchant, and Sam Salt, the Shanghai bookmaker, occupying opposite seats.

CHANG (glancing at his watch): Well, we're off on time—
SAM SALT (with an air of delicate approach): *Say, partner, d'you ever make a little bet? My name's Sam Salt*—(Snapping out a card and handing it to Chang.)—*I bet on everything under the sun going right or wrong—take your choice —and I'm willing to give you odds that this old rattler doesn't get into Shanghai on time!*
CHANG (with a queer, unfathomable smile): *Sir, let me remind you that China is in the throes of a civil war—and we'll be fortunate to arrive in Shanghai at all—*

Then door slides back and guard enters with Rev. Carmichael. Guard sullenly dumps bags on floor and exits. Rev. Carmichael, looking over his fellow-passengers as they do the same to him, puts his bags up in rack and fussily brushes off seat. Sam Salt turns his worldly eye on Henry Chang. Rev. Carmichael sits down, covertly surveying his companions with an air of grouchy contempt.

EXTERIOR: PEKING STREET—FULL SHOT—

of Shanghai Express slowly puffing down middle of busy Chinese street decorated with banners and dragons. We have left modern China behind at railroad station and are entering a China that is age-old. The street is teeming with ancient traffic. Woman bargaining with shopkeepers. Hucksters crying their wares. Shopkeepers and patrons coming

out to watch train pass. Two coolies darting by with a sick man in a hammock.

Farmer staggering by with a crate of chickens. Mothers running out and screaming at children to get off track. Engine approaches, slowly gathering headway. Two coolies carrying a squealing pig in a sling dart across track ahead of engine. Engineer waves to Chinese girl in window above shop. Her father comes out and curses engineer. Latter grins and gives him a toot from whistle. Shopkeeper runs into shop and comes out wearing dragon's head and screaming fresh curses, shaking his fist after Shanghai Express as it slowly pulls by down street—soldiers and passengers sticking heads out of windows of coaches. Engine whistle suddenly begins to blow a frantic warning.

FULL SHOT—

of cow nursing calf in middle of track. Engine enters with screaming whistle and brakes. Stops ten feet away from cow, which calmly continues to chew cud. Trainmen alight from train and run forward. Crowd swiftly gathers. Owner of cow excitedly enters. Trainmen bawl him out in Chinese as he removes cow and calf. Owner and crowd bawl out trainmen. Brakeman motions them back and raises flag to signal engineer to go ahead. He pauses as he sees a Chinese funeral procession starting across track.

FOLLOW SHOT—

along train as passengers lean curiously out of windows to see cause of delay. Hucksters come up, crying their wares. Coming to first-class car, we see Sam Salt looking out of vestibule window.

SAM SALT (as camera passes him): *Even money we don't get away for an hour!*
CARMICHAEL (sticking out head): *What's wrong now?* (He turns to Henry Chang, who is looking out next window.)
CHANG (sarcastically): *You're in China now, sir—where time and life have no value—*

The "Dreiser breather" has done Sternberg good. He returns to Dietrich more the cinema Ingres than ever with *Shanghai Express*— the most famous train journey in screen annals—in a film of the purest lambency. Clive Brook and Dietrich. (1932)

CAMERA PASSES ON to Captain Harvey, who is leaning out of adjoining window. Shot should include Lily, who is looking out of window behind him. Harvey turns and sees Lily in adjoining window. She glances at him. They slowly recognize each other.

HARVEY (in amazement): *Magdalen!*
LILY (with a smile): *Well, Doctor—I haven't seen you in a long time—*

They study each other intently for a moment, both smiling. Finally Lily says:

*You haven't changed a bit, Doctor—maybe a little grayer —that's all—*

HARVEY: *You've changed a lot, Magdalen—*
LILY: *Have I, Doc? D'you mind me calling you Doc? Or must I be more respectful?*
HARVEY (smiling): *No. You never were respectful. And you always called me Doc.*

Lily looks at him with a faint smile, half-affectionate, half-reminiscent.

There is a toot-toot from the engine, the sigh of released air-brakes, and train starts with a jerk.

FOLLOW SHOT—

of Lily and Captain Harvey turning away from window. He goes with her to door of her compartment. The past has reached out and subtly touched them. The years have rolled up like smoke. They are looking at each other— both deeply stirred.

*I didn't think I'd ever run into you again, Magdalen—*
LILY: *Have you thought of me much, Doc?*
HARVEY: *How long has it been?*
LILY: *Five years—almost.*
HARVEY: *Well, for five years I've thought of nothing else, Magdalen.*

First-class compartment from Pekin to Shanghai on the Shanghai Express and two of its assorted passengers, Hui Fei (Anna May Wong) and the "notorious coaster," Shanghai Lily (Marlene Dietrich).

LILY (smiling): *You were always polite, Doc. You haven't changed at all.*

HARVEY (after a moment): *You have, Magdalen—you've changed a lot.*

LILY (in mock alarm): *Have I lost my looks?*

HARVEY (soberly): *No—you're more beautiful than ever.*

LILY (puzzled): *Well, how have I changed?*

HARVEY: *I don't know—I wish I could describe it—*

LILY: *Well, Doc, I've changed my name.*

HARVEY: *Married?*

LILY (shaking her head): *No! It took more than one man to change my name to Shanghai Lily—*

HARVEY (staring at her): *Shanghai Lily?*

LILY (smiling): *Yes—the white flower of China—you've heard of me—and you've always believed what you've heard—*

HARVEY (smiling): *I still do.*

She shrugs and opens door of compartment. Hui Fei sits at table still smoking and playing solitaire. She glances up at them—then goes on with her game. Captain Harvey, constricted by the presence of the Chinese woman, looks at Lily in silence for a moment. Rev. Carmichael, passing by in vestibule, gives them both a curious stare over his shoulder as he exits.

*Well, it was nice to see you again, Magdalen—*
LILY (looking at him): *Oh, I don't know—*

She turns to chair upon which is case containing Victrola. She opens case, puts on record, and touches lever. There is a noisy blare of music and song as Lily lifts her eyes at Captain Harvey.

INTERIOR: MRS. HAGGERTY'S COMPARTMENT— FULL SHOT—

of Mrs. Haggerty hearing music in adjoining compartment. She brightens up, rises, and exits into vestibule.

INTERIOR: LILY'S COMPARTMENT—FULL SHOT—

of Lily and Captain Harvey looking at each other in silence while Victrola plays record. Mrs. Haggerty, entering in vestibule, smiles at Captain Harvey and sticks her head into compartment, nodding affably to Lily and Hui Fei.

MRS. HAGGERTY: *I heard your gramophone, ladies—and thought I'd come in and get acquainted—if you don't mind?*
LILY (welcoming the interruption): *Not at all—come in—*

Mrs. Haggerty flutters in and sits down. Captain Harvey starts to go.

MRS. HAGGERTY (calling to him in coquettish alarm): *I'm not driving you away, I hope?*
HARVEY (politely—as he exits): *Oh, no—*

Lily, winding up Victrola, looks after him. Hui Fei looks up at Lily—and continues to regard her, lighting another cigarette.

MRS. HAGGERTY (with her best social air): *It's a bit lonely on a train, isn't it? I'm used to having people around. They put my dog in the baggage car—that's why I dropped in on you—*

Lily smiles. Hui Fei, without looking up—laughs softly. Mrs. Haggerty, feeling the ice is broken, chatters on.

*I been visiting my niece in Peking—she married a sea-faring man—he hasn't been home in four years—and she ain't been very cheerful—I has a boarding-house in Shanghai—Yorkshire pudding's my specialty—and I only take the most respectable people—*(She hands out cards to Lily and Hui Fei.)

LILY (as she looks at card): *Don't you find respectable people terribly dull?*
MRS. HAGGERTY (startled out of her wits): *You're joking, ain't you? I've only known the most respectable people— you see, I keep a boarding-house—*

LILY (puzzled): *What kind of a house did you say?*
MRS. HAGGERTY (icily): *A boarding-house!*
LILY (thus enlightened): *Oh!*

She laughs in great amusement, and Mrs. Haggerty haughtily turns her back on her.

MRS. HAGGERTY (ingratiatingly to Hui Fei): *I'm sure you're very respectable, Madame*—(But her rising inflection indicates a faint doubt.)
HUI FEI (smiling—and in good English): *I'm sure I don't quite know the standard of respectability that you demand in your boarding-house, Mrs. Haggerty—*
MRS. HAGGERTY (suspicious of Chinese humor): *I'm afraid I've made a terrible mistake*—(Haughtily rising and starting toward door.)—*I better look after me dog!*

She goes to door. As she exits into vestibule, native guard enters with hatful of telegrams. He speaks to Hui Fei in Chinese and gives her a telegram.

LILY (to guard—as Hui Fei eagerly opens telegram): *Nothing for me?*

Guard looks through telegrams, shakes head, and exists. Hui Fei, who has read telegram with very happy expression, turns to Lily.

HUI FEI: *Are you going all the way to Shanghai?*
LILY: *Yes.*
HUI FEI: *So am I—and I am very happy about it—*
LILY: *So am I—*
HUI FEI (shy yet proud): *I'm going to be married when I arrive—*
LILY (with womanly interest and pleasure): *Are you very much in love with him?*
HUI FEI (simply): *yes, I am—*

DISSOLVE TO:

END OF SEQUENCE

# ANATAHAN
## (THE SAGA OF ANATAHAN)

### Narration

The text which follows is that of the complete English commentary (written and spoken by Sternberg) that accompanies the images of the film and is superimposed on the sound track over the Japanese dialogue, thus obviating the need for subtitles. Besides translating the dialogue, usually in condensed form, although sometimes word for word when a particular point is accented, the commentary does just that, it comments on the action, not only in terms specific to the action but also in universal terms. "The Anatahan incident," said Sternberg, "gave me the opportunity to depict the Japanese not subjected to a Japanese problem which might not be understood abroad. The Japanese on Anatahan were part of a sudden misfortune which could happen to anyone anytime. And, therefore, this incident could help to bridge the distance between the legend of this country and the readiness (or lack of it) to understand this country by others." In short, not a Japanese film but an international film. Inspired by an actual episode of the late war in the Pacific, and adapted by the director from a book on the subject subsequently written by one of the survivors of "the battle of Anatahan," the commentary is written, as is the book, in the first person.

### REEL #1

Nineteen days out of Yokohama, we were drifting toward Saipan at six knots an hour. The convoy consisted of five old bonito vessels. Our engines were in poor shape. We carried

badly needed supplies to our island outposts. We were fishermen, proud to be drafted into service, and had two soldiers posted on each boat—no need for more we thought. We are not prepared for defeat. Who is?

The lead boat, the Heiske Maru, was captained by an old salt who knew nothing about this watery arena. His maps showed some 2000 islands, like sprinkled crumbs on a vast surface. We were now passing the Mariana archipelago. Once it had belonged to Spain—then to Germany—and finally to Japan, and we intended to keep it. This tropical world was a geological joke of coral and volcano. Some islands lasted, some disappeared. Some were inhabited, others were not. Who would want to live here anyway? This giant body of water, and all that was in it, was ours. Our belief in victory was unshakable. We had stopped looking at the stepping stones that paraded by—they were of no interest to us—we wanted to return home.

We now sighted Anatahan—a jungle rock that stood high out of the sleeping waters—so it was duly recorded in the log that morning—June 12, 1944, the fourth year of a war to which we had dedicated our lives, like children playing a game without vision or foresight.

Four bells and our chief cook and bottle washer appeared promptly with *asameshi*, breakfast for the skipper. His American sailor's hat was a reminder of a defeated enemy ship.

At first, we thought it was one of our own planes.

The barren map of the world makes no note of where misfortune strikes. We went down fast, few survived. The Mariana trench over which we swam ashore was over 35,000 feet deep—the fiery center of the earth had blown this rock of Anatahan a long way from the ocean floor. How we got ashore, no one remembered. We were dumped like garbage on a hot coast—left to rot—the change from a human being with dignity to a helpless worm takes but a second. A merciful narcosis kept us from suffering too much.

One of the men had not only saved his hide but accomplished the heroic feat of bringing a machine-gun ashore. A warrant officer with a long service record—he was the only one who knew what to do—to defend this island for a couple of months was not a difficult task, he thought. He knew the enemy, and he knew the Imperial Navy would not permit us to stay abandoned very long.

Yes—we had picked the deepest part of the Pacific Ocean —deep and solemn.

We were to be here for seven long years and little did we know that the enemy was not in planes overhead, nor was it the lack of food, the lack of water and medicine—nor the venomous jungle that hemmed us in. How could we know that we had brought the enemy with us—in our own bodies —an enemy that would attack without notice.

One of our men had spotted a deserted village. This was good news, after many weeks of hardship.

And so we entered the twisting, haunted labyrinth of an unfamilar jungle—a beautiful but vicious world from which many of us never returned.

What kind of a Japanese was this? His name was Kusakabe —said he lived alone on the island—the others had left when the war started. He had been plantation foreman—exported copra—but the jungle had taken over—an unfriendly man, unfriendly to us—and unfriendly to himself.

Imagine living on an island like this by choice—thousands of miles from nowhere—all by himself—or was he all by himself?

That's how we met Keiko. At first, she was only another human being stranded on this pin-point on the map. Then, she was to become a female to us, and finally a woman—the only woman on earth.

REEL #2

The horizon stayed empty and remote. We lost track of time. The rains had started. They seemed never to end. We built boats—toy boats to carry us home on the wings of our longing. This lonely island was our whole world. We went to sleep at night and dreamt of home—each morning we were back on Anatahan.

Like a rare bird of the wet jungle—we caught an occasional glimpse of Keiko.

Some of us—sooner than the others, longed for something more than bread alone—and we watched her—and we watched each other.

The walls of the huts were thin. There were no secrets.

She had been out collecting shells as usual—his way of paying her a compliment was to call her "shell crazy."

The rains stopped—nothing lasts forever—though the waves of the ocean lasted long.

First thing we did when the hot rays of the sun came again was to build a Shinto Shrine to speed our prayers. Most of us believed in Shintoism. There were two Christians—four Buddhists—others believed only in Japan.

We extracted salt from the sea—hunted lizard and bat—found wild potatoes—lived on food that pigs would have rejected—but best of all, we found a way of making fire.

We had sunk to the level of prehistoric man—but our progress was not slow. We achieved in weeks what the cave man had taken centuries to accomplish.

And so we faced our new life—half way between Japan and New Guinea on a deserted sea-lane, 1500 miles from the Philippines—some 16 degrees above the Equator—resigned to wait.

The first typhoon struck us with an unjust fury. What had we done to reap all this? Why did man and nature conspire to make us helpless? The rocks that were so formidable when we crawled ashore were pebbles now in a giant sea. It raged for three days. The elements are cruel. To the winds and to the sea, man and his problems—is as nothing.

The typhoon pounded at us—the ocean wanted to wipe us out. The island rock that was anchored firmly to the bottom of the deep sea seemed to tear loose and join the storm.

One year on Anatahan! This was our home, now. Three miles long—one mile wide—most of it impenetrable. We stood guard in turns to wait for our Navy to come—it never came—for the enemy to come—he never came.

Nothing came but the waves—tides lifted and the tides fell. We watched the waves approach and we watched them recede, and we tried to find a meaning where there was none.

We now took another step away from prehistoric man. We had found empty beer bottles—and now we found a way of filling them—with coconut wine. If we drank quickly, before it turned to vinegar—it made us forget where we were and who we were.

We were scolded, of course, but since when has alcoholism been cured by scolding?

"Who are you combing your hair for?" "For you, naturally." Was she combing it for him?

Takahashi was the first man to break the social ice. He brought a peace offering. More shells for the wife as if she needed them. At that time, we still thought they were man and wife. And—we had not yet become savages.

The difference between a child and a grown-up is in the way the brain is in control of the emotions. Kusakabe objected to any one paying attention to Keiko. That was easy to diagnose—more difficult to understand was why he was so antagonistic—to us—and to himself.

Our leader, the boss of the island—that is, boss for a while, was not opposed to a display of his authority. Some men are drunk on wine—some are drunk on power.

So far, all these things that happened to us on Anatahan were small—our life now consisted of nothing but trifles. How were we to know what was important and what trifle was not?

She was a pretty woman—she was a Japanese woman—trained to obedience. When she was young, she followed her father—never dreamt of walking at his side. When she married, she walked behind the husband—obedience to a husband is considered to be the prime virtue of Japanese womanhood.

REEL #3

The full moon of the autumn equinox is the time for the "Ohigan" festival when we pay respect to our ancestors. Our thoughts then go from them to our families. The word *Higan* means the other shore. It is taken from the Buddhist legend that there is a river marking the division of this earthly world to a future one. This river is full of illusion, passion, pain, and sorrow. Only when you cross the river, having fought the currents of temptation to gain the far shore, do you reach enlightenment. This was the time when we thought of our families far away.

This was the time when we thought of our families—all of us—and so did Kusakabe. He had brought with him, when he came, wife and child. At the outbreak of the war, four years now—they had left him to go to Saipan—for safety. Keiko too

had a husband who had left on the same boat. She too had not heard from him again. All this, we found out later.

Carelessly as we might wish to be in our human relations —there is a time of accounting.

Left alone in an empty world, it was natural for these two to have formed a bond of sorts—for a time they had forgotten everything but each other.

"Are you thinking of your home?" "Yes, but not when I see you." She was prepared to hear just that.

The longest journey begins with one step. Hers was to be quite a long journey.

This was Anatahan. We still kept track of the month, though we had forgotten the day of the week. A little while later, no one cared what year it was. Japan had forgotten us.

The horizon remained empty and remote, but the circle around Keiko enlarged; she was young, her body failed to remember the blows she had received. It also slipped her mind. She became better looking day by day. She became Queen Bee and the drones began to swarm.

"What's your husband doing?" "All I know, he's not out looking for another woman." "How would you like to be my bride tonight?" "I don't need two husbands."

Coconut wine had become our steady diet. With the coming of wine, discipline diminished. Some of us began to feel strongly about being told to stand guard day and night against an enemy that never came. Who was this man, anyway, who never allowed us to forget what it meant to be a Japanese soldier? All this talk of "stand up and salute" became more and more pointless.

It took him years to achieve his position, it took seconds to lose it.

Typhoons in human beings strike without much warning. There are few signals and only the skilled—the very skilled, can read them.

The loss of face to a soldier in command is not a pleasant experience. To lose the respect of our fellowmen is not pleasant to anyone—anywhere. A good part of our life is spent in trying to gain the esteem of others—to gain self-esteem, however, we usually waste little time.

REEL #4

We had thrown off the yoke of discipline. We were free—free of all restraint—which only meant that we were slaves to our bodies.

The *Tsundara Bushi*—an Okinawa folk song—had spread like a weed among the soldiers during the war.

"You and me—like an egg—I'm egg white, you're egg yellow, I embrace you."

The day started with a dispute over the words of a song. How the day would end, no one knew at the time. We were looking for trouble—and we found it.

"Keiko, Keiko . . . . . . . . . . . come out, come out." Those were the right words!

Semba was 19, with the beard of a man and the brain of a grasshopper. He was next in line for Keiko's favors. We gave little thought to our actions. There is no medicine against stupidity—and it was epidemic among us.

Then came the unexpected!

"To all Japanese Forces! Three months ago—August 15—Japan accepted unconditional surrender. The Japanese Emperor himself is asking you to lay down your arms. The war is over. An American ship will take you home. Hostilities have ceased. All Japanese men and officers surrender—surrender at once!"

The unbelievable had happened. This could not be true. We had just begun the war. We were prepared to fight for a thousand years. We had overrun Asia, almost the entire Pacific—how could we have lost so suddenly?

This was an enemy trick. It could fool no one. We came to ask him to lead us again. There are those who lead and those who wish to be led. There is not necessarily any other bond between them.

"The sacred soil of Japan cannot be conquered. So long as we have one drop of blood in our veins—we will not give up. Rather die than surrender!"

But far away in Japan—our country had faced the reality of defeat. The Emperor had called the troops home. And millions streamed back—away from the nightmare of trying to conquer a world.

Father and son—wife and husband—mothers, daughters—friends—all those who feared they might never meet again. The men who had fought in vain came back home—there also were many that did not come back.

REEL #5

But we knew nothing about what took place in a new Japan. We were still on Anatahan—deserted by the world—we were defending this volcanic rock—against what enemy?

The only real enemy most of us ever have is lonesomeness.

The jungle had disgorged a rare prize. An enemy plane had been found wrecked, the bodies vanished.

This was a doubtful reminder of civilization. We fluttered around this sudden gift from the skies like vultures—what could we find to make our life better?

Some of the things were to make our life worse. Nishio found a .45 calibre weapon and a few bullets—Yananuma, too, hit the jackpot.

Keiko found a parachute—which meant elegance for us instead of clothes made of tree-bark—or no clothes at all.

Semba, our friend, the lady-killer, found a ring—the easy way to a woman's heart.

This lifeless mass of iron was the only sign of life from the outside world, so far.

Maruyama was seaman first class. Before joining the Navy he had been a first class musician. He had an idea how to make use of rusty wire. He was to convert a war machine into a musical instrument.

This was the first shot heard on the island—it was not to be the last one—two old pistols—two new masters.

Keiko was gone. She had been missing all night. This was a serious defection. Keiko missing? Kusakabe was more out of his mind than usual.

Away from all our troubles—our now useless leader kept the machine-gun ready to shoot. This gun was never to shoot.

Our search party went into action. Something must have happened to Keiko—was she dead? We were too stunned to count the men that were missing.

She was not dead—far from it—she was very much alive. This was the beginning of a new pattern on Anatahan—Keiko

had gone into circulation. To spy on the humiliating details of another human being's life would be unforgivable were we not concerned in finding a clue to our own behavior. Nothing that happens to a human being is alien to us—there but for the grace of God go I.

Nishio and his friend are not uncommon among those that we know. They had guns now, to take the place of thinking.

Of course they had seen no one—why should they reveal her whereabouts—they had plans of their own. We had now been on this island for a long time, for all we knew we would be there forever. It is easy to look back and label all the commotion about Keiko ridiculous. What we did there— we might not have done somewhere else—opinions differ on that point—it is said that human beings react according to a set pattern whether they are in a primitive or a civilized society—maybe so. To look back on something is not the same as living with it.

The relationship between a man and a woman is based on emotions which often may not be understood by others—who in one way or another fumble just as much. It is easy to see what wrong others do—we carry no mirror to reflect our own actions.

REEL #6

She was clearly the winner this time—a bargain had been made. When a woman threatens to leave—this has considerable influence on the behavior of a man—even when she is not the only woman on earth.

Our leader took the occasion to lecture on our behavior— our mission was to defend Anatahan—not to drink and chase after females. Someday the enemy would appear. But he missed the most important point—the enemy *was* on Anatahan—man's genius to destroy himself was in clear evidence.

The day began with a harmless little ditty—a prelude to violence.

Keiko wanted to be taught how to play the shamisen. "What about your husband?" But she knew how to handle him now! One more blow out of him and she would leave him again!

We were all in bondage to Keiko—some more and some less. She was the center of our universe. We had no one to call our own—no one to care for us. It is not good for man to be alone.

Kuroda was the oldest sailor among us and he took the occasion to confirm our suspicions about the marital status of Keiko and Kusakabe—as if legalistic technicalities made any difference, any more, in Anatahan society. It was he who noticed the photograph—and told us about it later. There was no law on our island—no police—there were only two pistols.

Not so long ago these two had been members of the Imperial Navy—disciplined and polite—but the Navy was all but forgotten—and forgotten was what they had once been. But they were still human beings, and that classification is sufficient to cover quite a variety of behavior.

Certainly, Kusakabe had promised not to beat Keiko but in turn he reminded her that she had promised not to fool around with others. The two gunmen suggested that they settle their differences where they could be under scientific observation. They had an idea. Keiko could cook for four as easily as for two—Kusakabe could provide food if he wanted to be friendly. She did not object—too much. It would have done little good, if she had! Now these were no longer trifles. The knife and the bullet had become law.

So the Queen Bee kept house for three drones. At all these events that began now, we were not present. We were not inside that hut. There is no way to check the story of violence that now unfolded swiftly. Even had we been there—all our versions would differ.

One man who did try to check what occurred on the "hill of fools"—as we subsequently call this corner of the jungle—was our old friend Semba.

A little while later, his body was found in the swing where only a week before he had enjoyed the company of Keiko. We can only guess how he got into that hammock.

We can only surmise how a second body came to be found on that hill—two bullets buried deep in Nishio's back helped us to guess correctly.

In some parts of Asia there is a God of Immediate Retribution, whose function it is to spare us long delays in deserved

punishment. Had he decided to become the deity of Anatahan?

Anyway, death was fishing in this jungle and on his hook
as bait he dangled Keiko.

REEL #7

So we buried the two victims of our ill-fated mission with
due Shinto ceremony. A little part of us went down with them
into the moist ground. We felt sorry for the dead. Even an in-
sect an inch long has half an inch of soul. Time had stopped
for these two but our miserable existence continued.

We had now been on Anatahan for five years—five years
can be short—for us they were endless—days can be as fatal
as bullets—all that kept us alive was the thought of our
country.

Somewhere to the north was another island—an island that
we loved and longed for and could never forget as long as we
had breath in our bodies.

We celebrated the New Year like good Japanese soldiers.
We paid our respect in the direction of the Imperial Palace
and sang our National Anthem.

We wished each other a happy New Year—*omedeto
gozaimasu*—and as if nothing had happened, thanked each
other for the friendship of the past year and hoped courteously
that this year would be as pleasant as the last.

At all this, too, no one else was present. We can only reconstruct the events from which we were barred. The King
and Queen had left our festival—that we knew—but we never
saw the King again. He had been marked for death, indelibly,
long ago. The only thing we did not know was—who would
be the executioner?

Now Kusakabe was royalty. Anatahan had a new overlord—
a new King for a short time—for a short time only.

She followed him obediently—but this was a travesty of
obedience. Obedience at the point of a gun—is no obedience
at all.

We put Yananuma to rest. He died young. He had no
chance to learn how to live properly. Someday we would bring

his ashes back home—and lie to his people that he had died like a good soldier—honorably.

REEL #8

The Queen had returned to the beehive. But there was little rejoicing. They should have attended the funeral. You do not beat the dead.

When human beings wish to quarrel—they soon find a cause. The litany is of no consequence. This time it was: no food in the hut—why doesn't he go out and get some? There was no love in the hut also.

Next in line was the ex-cook of the Heiske Maru—Yoshiri. He aspired to Keiko—the goal of his ambitions was not lofty. We are driven by forces about which we know nothing.

The King is dead! What price the new King? How long will the tyrannical house of Yoshiri last? He was to wield his power over Anatahan for less than 24 hours. Keiko was his and all the coconut wine he could guzzle. Untold riches! But the Queen was not to be his. She had not been partial to the murder of her previous consort. The bond between them had been strong—whatever the nature of the elastic might have been that binds together male and female. He wanted her as Queen and handmaiden—no insolence—no one was going to throw a cup at his feet.

Would he have laughed quite so much had he known that he would not see the light of another day?

All of us remember that night. The moon was low—the trees silent. The air was full of mist—the sea was deep—the rocks black—Nature was indifferent to the cruel destiny of man.

The history of this unfortunate is the history of an American sailor's hat.

The two pistols were thrown into the ocean—they were gone. There was to be no more bloodshed—we chose Keiko peacefully, that is—peacefully, for us.

But Keiko was not going to be chosen peacefully or otherwise. She was through.

We started the hunt for the prize that this time had been won in fair competition.

The foe had found us—the long looked for enemy. We

were to be bombed—we thought—for this we had been trained—this was a simple matter.

"To the Japanese Army on Anatahan!" The "bombs" that had dropped told us that war had been over for five years—a vessel would call and take us home.

This was, of course, another crude enemy trick—what did they think we were—children?

REEL #9

This was hardly the time for love letters from the enemy—let's find Keiko!

We did not see this. We never saw her again. She disappeared as if she had never existed. Long ago, I heard her say that if she had wings she would fly home.

Keiko had gone—there was no more trouble—there was also no more life. And then a ship came and a white flag was found in our jungle burial ground. Letters from Japan.

This one was from Keiko. She had notified our families—told them we were alive—Kuroda had no family so she thoughtfully thanked him and said she hoped her departure had not brought too much trouble to him. This was embarrassing but definitely not an enemy trick.

There was another letter—from the Governor of the prefecture. "The war ended six years ago—your families are waiting—this flag we send has surrendered a Japanese regiment—use it—we want you home!"

"You can return if you wish—I will never go back to a defeated Japan!"

The rest of us surrendered—gladly. We had lost the battle of Anatahan.

We soared like eagles over our sacred mountain. It took 10 hours to retrace a journey of 19 days and seven long years.

We were back in Japan—heroes to all but to ourselves—brother and sister were there—our friends were waiting—father and mother—our neighbors came. We saw our wives—our children—now seven years older—we would have to earn their affection all over again—we were home at last.

And if I know anything at all about Keiko—she too must have been there.

# Critical Reviews

### Some Reflections on the Art of
### Josef von Sternberg

So much has been written about Sternberg and his films that the director once remarked to me in real alarm that it was "inhuman." Perhaps in no countries more than America and France, however, have the most cogent and perceptive critical estimations and summings up of the Sternberg *daemon* been delineated. The following dozen excerpts (with the exception of a wry "pen portrait" published in London) appeared principally in New York and Paris. Trenchant and incisive, they have one thing in common: they attempt to get at the heart of the matter, e.g., his mordant art, so disconcertingly flecked with perverse humor as to, in the last analysis, confound even his most acute critics. A psychoanalyst, following the labyrinths of his psychological motivations, could conceivably throw up his hands in despair and say, "I can't figure out if he's in earnest or if he's kidding!"

Both, I'd say, but never at the same time—never.

*Peter Balbusch*
NOTES DURING THE FILMING OF
"SHANGHAI EXPRESS"
(extracts)

The night was glorious and one had to count it high in his favor. It is curious to think that all this exists only because a single brain wanted it to exist. The night, the searchlights,

Sternberg on the set for the opening scene of *Shanghai Express*
. . . . . "the intoxicating perfume of work" . . . . .

In nature, the crested crane; in the cinema, this. Dietrich garbed for her "Hot Voodoo" number in *The Blonde Venus*, a song, not a *danse lascif*, which another director would have made of such a costume. Ever present is the director's aesthetic equilibrium. (1932)

The art of the cigarette, a Dietrich specialty. Style is the servant of meaning, not an end in itself. In this portrait, Sternberg's meaning travels with the speed of light. Dietrich in *The Blonde Venus*—a tale, believe it or not, of mother love, like *The Case of Lena Smith*.

the dust, the wind—all this and the intoxicating perfume of work, an actuality now—because *he* thought of it. At times one can bodily feel how he thinks. I don't want to forget the locomotive that blew its puff of white steam into a yellow sky. It was unspeakably beautiful in this barren landscape.

.   .   .

They slander him a good deal and one is either for or against him. Curiously enough, there is not even the typical American well-tempered tolerance for success. So definite is his personality, one must either love or hate him and when you love him you smilingly accept all that which arouses antagonism in others.

.   .   .

Polished dialogue? The hell with it! To the capable director dialogue is no more than a spoken musical note of the final theme, infinitely varied and harboring hundreds of unspoken meanings.

.   .   .

Even the camera and the microphone can be inspired through barely noticeable movement and their own obstinate qualities, and I believe that the future directors will take strong advantage of the ideas proposed by the stubborn film machinery.

.   .   .

It would be interesting to find out what some of the Chinese extras think about the filming, the director, and the complicated apparatus. Probably we would all come off badly.

.   .   .

What I admire in him is not his cinematic genius that reveals itself in his bird-of-prey eyes and his lightning comprehension and control of any situation. That can be learned and may often be harbored in an individual. But what counts most and makes him great is his endurance, his mind forcing domination over his threadbare nerves, his stoicism and monklike humility toward his work.

*Written on a copy of the shooting script on the sets during the filming of "Shanghai Express." Hollywood, Autumn, 1931*

*Charles Graves*

### JOSEF VON STERNBERG

Josef von Sternberg walks like a cat, looks like a fallen archangel, wears Mongolian moustachios and black Chinese pyjamas, is never seen out of doors without a walking-stick, craves cornflowers, and always expects the head waiters to bring, unasked, seven iced black grapes when he enters a restaurant. He has wavy grey hair, steel-blue eyes, a horror of the cold, and a consequent love of the tropics. He talks epigrammatically, paints admirably, and has already sculptured his own tombstone—a brooding, monkish figure holding its head with one hand. The only things he has not yet done are to write his own epitaph or to direct Charles Laughton. And he is beginning on the latter early in the New Year.

Mr. von Sternberg lives at the Splendide, resents being put under the slightest obligation by strangers, always refers to Marlene Dietrich as "Miss Dietrich," visits lunatic asylums wherever he can find them, and has built himself an all-steel house in the San Fernando Valley. Here he has a valuable collection of portraits by Utrillo, as well as by Van Gogh, Picasso, Modigliani, and most of the other leading modern painters.

Born in Vienna of Polish and Hungarian parents forty-two years ago, he emigrated to the United States at the age of seven. Always possessed with a leaning toward chemistry, he found himself in the film industry on the laboratory side. Soon he became a film patcher, and finally was put in charge of the camera department. Today, he is the only director who has a union card as a camera-man. Not only that, he cuts and edits his own films. It was he who discovered Miss Dietrich, took her to America, directed her first six pictures, and earned the title of "Marlene's Svengali." He also gave their first real chance to Evelyn Brent, Herbert Marshall, Warner Oland, Gary Cooper, William Powell, George Bancroft, Victor McLaglen, Sylvia Sidney, Cary Grant, and Cesar Romero. *I, Claudius* will not be the first English picture with which he will have been associated. Fourteen years ago he was an

Paul Ivano, cameraman for *The Sea Gull*, and Von Sternberg, just before taking off for the Caribbean to shoot a hurricane for the next Dietrich film, but the hurricane failed to materialize and the project was abandoned. (1932)

Yes, the future has definitely arrived. Director and star, the subjects of more éclat than any team in screen history, dine out in Hollywood. They are at the pinnacle of their success. (1934)

assistant director at Twickenham, with the Alliance Film Company. Previously, during the war, he had been appointed motion-picture expert to the American G.H.Q. and taught them bayonet fighting on the screen. The picture that made him famous was *The Salvation Hunters*—and was incidentally the only one of his own he ever saw with an audience—which laughed.

Josef von Sternberg is ultra-sensitive to noise (he once told Miss Dietrich to stop her teeth chattering), secretive, cynical, and certain of himself. He says truthfully that he is neither morbid, sinister, nor particularly decadent. He is merely a realist. He thinks deeply, never evades issues, and enjoys trying to disconcert you. Quite incidentally, he is the greatest living director.

*The Bystander, London*
*Dec. 9, 1936*

### Kirk Bond

#### JOSEF VON STERNBERG REVISITED

. . . I think that, if anything, his stature increases. He is, beyond question, one of the great directors. He ranks in this country with Vidor, with Lubitsch, perhaps only a little below Griffith and Stroheim. . . . He is one of the richest, one of the subtlest of directors. He may not always be easy to follow, but to those who are ready to follow he is immensely rewarding. He combines, in a way that may be unique in art, a luxurious pictorial style with a detached, often sardonic point of view that seems almost grotesquely at odds with the warm imagery. But that is Sternberg . . .

Sternberg is a poet who writes of life as he sees it, standing somewhere off at the side, understanding, criticizing, yet loving it, too. And it is part of Sternberg that his love comes out in little tender moments almost awkwardly—and yet is so vital and basic to the whole fabric.

"You see," says Menjou in *Morocco*, "they love their men." "Perhaps," says Marlene in *Dishonored*, "[I did it] because I love him." Such tiny, almost Chinese-like cameos are worth more than vast epics of tumultous red passion.

A similar moment occurs in the opening scene of *Dis-*

*honored*. Marlene stands on the sidewalk as what appears to be a suicide is carried out. Someone in the small crowd growls, "They all end that way." In a tone that is indescribable Marlene says, "No, they don't!" Of course they don't. It is part of the dogma of our hard age that they *do*, and one of the wonderful things about Sternberg is that he has the courage and the compassion to say they don't.

And then there comes the other Sternberg, worldly, sardonic, but never cynical. "What a lovely evening we might have had," says Warner Oland in *Dishonored* with the meditative calm of a Buddhist monk, "if you weren't a spy and I a traitor." "Then," replies Dietrich, "we might never have met."

In the midst of the swooningly beautiful hubbub of the duel in *The Devil Is a Woman*, Edward Everett Horton as the mayor (complete with trim beard) arrives. "Good morning, gentlemen." (It is raining pitchforks.) "A pretty mess." And a few minutes later: "All professions have their compensations, even mine." Shaw could hardly do better.

The wonderful endings of *Morocco* and *Dishonored* deserve a special note. They are not to be excused or brushed aside as too bizarre. They are essential parts of Sternberg's work. And they bring tears to the eyes ...

*Film Courier, New York*
*Summer, 1959*


## Andrew Sarris

### THE CINEMA OF JOSEF VON STERNBERG

The cinema of Von Sternberg is the cinema of illusion and delusion, of men deluded by women, of men and women deluded by surface appearances. Von Sternberg has always worked within a studio enclosure where he could control the lighting and texture. When a French interviewer asked him why he had constructed a studio set for the Pacific Island of *Anatahan*, Von Sternberg replied simply, "Because I am a poet." Some critics have mistakenly confused his poetry with folly as if Von Sternberg himself had been as deluded as his characters ... Von Sternberg the man undoubtedly shared some of the follies of his characters, but Von Sternberg the

director never lost his formal grip on his material. The critical sentiment in the Thirties was that films were supposed to be short, snappy, and to the proletarian point. Von Sternberg was thus considered slow, decadent, and self-indulgent, and gloriously ambiguous Marlene Dietrich was judged too rich for the people's blood. This was a time for bread, not cake. Today, Von Sternberg and Dietrich look more dazzling than ever while most of the cinema of the bread lines looks excessively mannered. Time invariably vindicates form over topicality, and poetry always outlives journalism.

*Film Culture, New York, Spring, 1963*

## Jack Smith

### A BELATED APPRECIATION OF J.V.S.

People never know why they do what they do. But they have to have explanations for themselves and others.

So Von Sternberg's movies had to have plots even though they already had them inherent in the images. What he did was make movies naturally—he lived in a visual world. The explanations, plots he made up out of some logic having nothing to do with the visuals of his films. . . .

In this country the movie is known by its story. A movie is a story, is as good as its story. Good story—good movie. Unusual story—unusual movie, etc. Nobody questions this. It is accepted on all levels, even "the film is a visual medium" plane, by its being held that the visuals are written first then breathed to life by a great cameraman, director. In this country the blind go to the movies. There is almost no film an experienced and perceptive blind man couldn't enjoy. This is true. I was a Broadway barker once and was approached by a blind man! The B.M. was right—there must be others! The manager, nobody, thought it strange—at the time I didn't— and don't now. I do think it strange that nobody uses their eyes. . . .

I don't think Von Sternberg knew that words were in his way, but he felt it—and he invested his images with all the care he rightfully denied the words. And he achieved the rich-

est, most alive, most right images of the world's cinema—
in company with men like Von Stroheim, the genius of *Zero
de Conduite*, early Lang, and that limited company. . . .

Possibly he might have been afraid of reaction if it were
known that his visual fantasy world was really his own mind.
He might have deliberately obscured, distracted attention
from the shock that might have occurred, if his creation had
been understood through the eye. To close the ears would
have thrown the viewer into an undersea, under-conscious,
world where the realities were very different from what the
script purported. He needn't have worried. As it was, no one
had that ability to see. He was misunderstood and well understood. Well understood in that his covert world disturbed;
misunderstood in that no one knew why or appreciated the
wonder of being disturbed. Misunderstood and done an in-
justice to in that finally, when opinion turned against him,
it was for the wrong reason: (wrong not because people
should not be disturbed) the "insipid stories, bad acting, bad
dialogue," etc. Wrong reasons because they were, to be true
to his expression, deliberately "bad." Then he was punished
—turned out of Hollywood and never again allowed to work.
Only frightened people punish. Ostensibly because he had
violated good technique. Good technique being used as something people hide behind when they are frightened by
something they wouldn't like in themselves, therefore *is* in
themselves. And the hypocrisy of good acting, good this,
good that—GOOD MOVIES being perpetuated—GOOD
EMPTY—BANAL—UNTRUE MOVIES—IMPERSONAL
MOVIES.

*Film Culture, New York*
*Winter, 1963–64*

## Ado Kyrou

### STERNBERG AND THE MARLENE MYTH

There never was a more exalting association than that between Sternberg and Marlene. But to be more accurate, let
us say right away that Marlene only exists through Sternberg,
just as the work of this genial director only exists through
her and for her.

The next was a mad stunt, a "Carnaval Russe" on the theme of Catherine II ("the Great") with the Imperial Court peopled by gargoyles both human and sculptured, a film-*toccata* of relentless *brio* crackling with insolent wit. Sam Jaffe as the Grand Duke Peter and Dietrich as the newly arrived Sophia Frederika. *The Scarlet Empress.* (1934)

Byzantine luxury. Louise Dresser as the Empress Elizabeth admonishes her half-wit son, Peter (Sam Jaffe), as his bride-to-be, Sophia Frederika (Dietrich), looks on. *The Scarlet Empress.*

Detail from the wedding of Peter and Sophia Frederika in the Cathedral of Kazan, according to the Russian Orthodox ceremony. Done entirely *sans* the vocal ritual but accompanied by Rubenstein's "Kamenei Ostrow" as a musical interpretation of the ritual. *The Scarlet Empress.*

"Exit Peter—enter Catherine!" The procession following Peter's assassination, which heralds the ascendancy of Catherine to the throne.
Dietrich in hussar's uniform as a symbol of the male power she will
assume. *The Scarlet Empress*.

He used to say: "Cinema is a commercial profession which utilizes tools that could have been used for the creation of art." He and the few true men of the cinema (Chaplin, Eisenstein, Vigo, Buñuel, Fields) dared and were lucky enough to be able to utilize these tools to express themselves freely. They understood that only their personal vision of the world was of capital interest. Incapable of abiding by the commercial exigencies (he had innumerable problems with producers and critics), Sternberg gave us his world without worrying about the ridiculous question of true and false, real and unreal. His world, like any personal world charged with magnetism, is a mirror that we cannot grasp with our feeble means; the communion can only come about with sensivity. Sternberg's truth is beyond the subject matter, the people, and the ideas, and even when he makes a film imposed on him, he cannot help filming it in his own universe of dreams. Sternberg's universe, made up of the unusual and of eroticism, is purely surrealistic: he burns its visible envelopes with corrosive rays in order to explore its latent riches.

His first picture, *The Salvation Hunters*, was realized and produced with amateur means, but it already reveals that which will make Sternberg's majesty. The poetic aspect of things dominates the manifest aspect and man's forces (non-physical) are its subject matter. Each gesture, each spoken sentence is transfigured, a predominant search already appears, the search for the woman which will enable Sternberg to leave the *"marie-salope"* of *Salvation Hunters* and nearly find the ideal in *Underworld*. In it Evelyn Brent has the symbolic name of "Feathers," light and present, like the feathers she leaves in her path; she will make the killer, Bancroft, understand in one hour what a whole lifetime could not have taught him. A year later, Bancroft, a rough sailor in *The Docks of New York*, will meet a woman, Betty Compson, whom he will not immediately recognize as The Woman. He believes she is but a companion for the night and in the morning, while she is still asleep, he gets up to go after leaving her a few dollars on the night-table, but he turns around, looks at Betty's beautiful body, smiles, and adds two dollars. He comes back later and the couple unites in a real, mad love, braving the ribbing and the obstacles that surround them. "The rules of the established morality are not respected for a moment— the heart, pleasure, pride, a sense of personal dignity are the

only rulers of the people in this story." (J. G. Auriol, *Revue du Cinéma*, 1929). Now Sternberg knows the object of his desperate search; in the extraordinary *Case of Lena Smith* he enumerates the obstacles and the ignominious ways in which love is forbidden.

He goes to Germany in 1930 to make a picture based on a novel by H. Mann. It is the story of a beautiful woman and of a man who will live only for her, despite the consequences of this love. Sternberg thinks of Gloria Swanson or of Phyllis Haver for the main role, but in the musical show, *Zwei Krawatten* (*Two Neckties*), he notices a young singer who had already tried her luck in pictures, but failed to make it despite her interpretation in an unjustly forgotten film, *The Isle of Lost Ships* by Tourneur. Her name is Marlene Dietrich. She is The Woman and Sternberg makes her get up on the studio sound stage so that her legs can better be seen, he surrounds her with female "horses" to show off her beauty, he caresses her with his camera, with his lights, with his shadows, as no woman has ever been caressed before.

From now on Sternberg's work will be Marlene. He creates her in the image he has of her, he places her in his universe, he explodes with joy, his cries of happiness come up magnificent. He shows us his exultant happiness: it is not just a woman, it is not life as you believe you live it, it is Sternberg's woman in Sternberg's life, which changes everything. His reticence is over, Sternberg no longer searches, he has found, he will now make passionate films.

This huge gorilla who staggers onto a cabaret stage will pull off his ridiculous attire and Marlene, superb, will appear (*Blonde Venus*). A mad king drills holes in the eyes of sculpted angels on the walls to watch Marlene, who gets undressed next door (*The Scarlet Empress*). The burning desert sand becomes a moving rug under Marlene's feet (*Morocco*). Marlene is offered the most beautiful accessories, the maddest poses, she walks around the grottoes in a white lace dress (*Blonde Venus*). A clothes madness comes over Sternberg: a lunacy unequaled in the history of cinema, he braves all criticism concerning his "bad taste," he dresses Marlene in the most unusual and most erotic manner. I was never able to enumerate Marlene's outfits in *Shanghai Express*.

With such a woman events cannot follow their usual course; the unusual, the surrealistic, accompany her, and huge

How can you follow a bravura work like *The Scarlet Empress* without its being an anti-climax? For this was to be their last film together. You make the exasperatingly sado-masochistic *The Devil Is a Woman* because as you get older, she get's more and more beautiful. Something (someone?) has to give. Dietrich and goose, Lionel Atwill. (1935)

"Marlene is not Marlene, she is me," Sternberg once said. So was everyone else who ever acted in his films. Their composite is a portrait of the director more accurate than any single camera portrait of him can show. Dietrich as the devastating Concha Perez of *The Devil Is a Woman*, played in high parody and a stylized *tour de force*.

That ball of fire, the sun, gives light, and men have learned to manipulate light incandescently. Put to the service of the pan-sexual morality of Sternberg, in terms of the most silken chiaroscuro, the effect is truly promethean. Louys, from whose *Woman and Puppet* the story derives, left one man gutted at the end. Sternberg leaves two. Dietrich and Cesar Romero (as Don Antonio). *The Devil Is a Woman*.

White on white—sheer opalescence. Here the camera literally paints with light and the lattice-work on the door seems as if done with a painter's brush. Vermeer eliminated the brush-stroke in painting; Sternberg puts the brush-stroke in photography. Opposites become one. Dietrich in *The Devil Is a Woman*.

marble gargoyles lead her steps. If she is a spy, she will commit treason against her country to be faithful to her love (*Dishonored*) and in a make-believe Spain she becomes the frenzied heroine of a wildly romantic story (*The Devil Is a Woman*).

Sternberg now reigns over his own films, nothing will oust him. Thanks to *the* woman, he has achieved a sublime freedom and with ferocious joy he makes pictures, just as great poets write poetry for themselves. "My pictures are acts of arrogance," he used to say.

Then came Sternberg's separation from the ideal woman he had created. His universe should normally have become empty; the creator was so involved with the laces and jewels that covered his creature, the love between creator and creature was so strong, that they fused into one being (I mean in their pictures, I do not mention what may have happened outside their films). Sternberg feels lost for six years, his pictures still have the magnetic imprint of his universe, but he is obviously filming "to do his job." Yet it seems that his picture, *I, Claudius*, might have been a masterpiece.

Suddenly, in 1941, he makes *Shanghai Gesture* without Marlene and again this is very great Sternberg. He makes his picture, perhaps his most personal one, with melo-theatrical means. Through a curious sexual and cinemato-graphic mechanism he makes it a Marlene picture, her presence is felt (I nearly said that one smells her perfume), she is "seen" but she is now a split person: she is Gene Tierney, all woman with her unkempt hair; she also is Victor Mature, the man Sternberg himself. This Doctor Omar, "doctor of nothing, poet of Shanghai—and Gomorrah," has Marlene's lascivious poses, her great cruelty, her voluptuousness, but he is also Sternberg, himself, who made Marlene and who will be instrumental in the plot destined to crush Marlene—Gene Tierney.

A clever and instinctive complexity has always recreated the same woman in Sternberg's personal world. She appears again as Jane Russell in *Macao*. Sternberg had created a myth; he can no longer escape it. Sternberg and Marlene were never really separated. And if they now made a film together?

Josef von Sternberg is the most complex of *cinéastes*. He is also the most misunderstood. His flamboyant originality

Sternberg follows his former producer at Paramount, B.P. Schulberg, to Columbia Pictures, for whom he makes a perfunctory *Crime and Punishment*, after Dostoievski, and since it is not his adaptation and he lacks his usual autonomy, the picture looks it. Peter Lorre (Raskolnikov) and Marian Marsh (Sonia). (1935)

His follow-up picture for Columbia is *The King Steps Out,* from the Fritz Kreisler operetta, *Cissy.* Grace Moore (Cissy, afterwards Empress Elizabeth of Austria) and Franchot Tone (Franz Josef, afterward Emperor) on a spree in the Prater. (1936)

Sternberg returns from a trip around the world to direct *I, Claudius* for Alexander Korda in London. In high leather safari boots and Hindu turban he is, at first, an intimidating sight on the set. Later, his graciousness will dispel all his cast's fears. (1937)

Charles Laughton (as the imbecilic Roman emperor, Tiberius Claudius Drusus) and Flora Robson (as his mother, the Empress Dowager, Livia). Laughton, though marvelous in the part, develops some eccentricities that contribute toward the abandonment of the film in its early stages. (1937)

Emlyn Williams as Caligula in *I, Claudius*—seldom has evil incarnate been so acidly portrayed. The eyes of a basilisk in a human face. Sternberg later said it might have been his best work had he been given the chance to finish it.

After a number of non-realized projects, Sternberg returns to Hollywood to fulfill an old contract with MGM where he is assigned a picture to which he is totally unsympathetic. "There is nothing of me in it," he said. Wallace Beery in *Sergeant Madden*. (1939)

But he is back in Hollywood again, and in this photo with old friends at Ciro's. L. to R.—René Clair (then directing Dietrich in *The Flame of New Orleans*), the lady herself, Joe Pasternak, that film's producer, and Sternberg. (1941)

Then "from out of the blue" comes the offer to direct with complete autonomy again, as in the old days. An all but impossible assignment—the lurid *The Shanghai Gesture*—whose deadly attack on moral hypocrisy had somehow to be deflected to pass the censors. Sternberg's adaptation fooled them—and no one else. Notable for the hieratic beauty of Gene Tierney (Poppy) and the corrosive spleen of Ona Munson, Sternberg's "Chinese Dietrich," as "Mother Gin-Sling." (1941)

Next came an assignment about an American jet ace and a female Soviet jet ace for Howard Hughes, *Jet Pilot*, Sternberg's first color film, and a comedy (his only one). Some amusing "aerotics" were almost the only sternbergian touches that survived the wholesale reshooting and re-editing this picture suffered. John Wayne and Janet Leigh were starred. (1951, but not released till 1957)

A second assignment for Mr. Hughes was *Macao*, about diamond smugglers in the mysterious East. Despite Sternberg's previous successes with exotic locales, the picture was almost totally reshot by another director (Nicholas Ray). Only some telling atmospheric shots remained of Sternberg's work. Jane Russell starred (with Robert Mitchum). William Bendix is her vis-à-vis here. (1951)

places him outside commercial limitations. The unusual, the magic, the eroticism of his films, lead us beyond everything. The elements of his subject matter only lead us, however rationally, toward the irrational. He minutely details events that are of minor importance in order to get to scenes that take place in the depths of the unexplored. I think of the final sequence in *Morocco*, of the demonic faces in *The Case of Lena Smith*, of the dinner in *Shanghai Gesture*, where a lame man plays a romantic tune on the piano while a giant coolie opens the window, enabling the customers to see half-naked women hanging high up in birds' cages; the chase through the labyrinth of the fisherman's nets in *Macao*, and of all the other images that constitute this unique entity in the history of cinema. His lashes wake our numbness, his flashes of light touch the innermost depths of our sensitivity, while his work remains that immense and marvelous hymn to woman and to love.

"Here nothing is impossible!" says one of his protagonists. Eroticism upsets daily habits and a perpetual carnival is bound to release its monsters.

Sternberg's last picture, *The Saga of Anatahan*, is, perhaps, more disconcerting than even his preceding masterpieces. Total author (he directed it, wrote the scenario, narrated it, and photographed it), the great director went to Japan to film the true story of twelve Japanese sailors who, isolated on a jungle island, continue to believe for years that the war is not yet over. But he realized that the settings of Japan were not what he wanted so he built a jungle in a studio and he himself painted "Japanese clouds" for his sets. This is one of those rare films in the history of cinema in which sexual desire is the only subject matter, because, before these men, isolated from the rest of the world, is a young and beautiful woman whom Sternberg calls "The Queen Bee." The sailors all sing around her: "You and I, like an egg—you, egg yellow: I, egg white—I embrace you!" Sea shells, jungle vegetation, and exacerbated feelings take us back into Sternberg's world, while we cannot help noticing an unusual calm, a calm distilled of passion, which reminds us of the same kind of calm in Buñuel.

*Le surréalisme au cinéma*, Éditions Arcanes, 1953, re-published by Éditions du Terrain Vague, 1963.

*René Jeanne and Charles Ford*

PRIMITIVE VIOLENCE

The three pictures, *Underworld, Docks of New York, Dragnet,* form a homogeneous ensemble, which one seldom finds in the work of an American director, and in that respect Sternberg is set apart from Stroheim, who despite his intransigency—and perhaps because he had a richer personality—tried his luck in very different directions. With *Underworld* Sternberg found the climate that suited him. Very reasonably, he stuck to it and he is perhaps best judged on these three pictures because he feels at ease only when he is confronted with violently dramatic action. He does not care whether or not his characters resemble those of headline stories, as long as the filmic life he has to struggle with is ardent, and he is quite indifferent if it happens to be brutal and sordid. The personages he most incisively animates are those who are devoid of complications and psychological subtleties, and who are moved by primitive feelings of extreme violence—as one finds them in the romantic repertory. Georges Charensol does not hesitate to say of them that "like the heroes of antiquity, fate destines them to the worst catastrophies." However, these characters are never simple, because their animator knows how to enrich them throughout the action that motivates them, without being obvious about it and without ever slowing down that action. From the very start he holds his public in thrall and doesn't let go until he has achieved a knockout. The screen had never presented anything similar to its faithful under anybody's signature, unless it was under Stroheim's. One must add for another thing that Sternberg never lost the qualities for which Paramount first hired him, as "technical adviser for lighting and photography," e.g., he was a virtuoso of lighting, particularly when he had to compose in chiaroscuro. On the other hand, he knew at least as well as Griffith how to get the best out of his actors—it is not an exaggeration to say that he revealed Bancroft to himself, that he discovered Evelyn Brent, and that under his direction Olga Baclanova was once a very fine screen actress. These are some of the

reasons—the least debatable—which make Sternberg one of the great men of the American cinema during that richly creative period that preceded the advent of the sound film.

*Histoire Encyclopédique du cinéma,*
Vol. 3, *Le Cinéma Americaine,*
Éditions Robert Laffont, 1965.

## Philippe Demonsablon

### A HEART LAID BARE

If one looks at *The Saga of Anatahan* it presents the example of a fight between hazardous production circumstances and a definite will to create, between a poverty of means to realize and the density through which the author expects to express himself. But the picture also presents a definite triumph of one over the other—a just revenge if one remembers to what extent Sternberg's career had been upset almost twenty years before and if one imagines the feeling of a creator to whom creating has been denied. However these years of silence and of half-silence were not in vain and now Sternberg gives us with *Anatahan* a mature work, with a more demanding precision and a more complex design than ever. For this work has two closely connected aspects, each one of which corresponds to the feelings it inspires: first in the succession in which we see the images, with their own powers of fascination, which justifies the admiration one has for them; then the reflection, or rather the projection, extremely willful, of the man who created them. These two levels will facilitate the understanding of what has been achieved.

The newspapers have published this ridiculous and tragic episode of the last war: a group of fishermen and Japanese soldiers were stranded on the island of Anatahan in 1944. With the exception of one couple, the island was deserted. Refusing to believe that Japan had been defeated, they waited for the arrival of the enemy who no longer existed, they ended up by fighting among themselves for the possession, they thought, of the woman. This went on for seven years. It could just as well still be going on while I write

these lines. Based on these true events of our time, and with great respect for the truth, Sternberg conceived a work decidedly nonrealistic. The film offers many examples of this: the most striking ones showing that provocation is always present, also a certain aristocratic pleasure to displease; but it displeases only the stupid ones. And as if to baffle completely those who might misunderstand, Sternberg went across the Pacific to build a jungle set in a Kyoto studio, probably a small one, because he is more at ease when confined to little space (one remembers *Shanghai Gesture* and the docks setting of *Macao*), and he engaged a troupe of Kabuki dancers to play the actors of this drama.

One already conceives what transfiguration this procedure accomplished. The author thus acquired a greater freedom to express a poetic truth. What could be more abstract than this arid and parched jungle, rather than the steaming jungle we have seen in so many films? There were still other conventional things that had to be done away with. First of all, the dramatic conventions—and the style of the actors' playing contributes to eliminate those. A unique thing in a "Japanese film": expressive gestures have been replaced by the magic of their looks, often directed at the prodigious unknown of their vision. One cannot help recognizing the stylization of the German movie men, Fritz Lang and Murnau, who are much more concerned with plunging their characters into an abstract universe than confronting them with each other. This effacement of all dramaturgic structure is accentuated by the commentary throughout the duration of the film. I presume that this procedure was deemed necessary for the exploitation of the film in the United States. But Sternberg himself wrote this commentary and it is his voice we hear for one and a half hours over the images; this was not just to sum up the speech of the characters, but to comment upon their actions, thus introducing a time-lag between the images and the thoughts regarding the images. These actions are even announced in advance quite often and the dramatic interest then gives place to a stupefied feeling of fatality; the account becomes a horrible and necessary ceremony that gives reality to the words of the one who gives the account. In short, if the commentary could invite the attitude of a moralist, such an attitude is quickly bypassed. It is impossible here to attain, or to keep, the detachment which moralists try to have

and which often is only coldness; the images of passion on the screen would immediately contradict it, and the spectator thus solicited in contrary directions by the images and the commentary (or should we say by the commentary and its images) cannot help having a bad conscience in this duality.

But we must not go any further if we want to explain a feeling that owes everything to a work of such sincerity, a work that Sternberg created with such meticulous care. It even seems as if he had made *The Saga of Anatahan* primarily for himself. The spectator is an intruder in the theatre, but since he is now involved, let him into the secret, even if it is one he did not want to hear.

I know that those who consider even an artistic production solely as a means of entertainment will be indignant that behind the work one is curious about the man who created it and that through this work one attempts to communicate with him. But isn't man a phenomenon surprising enough so that all the aspects of his activity are worthy of our interest? What do I get out of listening to all those brilliant conversationalists who can tell me nothing? I prefer the company of Rossellini, Aldrich, Sternberg, and a few others. Those are my dear friends; even the shadows of their anxious faces speak to me from the screen. *The Saga of Anatahan* appears to me like that impossible work Edgar Allan Poe wanted to write and call "My Heart Laid Bare"; indeed, the screen is nearly in shreds and ablaze from the fulminations that Sternberg projects on it and that, without a doubt, come from deep within him. Although it offers us some thoughts on the meaning of existence, this reverie is not satisfied to give us merely the fruit of an experience. The dream itself becomes a subject for our reflection. In his soliloquy, the narrator retraces his experience, he observes it with detachment, as if brooding over what was unique and irreversible in it. An erotic experience of which Woman is the center, inevitable source of fascination, object of adoration and terror that inspires cruel and impossible divinities, her erotic power crowns her Queen, or Goddess; her dwelling is a temple decorated with the multitudinous fetishes of the Woman, and these adorn every gesture of hers, a ritual her court observes with fervor.

Absolute and inaccessible sovereign, her power destroys

those who come near her; but she is also only a ridiculous means because she did not seek this power and the men who surround her are determined to see her dethronement and her destruction through the myth they created to maintain their passion. Thus Keiko joins Sternberg's most famous heroines. It is known how the seven years of his "baudelairian" concept of Woman made him idolize Marlene Dietrich and how several years later he chose an actress in the image of the other: Ona Munson. Twenty years later, in *The Saga of Anatahan*, we "meet" Sternberg himself in the person of the husband. The knot to *The Blue Angel* is here tied, and it is probably not by chance that the account of the same humiliations appear in the same scenes. But this time Sternberg *lived* them and he put into them an all but unbearable veracity. Without a doubt, the husband's frightened look, his fits of panic and submissiveness, would be impossible to watch if such scenes did not enable Sternberg to look back lucidly and without illusion at the sorceries of his own past.

"The relationship between husband and wife is based on sentiments, often misunderstood by others, whose behavior, however, is not less blameable," a 60-year-old Sternberg tells us, while a 35-year-old Sternberg on the screen falls to his knees before his wife, who walks away. Let's remember the lesson. The essential thing is to grow old gracefully, but it also is more difficult.

*Cahiers du Cinéma*, No. 58, April, 1956

### Henri Agel

It would be just as inopportune to gauge Sternberg according to his coefficient of social reality and his "negating anarchy" as it would be incongruous to evaluate *Les Fleurs du Mal* from the point of view of nineteenth-century historic truth. We do not cite Baudelaire by chance. There is more than one affinity between the author of "Spleen de Paris" and the director of *The Shanghai Gesture*: cruel masochism that explodes in *The Devil Is a Woman* (whose protagonist, Lionel Atwill, physically resembles Sternberg, vampirized by Marlene Dietrich), an ambivalence sustained by a morbid voluptuousness with regard to the woman, perverse and insensitive goddess, who reigns in insolent splendor, enhanced by

make-up, jewels, and the most vertiginous costumes: this taste for carnival and disguise used to obsess Baudelaire and the theme of the androgyne appeared in *Les Journaux Intimes* as it does in *The Blonde Venus*.

Just as the poet Sternberg seems to abhor everything "natural." Therefore his metamorphosis of the 1929 Marlene, plump and slightly bovine. It did not suffice him to hollow her cheeks, to widen the look of her eyes like those of an opium smoker, he invented for her mythological moltings of garb, each more fabulous than the other, the total effect of which was delirious with exhibitionism. *The Blonde Venus* would have been the apotheosis of the erotic, with all the phases of decadence illustrated by glittering rags among which there is the barbaric outfit of a gorilla, had there not been *The Scarlet Empress*, a kind of petrified parade of Russian-American music hall, in which the sexual awakening and awareness of her power makes Catherine's itinerary the reverse of that of Lola Montez. But the swan song of this duo, which defied the most extravagant wagers, was a dreamlike and funereal adaptation of Pierre Louys's novel, *Woman and Puppet*. The Vamp, incarnated here by Concha Perez, a species of super-Carmen, hideous as a result of so much cruel and metallic splendor, evoked those devouring females of the Italian silent screen as in d'Annunzio's deliriums. She appears at the end all in black, adorned with sinister magnificence, shortly before which she has sung a ballad the very German sadism of which blends well with the atmosphere of a decadent Spain, just as Cocteau might have dreamed it. An image where one could easily recognize the fusion of Goya and Léonor Fini, the implacable triumph of a funereal Eros, as imagined by Pierre Jean-Jouve, and the crystallization of the haggard and tormented imagination of an obsessed dream.

Ado Kyrou, who consecrated a very beautiful chapter to Sternberg in his book, *Armour, Erotisme et Cinéma*, sees in this film the hopeless expression of erotic potency in woman.

Between the suicidal lyricism of *The Devil Is a Woman* and the infernal engulfment of *Shanghai Gesture* there is no discontinuity. There is, however, one difference. The "femme fatale" who clothed her bewitching carnality in all climates, the aridity of Africa (*Morocco*), the Vienna of *Dishonored*, the China of *Shanghai Express*, the Hispano-Hollywood of

*Devil Is a Woman,* has become in *The Shanghai Gesture* a fatal man, and androgyne as well, with the oily and animal face of Victor Mature, so that he may exercise his ravages in a brothel, again suffocating with exoticism. The sumptuous decomposition of a décor runny with byzantinism, asphyxiating us with all it implied of sweat and enervating scents, was perhaps never better "harmonized" than with the circulation of this species of human fauna, whose "rotten grandeur" was once more all baudelairian in essence.

This poetic décor, totally unrealistic and oozing every wretched emanation bewitching the author, whether or not he is steeped in the *Kammerspiel* tradition—we find it all through a work as meticulous in its extravagances as that of Ophuls. Sternberg painted white the sets for *The Case of Lena Smith,* the train in *Shanghai Express,* and the set of the gambling hall of *The Shanghai Gesture.* He made use of the most willfully baroque compositions, limned by a rigorous control of lighting, beginning with his silent films, even the first of which, *The Salvation Hunters,* already expressed his unique mythology. Curtis Harrington reminds us that the America of *The Blonde Venus,* with its low dives, its night clubs, its hotel rooms, its flophouses, which became the archetypes of a whole future of Hollywood cinema, is really strictly Sternbergian, just as is the Peterhof Palace of *The Scarlet Empress.* Sternberg's baroque style sometimes reminds us of Welles's and it is not pure chance that one finds a Goya trait in both men (see *Mr. Arkadin*) as in *The Case of Lena Smith,* in which an amusement park with its distorting mirrors and fantastic tunnels is echoed later in *The Lady of Shanghai.* On the other hand, no cinéaste was ever able to produce from the cadre of the Foreign Legion a dreamlike quality as subtly sophisticated as that of *Morocco,* where the trio, Menjou–Gary Cooper–Marlene, forms a perfect romantic and "decadent" constellation. Here this farrago of a story serves its purpose, as Harrington remarks: to evoke an unusual place, peopled with extraordinary characters thrown into adventures as melodramatic as they are erotic.

This is doubtless the perspective in which we must view our author's silent films: *The Salvation Hunters,* Sternberg's first film, is the one in which he expresses naive confidence in the interior redemption of the most dejected souls des-

pite their nightmarish and putrefied background; *Underworld*, which already bore, unfortunately, the mark of commercial concessions and which was to shape the style and atmosphere of the gangster movies; *The Docks of New York*, a revelation in simplicity. Certainly the psychological study of human wrecks always held his interest. Bancroft, the leader of the gang in *Underworld*, was the vindicator who saved a prostitute from suicide, then married her in an atmosphere of picaresque lyricism that reminds us at once of Pabst and Borzage. But it was really the taste for dank interiors, for musty and acrid smells, drenched textures, and the search for moments when truth blends with bad dreams—the night in the port, the bunker-hands in the stokeholes, the pathetic and derisory wedding before an improvised altar—that was the object of his aesthetic interest.

But this atmosphere, no more than in *The Shanghai Gesture*, is not simply virtuosity. For Sternberg, it has to reveal an inexorable festering of fatality. The tradition of the *Kammerspiel* is not far removed. Later on, it will limn Marlene's face without neglecting the décor that he will illumine with his strange emanations. In this respect, Sternberg's masterpiece—at least his most famous work—remains *The Blue Angel*. Let us not look for the delineation of a certain social reality that crumbles under the author's satire, as in Heinrich Mann. From now on, however, he will affirm the demolition of that aesthetic, the unnameable work of Time fused with the proliferation of a spiritual cancer inside a brain and a society. Here is not only the paroxysm of expressionism but above all the false exorcism of one obsessed and already a prisoner of his morass. *The Blue Angel* was almost insupportable in its excesses, extending the limits of bad taste (which some scenes of *The Shanghai Gesture* will extend even further), emphasizing the sensuous spell of that Germany whose vulgar fascination was embodied in Marlene Dietrich's costumes in it. Epic of filth and abjection, this film is undoubtedly a clinical document, a case-history like the Marlene series that is to follow.

Every cinéaste is haunted by an obsession. Sternberg's is desire, so obvious from one of his most recent works, *Anatahan*. In June of 1944, a group of Japanese military was stranded by an air attack on their convoy on the island of Anatahan and lived there for seven years on the margin of the war.

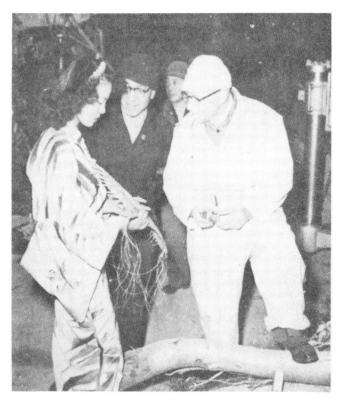

Two years later Sternberg is invited to Japan to make a film and given "carte blanche" and complete autonomy one last time. The result is *Anatahan*, a bizarre postscript to the late war in the Pacific. He discovers in Tokyo a "Japanese Dietrich"—Akemi Negishi—seen here on the set with him and the interpreter. (1953)

*Anatahan* turns out to be his most personal work, as much a study in behaviorism on a universal scale as a retelling of a true and violent anecdote about some shipwrecked Japanese sailors stranded on a jungle isle. A narration written and spoken by the director gives the film that rarest quality—a fourth dimension. Sternberg's last film. (1953)

Sternberg imagined * that this island was inhabited by a young and seductive woman whose very presence will mean provocation and murder to the stranded men. There no longer will be soldiers or friends, but primitive man, whom forced confinement suddenly confronts with his own demons, obscure forces that rule and submerge him. Stroheim's and Buñuel's names were mentioned in connection with this film. But a beautiful theme is not enough: the essential is to know whether Sternberg was really able to master it. Such was not the opinion of Lotte Eisner, who was dismayed by this "bric-a-brac of bazaar eroticism." There may be reasons to argue about the unrealistic style and certain insistent expressions, but we cannot negate the heart-rending seriousness and autobiographical significance of the film, as testified by a commentary written and read by the director himself. As a result, according to Philippe Demonsablon's trenchant observation, "The account becomes a horrible and necessary ceremony that gives reality to the words of the one who gives the account." *Anatahan* thus appears as the result of a meditation directed toward woman and love, a last exorcism of eroticism, the very ambiguity of which accounts for its savor. "I cultivated my hysteria with delight," wrote Baudelaire. Is Sternberg a modern or a decadent patrician? Perhaps this cinéaste was lacking just that which the author of *Les Fleurs du Mal* possessed: an intelligence and a willpower strong enough to discover beyond his nerves a "new thrill" that was not just a spasm and convulsion.

*Les Grandes Cinéastes*, Éditions
Universitaires, 1959.

### Michael Aubriant

And here once more is *The Blue Angel*, not in any of those ciné-clubs, to impress the *aficionados*, but on view in two Paris theatres, as a regular show, as if this film had been made yesterday. I was trembling when I bought my ticket, less afraid for Sternberg, whose glory never stops growing, or

* The principal ingredients of the plot of *Anatahan* were not imagined by Sternberg but were based on actual fact, reported in the press—including the woman. (Ed. Note)

Jannings, that pachyderm ham, but for Marlene, the Marlene whose picture we used to pin inside our school books.

She has changed a great deal and the film along with her. It no longer tells us the exact same story. We probably all were victims of an illusion, the cinema historians above all. What is *The Blue Angel?* The adventure of an honorable high-school professor whom a trollop performing in some deadfall reduces to a crawling worm? Jannings damning himself for a Marlene who incarnates all sensuality, perversity, and female trickery? This is not at all certain.

Compared to today's amazons, the Marlene we rediscover is candor personified; a good-hearted little trouper, a bit overly romantic, perhaps, flattered by the attentions of a pedant old enough to be her papa, dragging him along for four years like a ball and chain, flattered to have been chosen by that solemn ninny. Not a trace of malice. She prefers this clod to her gilded coxcombs. Of course she ends up cuckolding him, but almost against her own will. The idiot dies from it. Good riddance!

A pretty gretchen, cutely set on her sturdy peasant legs, more touching than sensual and more disquieting, in fact, with her alluring lace panties attracting passing sailors and provincial schoolboys, set ablaze by a bit of naked thigh, with her broken little voice of a honky-tonk singer, whom the first ruffian can buy for a bottle of champagne. All this, seen at this distance, now appears like a sad farce, a satire half-ferocious, half-tender, typical of a certain kind of German sentimentality, of a certain German taste for tinsel, exuberance, and misery.

It is not certain that Sternberg, under the impression that he was making a German *Nana,* was fully aware of this. No doubt he was the first victim of the myth he had created, chained to Marlene, polishing her from film to film to transform her into a diaphanous idol with a laquered face who soon would no longer need her Pygmalion.

*France-Soir—Paris Presse*
January 20, 1966.

*Jean de Baroncelli*

#### A FORMIDABLE VOICE

Sure, Marlene is there in a role tailored to her measure. We see her as a frightened young girl, her face smooth and candid, little by little metamorphosized into a redoubtable woman who will reign under the name of Catherine II of Russia. Loving, hating, revolted, jilted, and triumphant, she hardly ever leaves the screen. And we wait for her and we spy on her because she is so famous. But fascination is no longer a part of the game, time has passed, the myth has turned into a memory. As Catherine, Marlene is but an actress, an excellent actress, like many others . . .

That which attracts us, which puts us under a spell, however, which stupefies us (and helps us forget that somewhat absurd gallop up the palace steps)* is another presence, an invisible one, but much more obsessive than the first one. It is a formidable voice. It is Sternberg in person.

He said it in his book, he did it all by himself. "With one exception, the story, the décor, the settings, the sculptures, the costumes, the photography, all were mine." Prodigious pride, the morbid jealousy of an artist? Perhaps. But mainly an irresistible need to create and to carry alone the weight of his creation. *The Scarlet Empress* is, in fact, a pure artistic creation, a visual symphony, based on the triple theme of ambition, voluptuousness, and death, an unfurling of images whose freedom of design reminds one at moments of the silent film, a baroque frenzy of flesh and marble monsters that leads us straight into this "universe," to which Sternberg dreamed of attracting crowds.

It is unnecessary to evoke Flaubert with his famous "*Madame Bovary, c'est moi.*" We don't doubt for a moment that the real "scarlet empress" is not that blonde shadow agitating the screen. The Hollywood people were right: Josef von Sternberg just made his own portrait! but they

* At the Sandhurst military academy in England, there is a traditional ritual calling for an officer to gallop his horse up the steps of the grand entrance through the doorway, following the passing-out parade. (Ed. Note)

don't know—besides, it does not matter to them—that without dreamers and egocentrics of that kind art would never flower.

*Le Monde*, March 2, 1966.

## Michel Cournot

### A DREAM "CINEMATIQUE"

*The Scarlet Empress*, the story of which is, in a way, the youth of Catherine the Great up to her ascension to the throne, is, to its smallest detail, the work of one man. Sternberg wrote the story and dialogue, suggested the décor and the ikons, designed the statues—which are more numerous in the film than the actors—sketched the costumes, arranged the lights, composed some of the music and personally directed the Los Angeles Philharmonic Orchestra which plays the score.

That basic fundamental of cinema, movement, was approached by Sternberg in *The Scarlet Empress*, paradoxically enough, through his immobile chimeras: the statues. The very first scene foretells these statues through a doll that the future empress, still a child, holds in her arms. Let us note here that when the Czar Peter is suddenly awakened the night of his assassination, he holds another doll-like figure in his sleep: one of the toy wooden soldiers he used to drop all over the palace.

Reduced in size or gigantic, but often of the same size as the actors, this crowd of statues, tortured or placid, twisted or straight, constantly help or disturb the living action of the film. The characters cannot sit down, they can only lie down against, next to, and even inside the statues. They must go around them to move. The statues are erect when characters prostrate themselves, or they lie prostrate when the characters themselves are erect.

Obviously condemned, these statufied beings have a part in the events: they observe a world forbidden to them, they spy on it, defy it, are resigned to it, indifferent to it, they disapprove of it, they refuse to have anything to do with it, they sometimes become human, incredibly they even change

their poses, according to the inflections of the film, so much so that eventually their presence, with all its intentions and judgments, far exceeds that of the living protagonists, the historical personages, the actors.

Constantly judged by these mute presences, as insinuating as they are stubborn, what can the players do? They can "play," which is to say *"they can proceed with the reconstitution of motives which are the cause of their actions and their words."* But *"the cinema is only a highly developed theatre of shadows, and wishing to manipulate humans as if they were puppets is to get into trouble.*\* It seems that every personage of *The Scarlet Empress* spontaneously finds his way toward animation as if it were a reaction, or a reference, to the anti-cinema accusation of the motionless statues. Czar Peter and Sam Jaffe, who portrays him, decompose several motionless "moments" into an animation, broken and cut, which is that of automatons: Sam Jaffe never connects his gestures, he goes from one prostration to another prostration, he seems to leap over life. The Master of the Hounds, and John Lodge, who plays him (after this picture Lodge became Congressman, Governor of Connecticut, and United States Ambassador to Spain), get into a false situation, an affected, behavior-mimicking impassability. As for Catherine, Marlene Deitrich is the only one whose guileless transports sometimes escape the clutches of the statues, because of her vital life force, and yet, when Marlene Dietrich, too, stands completely still, Sternberg lingers and strolls over her fabulous face with his lens as if he were traversing a beach in the morning (*"the forehead is a fragment of the sky, the hair are clouds"*).† When she, too, is paralyzed like an object, her presence succeeds in overwhelming, though not without a struggle, the demonic presence of the sculptured monsters that engulf her.

It is quite certain that each tenth of a second in the film, each aspect of immobility or of movement, has in addition a precise significance, a responsibility to the events described and the spirits evoked, and the expressions of the statues change as much as those of the actors. If for once one wishes to watch a living mediation regarding one of the mysteries of cinema, movement, one must look straight at those statues and those

---

\* These quotations are from Sternberg's autobiography, *Fun in a Chinese Laundry.* (New York: The Macmillan Co., 1965)
    † Ibid.

actors, and observe how the moving image modifies the meaning of the inanimate one and in what way.

On the studio set, statues and players stand in space, whereas the white screen is flat: here is another simple cinema element upon which Sternberg now acts, by animating other images, the innumerable paintings and ikons which cover the walls, the pillars, the doors, the sleighs, the bells, the backs of mirrors, everything. He sometimes makes these flat images of the paintings move in such a hallucinatory way that the screen itself seems to "turn on its hinges," and it is the screen itself that looks when Peter, to spy on his wife, drills a hole into the eye of a saint who is, incidentally, armed with a large knife. The paintings are as flat as the screen, but the image of cinema remains, here as everywhere else, "*restive and trembling with emotion.*" It is when the paintings take over the relay from the statues that Sternberg "*mingles the real and the imaginary until the spectator is confounded.*" He also intermingles them with incredible audacity as when, to show for the first time the Russia of the peasants, he superimposes on the slow traveling shots of models in relief and flat ikons lightninglike flashes of white cavalry, against the sombre background, charging across the screen.

Between the reliefs of both statues and actors flattened on the screen, and the flat of the ikons to which the movement of the camera gives imaginary perspectives, Sternberg leads a game of make-believe that is a breath of cinema in a rough stage. This same obsession of the spirit also gives us that frenzy characterized by his filming of doors. *The Scarlet Empress* is an organized nightmare of doors, also foretold in the first sequence, even before Catherine's doll, when the shadow of who knows what dead tree appears on the open door of the little girl's room. What can one say about the painted doors in Peter's palace, doors a hundred times as large as the characters, the tops of which one never sees, elaborately decorated doors, the opening and closing of which each time seem to demand momentarily insoluble problems and superhuman efforts?

The eyes rest on another door, less noticeable, the door behind a mirror, or by chance behind the mirror of the Empress's bedroom, the secret door through which come and go the lovers for a night. A simple wooden door, rather small this one, half-lost in the dark, and on which one nevertheless

sees the shadow of a monster statue with horns and vampire wings, a surface of mystery and lies, a sombre screen on which shines only the golden chimera of a handle. It looks as though this cinema screen, which we are so used to, is entirely occupied by the motionless and dimly lit surface of this simple door; it is then we immediately plunge into an abyss of dreams from whose depths *"the sighs of the queen and the cries of the fairy-queen"* of Nerval begin to fill the universe.

Two well-known sequences of *The Scarlet Empress* are among the strongest of the cinema.

The first is a single shot. The camera plunges down onto the table set for a wedding feast. We advance slowly along this table. As our gaze glides along, we see statues of naked women, peelings, melted candles, cadavers of animals, wigs, horns, a soup simmering like a witch's brew, feathers, a crown, fruit. There is a disorder of blacks and whites, which is the disorder of objects "naturally" to be found on a festive table at the court of Imperial Russia but we move further into this nightmare, into this hallucinating landscape of injustices and tortures. The camera, having slowly reached the end of the table, now rises almost imperceptibly and moves slowly back. This time, each side of the table, we see the guests, seated between the gargoyle-statues, almost motionless, absolutely silent, the living are dead, one hears only the faint sound of a violin playing a gypsy tune. Nothing has been said and yet, with a single shot, through the magic of the cinema, all has been said about the palaces of the Czars. It is the summit of art.

The second is the marriage of Catherine and Peter at the Cathedral of Kazan. This sequence is filmed in 29 shots that require the special attention of the spectators, particularly shots 15, 17, 19, and 22, which are close-ups of Marlene Dietrich and of a candle behind a veil, as well as close-up 27, of the hands of the betrothed pair. I know Russia and it seems to me that all the poetry of an ancient country is there. One cannot help admiring also shots 1 and 28 which describe the same path in space, but reversed, penetrating and surrounding the total ensemble of the scene. Yes, the sequence on Kazan, alone, is a monument. To evoke the Russia of another time, Eisenstein did something else, but he did not do better.

A last word regarding the sound track of *The Scarlet Em-*

# Filmography

> "*Where is this division of labor to end and what object does it finally serve? No doubt another may also think for me, but it is not therefore desirable that he should do so to the exclusion of my thinking for myself.*"
>
> —THOREAU

(Screen credits that appear on a film can often be a matter of company policy and/or contractual obligation. The following credits are not in every case those which appeared on the screen, but they represent the true credits, according to Von Sternberg.)

In 1924 Sternberg acted as scenarist, photographer, and assistant director on *By Divine Right*,* a P.R.C. film for F.B.O., directed by Roy William Neill starring Elliot Dexter and Anna Q. Nilsson. That same year he directed his first scene, in the same company's *Vanity's Price*, for which Neill was also the director, an adaptation of Gertrude Atherton's novel *Black Oxen*, again with Anna Q. Nilsson. The scene, of a rejuvenation operation, became famous, even after the film was forgotten. It marked Sternberg's debut as a director. "A long journey," said Lao Tse, "begins with a single step."

## 1925

### THE SALVATION HUNTERS

*Original scenario* by Josef von Sternberg.
*Photography*: Edward Gheller. A Josef von Sternberg production released by Academy Pictures and distributed by United Artists.
*Première*: February 15, 1925

---

\* It was in this film that Sternberg discovered Georgia Hale as an extra. She was subsequently to become his first female star.

*Players:* George K. Arthur (The boy), Georgia Hale (The girl), Bruce Guerin (The child), Otto Matiesen (The man), Nellie Bly Baker (The woman), Olaf Hytten (The brute), Stuart Holmes (The gentleman).

## THE EXQUISITE SINNER

*Scenario:* Josef von Sternberg and Alice Deuer Miller, from the novel, *Escape,* by Alden Brooks. *Assistant:* Robert Florey. *Photography:* Maximilian Fabian. *Distributed by* Metro-Goldwyn-Mayer. *Première:* March 28, 1926.

*Players:* Conrad Nagel (Dominique Prad), Renée Adorée (Gypsy girl), George K. Arthur (Captain's orderly), Paulette Duval (Yvonne), Frank Currier (Captain), Matthew Betz (Gypsy chief), Helene d'Algy and Claire Dubrey (Dominique's sisters), Myrna Loy ("Living Statue").

This film was remade by Phil Rosen for MGM and therefore was not recognized in its released version by Sternberg.

## THE MASKED BRIDE (Abandoned)

*Scenario:* Carey Wilson, after a novel by Leon Abrams. *Photography:* Oliver Marsh. *Assistant:* Robert Florey. *Distributed by* Metro-Goldwyn-Mayer. *Première:* December 13, 1925.

This film was quickly left unfinished by Sternberg, the major part of it being completed by W. Christy Cabanne for MGM.

*Projects:* A project for Mary Pickford, *Backwash*. Not realized.


### 1926

## THE SEA GULL (WOMAN OF THE SEA) Unreleased.

*Original scenario* by Josef von Sternberg. *Photography:* Paul Ivano. *Settings:* Danny Hall. *Produced by* Charles Chaplin.

*Players:* Edna Purviance, Eve Sothern, Gane Whitman.

A simple love story served as the basis for this film, in which

the changing patterns of the sea were used for psychological and atmospheric underscoring of the action, which was photographed largely on the sea coast of Monterey, California. The film was previewed only once in Beverly Hills, after which Chaplin decided, for reasons of his own, not to release it. In the late Twenties, John Grierson, one of the few people who saw it, called it, "The most beautiful film ever shot in Hollywood."

In 1927, Sternberg directed the final scenes of Clara Bow's hit, *It*, from the novel by Elinor Glyn, when its director, Clarence Badger, was unable to finish his work. (For Paramount.)

The same year he served in a similar capacity on Frank Lloyd's *Children of Divorce*, starring Esther Ralston, Gary Cooper, and Clara Bow. (For Paramount.)

## 1927

## UNDERWORLD

*Original idea:* Ben Hecht. *Scenario:* Josef von Sternberg. *Photography:* Bert Glennon. *Settings:* Hans Dreier. *Distributed by:* Paramount. *Première:* September 3, 1927.

*Players:* Clive Brook ("Rolls Royce"), Evelyn Brent ("Feathers" McCoy), George Bancroft ("Bull" Weed), Larry Semon ("Slippery" Lewis), Fred Kohler (Buck Mulligan), Helen Lynch (Mulligan's girl), Jerry Mandy (Paloma).

## 1928

## THE LAST COMMAND

*Original scenario:* Josef von Sternberg, based on an idea told to Sternberg by Ernst Lubitsch. *Photography:* Bert Glennon. *Settings:* Hans Dreier. *Distributed by:* Paramount. *Première:* January 23, 1928.

*Players:* Emil Jannings (Grand Duke Sergius Alexander), Evelyn Brent (Natasha Dobrowa), William Powell (Leo

Andreiev), Nicholas Soussanin (Adjutant), Jack Raymond (Assistant Director), Michael Visaroff (Valet).

*The Street of Sin,* an original scenario by Sternberg for Emil Jannings, whose direction was begun by Mauritz Stiller, continued by Lothar Mendes, and finished by Ludwig Berger for Paramount. With Fay Wray and Olga Baclanova. The setting was London's Soho district. *Subject:* The Salvation Army.

At the request of Paramount and with the approval of Stroheim, Sternberg recut the latter's *The Wedding March,* to reduce its length. Paramount subsequently divided Sternberg's version into two parts (the second was called: *The Honeymoon*). Part One was released for its première October 6, 1928. The second part was never shown in the United States.

## THE DRAGNET

*Original story:* "Night Stick" by Oliver H.P. Garrett. *Scenario:* Jules Furthman. *Photography:* Harold Rosson. *Settings:* Hans Dreier. *Distributed by:* Paramount. *Première* May 26, 1928.

*Players:* George Bancroft ("Two Gun" Nolan), Evelyn Brent ("The Magpie"), William Powell ("Dapper" Frank Trent), Fred Kohler ("Gabby" Steve), Francis McDonald ("Sniper" Dawson), Leslie Fenton (Donovan).

## THE DOCKS OF NEW YORK

*Original scenario:* Jules Furthman, suggested by "The Dock Walloper" by John Monk Saunders. *Photography:* Harold Rosson. *Settings:* Hans Dreier. *Distributed by:* Paramount. *Première:* September 29, 1928.

*Players:* George Bancroft (Bill Roberts, the stevedore), Betty Compson (Sadie), Olga Baclanova (Lou), Clyde Cook ("Sugar" Steve), Mitchell Lewis (Third Engineer), Gustav von Seyffertitz ("Hymn Book" Harry), Lillian Worth (Steve's girl).

1929

## THE CASE OF LENA SMITH

*Original scenario:* Josef von Sternberg.
*Photography:* Harold Rosson. *Settings:* Hans Dreier.
*Distributed by:* Paramount. *Première:* January 19, 1929.

*Players:* Esther Ralston (Lena Smith), James Hall (Franz Hofrat), Gustav von Seyffertitz (Herr Hofrat), Emily Fitzroy (Frau Hofrat), Fred Kohler (Stefan), Betty Aho (Stefan's sister), Lawrence Grant (Commissioner), Alex Woloshin (Janitor), Ann Brody (Janitor's wife).

## THUNDERBOLT *

*Original story:* Jules and Charles Furthman.
*Scenario:* Josef von Sternberg. *Photography:* Henry Gerrard.
*Settings:* Hans Dreier. *Distributed by:* Paramount.
*Première:* June 22, 1929.

*Players:* George Bancroft ("Thunderbolt"), Richard Arlen (Bob Morgan), Fay Wray ("Ritzy"), Tully Marshall (Warden), Eugenie Besserer (Mrs. Moran), James Spottswood ("Snapper" O'Shea), Fred Kohler ("Bad Al" Frieberg), Mike Donlin ("Kentucky" Sampson), S. S. Stewart (Negro convict), George Irving (Bank officer), Robert Elliott (Priest), William Thorne (Police inspector), E. H. Calvert (District Attorney).

1930

## THE BLUE ANGEL

*Scenario:* Josef von Sternberg, freely adapted by him from the novel, *Professor Unrat,* by Heinrich Mann.
*Photography:* Gunther Rittau, Hans Schneeberger.
*Settings:* Otto Hunte, Emil Hasler.
*Lyrics and songs:* Friedrich Hollander.

* Von Sternberg's first sound film. There was no musical background.

*Produced by:* Erich Pommer for Ufa, Berlin, and produced in two versions, German and English.
*Distributed by:* Paramount (U.S.).
*Première:* January 3, 1931.
*Berlin Première:* April 1, 1930.

*Players:* Emil Jannings (Prof. Immanuel Rat), Marlene Dietrich (Lola Froehlich), Kurt Gerron (Kiepert, a magician), Rosa Valetti (Guste, his wife), Hans Albers (Mazeppa), Eduard von Winterstein (Principal of the school), Reinhold Bernt (The clown), Hans Roth (The beadle), Rolf Mueller, Roland Varno, Karl Balhaus, Robert Klein-Loerk (students), Karl Huszar-Puffy (The publican), Wilhelm Diegelmann (Captain), Gerhard Bienert (Policeman), Ilse Fürstenberg (Rat's housekeeper).

Four songs: "Nimm Dich in acht vor blonden Frauen," "Ich bin von Kopf bis Fuss auf Liebe eingestellt," "Ich bin die fesche Lola," "Kinder, heut' abend such' ich mir was aus."

## MOROCCO

*Scenario:* Josef von Sternberg, based on the novel *Amy Jolly*, by Benno Vigny.
*Photography:* Lee Garmes and Lucien Ballard.
*Settings:* Hans Dreier.
*Songs:* "Give Me the Man Who Does Things" and "What Am I Bid for My Apples?" by Leo Robin (lyrics) and Karl Hajos (music). "Quand l'Amour Meurt" by Millandy and Cremieux.
*Distributed by:* Paramount. *Première:* December 6, 1930.

*Players:* Gary Cooper (Legionnaire Tom Brown), Marlene Dietrich (Amy Jolly), Adolphe Menjou (LeBessière), Ullrich Haupt (Adjutant Caesar), Juliette Compton (Anna Dolores), Francis MacDonald (Corporal Tatoche), Albert Conti (Col. Quinnevières), Eve Sothern (Mme. Caesar), Paul Porcasi (Impresario, Lo Tinto), Émile Chautard (French General), Michael Visaroff.

1931

DISHONORED

*Original scenario:* Josef von Sternberg.
*Photography:* Lee Garmes. *Settings:* Hans Dreier.
*Distributed by:* Paramount. *Première:* April 4, 1931.

*Players:* Marlene Dietrich (X-27), Victor McLaglen (Lt. Kranau), Lew Cody (Col. Kovrin), Gustav von Seyffertitz (Austrian Secret Service Head), Warner Oland (Capt. von Hindau), Barry Norton (Young Lieutenant), Davison Clark (Court Martial presiding officer), Wilfred Lucas (General Dymov).

*Music:* Ivanovici's "Danube Waves," Beethoven's "Moonlight Sonata," and original music by Sternberg.

AN AMERICAN TRAGEDY

From the novel by Theodore Dreiser. *Adaptation:* Josef von Sternberg and Samuel Hoffenstein.
*Scenario:* Josef von Sternberg.
*Photography:* Lee Garmes. *Settings:* Hans Dreier.
*Distributed by:* Paramount. *Première:* August 22, 1931.

*Players:* Phillips Holmes (Clyde Griffiths), Sylvia Sidney (Roberta Alden), Frances Dee (Sondra Finchley), Irving Pichel (Orville Mason), Frederick Burton (Samuel Griffiths), Claire McDowell (Mrs. Samuel Griffiths), Wallace Middleton (Gilbert Griffiths), Vivian Winston (Myra Griffiths), Emmett Corrigan (Belknap), Lucille La Verne (Mrs. Asa Griffiths), Charles B. Middleton (Jephson), Albert Hart (Titus Alden), Fanny Midgely (Mrs. Alden), Arline Judge (Bella Griffiths), Evelyn Pierce (Bertine Cranston), Arnold Korff (Judge), Elizabeth Forrester (Jill Trumbell), Russell Powell (Coroner), Imboden Parrish (Earl Newcomb), Richard Kramer (Deputy Sheriff).

## 1932

### SHANGHAI EXPRESS

*Scenario:* Josef von Sternberg and Jules Furthman. From a story idea by Harry Hervey.
*Photography:* Lee Garmes. *Settings:* Hans Dreier.
*Distributed by:* Paramount. *Première:* February 12, 1932.

*Players:* Marlene Dietrich (Shanghai Lily), Clive Brook (Capt. Donald Harvey), Anna May Wong (Hui Fei), Warner Oland (Henry Chang), Eugene Pallette (Sam Salt), Lawrence Grant (Mr. Carmichael), Louise Closser Hale (Mrs. Haggerty), Gustav von Seyffertitz (Eric Baum), Émile Chautard (Maj. Lenard).

### THE BLONDE VENUS

*Original scenario:* Josef von Sternberg.
*Photography:* Bert Glennon. *Settings:* Wiard Ihnen.
*Songs:* "Hot Voodoo" and "You Little So and So" by Sam Coslow and Ralph Rainger; "I Could Be Annoyed" by Leo Robin and Dick Whiting.
*Distributed by:* Paramount. *Première:* Sept. 16, 1932.

*Players:* Marlene Dietrich (Helen Faraday), Herbert Marshall (Edward Faraday), Cary Grant (Nick Townsend), Dickie Moore (Johnny Faraday), Gene Morgan (Ben Smith), Rita La Roy ("Taxi Belle" Hooper), Robert Emmett O'Connor (Dan O'Connor), Hattie McDaniel (Negro maid), Sidney Toler (Detective Wilson).

In November, 1932, Sternberg and his cameraman of *The Sea Gull*, Paul Ivano, went to the Caribbean to shoot scenes of a hurricane for a projected circus story by Miss Dietrich. The hurricane failed to materialize and they returned to Hollywood with the project abandoned.

## 1934

### THE SCARLET EMPRESS

*Scenario:* Josef von Sternberg, based on a diary of Catherine the Great.
*Photography:* Bert Glennon. *Settings:* Hans Dreier, Peter Balbusch, Richard Kollorsz.
*Music:* From Tchaikovsky, Mendelssohn, and Wagner, arranged by John M. Leipold and W. Frank Harling.
*Distributed by:* Paramount. *Première:* September 7, 1934.

*Players:* Marlene Dietrich (Sophia Frederika, later Catherine II), John Lodge (Duke Alexei), Sam Jaffe (Grand Duke Peter), Louise Dresser (Empress Elizabeth), Maria Sieber (Catherine as a child), C. Aubrey Smith (Prince August), Ruthelma Stevens (Countess Elizabeth), Olive Tell (Princess Johanna), Gavin Gordon (Gregory Orloff), Jameson Thomas (Lt. Ovtsya), Hans von Twardowski (Ivan Shuvolov), Davison Clark (Archmandrite and Arch Episcope Simeon Tevedovsky).

## 1935

### THE DEVIL IS A WOMAN

*Scenario and adaptation:* Josef von Sternberg, after the novel *Woman and Puppet*, by Pierre Louys.
*Photography:* Josef von Sternberg, assisted by Lucien Ballard.
*Settings:* Hans Dreier and Sternberg. *Music:* Arranged by Ralph Rainger and Andrea Setaro, from Rimsky-Korsakov's "Caprice Espagnole" and Spanish folk-songs. *Song:* "Three Sweethearts Have I" by Leo Robin and Ralph Rainger.
*Distributed by:* Paramount. *Première:* May 3, 1935.

*Players:* Marlene Dietrich (Concha Perez), Lionel Atwill (Don Pasqual), Cesar Romero (Antonio Galvan), Edward Everett Horton (Don Paquito), Alison Skipworth (Señora Perez), Don Alvarado (Morenito), Morgan Wallace (Dr. Mendez), Tempe Pigott (Tuerta), Jill Dennett (Maria), Lawrence Grant (Conductor), Charles Sellon (Letter writer),

Luisa Espinal (Gypsy dancer), Hank Mann (Foreman, snow-bound train), Edwin Maxwell (Superintendent, tobacco factory).

Prize at the Venice Film Festival, 1935, for the best photography.

CRIME AND PUNISHMENT

*Scenario:* S. K. Lauren and Joseph Anthony, after the novel by Fyodor Dostoievski.
*Photography:* Lucien Ballard. *Settings:* Stephen Goossens.
*Costumes:* Murray Mayer. *Music:* Louis Silver.
*Edited:* Richard Calhoon. *Produced by:* B. P. Schulberg.
*Distributed by:* Columbia. *Première:* November 20, 1935.

*Players:* Peter Lorre (Raskolnikov), Edward Arnold (Inspector Porfiry), Marian Marsh (Sonya), Tala Birell (Antonya), Elizabeth Risdon (Mrs. Raskolnikov), Robert Allen (Dmitri), Douglas Dumbrille (Grilov), Gene Lockhart (Lushin), Charles Waldron (University Rector), Thurston Hall (Editor), Johnny Arthur (Clerk), Mrs. Patrick Campbell (Pawnbroker), Rafaelo Ottiano (Landlady), Michael Mark (Painter prisoner).

1936

THE KING STEPS OUT

*Scenario:* Sidney Buchman, from the operetta *Cissy*, by Herbert and Ernst Marischka, with music by Fritz Kreisler.
*Assistant director:* Wilhelm Thiele.
*Photography:* Lucien Ballard. *Settings:* Stephen Goossens.
*Ballet:* Albertina Rasch. *Costumes:* Ernst Dryden.
*Music:* Arranged by Howard Jackson, from themes by Fritz Kreisler.
*Distributed by:* Columbia. *Première:* May 15, 1936.

*Players:* Grace Moore (Cissy, afterwards Empress Elizabeth), Franchot Tone (Franz Josef, afterwards Emperor), Walter Connolly (Maximilian), Raymond Walburn (von Kempen), Victor Jory (Palfi), Elizabeth Risden (Sofia), Nana Bryant (Louise), Frieda Inescourt (Helena), Thurston Hall (Major),

Herman Bing (Pretzelberger), George Hassell (Herlicka), John Arthur (Chief of Secret Police).

## 1937

I, CLAUDIUS (Unfinished)

*Scenario:* Josef von Sternberg, based on the historical novel *I, Claudius,* by Robert Graves. *Photography:* Georges Périnal. *Settings:* Vincent Korda. *Costumes:* John Armstrong. *Choreography:* Agnes de Mille. *Produced by:* Alexander Korda for London Films.

*Players:* Charles Laughton (Tiberius Claudius Drusus), Merle Oberon (Messalina), Flora Robson (Livia, Empress Dowager, mother of Claudius), Emlyn Williams (Caligula), Robert Newton, Ralph Richardson, John Clements, Basil Gill, Everley Gregg.

Sternberg's difficulties in handling Laughton, who had suddenly developed some eccentricities, and an automobile accident injury sustained by Merle Oberon, brought production to a halt early in the film. Some 20 minutes of edited footage of several scenes remain in the collection of the National Film Archives in London and have been incorporated into the BBC television film, *The Epic That Never Was,* recounting via interviews with some of the principals involved, including the director, the reasons for the curtailment of this ambitious project.

*Other projects: Germinal,* from the Zola novel, of which a treatment exists. To have starred Jean-Louis Barrault and Hilde Krahl. The director's illness put a halt to this. Pirandello's *Six Characters in Search of an Author,* with Max Reinhardt playing the stage manager, was another unfulfilled project. Also unrealized was the plan to film *Austrian Peasant Wedding,* after a ballet, in Austria. An abortive attempt to direct Hedy Lamarr (October, 1938) in a film, *New York Cinderella,* from a story by Charles MacArthur, followed, but after 18 days Sternberg gave up and Frank Borzage took over. The picture was not released however until two years later when W. S. Van Dyke re-shot it. Under its new title, *I Take*

*This Woman*, and with Spencer Tracy and Laraine Day also in the cast, MGM finally launched it to a disastrous press. While at MGM Sternberg added some touches to its big Johann Strauss film, *The Great Waltz*, which Julien Duvivier had directed, and remained just long enough to complete his contract at the studio with the perfunctory *Sergeant Madden*.

## 1939

### SERGEANT MADDEN

*Scenario:* Wells Root, from the story "A Gun in His Hand," by William A. Ulman.
*Photography:* John Seitz. *Settings:* Cedric Gibbons, Randall Duell. *Special effects:* Peter Balbusch.
*Music:* William Axt. *Distributed by:* Metro-Goldwyn-Mayer.
*Première:* March 24, 1939.

*Players:* Wallace Beery (Sean Madden), Tom Brown (Al Boylan, Jr.), Alan Curtis (Dennis Madden), Laraine Day (Eileen Daly), Fay Holden (Mary Madden), Marc Lawrence ("Piggy" Ceders), Marian Martin (Charlotte), David Gorcey ("Punchy").

## 1941

### THE SHANGHAI GESTURE

*Scenario:* Josef von Sternberg, adapted from the play by John Colton.
*Photography:* Paul Ivano. *Settings:* Boris Leven, Howard Bristol. *Murals:* Keye Luke. *Music:* Richard Hageman. *Miss Munson's costumes:* Royer. *Miss Tierney's costumes:* Oleg Cassini. *Produced by:* Arnold Pressburger. *Distributed by:* United Artists. *Première:* February 6, 1942.

*Players:* Gene Tierney ("Poppy"–Victoria Charteris), Walter Huston (Sir Guy Charteris), Victor Mature (Doctor Omar), Ona Munson ("Mother Gin Sling"), Phyllis Brooks (Dixie Pomeroy), Albert Basserman (Commissioner), Maria Ouspenskaya (Amah), Eric Blore (Bookkeeper), Ivan Lebedeff

(Gambler), Mike Mazurki (Coolie), Clyde Fillmore (Comprador), Rex Evans (Counsellor Brooks), Grayce Hampton (Socialite), Micharl Delmatoff (Bartender), Marcel Dalio (Croupier), Mikhail Rasumny (Cashier), John Abbott (Poppy's escort).

## 1943–44

### THE TOWN

*Scenario:* Joseph Krumgold.
*Photography:* Larry Madison. Philip Dunn in charge of production for the United States Office of War Information.
*The town:* Madison, Wisconsin.

A one-reel documentary made during World War II to show the many diverse elements that go into the making of a typical American town.

## 1946

Color consultant for David O. Selznick's *Duel in the Sun*. Sternberg also directed some scenes during a brief illness of the film's director, King Vidor.

*Project: The Seven Bad Years* (1949) an essay that was to be the prelude to a film examination of the roots of aggressiveness in man that are to be found in his first—formative—seven years "and from which he could extricate himself were he to recognize that an irresponsible child was leading him into trouble." (J.v.S.) No support for this project could be found.

## 1950

### JET PILOT

*Scenario, Co-Producer:* Jules Furthman.
*Photography:* Winton C. Hoch. *Aerial photography:* Philip C. Cochran.

*Settings:* Albert S. D'Agostino and Field Gray.
*Music:* Bronislaw Kaper.
*Costumes:* Michael Woulfe.
*Edited by:* James Wilkinson, Michael McAdam, Harry Marker, William Moore.
*Produced by:* Howard Hughes.
*Distributed by:* R.K.O.

*Players:* Janet Leigh, John Wayne, Hans Conreid, Richard Rober, Paul Fix, Jay C. Flippen, Roland Winters, Ivan Triesault, John Bishop, Perdita Chandler, Joyce Compton.

1951

MACAO

*Scenario:* Barnard C. Schoenfeld and Stanley Rubin, from a story by Bob Williams.
*Photography:* Harry J. Wild. *Settings:* Albert S. D'Agostino, Ralph Berger.
*Music:* Anthony Collins.
*Costumes:* Michael Woulfe.
*Produced by:* Howard Hughes. *Co-producer:* Alex Gottlieb.
*Associate producer:* S. Rubin. *Edited by:* Samuel E. Beetley and Robert Golden.
*Distributed by:* R.K.O. *Première:* April, 1952.

*Players:* Jane Russell, Robert Mitchum, William Bendix, Thomas Gomez, Gloria Grahame, Brad Dexter, Edward Ashley, Philip Ahn, Vladimir Sokoloff, Don Zelaya.

Neither *Jet Pilot* nor *Macao* represent authentic works by Von Sternberg, having been so altered for their commercial distribution that little of the director's original intentions was preserved. *Jet Pilot*, for instance, Sternberg's first film in color, retains almost nothing of his experiments in the medium of the color film. As for *Macao*, it was almost entirely re-shot by Nicholas Ray. Of these two films, Sternberg said: "They were for me unsuccessful assignments as the controlling factors were a dozen assorted and constantly shifted producers— never the director—and the only reason I accepted these doubtful conditions was that Howard Hughes promised to give

me support and authority for years to come—a promise that was to remain as elusive as he was."

1953

THE SAGA OF ANATAHAN

*Scenario:* Josef von Sternberg, adapted by him from a book by Michiro Maruyama, based on an actual incident of World War II in the South Pacific reported by *Life* magazine. Narration in English written and spoken by Von Sternberg. *Photography:* Josef von Sternberg. *Settings:* Kono. *Music:* Akira Ifukube. *Japanese dialogue:* Asano. *Produced by:* Yoshio Osawa and Nagamasa Kawakita for Daiwa-Towa Productions, Japan. *Première:* 1953.

*Players:* Akemi Negishi, Tadashi Suganuma, Shoji Nakayama, Hiroshi Kondo, Jun Fujikawa, Kisaburo Sawamura, Tadashi Kitagawa, Shozo Miyashita, Rokuriro Kinoya, Dajiro Tamura, Takeshi Suzuki, Shiro Amikura, Kikuji Onoe, Tsuruemu Bando.

Filmed in Kyoto, Japan, in a studio specially built for the film where the sub-tropical island of Anatahan, one of the Marianas group, was reconstructed.

In 1954, Sternberg planned with Gabriel Pascal, in their respective director and producer capacities, to film Shaw's "The Doctor's Dilemma." Not realized.

In 1959, Sternberg acquired an option to film Shelby Foote's novel of a *crime passionel* set in the deep South, *Follow Me Down.* The film was to have been called *The Temptation of Luther Eustus.* Not realized.

. . .

With the exceptions noted above, Sternberg wrote or supervised the scenarios of all his films and edited them himself. Being himself a cameraman, he also supervised the photog-

raphy of all his films, determining the angles, lighting, and composition. Two he photographed himself—*The Devil Is a Woman* and *Anatahan*. As to the music, he specified all the sounds, including the music and songs, that were to serve as backgrounds to or source music from the images. Although ideas for sets and costumes were sometimes submitted to him by the set designers and wardrobe people, their essential style was determined by Sternberg. Often they were based on prior fantasies by painters and illustrators of long ago. Just as often, they were products of his own imagination.

# Bibliography
(Selective)

I. WRITINGS BY STERNBERG

## Books

*Daughters of Vienna*, a novel, Vienna, 1922. (Translated from the German of Karl Adolph.)
*Fun in a Chinese Laundry*, an autobiography, Macmillan, 1965. British edition: Secker & Warburg (London), 1966.
*Souvenirs d'un montreur d'ombres*, French translation of the autobiography, Éditions Robert Laffont (Paris), 1966. (A German edition of the autobiography, by Friedrich-Verlag [Hanover], is to be published this year.)

## Articles

"The Waxen Galatea," *The Director* (Hollywood), 1925. (This was a short story.)
"Come studio i mei film," *Cinema* (Rome), No. 3, 1936.
"On Life and Film," *Films in Review* (New York), October, 1952.
"Acting in Film and Theatre," *Film Culture* (New York), No. 5–6, Winter, 1955.
"More Light," *Sight & Sound* (London), Autumn, 1955.
"Plus de Lumière," *Cahiers du Cinéma* (Paris), Oct.–Nov., 1956.
"Le Jeu au Théâtre et au Cinéma," *Cahiers du Cinéma* (Paris), Noël, 1956.
"Créer avec l'oeil," *L'Art du Cinéma* par Pierre Lherminier, Éditions Seghers (Paris), 1960.
"Del Estetismo a la Filosofia," *Gaceto del Festival Mar del Plata*, March 21, 1963.

"A Taste for Celluloid," *Films and Filming* (London), July, 1963.
"The Von Sternberg Principle," *Esquire* (New York), October, 1963.


II. WRITINGS ABOUT STERNBERG

*Books*

Josef von Sternberg, *The Filmcritic*, Tokyo. (The entire issue of 108 pp. was given over to a critical study of his work.) Part One—1928; Part Two—1933.
*The Films of Josef von Sternberg*, by Andrew Sarris, Museum of Modern Art, New York, 1966.
*Josef von Sternberg/Dokumentation/Eine Darstellung*, Verband der Deutschen Filmclubs E.V., Mannheim, 1966.
*l'Ange Bleu* (Screenplay), *L'Avant-Scène du Cinéma*, No. 57, Paris,. March, 1966.
*Josef von Sternberg*, by Herman G. Weinberg, Éditions Seghers, Paris, 1966.
*The Celluloid Sacrifice* by Alexander Walker (Chapter 4), Hawthorn Books Inc., New York, 1967.


*Interviews*

Jean-Claude Bellanger, Dennis Freppel, Bertrand Tavernier, Interview de Josef von Sternberg, *Cinéma 61* (Paris), No. 54, March 1961.
Peter Bogdanovich, Encounter with Josef von Sternberg, *Movie* (London), No. 13, Summer, 1965.
Kevin Brownlow, Sternberg, *Film* (London), Spring 1966.
Felix Bucher, Interview mit Josef von Sternberg, *Film Magazin*, No. 14, 1960.
Serge Daney, Jean-Louis Noames, Recontres avec un solitaire, *Cahiers du Cinéma* (Paris), No. 168, July 1965.
Vitus B. Dröscher, Der Weg zur absoluten Filmkunst— Gesprach mit Josef von Sternberg, *Frankfurter Rundschau*, Dec. 17, 1960.
Philippe Esnault, Michèle Firk, Entretien avec Josef von Sternberg, *Positif* (Paris), No. 37–38, Jan. 1961, March 1961.

Manfred Georg, Eine Begegnung mit Josef von Sternberg, *Die Neue Zeitung*, No. 71, March 25, 1954.
Erich Krünes, Erstes Interview mit Josef von Sternberg, *Film-Magazin* (Berlin), Aug. 25, 1925.
F. A. Macklin, Interview with Josef von Sternberg, *Film Heritage* (Dayton, Ohio), Winter 1965–66.
John Nugent, Total Recall, *Newsweek*, March 29, 1965.
John Pankake, Sternberg at 70, *Films in Review*, May 1964.
Bert Reisfeld, Gespräche mit Josef von Sternberg, *Stuttgarter Zeitung*, Aug. 21, 1959; A Taste for Celluloid, *Films and Filming* (London), July 1963; Le Montreur d'ombres: Déclarations de Josef von Sternberg, *Cahiers du Cinéma* (Paris), No. 168, July 1965; Interview with Sternberg, *Cinema 61* (Paris), No. 54, March, 1961.


Articles

"The Salvation Hunters,"* *The Director* (Hollywood), Dec. 1924.
E.E.B.: "The Luck of von Sternberg," *Picture Goer* (London), January, 1925.
Jim Tully: "Josef von Sternberg," *Vanity Fair* (New York), July, 1928.
Robert Desnos: "Cinéma d'Avant-Garde," *Documents No. 7* (Paris), 1929.
Jean Lenauer: "Dix Jours à Berlin," *La Revue du Cinéma* (Paris), June, 1930.
Jan & Cora Gordon: "Star-Dust in Hollywood" (Edinburgh), 1930.
Louis Chavance: "Le Cas de Josef von Sternberg," *La Revue du Cinéma*, July 1930.
——: "Le Calvaire de Lena X," *ibid.*
Jacques Spitz: "L'Ange Bleu," *La Revue du Cinéma*, October, 1930.
Heinrich Mann: "Le Prof. Unrat," Chapter 1, *La Revue du Cinéma*, December, 1930.
M. Gibbons: "Sternberg," *Film Mercury*, January 2, 1931.
Jean Lasserre: "La vie brûlante de Marlene Dietrich," *Nouvelle Librairie Française* (Paris), 1931.

* Sternberg's first review.

## 250  Bibliography

William Ortoni: "Hollywood Has Nothing to Learn," *Atlantic Monthly* (New York), June, 1931.

Henry F. Pringle: "Profile of Josef von Sternberg," *The New Yorker* (New York), March 28, 1931.

Denis Marion: "Un Ethique du Film," *La Revue du Cinéma* (Paris), January, 1931.

Heinrich Mann: "Le Professeur Unrat," (Excerpts), *La Revue du Cinéma* (Paris), December, 1930, January–February, 1931.

Germaine Decaris: "Le Calvaire de Lena X," *Le Soir* (Paris), June 27, 1931.

Robert E. Sherwood: "Shanghai Express" *Hollywood Spectator*, March 1932.

Jean Talky: "Marlene Dietrich, femme enigme," *Nilsson* (Paris), 1932.

Ron Landau-London: "Begegnungen mit amerikanischen Titanen," *Der Ouerschnitt* (Berlin), August, 1932.

"Marlene, hallucinante obsession de Sternberg," *Pour Vous* (Paris), January 12, 1933.

Rudolf Arnheim: "Josef von Sternberg," *Scenario* (Rome), No. 2, 1934.

H.S.: "Von Sternberg als Absolutist," *Filmliga* (Holland), August, 1934.

Andre Sennwald: "J.v.S.—Stylist," *New York Times*, September, 23, 1934.

Andre Armandy: "L'Imperatrice Rouge," *La Revue du Paris*, November 1, 1934.

Arne Bornebusch: "De lever Ett Rikt Livt" (Stockholm), 1935.

Alberto Consiglio: "Attore o regista?" *Cinema* (Rome), No. 1, 1936.

Charles Graves: "*Celebrities in Cameo, No. 50—Joseph von Sternberg*," *The Bystander* (London), December 9, 1936.

"Marlene Speaks," *Daily Sketch* (London), December 19, 1936.

A. E. Mackenzie: "The Leonardo of the Lenses," *Life and Letters Today* (London), Spring, 1936.

"The Man Who Knows 20,000,000 Minds," *Hong Kong Daily Press*, September 19, 1936.

Eric H. Rideout: *The American Film* (London), 1937.

Pasinetti & Puccini: *La Regia* (Venice), 1943.

John Grierson: "Grierson on Documentary" (London), 1946. (Pub: Collins).

Roberto Paolella: "Grandezza i decadenza di J.v.S.," *Cinema* (Milan), No. 26, 1946.

Robert Florey: "Ma carriere à Hollywood," *Hollywood, d'Hier et d'Aujourd'hui* (Ed. Prisma, Paris), 1948.

Curtis Harrington: "An Index to the Films of Josef von Sternberg" (Edited by Herman G. Weinberg), Index Series, No. 17, *The British Film Institute* (London), February, 1949.

Curtis Harrington: "The Dangerous Compromise," *The Hollywood Quarterly* (Berkeley, Cal.), Vol. 3, No. 4, 1949.

Herman G. Weinberg: "Director's Return," *New York Times*, Nov. 6, 1949.

Robert Florey: "Escape" (The Exquisite Sinner), *Cinémonde* (Paris), February 7, 1949.

"A Native Returns," *New York Times*, September 10, 1950.

Jorge Luis Borges: Prologue, *La Muerte y la Brujula* (Buenos Aires) 1951.

Curtis Harrington: "Josef von Sternberg," *Cahiers du Cinéma* (Paris), October–November, 1951.

Leslie Frewin: "The Blonde Venus," *Roy Publishers* (New York), 1953.

Giovanni Scognamillo: "Sternberg, le donne e i gangsters," *Bianco e Nero* (Rome), November–December, 1954.

Guido Cincotti: "Filmografia di von Sternberg," *Bianco e Nero* (Rome), No. 11–12, 1954.

"Hollywood and Von Sternberg," *New York Post*, January 26, 1956.

Philippe Demonsablon: "Un coeur mis à nu," *Cahiers du Cinéma* (Paris), April, 1956.

Curt Riess: "Unternehme 'Blauer Engel' " *Das Gab's Nur Einmal*, Hamburg (Germany), 1956.

Andre Labarthe: "Un metteur en scène baudelairien," *Cahiers du Cinéma* (Paris), April, 1956.

Ado Kyrou: "Josef von Sternberg" (in *Amour-Érotisme et Cinéma*), Le Terrain Vague, Paris, 1957.

Gert Wolfram: *Der Sex-Appeal* (Munich), 1957.

"Josef von Sternberg," Kultur Fahrplan (Berlin), 1958.

Kirk Bond: "Joseph von Sternberg Revisited," *Film Courier* (New York), Summer, 1959.

Herbert G. Luft: "Erich Pommer, Part II," *Films in Review* (New York), November, 1959.

Richard Griffith: "Marlene Dietrich—Image and Legend," Monograph, *Museum of Modern Art* (New York), 1959.

Giulio Cesare Castello and Claudio Bertieri: "The Devil Is a Woman," *Venezia 1932–1939 Filmografia Critica, Bianco e Nero* (Rome), August–September, 1959.

Henri Agel: "Josef von Sternberg," *Les Grandes Cinéastes* (Paris), 1959.

"The Blue Angel," *La Razon* (Caracas), April 3, 1960.

Franco Berutti: "La seconda giovinezza del regista che ha inventato Marlene Dietrich," Venice, 1960.

"Omaggio à Josef von Sternberg," *Festival Bulletin—Locarno,* 1960.

L. KN.: "Josef von Sternberg," *Neues Oesterreich* (Vienna), April 19, 1960.

"Josef von Sternberg," Revista bimestrial de Cinema (Sao Paulo) September, 1960.

"Der Schoepfer des *Blauen Engels,*" *Der Kurier* (Berlin), June 28, 1960.

"Joseph: Figura Central de la IV Reseña," *El Grafico* (Acapulco), November 22, 1961.

Ortiz Gonzalez: "Primer Encuentro con el Gran Realizador Aleman—Josef von Sternberg," *Cine Mundial* (Mexico, DF), November 22, 1961.

Octavio Albee: "Canas de Josef von Sternberg," *Cine Mundial* (Mexico, DF), November 30, 1961.

"Sternberg da en el Blanco," *Cine Mundial* (Mexico, DF), December 3, 1962.

"Josef von Sternberg," *Wer ist Wer,* Arani Verlag (Berlin), 1962.

Herman G. Weinberg: "The Lost Films" (Part One), *Sight and Sound* (London), August, 1962.

Jean Douchet: "Sternberg," *Cahiers du Cinéma* (Paris), No. 137, November, 1962.

S. M. Eisenstein: *"Erinnerungen"* (Die Arche Verlag) (Zürich), 1963.

H. Alsina Thevenet: "Josef von Sternberg," *Tiempo de Cine* (Buenos Aires), October–November, 1963.

Walter Khouri: "Filmografia de J.V.S.," *Tiempo de Cine* (Buenos Aires), October–November, 1963.

Carlos Ferreira: "Cineatalya," *La Capital* (Mar del Plata), March 23, 1963.

Ado Kyrou: "Sternberg et Marlène" in *Le Surrealism au Cinéma* (Paris), 1963.

"The Devil Is a Woman & Anatahan," *Protocole du Troisieme Congres International du Cinéma Indépendant*," SIDOC (*Lausanne*), *August 25, 1963—September 1, 1963.*

"Von Sternberg—del estetismo a la filosofia," *Gaceta del Festival* (Mar del Plata), March 21, 1963.

"Josef von Sternberg," *El Tiempo* (Bogota), March 24, 1963.

Herbert G. Luft: "J.V.S.—A Study," *Film Journal* (Melbourne) No. 24, December 1964.

Jack Smith: "A Belated Appreciation of Von Sternberg," *Film Culture*, No. 31 (New York), Winter 1963–64.

Al Milgrom: "The Cinema of J.v.S."—Symposium, University of Minnesota, 1964.

Patrick Brion: "Filmographie de Josef von Sternberg," *Cahiers du Cinéma* (Paris), No. 168, July, 1965.

O. O. Green: "Six Films of Josef von Sternberg," *Movie* (London), No. 13, 1965.

Elliott Stein: "Fun in a Chinese Laundry," *Sight & Sound* (London), Autumn 1965.

Herman G. Weinberg: "Sternberg & Stroheim" (letter), *Sight & Sound* (London), Winter 1965–66.

"V.S.—Puppe für Bauchredner," *Der Spiegel*, April 21, 1965.

"Josef von Sternberg ou le cinéma de l'enthousiasme," *Cahiers du Cinéma* (Paris), No. 168, July, 1965.

Ulrich Gregor: "Der Blaue Engel," *Filmkritik* (Frankfurt A.M.), No. 4, April, 1965.

Michel Cournot: "Une cinématique du rêve," *Le Nouvel Observateur* (Paris), February 23, 1966.

Michel Ciment: "Fun in a Chinese Laundry," *Positif* (Paris), No. 75, May 1966.

Bernard Eisenschitz: "L'Oeuvre de Josef von Sternberg," *L'Avant-Scene du Cinéma* (Paris), No. 57, March 1966.

Ado Kyrou: "Sternberg, avant, pendant, après Marlene," *Positif* (Paris), No. 75, May 1966.

Herbert G. Luft: "Josef von Sternberg," *Filmkunst* (Vienna), No. 45, 1966.

Claudio Rispoli: "Il Labirinto sentimentale di Sternberg," *Filmcritica*, No. 166, April, 1966.

Albert Winblad: "Josef von Sternberg," *Kosmorama* (Copenhagen), No. 73, February, 1966.
Ulrich von Thuna: "Ueber die Modernität bei Josef von Sternberg," *Neu Zürcher Zeitung* (Zürich), June 11, 1966.
Herman G. Weinberg: "Fun in a Chinese Laundry" (Review), *Film Heritage* (Univ. of Dayton), May, 1966.
Kirk Bond: "Josef von Sternberg: Three Books," *Film Comment* (New York), Vol. 4, No. 2, 1967.
"Joseph von Sternberg"—*Chaplin 68–70* (Stockholm), December, 1966, February, 1967.

Although this is only a partial listing, it should be stated that a large number of additional articles appeared on Sternberg in late 1966 and early in 1967 in Mannheim, Lyons, Paris, London, Algiers, Oran, Tlemco, Stockholm, Uppsala, Lund, Copenhagen, and Sydney, as a result of his visits to those places.

MEMORIAL FOR JO
December 24, 1969

*You are not here*

*among dead mourners*

*blatant flowers*

*fumbling praise*

*your sham-defying*

*laughter*

*your terrible fury*

*somewhere out of sight*

*focus the camera eye*

*that probes these ghosts*

*to the depth of empty hearts*

*made less than flesh*

*by your departure.*

Elva Kremenliev

HERMAN G. WEINBERG was born in New York City in 1908. After attending the Institute of Musical Art where he studied the violin under Louis Svecenski, preparing for a concert career, he changed his mind and entered the field of motion pictures, first scoring foreign films at the Fifth Avenue Playhouse, then subtitling them when sound came in. Since then he has provided the screen captions for over 400 French, German, Italian, etc., pictures. Beginning with Close-Up in 1928, he has contributed articles on the aesthetics of the cinema to most of the leading film journals throughout the world, has lectured extensively on this subject in universities in the United States and Canada, inaugurated the Index Series on directors for the British Film Institute as well as a column, Coffee, Brandy and Cigars, now in its seventeenth year (and currently appearing in Film Culture magazine), comprising "notes for an as yet unwritten history of the cinema." In 1960–61 he served as a juror at the San Francisco and Vancouver International Film Festivals and in 1964 mounted an elaborate exhibition, "Homage to Erich von Stroheim," at the Montreal International Film Festival. The following year he delivered a memorial address on Stroheim at the New York Film Festival and in 1966 at the Canadian Film Institute. He translated and edited the American editions of 50 Years of Italian Cinema and 50 Years of Ballet and Opera in Italy and has contributed to many anthologies on the film here and abroad. He was for ten years American Correspondent for Sight & Sound (London) and served in a similar capacity for Cahiers du Cinéma (Paris), among other film periodicals. His short film, Autumn Fire, an early classic of the first American avant-garde, is now in the collections of most of the principal film museums here and abroad. He has been "profiled" in The New Yorker's "Talk of the Town" and in Esquire and has been working on a "magnum opus," Sin and Cinema, a moral history of the movies, off and on for the past decade. Currently he is preparing a biography of Ernst Lubitsch, to be published by Dutton in the fall of 1968. Since 1960 he has been teaching a course on the history of the motion pictures as an art at The City College in New York.

# ASPECTS OF FILM

*An Arno Press Collection*

Adler, Mortimer J. **Art and Prudence.** 1937

Conant, Michael. **Anti-Trust in the Motion Picture Industry.** 1960

Croy, Homer. **How Motion Pictures Are Made.** 1918

Drinkwater, John. **The Life and Adventures of Carl Laemmle.** 1931

Hacker, Leonard. **Cinematic Design.** 1931

Hepworth, T[homas] C[raddock]. **The Book of the Lantern.** 1899

Johnston, Alva. **The Great Goldwyn.** 1937

Klingender, F.D. and Stuart Legg. **Money Behind the Screen.** 1937

Limbacher, James L. **Four Aspects of the Film.** 1969

Manvell, Roger, ed. **The Cinema 1950.** 1950

Manvell, Roger, ed. **The Cinema 1951.** 1951

Manvell, Roger, ed. **The Cinema 1952.** 1952

Marchant, James, ed. **The Cinema in Education.** 1925

Mayer, J.P. **British Cinemas and Their Audiences.** 1948

Sabaneev, Leonid. **Music for the Films.** 1935

Seabury, William Marston. **Motion Picture Problems.** 1929

Seldes, Gilbert. **The Movies Come from America.** 1937

U.S. House of Representatives, Committee on Education. **Motion Picture Commission: Hearings.** 1914

U.S. House of Representatives, Committee on Education. **Federal Motion Picture Commission: Hearings.** 1916

U.S. Senate, Temporary National Economic Committee. **Investigation of Concentration of Economic Power.** 1941

Weinberg, Herman G. **Josef von Sternberg.** 1967

The Irish Theatre Series 6
*Edited by* Robert Hogan, James Kilroy *and* Liam Miller

The Modern Irish Drama, *a documentary history*
I: The Irish Literary Theatre 1899-1901

The Modern Irish Drama
*a documentary history* I

# The Irish Literary Theatre
1899-1901
by Robert Hogan and James Kilroy

The Dolmen Press

Humanities Press Inc.

Set in Times Roman type and printed
and published in the Republic of Ireland
by The Dolmen Press Limited
North Richmond Industrial Estate, North Richmond Street, Dublin 1

Distributed outside Ireland, except in the United States of America
and in Canada, by Oxford University Press.

Published in the United States of America and in Canada
by Humanities Press Inc.,
171 First Avenue, Atlantic Highlands, N.J. 07716

First published 1975

HARDBACK EDITION
ISBN 0 85105 222 3: The Dolmen Press
ISBN 0-391-00377-1: Humanities Press Inc.

PAPERBACK EDITION
ISBN 0 85105 274 6: The Dolmen Press
ISBN 0-391-00378-X: Humanities Press Inc.

147151

# Contents

# Acknowledgements

Grateful acknowledgement is made to:

Ernest Benn, Ltd., for quotations from F. R. Benson, *My Memoirs*.

Srimati Rukmini Devi, for quotations from *We Two Together* and manuscripts by James Cousins.

J. M. Dent & Sons, Ltd., for quotation from W. H. Reed, *Elgar*.

Faber & Faber, Ltd., for quotation from 'The Day of Rabblement' in *Critical Writings of James Joyce*.

Stephen Fay, for quotations from the writings of F. J. Fay.

Nevin Griffith, for quotations from *The United Irishman*, and writings of Arthur Griffith.

Harcourt, Brace & World, Inc. for quotations from W. G. Fay and Catherine Carswell, *The Fays of the Abbey Theatre*.

Rupert Hart-Davis, Ltd., for quotations from Max Beerbohm, *Around Theatres*.

William Heinemann, Ltd., for quotations from Max Beerbohm, 'In Dublin'.

*The Irish Independent*, for quotations from *The Daily Nation, The Freeman's Journal* and *The Irish Daily Independent*.

*The Irish Times*, for quotations from *The Daily Express, The Dublin Evening Mail* and *The Irish Times*.

Gerald MacDermott, for quotations from the journals of Joseph Holloway.

The Society of Authors, for the Estate of Bernard Shaw, for quotations from the writings of G. B. Shaw.

A. P. Watt & Son, for quotations from W. B. Yeats, *Letters*.

The National Library of Ireland, for quotations from manuscript collection.

Percy M. Young, for quotations from *Elgar*.

# Introduction

In this history, we have attempted to recreate something of the immediacy felt by those writers and actors and playgoers who, in the years from 1899 to 1901, were laying the foundations of a national drama for Ireland. Most histories, quite properly, are compilations of fact and assessments of value, and so also, we hope, is this one. Nevertheless, we have attempted to do more than set down a judicious appraisal of what happened. There are several such accounts, although none, we believe, so full and accurate as we have tried to make this one. Here, we have primarily attempted to recreate a sense of how it was at the moment, and to achieve this feeling of immediacy we have allowed the story to be told as much as possible by the people who were involved in it. W. B. Yeats, George Moore, Frank Fay have been our collaborators, and we have made great use of contemporary documents — of letters, memoirs, and forgotten newspaper accounts and reviews.

Perhaps more than most historians, the chronicler of the theatre is always thwarted by the fact of time. A theatrical performance exists for the moment, and even the vivid memories of those who saw a play are but dim and distorted reflections of the lost reality. How Burbage sounded, how Garrick looked, whatever was so inimitable about Nell Gwynn or Mrs. Siddons or Molly Allgood — these matters of purely visual or aural appeal are central to a great player's genius, and yet so rarely, so vaguely recorded.

We have attempted, then, to reconstruct what still can be reconstructed of the actuality and the excitement of these formative years in Dublin, when a new drama was being created from nothing. It is particularly appropriate that we allow the principals to tell the story largely in their own words, for the principals included people like Yeats, Moore, John Synge, the Fay brothers, Arthur Griffith, Joseph Holloway, Lady Gregory, Douglas Hyde, Miss Horniman, and Maud Gonne. The intrigues, the quarrels, the problems, as well as the wit, the humour, and the charm reside in their own words far more than they could in any paraphrase of ours.

ROBERT HOGAN
JAMES KILROY

# 1899

The centuries-long struggle of Ireland for its national independence was not an ever-growing movement whose final cumulative intensity was the 1916 Rising. Over the centuries, Irish nationalism has risen to many waves of intensity between many troughs of despair. One such intense movement reached its peak in 1890 under the inspiring leadership of Charles Stewart Parnell. When Parnell lost the leadership of the Irish party and then, in 1891, died struggling to regain it, the cause of Irish freedom received a reversal from which it did not recover for years. But, as Edmund Curtis remarked, 'in the grand disillusionment that followed Parnell the national cause took new and deeper channels than mere politics.'[1] One such channel was the intensification of an already growing movement in literature. It was a movement which looked directly to Ireland, to Irish legend and Irish history, for its inspiration. It was a movement which was abruptly to blossom into what has been justly called the Irish Renaissance.

There had been, of course, Irish writers before the 1890's who had written about Ireland. Maria Edgeworth and William Carleton had both taken Ireland for their subject, but both in different ways had not quite attained what Lennox Robinson was to call 'this Irish thing'. Maria Edgeworth, for all her knowledge, was an outsider painting with sympathy, but with an outsider's incomplete understanding. Carleton, the son of a peasant, did know intimately what he was writing about, but he grafted an alien style onto his subject, thus exaggerating and distorting it. Similarly, the fervent patriotic poems of the Young Ireland group suffered as much from English poetic diction as they did from their authors' minor talents. However, with the poems of James Clarence Mangan and Sir Samuel Ferguson, and perhaps even with the flawed novels of Charles J. Kickham, the first indications of an Irish literature that was both Irish and literature began to appear.

Ernest Boyd dates the true beginnings of modern Irish literature with the publication of two volumes by Standish O'Grady: his *History of Ireland : The Heroic Period* in 1878, and his *History of Ireland : Cuculain and his Contemporaries* in 1880. These volumes were an exultant celebration of Irish legendary materials, and, although in prose, were vibrant with poetic fervour. As Æ wrote in

1902, 'Years ago, in the adventurous youth of his mind, Mr. O'Grady found the Gaelic tradition like a neglected antique dún with the doors barred. Listening, he heard from within the hum of an immense chivalry, and he opened the doors and the wild riders went forth to work their will.'[2] To this, W. B. Yeats added the footnote that, 'I think it was his *History of Ireland, Heroic Period*, that started us all. . . .'[3]

What it had started was this: In 1888 the Dublin firm of M. H. Gill and Son published *Poems and Ballads of Young Ireland*, which included the work of most of the new poets — Yeats, T. W. Rolleston, John Todhunter, Katherine Tynan, Rose Kavanagh, and others — and which, according to Boyd, 'announced the co-operative, concerted nature of the effort of the younger generation to give a new impulse to Irish poety'.[4] In 1899, Yeats published *The Wanderings of Oisin*. In 1891, at a meeting at Yeats's house in London, he, Rolleston, Todhunter, and others initiated what was to become in the next year the Irish Literary Society of London. Also in 1892, a sister organization, the National Literary Society, was formed in Dublin, and Douglas Hyde gave before it his influential lecture on 'The Necessity for De-Anglicising Ireland'. In that same year Yeats published his play *The Countess Cathleen*. In 1893, Hyde published his beautiful *The Love Songs of Connacht* and founded the Gaelic League for the propagation of the Irish language. In 1893 also, Yeats's volume *The Celtic Twilight* gave a descriptive tag to the whole movement. In the next year he published another play, *The Land of Heart's Desire*, and it was produced in March in London together with Todhunter's *A Comedy of Sighs*. In 1897, George Sigerson published his *Bards of the Gael and Gall*. In 1899, Hyde published his monumental *Literary History of Ireland*. And in 1899, the Irish Literary Theatre made its first appearance.

\*    \*    \*

The originality of the Irish Literary Theatre in 1899 can probably best be appreciated by a knowledge of what the other Dublin theatres were doing.

The New Theatre Royal had been originally opened in January, 1821, and on that occasion Colman the Younger wrote an opening address which began:

Hail, generous Natives of Green Erin's Isle;
Welcome, kind Patrons, to our new-rais'd Pile.

After noting that all of the labour on the new building had been
done by Irishmen, he briefly charted the history of the site.

Here once a Market reared its busy head,
Where sheep, instead of tragic heroes, bled;
Bright cleavers form'd a band to charm the ears;
Joints dangled in the place of Chandeliers.
Stout Butchers, stern as Critics, had their day,
And cut up oxen, like a modern Play.
Soon Science came; — his steel the Butcher drops,
Removes, with awe, the shambles and the shops,
And Learning triumphed over Mutton Chops![5]

Although Colman's verses will never rank among the flowers of
English poetry, they seem masterly indeed when compared to the
address written by Edwin Hamilton, Esq. on the occasion of the
re-opening of the theatre after restoration on 13 December 1897.
In charting the theatre's history, Hamilton wrote:

Here, in sublime, soul-stirring, stately scenes,
Appeared Charles Young, the Kembles, and the Keans,
Macready, Brooke, bright stars of long ago;
Here — in his line unrivalled — Boucicault:
Then — loved as player, patriot, and man —
Our home-born genius, Barry Sullivan.[6]

No home-born genius was to tread the boards of the new Royal
under the directorship of H. H. Morrell and Frederick Mouillot,
for the theatre depended almost entirely upon English touring companies doing light drama and comedy. Some typical productions
of 1898 and 1899 were George Alexander's Company with Scenery,
Furniture and Effects from the St. James's Theatre, London, in
*The Man of Forty* by Walter Frith, in which Alexander was supported by H. B. Irving and C. Aubrey Smith; the celebrated actress,
Miss Annie Hughes, Mr. Edmund Maurice and Company in Robert
Buchanan's comedy *Sweet Nancy*; Mrs. Brown Potter and Mr.

Kyrle Bellew supported by their London company in Bulwer-Lytton's *The Lady of Lyons* and *Camille* of Dumas *fils*; Mr. J. L. Shine, supported by the Globe Theatre, London, Company, in an original play entitled *An Irish Gentleman* by David Christie Murray and Shine; George and Weedon Grossmith in *Young Mr. Yarde*, a farce by Harrold Ellis and Paul A. Rubens. There were many productions of light operas, such as *The Bohemian Girl, The Daughter of the Regiment* and *The Lily of Killarney* by travelling groups like the Moody Manners Opera Company. There were also many musical comedies, such as the popular *The Belle of New York, Little Miss Nobody, Topsy-Turvey Hotel, The Skirt Dancer, A Greek Slave* and *The Squatter's Daughter*. Occasionally there was the spectacular melodrama, which still had not quite gone out of style, such as that 'Up-to-date Drury Lane Sporting Drama' *The Prodigal Daughter* by Henry Pettitt and Sir Augustus Harris, 'with all the Original Drury Lane Scenes, Dresses, and 6 Blood Horses including the Grand National Winner VOLUPTUARY.' And not at all infrequently there was even an accomplished artist in an interesting, if un-Irish play. Mrs. Patrick Campbell played at the Royal in *The Second Mrs. Tanqueray, The Notorious Mrs. Ebbsmith* and *Magda*. Julia Neilson, Louis Calvert, William Mollison and Lillian Braithwaite appeared in *As You Like It*. The Benson Company, with such fine actors as Oscar Asche and Frank Rodney, appeared in *Antony and Cleopatra* and *The School for Scandal*. Winifred Emery and Cyril Maude appeared in Barrie's *The Little Minister*, and Martin Harvey appeared in *The Only Way*, the popular adaptation of *A Tale of Two Cities*.

However, about the only nod to Irish drama given by the Royal was a run in July, 1899, by E. C. Matthews' Company of Boucicault's *Arrah-na-Pogue* and *The Colleen Bawn*. Frank Fay, reviewing the plays in *The United Irishman*, greeted them with only faint praise:

> For the stuff that ordinarily goes by the name of "Irish Drama", the company would probably be quite adequate. But, with the exception of Mr. Somerfield Arnold, it does not contain anyone who, by even a stretch of imagination, could be called an artist; and if we are to feel the poetry, the laughter, mingled with tears, so predominant in the Irish character, we must have Boucicault's Irish plays interpreted by *artists*. When

11

the managers of the Scotch theatres revive, as they do each year, *Rob Roy* (Pocock's miserable travesty of the novel), *Jeannie Deans* (another of Boucicault's plays, by the way), *The Lady of the Lake*, &c., they engage artists of the calibre of William Mollison, so well known to Dublin playgoers as a Shakespearian actor. Except Ada Rehan, there is not, unfortunately, a single Irish dramatic artist of the first rank at present on the stage, and she is Irish by birth only; therefore we cannot hope to see worthy revivals of Irish plays by first-class Irish artists. But when we go to the Theatre Royal, which poses as a first-class house, to see Irish Drama, we have every right to expect to find the best Irish talent available in the cast. Why is not that admirable and versatile actor, Mr. Frank Dalton, in the cast? Where is his sister, Mrs. Charles Sullivan? Where is Mr. Tom Nerney (so long associated with Boucicault)? I suppose Mr. E. C. Matthews is the best Irish comedian to be had at present, but as Shaun he is only passable. Like his kind and doubtless because he plays more often in England than in Ireland, he "plays for the laugh" all the time, and the audience punish him by laughing at his pathos, and this is exasperating to one who considers that their poetry, pathos and tenderness are the only qualities which distinguish *The Colleen Bawn, The Shaughraun* and *Arrah-na-Pogue* from ordinary melodrama.[7]

In another review, Fay scored the audience as much as the players:

A very large audience assembled in the popular portions of the house to witness the performance, but with regret, I find myself compelled to say that the majority of them seemed to be of the intensely uncritical and ignorant type, only too common in Dublin, the class who will madly applaud a singer or an instrumentalist, no matter how much out of tune the former may sing or how wretchedly the latter may play, provided they finish with the conventional bluster. That they were noisy and ill-behaved is nothing, because one does not expect much from such people; but that they should scream with boorish laughter, when one of the characters in the play spoke a few words of Irish, will scarcely be credited by anyone who was not present.[8]

12

Fay found little of Irish interest to intrigue him at Dublin's other first-class house, the Gaiety, which from 27 December 1897 to 1 May 1909 was managed by the Gunn family. As with the Royal, there was practically never during this entire period a programme at the Gaiety that was about Ireland or that used local talent. This theatre also depended chiefly on English touring companies, bringing the latest farce or melodrama to the provinces. Occasionally a great actor or actress, such as Coquelin or Bernhardt, would appear briefly; and occasionally an accomplished touring company, such as F. R. Benson's or Edward Compton's, would appear in Shakespeare or the classic English comedies. But for the most part, the Gaiety, like the Royal, was given over to crowd-pleasing entertainments.

In 1899, for example, the D'Oyly Carte appeared twice: in February and again in November. The George Edwardes Company was featured three times during the year, playing *A Runaway Girl* two of the times. The always popular *Charley's Aunt*[9] would run for one week, followed by Sardou's *La Tosca* the next. On 17 April, Thomas E. Murray's Company opened in a play called *Our Irish Visitors.* Murray was an Irish-American comedian whose 'primitive funniments and outlandish dialect' Bernard Shaw had once found mildly amusing, although they smacked to him more 'of the village rather than of the West End. But he is imperturbably good-humoured, sings in tune, and surprises the audience into laughing at his childlike jokes several times on which scores much is forgiven him.'[10] *Our Irish Visitors* was not an Irish but an American farcical comedy, and its pretensions are adequately described in the Gaiety advertisement: 'Constructed for Laughing Purposes Only. 180 Laughs in 180 Minutes!' Henry Arthur Jones's *The Manoeuvres of Jane* and several plays by Arthur Wing Pinero were presented in the spring; and on 23 June, Coquelin and his company played in French Rostand's *Cyrano de Bergerac* and, on the following day, *Tartuffe* and *Les Précieuses Ridicules.* On 2 October, Mrs. Lewis Waller and her London Company, including Mr. Robert Loraine and Miss Mary Rorke, appeared in *The Three Musketeers.* Mrs. Waller was, of course, the wife of the reigning matinee idol of the English stage. Rather more interesting than the romantic heroics of Dumas was the company's other presentation, James B. Fagan's *The Rebels,* described as 'A New Romantic Irish Play', and with H. B. Warner in the cast. Fagan in later years was to write some

13

extremely popular plays and to have a distinguished career in London as a producer of both continental masterpieces and Irish dramas. *The Rebels* was Fagan's first play, and unfortunately appears not to have been published.[11] In December, the Compton Company played its usual repertoire of Sheridan, Goldsmith and some new plays. And on Boxing Day the pantomime opened as usual, this year's being *Little Red Riding Hood*.

One other theatre was licensed to present plays. This was a second-class house, The Queen's Royal Theatre — or, as it was usually called, The Queen's. At this time the theatre was managed by J. W. Whitbread, an Englishman who was writing a number of popular, very broad and very bad, neo-Boucicaultian melodramas. In the 1890's, the Queen's was given over either to the production of patriotic pieces *à la* Boucicault or to the production of old-fashioned, but still popular, spectacular melodramas. Both the quality of the plays and of the productions was considerably lower than what might be seen at the Theatre Royal or at the Gaiety.

A typical Queen's melodrama of the period was *The Bandit King,* which the indefatigable playgoer Joseph Holloway saw on the evening of 24 September 1895. It was, he wrote:

> . . . a drama written round four trained horses. Mr. J. H. Wallick took the part of "Jesse James", the outlaw, and although he has been playing it for fifteen years he struck me as not being up to much as a melodramatic actor. . . . The other parts were indifferently filled. The piece was rot. The house was full. There was so much shooting during the unfolding of the incidents, that you would at times imagine you were at a "field day" in the Fifteen Acres in the Park.[12]

On 15 September 1896 Holloway went to the Queen's, and saw

> . . . a noisy, rough-and-tumble, song and dance, American sensational play, entitled *One of the Bravest*, with a realistic fire scene, including fire engine, etc., complete. The play, in fact, seemed to have been written round this tableau. The piece, like most American dramas, has no plot to speak of, and plenty of knockabout, grotesque characters.[13]

On 6 October Holloway saw one of the few pieces at the Queen's with any pretentions to literature, Charles Reade's *Drink*, an adaptation of Zola's *L'Assommoir*. Charles Warner had made a minor

14

reputation playing the lead, and his death scene seems to have been in the best tradition of nineteenth century melodramatic acting. 'The shattered wreck of humanity, foaming at the mouth and almost tearing himself to pieces in his frenzy, will always remain a nightmare recollection in my mind,' remarked Holloway, who was impressed even by the scenery and reported that the fall from the scaffold in Act 4 caused many of the audience to cry out, 'My God, is he killed!' [14]

The Queen's audience demanded strong situations, and the play which Holloway saw there on 4 May 1897, certainly provided them. The piece was *The Trail of the Serpent* by F. Marriot Watson, and Holloway remarked that the scene in the smelting works 'was intensely realistic, and a thrill of fear passed through the house as the lever bearing the fainting form of the heroine moved towards the furnace to deposit her therein. It was certainly admirably managed, and her rescue in the nick of time was a great relief to all.' [15] On 29 June Holloway saw a Western Romance by Fred Darcy entitled *The New World*, which he described as 'a most interesting, exciting well-made drama of its class, with endless pistol-shooting, knife-flashing, hair-breadth escapes, lynching songs, dances, and fun.' He was particularly impressed by the lynching scene in Act 1, in which 'the man was actually dangling in mid-air before the rope was shot in twain above him.' [16] On 9 November, he saw a play called *Shaft No. 2*, 'the first drama that has been written around electricity which we have seen in Dublin.' The highpoint of the drama was 'a realistic representation of one on the point of being put death in an electrocution chair.' [17]

On 21 December he saw Mr. Herbert Barr's Company play George Gray's four-act drama, *The Football King*, a piece whose myriad excitements are worth describing at some length:

> The novelty round which the piece is written . . . is an Association Football Match — the final for the English Cup at Kennington Oval — played in full view of the audience with cheering multitude of small boys, goal posts, and all — an exciting episode as the ball was twice kicked across the footlights into the pit despite the netting placed almost across the stage between the audience and the players. The general shindy at the end of the match was realistic as well as amusing. The whole bag of tricks of melodrama was used in the construction

15

of the work, and the hero was as loud-voiced, declamatory, and spotless as they make them, while the villain would stop at nothing, and committed murders, poisoned, seduced, and abducted every other minute for the mere fun of the thing, it would seem. And, of course, he was well-dressed, deep-voiced, long-haired, black-moustached and eyebrowed, and smoked cigarettes beyond counting. One of the most amusing incidents occurred in Act 4, Scene 3, where the villain places his discarded mistress on the rails in an insensible[18] condition as the train is approaching, and she is supposed to be rescued by the hero in the nick of time. The hero on this occasion being a moment late had to forceably stop the train with his strong right hand in order to take the lady out of harm's way.[19]

On 3 August 1898 Holloway saw *The Terror of Paris* by E. Hill-Mitchelson and Charles H. Longdon, and was much thrilled by the scene 'in the Glassworks at St. Cloud, when the spy "Laroche" is denounced, and his eyes are about to be gouged out with molten glass from the furnaces. . . .'[20] On 9 August he saw Mr. John H. Preston's Company in an Oriental drama by Max Goldberg, entitled *The Secrets of the Harem, or The Cross and the Crescent.* The plot is the usual involved and thrilling hokum about a beautiful Christian girl caught in the toils of a lustful Pasha and rescued by the brave young Englishman, Lieutenant Herbert Markman, R.N. From the point of view of the emerging Irish drama, the scene in which the heroine is being sold at the slave auction is of some interest. As Holloway described it:

> The Lieutenant is determined to purchase her, but is outbid by the sensual Pasha who is about to claim her when "Markman" draws the Union Jack around her and defies them in the name of his country to touch it. The curtain descending in a very effective tableau amid cheers from the audience. This was the first time I ever heard an Irish audience cheer the Union Jack, or English pluck on the stage.[21]

We can hardly leave this discussion of the Queen's spectacular melodrama without mentioning Charles Locksley's amazing drama *Humanity,* which Holloway saw John Lawson's Company perform on 3 November 1898. The play's advertisements boasted:

16

Such a dénouement never before witnessed on the British Stage. Complete wreckage and demolition of a magnificently furnished Drawing Room. Smashing of windows, pier glasses, statues, ornaments, and *the fight until death on the collapsing staircase!* The breakages alone amounting to a Star's salary.[22]

This, of course, was sheer delight for the Queen's audience, and Holloway reported that 'as each article came crashing down a cry of suppressed astonishment escaped the lips of most who witnessed this truly appalling scene of destruction.' The room was destroyed in a fight between the hero and the villain, and Mr. John Lawson, remarked Holloway, gave a remarkable impersonation of the hero— 'quiet and artistic, as well as realistic. . . .'

In addition to these spectacular melodramas, the Queen's produced the Irish plays of Boucicault and the patriotic melodramas which J. W. Whitbread was turning out according to the Boucicault formula. That formula — a mélange of thrills, laughter, pathos and patriotism — offered an exaggerated and unrealistically simple view of Ireland, and it was this kind of drama against which W. B. Yeats and his colleagues were to rebel. Their rebellion so successfully swept the stage-Irishman off the stage that it was not immediately apparent how several of the masterpieces of the new Irish drama — such as Synge's *The Playboy of the Western World*, O'Casey's *Juno and the Paycock*, M. J. Molloy's *The King of Friday's Men*, and Brendan Behan's *The Hostage* — owed a very considerable debt to the Boucicaultian melodrama. In the last five or ten years there has been a revival of interest in melodrama and even a re-appraisal of Boucicault. In the World Theatre Festival at the Aldwych Theatre, London, in May, 1968, the Abbey Theatre's entry was an enthusiastically received revival of Boucicault's *The Shaughraun*, and Ronald Bryden heralded that occasion with a perceptive and convincing defence of melodrama in *The Observer* Sunday magazine. The cycle of taste again seemed to have come full circle.

Whatever their intrinsic merits, the Boucicault melodramas at the Queen's were at best unevenly presented, and the bald Whitbread imitations intended to evoke only cheap thrills and easy laughter. In 1899 the time had almost passed for Irish melodrama. The form was shortly to receive a new injection of vitality from the movies, but to the playgoer it was beginning to seem old-fashioned. On 26

17

August 1899, Frank Fay reviewed a revival of Whitbread's *Wolfe Tone*, and his dissatisfaction is beginning to be apparent.

> Of the many plays written and produced at the Queen's Theatre by Mr. J. W. Whitbread, *Wolfe Tone*, his latest, is to my mind, his best. The theatre-going public were evidently of the same opinion, for the play continued to attract large audiences for a full month after its production on St. Stephen's Day, 1898. . . . We have not yet had a real historical Irish drama, and the author of *Wolfe Tone* cannot give us one, but with the skill born of long connection with and knowledge of the boards and of the class of audience to which he appeals, Mr. Whitbread has construced an exceedingly effective play, which he calls "A Romantic Irish Drama". It is really neither more nor less than a well-constructed melodrama. . . .[23]

Later in the year Fay wrote a much more caustic review of Whitbread's play, *The Irishman*:

> Each time I have seen it the play was interpreted by thoroughly competent players; but *The Irishman* remains a crude piece of unconvincing conventionalism, without any right to its name. Before the first act was half through, all my old friends, whom I never met outside melodramas, had made their appearance. . . . I positively loathe the virtuous persons of melodrama, and would have their blood were it not that, between us, intervenes that horrible instrument of torture, the orchestra of the Queen's theatre.[24]

Later in the month the Kennedy Miller Combination revived John Baldwin Buckstone's *The Green Bushes*, which had originally been produced in 1845, and Fay remarked that a large audience treated the old play with 'amusing toleration'. He concluded, 'I suppose the day of *The Green Bushes* is nearly over.'[25]

Of course, as the clientele of the Queen's was an undemanding one, which was easily delighted with simple characterization and broad effects, the acting tended to be, with some notable exceptions, rather slovenly exaggerations of a nineteenth century broad style. When Joseph Holloway went to the Queen's on 13 August 1895, to see Fred Cooke's company in Cooke's drama *On Shannon's Shore, or The Blackthorn*, he remarked:

18

Oh my! it was shockingly bad! Too absurd for anything! Mr. Fred Cooke, the author, behaved in the character of "Barney Shanaghan" as a blithering idiot right through and nearly made me ill by his exaggerated tomfoolery.[26]

It was, of course, the Boucicault productions at the Queen's that came closest to nature, and a more tolerant Holloway reminiscence may indicate how close, at best, the Queen's came to giving a realistic view of Ireland.

A typical Queen's audience, noisy and full of suggestions to the players, filled the cosy little theatre to see Dion Boucicault's admirably constructed and most interesting Irish drama, *Arrah-na-Pogue*, acted by Kennedy Miller's Favourite Company of Irish Players. The Queen's is the home of Irish drama. There you may always reckon to see this form of piece well played by genuinely Irish actors; and, as the audience knows every line of the text and every bit of by-play in the various parts, it sees that it gets the full value for its money, or lets those on the stage know why. Such genuine, innocent, hearty laughter as the racy dialogue and droll situations brought to life became so infectious that I had to join in the laughter myself.... A more uproariously funny scene, intermingled with pathos and patriotism, than the Court Martial Scene in Act 2 where poor "Séan the Post" is tried and condemned for the robbery of money from the process server, "Michael Feeny", or one better played all-round, is seldom seen.

And the Queen's stage seemed made for the wedding scene in the barn, as the gates at the rear of the stage only have to be opened to allow the cars to pass up the laneway, and one can see from the theatre the College wall and position of the College buildings in the dim light of the dark-black night outside. Nature forming a background to the stage picture! Instead of the noisy rattling of horses' hoofs on the boards, they drive up the natural road of the laneway and discharge their load right onto the back of the stage in the most natural way possible, and when big Kitty Walsh arrived on her private ass and cart, there was a roar of delight from the house.[27]

19

But despite the pleasure that Fay and Holloway could still derive from Boucicault, if not from his imitators, the acting was usually overdone and sometimes outrageously false. What was happening at the Queen's was the last twitch of a dying convention. A new drama which would truly reflect contemporary Ireland would have to be different and would have to be acted differently.

\*     \*     \*

To round out the picture of the Dublin stage at the end of the last century, it should be mentioned that the city had one or two variety houses, which seldom or never included dramatic pieces on their bills. The most popular, and a still functioning theatre, was the one which is now called the Olympia in Dame Street. In 1896 the theatre had been called Dan Lowrey's Star Theatre of Varieties, but in 1897 its name was changed to the Empire Palace Theatre. Its Grand Opening Programme of Monday, 15 November 1897, is a quite typical one:

1   Overture, "Rosamunde", Schubert.
2   Mr. Lester King, Character Baritone Vocalist.
3   Celest, Novelty Wire Act.
4   Miss Dulcie Laing, Contralto Vocalist and Dancer.
5   Virto, the Man of Many Instruments.
6   Griff, Comic Juggler.
7   Werner & Rieder, Duettists and Swiss Warblers.
8   Frantz Family, Lady and Gentlemen Acrobats.

Interval of 10 Minutes

9   Selection, *Maritana*, Wallace.
10   Miss Florence Esdaile, Australian Soprano Vocalist.
11   Lumiere Triograph, With Special Local Views, &c.
12   Charles Coborn, Favourite Comedian and Vocalist.
13   Eight Eldorados, Vocalists and Expert Dancers.
14   Morris and Morris, American Acrobatic Grotesques.[28]

In 1898 and 1899, the theatre billed such attractions as Zaro and Arno, 'The Heathen Chinee', in their Great Horizontal Bar Act; Minnie Ray, Champion Lady Clog Dancer of the World; Professor

20

Vox, the popular singing Ventriloquist; and Franks' Roosters, a Novelty Act with Roosters, Dogs and Bantams. The bill at the Empire Palace was not greatly different from what was to be seen at the Lyric Theatre of Varieties, while in the Round Room of the Rotunda one was likely to see a home-grown concert show featuring Miss Clara Butt.

*    *    *

In his reviews in *The United Irishman*, Frank Fay was fond of pointing out that, 'In the last century we gave Quin, Macklin, Barry and Peg Woffington, Mossop and Sheridan (father and son) to the English stage. What has become of our histrionic ability? Is it that we lack the perseverance necessary?' [29]

There was, of course, still professional Irish acting and entertaining. Actors such as Chalmers Mackay, Frank Breen and Frank Dalton achieved some professional success, although none became widely known outside of Ireland. Mainly, the Irish professional actor played in Boucicault or imitations of Boucicault, and so offered nothing new to the development of an indigenously Irish style of acting. Mr. and Mrs. McHardy Flint conducted classes in acting in Dublin, and occasionally gave recitals which might include scenes from Shakespeare or the eighteenth century comic dramatists. Percy French could often be seen in his medley of songs, comic monologues and lightning sketches.

Frank Fay's brother, W. G., had a good deal of experience in fit-up companies. He toured Ireland and England with J. W. Lacy's Company, H. E. Bailey's Comedy Company, Lloyd's Mexican Circus, and even with what was probably the first production in Ireland of *Uncle Tom's Cabin* in a company headed by an American Negro actor, R. B. Lewis. Both the Fay brothers were hopelessly stagestruck, and from 1891 to 1903 they played in and around Dublin with their own amateur company, which was first called the Ormond Dramatic Society, and later W. G. Fay's Comedy Combination or W. G. Fay's Celebrated Variety Group. Some of the actors attracted to the group, such as Dudley Digges and Sara Allgood, were later to become famous, and of course several of them formed the nucleus of the Irish National Theatre Society.

In 1899 W. G. Fay had returned from his wanderings and taken a job as an electrician, and Frank was secretary to a firm of

21

accountants, but their main energies were devoted to the production of plays in the evening. As W. G. Fay remarked, 'As we never put on any plays that took a full evening to perform, it was possible to have always on hand a programme of short plays, which demanded a minimum of rehearsal and gave us a reasonable chance of replacing actors who moved on to other things or left the town.' [30] The plays were nothing remarkable — *Box and Cox, His Last Legs, Paddy Miles' Boy, That Rascal Pat, The Irish Tutor, The Secret, Who Speaks First?* — and the programmes were usually filled out by poems, songs and recitations.[31]

Despite almost thirteen or fourteen years of experience, the productions of the Fays' amateur group should not be overestimated. As late as 3 December 1897, Joseph Holloway could view one of their performances and remark:

> The Ormond Dramatic Society gave a triple bill and concert in the Molesworth Hall before a large and friendly audience. The Society had a shot at Buckstone's comic drama, *A Rough Diamond*, and failed to score. Mr. C. William Crowe's "Sir William Evergreen" was chiefly noted for the vagaries of his moustache. Miss E. Knowles put on an antic disposition as "Margery", the untutored country lass who weds above her station, and everyone saw that she did. Her dialect was a mixture of Dublin accent and cold in the head. Mr. Frank Evelyn [F. J. Fay] was a colourless "Lord Plato" (his face, though, had on a liberal supply of colour). The one-act pieces, *The Limerick Boy* and *Advice Gratis*, were also played, but I had enough, thank you, for one evening.[32]

\*     \*     \*

Despite the literary revival, a good deal of the original writing in Ireland continued for several years yet to imitate English models. Much of the popular fiction was a romantic or a melodramatic treatment of the English upper class. It is scarcely an exaggeration to say that, in such popular journals as *The Weekly Freeman* and *The Weekly Independent*, there were just two types of illustration for stories and serials. One type showed a moustachioed gentleman in evening dress either plaintively kneeling at the feet or deferentially bending over the hand of an imposing and rather large

22

maiden. The second type showed one moustachioed gentleman threatening to stab, shoot, or push over a cliff another moustachioed gentleman. George Fitzmaurice, who began his brilliant career with a series of comic stories of Irish life in these journals remarked satirically in one of his stories that the heroine

> from being an occasional purchaser had developed into a regular weekly reader of the *Family Speaker*, a periodical whose four serials were always written in the most highflown language, though now and then a little obscure in meaning. The contents were invariably devoted to depicting life in aristocratic circles, and it was an odd hero who was not a duke, a marquis, an earl, or at the very least a mere ordinary lord. The heroines in like manner were mostly "my ladys" or misses of high degree, and if a plebeian was now and then thrown in for the sake of contrast she was bound to change her state in due time by hooking a lord.[33]

What little dramatic writing there was also tended to be conventional imitation of English models. For instance, Mary Costello, a prolific writer of popular fiction, published in a woman's magazine, *The Lady of the House*, in 1893 and 1894 a play in two scenes called *The Tragedy of a Simple Soul*. Its nature may be inferred from its principal characters: the Hon. Edgar Haldane, Captain, Knightstream Guards; Miss Constance Pennefather and Miss Edith Pennefather; and Miss Nancy Hart, daughter of a bankrupt sporting squire. In the same magazine for the Christmas issue of 1900, Miss Costello published another short play called *A Daughter to Marry*. The characters included the Marquise De Montliva, who is described as an American heiress; Mrs. Harry B. Vandenhoff, her cousin; Claire De Montliva, her stepdaughter, described as a Convent Ingenue; and Captain Bodin, who wears a French uniform of the Line and has a deep sabre cut from eye to chin. The nature of the play may be inferred from the following sample of dialogue:

CLAIRE     [*Sweeping past*]: At last you realise my sentiments, Monsieur. [*At door*] Your conduct inspires me with detestation. [*Exit*]

CAPTAIN BODIN     [*In a fury*]: Criée nom d'un nom! What does it mean — this insult, this infamy? [*Pacing*

23

*stage*] If she were a man, a man! [*Gripping his sword*] How her eyes blazed, her voice quivered with contempt![34]

This, then, was the theatrical and literary background of Dublin in the year 1899. It was time for a new inspiration.

\* \* \*

The idea of a literary theatre for Dublin originated with W. B. Yeats, and originally seemed a most incongruous notion. As George Moore put it, when Yeats and Edward Martyn first spoke to him of the project, 'to give a Literary Theatre to Dublin seemed to me like giving a mule a holiday. . . .'[35]

Yeats in the 1890's was an increasingly appreciated young poet who had always been interested in the theatre. Indeed, much of his juvenilia had been plays, and in an article published late in his life he wrote that he used to read his early dramatic poems to a school friend, Charles Johnston. 'I recall three plays,' he wrote, 'not of any merit, one vaguely Elizabethan, its scene a German forest, one an imitation of Shelley, its scene a crater in the moon, one of somebody's translation from the Sanscrit, its scene an Indian temple.'[36]

One of Yeats' very first published pieces was *The Island of Statues*, 'an Arcadian Faery Tale — in Two Acts', which was published in *The Dublin University Review* in the number of April-July, 1885. The same magazine published in its September, 1885, number *The Seeker*, 'a Dramatic Poem — in Two Scenes', and in the June, 1886, number *Mosada*, a dramatic poem. The last play, published separately later in the year, was Yeats's first book, and all three of these early pieces, with one other slight dramatic work, were included in Yeats's second book, *The Wanderings of Oisin*, published in 1889.

Yeats's first active experience of the stage came five years later when his play *The Land of Heart's Desire* was produced on 29 March 1894, at the Avenue Theatre, London. Florence Farr, a friend of his and an amateur actress of note, had, with financial backing from Miss A. E. F. Horniman, leased the theatre for a short season of plays, and Yeats's piece was a curtain raiser first to John Todhunter's *A Comedy of Sighs* and then to Bernard

Shaw's *Arms and the Man*. Yeats's biographer, Joseph Hone, described the first night as 'a complete disaster', but also remarked that, 'Yeats was in the theatre almost every night for several weeks, noting in the light of the performances the changes he might make in the monosyllabic verse, in which his interpreters were ill at ease.' [37]

In a letter describing the productions to John O'Leary, the old Fenian, Yeats wrote, 'The whole venture will be history anyway for it is the first contest between the old commercial school of theatrical folk and the new artistic school.' [38]

The idea of a literary theatre for Dublin now strongly began to take shape in Yeats's mind, and in 1897 he discussed the matter first with Lady Augusta Gregory and then with Edward Martyn. Lady Gregory and Martyn were near neighbours in the West of Ireland, and Martyn, a rich Catholic landlord, had already written two plays which had been offered unsuccessfully to an English actor-manager. Lady Gregory, the widow of an ex-Governor of Ceylon, had edited her husband's autobiography and was eager to help in the Literary Revival. The immediate result of their conversations was a letter signed by the three of them and sent to various prominent Irishmen. Part of it was quoted in Lady Gregory's *Our Irish Theatre*:

> We propose to have performed in Dublin, in the spring of every year certain Celtic and Irish plays, which whatever be their degree of excellence will be written with a high ambition, and so to build up a Celtic and Irish school of dramatic literature. We hope to find in Ireland an uncorrupted and imaginative audience trained to listen by its passion for oratory, and believe that our desire to bring upon the stage the deeper thoughts and emotions of Ireland will ensure for us a tolerant welcome, and that freedom to experiment which is not found in theatres of England, and without which no new movement in art or literature can succeed. We will show that Ireland is not the home of buffoonery and of easy sentiment, as it has been represented, but the home of an ancient idealism.[39]

The intention of the letter was to raise a guarantee of £300 for the production of plays in Dublin in the spring of the next three years. According to Lady Gregory, the response to the letter varied considerably, but the real setback was that the patent theatres in Dublin were too expensive, and that an old law prohibited theatrical performances for money in buildings not licensed for dramatic performance. However, with the help of W. E. H. Lecky and other Irish Members of Parliament, Yeats, Martyn and Lady Gregory succeeded in getting the law amended. Then Martyn applied to the Dublin Town Clerk for permission to give performances in May, 1899. To forestall opposition from the established theatres, Martyn emphasized the non-commercial nature of the plays to be presented.

> The plays proposed to be acted are of a more literary nature than are usually acted in theatres, and are not expected to appeal to a popular audience. . . . There are two plays proposed to be acted, namely a play by Mr. W. B. Yeats called *The Countess Cathleen*, and a play by Mr. Edward Martyn called *The Heather Field*, both being exemplifications of Irish life, and copies of the plays, which are published works, can, if desired, be submitted to you or to any person named on behalf of the Council. Also it is possible that there may be a short dialogue in the Irish language.[40]

That accomplished, Yeats and his friends turned their attention to publicizing their venture and to the practical problems of hiring a hall, contracting actors, and conducting rehearsals. During this time, Æ (George W. Russell) wrote to Martyn, giving an imaginative suggestion for set design. Although he claimed to 'know nothing about stage mechanism', he proposed:

> The scene painting must be a large item in the expense of production. . . . Would it not be possible to get over this difficulty by the use of coloured photos of scenery, the castles at Gort, etc. used as magic lantern slides and flung from behind a thin hanging? It would be infinitely more illusive in its effect than any painting. The same could be done for most of the scenes in Yeats's *Countess Cathleen*. In fact the idea seems so simple that I imagine it must have been used already. I think it would be worth while thinking it over anyhow. If not capable of use just now, the idea may be of value at another time. It would be also very easy to change one scene to another. If you thought it worth while to ascertain the pos-

26

sibility of this, I imagine it would be well to write to some of the popular entertainers who use limelight views or the instrument makers. They would know to what extent the views could be enlarged.[41]

It was apparently about this time that Yeats and Martyn first discussed the project with George Moore, a close friend of Martyn and an expatriate Irish landlord, who was now widely touted as 'the English Zola' for his excellent realistic novels such as *Esther Waters*. In his droll three-volume reminiscence, *Hail and Farewell*, Moore gives probably only a semi-accurate account of this meeting and of the subsequent ineptitudes of Yeats, Martyn and Florence Farr at rehearsal. The entire tone of this section of *Hail and Farewell* is wittily condescending, and describes how the expert, Moore, takes pity on the follies of the feckless amateurs.

It is true that Moore did have some practical experience of the stage. He was a frequent tilter at the London critics and had early advocated the establishment in London of an equivalent of Antoine's Théâtre Libre. He was on the committee of J. T. Grein's Independent Theatre, an historic group which, whatever its artistic shortcomings, did champion Ibsen and did give to Bernard Shaw his first production. In response to a challenge by a popular boulevard dramatist, G. R. Sims, Moore polished up an earlier rejected play, *The Strike at Arlingford*, and it was presented by the Independent Theatre on 21 February 1893. One typical contemporary review remarked, 'With much to be commended in Mr. Moore's play, there is much to be deplored.' What was to be deplored was that:

. . . the central theme is tamely handled. There is no fight between the women — typical of Capital and Labour — for the omnipotent Reid. Lady Anne gets him for the asking. The momentous nature of the struggle was never felt. The scent of the strikers was never got over the footlights. The play did not palpitate as it should with the passions of the starving miners. Reid reflected nothing but himself. Lady Anne seemed fighting for no stake in particular. Worst of all, the people expressed themselves in language over which lay the trail of the literary man. Nothing destroys the sense of reality like high falutin' phrases, and in *The Strike* Mr. Moore's heroine being a little

27

upset is "distraught", his hero's thoughts "throng his brain in giddy exultation", and so on — the result being that half the house comes to the conclusion that not one of the characters, save the Baron, has anything in his veins but midnight oil and ink.[42]

J. T. Grein himself thought that the play was a *succès d'estime* which failed largely because the leading actors were inadequate. The result, he wrote years later, was 'totally unmagnetic'.[43] Actually, although the review quoted above is generally just in its disparagements, the language was less stiff than Moore's later *The Bending of the Bough*. And although the play is now dated, and was even in 1893 a far cry from Ibsen or Shaw, it was better than, say, Henry James' attempts at dramatic writing. One might conclude that, while Moore did have a greater knowledge of the stage than either Yeats or Martyn, he was far from being the maestro that *Hail and Farewell* suggests.

*    *    *

Florence Farr, who began the rehearsals, was an amateur actress who had the distinction of having love affairs with both G. B. Shaw and W. B. Yeats. 'She attached,' Shaw remarked, 'no more importance to what you call love affairs than Casanova or Frank Harris; and she was too good-natured to refuse anything to anyone she really liked.' The daughter of a well-known sanitary reformer, she was in many ways an English prototype of the New Woman, and she was potentially a fine actress. She made a great impression in an early production of Ibsen's *Rosmersholm*, and she was the original Blanche Sartorius of Shaw's *Widowers' Houses*. With backing from Miss Horniman, as has been mentioned, she produced for the first time, in 1894, Yeats's *The Land of Heart's Desire*, Shaw's *Arms and the Man*, and Todhunter's *A Comedy of Sighs*. Her involvement with Yeats in the Irish Literary Theatre led to her chanting poetry to the accompaniment of the psaltery as an illustration of Yeats's theories of poetic speaking. Yeats regarded her as 'an almost perfect poetic actress' who possessed a beautiful voice. St. John Ervine more caustically remarked that she chanted 'poetry in a rasping manner while she plucked a stringed instrument whose single merit was that it had only one string which was easily broken. This chanting was called 'cantilating', and was a melancholy noise.' Shaw regarded cantilating as nothing at all new:

> Yeats thinks so only because he does not go to church. Half the curates in the kingdom cantilate like mad all the time. Toastmasters cantilate. Public speakers who have nothing to say cantilate. . . . Sarah Bernhardt's abominable "golden voice", which has always made me sick, is cantilation, or, to to use the customary word, intoning. It is no use for Yeats to try to make a distinction: there is no distinction, no novelty, no nothing but nonsense.[44]

According to Shaw, Florence Farr's real difficulty was that she would never exert herself sufficiently to learn her craft. He must probably be considered on these matters a better judge than Yeats, and his letters to Miss Farr are full of exhortation to work at the technique of acting rather than to rely on the inspiration of the moment. He advised her, for instance, to study phonetics under Henry Salt. 'I have never been able to knock enough articulation into you, though you are much better than you were,' he wrote.

> You still think of how you are doing your recitations instead of what you are saying. The final consonant withers, and the light of the meaning goes out every now and then as you attend to your psaltery instead of to your business. At which moments I feel moved to throw things at you. And Yeats is heaping fresh artificialities and irrelevances and distractions and impertinances on you instead of sternly nailing you to the simple point of conveying the meaning and feeling of the author.[45]

The following account by George Moore of the rehearsal of *The Countess Cathleen* seems to make the same point, that Miss Farr was an attractive amateur dazzled by the glamour of art and bored by the labour necessary to achieve it. He and Yeats, he writes:

> . . . sat down together to listen to *The Countess Cathleen*, rehearsed by the lady who had put her psaltery aside and was going about with a reticule on her arm, rummaging in it from time to time for certain memoranda, which when found seemed only to deepen her difficulty. Her stage-management was all right in her notes, Yeats informed me:

"But she can't transfer it from paper to the stage," he said, without appearing in the least to wish that the stage-management of his play should be taken from her. At that moment the voice of the experienced actress [May Whitty] asking the poor lady how she was to get up the stage drew my attention from Yeats to the reticule, which was searched unsuccessfully for a satisfactory answer. The experienced actress walked up the stage and stood there looking contemptuously at Miss Vernon [Moore's name for Miss Farr], who laid herself down on the floor and began speaking through the chinks. Her dramatic intention was so obscure that perforce I had to ask her what it was, and learned from her that she was evoking hell.

"But the audience will think you are trying to catch cockroaches." [46]

*     *     *

There were other difficulties than those of casting and rehearsing. Edward Martyn, who had guaranteed the money for the production, began to worry about the orthodoxy of *The Countess Cathleen*, and submitted it to a clerical friend who denounced it. For a time it seemed as if Martyn might withdraw his support, but Yeats submitted the play to two other clergymen and received approving opinions, which helped to calm Martyn's fears. The only person who seemed disappointed by this happy outcome was George Moore, who lost the opportunity to write an essay on Edward Martyn and his Soul. Yeats wrote to Lady Gregory that Moore said, 'It was the best opportunity I ever had. What a sensation it would have made! Nobody has ever written that way about his most intimate friend. What a chance! It would have been heard of everywhere.' [47]

Reading *The Countess Cathleen* today, one finds it difficult to understand its controversial nature. However, the reasons for the opposition to the play were basically the same as those impelling the better-known later controversies surrounding Synge's *The Playboy of the Western World* and O'Casey's *The Plough and the Stars*. The reasons are probably three. Ireland was, and to some extent still is, in the grip of a hyper-sensitive, hyper-puritanical public morality, that was quick to sense slights, whether intentional or not and whether blatant or obscure, against religion and a rather narrow morality. Second, this tender moral sensitivity was paralleled by a

30

patriotic sensitivity that was just as quick to take offence, and whose tenderness had no doubt been exacerbated by the political futilities since the Parnell split. Third, there was an element of strictly personal rancour, which in this case was directed against Yeats by an old political opponent, F. Hugh O'Donnell, who had been expelled years earlier from the Irish Party by Parnell. Yeats's biographer, Hone, describes O'Donnell as 'a very clever man but half mad from vanity, long political contention and the strain of impecuniosity.' [48]

O'Donnell published a vindictive attack against the play in *The Freeman's Journal*, and when a second letter on the subject was refused publication he published both letters together in a pamphlet called *Souls for Gold*. The pamphlet was distributed in letter-boxes all over Dublin, and the journalistic outcry became so strident that Cardinal Logue, the Primate of Ireland, wrote a letter to the press stating that if Yeats's play was as O'Donnell had represented it no Catholic should attend a performance. The recently re-assured Edward Martyn for once behaved unpredictably and was not influenced by the cardinal's statement, for the cardinal admitted in his letter that he had not read the play.

O'Donnell's pamphlet is frequently referred to but seldom quoted, and indeed it is not worth quoting in full. However, some few excerpts will serve to indicate the nature and tone of the attack:

In this "Celtic drama" I saw at once many reasons why it continues to lie unrepresented, but not a single reason why it should be called Celtic. . . .

Out of all the mass of our national traditions it is precisely the baseness which is utterly alien to all our national traditions, the barter of Faith for Gold, which Mr. W. B. Yeats selects as the fundamental idea of his Celtic drama! . . .

I shall cite but two specimens out of this "Celtic Drama" at present, the one where Celtic peasant, Shemus Rhua, kicks the shrine of the Blessed Virgin to pieces, and the one where the Demon, disguised as an Irish pig, hunts down and slays "Father John the Priest" while reading his breviary, and sticks his soul into his black bag. I crave the pardon of my readers, Catholic or Protestant, for offending their sight with such grotesque impiety. . . .

Good old Father John, in spite of his prayers and his

breviary, killed by the devil in the shape of a brown pig! How Irish! How exquisitely Celtic!

In another scene Mr. W. B. Yeats introduces a Celtic peasant woman who is false to her marriage vows. How very Irish that is too. In another scene there are a pair of Celtic peasants who are thieves, and particularly mean thieves. Is that Irish likewise? . . . Mr. W. B. Yeats seems to see nothing in the Ireland of old days but an unmanly, an impious and renegade people, crouched in degraded awe before demons, and goblins, and sprites, and sowlths, and thivishes, — just like a sordid tribe of black devil-worshippers and fetish-worshippers on the Congo or the Niger. . . .

He has no right to outrage reason and conscience alike by bringing his degraded idiots to receive the kiss of the Mother of God. . . .

Mr. W. B. Yeats is a literary artist. He has found for his English readers what is described as a new vein of literary emotion. The transfusion of what is alleged to be the spirit of the Celtic past into modern English is hailed as quite an agreeable diversification of the Stage Irishman dear to the London caricaturist. Instead of Donnybrook and Ballyhooley, or rather by the side of these types, and, as it were, suggesting their development, the genial Anglo-Saxon is asked to regard the fine old Celtic peasant of Ireland's Golden Age, sunk in animal savagery, destitute of animal courage, mixing up in loathsome promiscuity the holiest name of the Christian Sanctuary with the gibbering ghoul-and-fetish worship of a Congo negro, selling his soul for a bellyful, yelling alternate invocations to the Prince of Darkness and the Virgin Mary. Surely this is a dainty dish to set before our sister England. . . .

What hideous silliness, and what hideous profanity! . . . But the utter idiotcy [sic] of it all puts even the impiety in the shade. I will not ask if Mr. W. B. Yeats has any sense of reverence. But has he any good taste, any sense of the becoming and the decent? . . . What is the meaning of this rubbish? How is it to help the national cause? How is it to help any cause at all? . . . There is no reason for tolerating the preposterous absurdity . . . which would degrade Ancient Ireland into this sort of witch's cavern of ghouls and vampires, and abject men and women, and blaspheming shapes from hell. . . .[49]

32

This was silly, but the bluster, the repetitions, and the judicious selection of certain passages out of context all helped to incite an hysterical reaction, that made the opening of the Irish Literary Theatre seem at the time dangerous and problematical.

*   *   *

Nevertheless, the project was publicly launched in early January by a letter from Yeats, which was published in *The Freeman's Journal*.[50] In it, he remarked that he and some friends had hoped a year or so earlier to found an Irish Literary Theatre, 'to do for Irish dramatic literature . . . what the Théâtre Libre and the Théâtre de L'Oeuvre have done for French dramatic literature.' He recounted their hopes to take a theatre or hall for a few days each spring, and also the difficulties they had had in getting the law changed so that they would be able to perform. Now the law had been changed, and so in May two plays would be presented — Martyn's *The Heather Field* and his own *The Countess Cathleen*. He also mentioned that Standish O'Grady, George Moore, and Miss Fiona MacLeod[51] had become interested in writing plays for the theatre in subsequent years. Finally, he listed the names of some of the more impressive guarantors for the theatre, and remarked that the National Literary Society was also assisting with the project.

On 16 January there was a meeting of the National Literary Society, and the following is an extract from the Minutes:

> Mr. W. B. Yeats and Mr. Edward Martyn being in attendance, by arrangement, the project of an "Irish Literary Theatre" was discussed. Mr. Yeats stated that he wished the project developed and carried out under the auspices of the National Literary Society. After a long discussion the following three resolutions were drafted: —
>
> I. "That this Council do hereby appoint a Sub-Committee to be called 'The Irish Literary Theatre Committee' consisting of Dr. George Sigerson, F.R.U.I., W. A. Henderson, W. B. Yeats, Edward Martyn, D.L., and Mrs. George Coffey."
>
> II. "That said Committee have power to co-opt additional members, and to take all steps in furtherance of the project of

'The Irish Literary Theatre' provided that they shall not subject the Council to any liabilities without first obtaining the express sanction of this Council by resolution."

III. "That in the event of any surplus of receipts over expenditure accruing from the performances, the amount shall be retained by the National Literary Society, and reserved for the promotion of the objects of the Irish Literary Theatre."

Mr. Joseph Holloway moved and Miss Edith Oldham seconded the adoption separately of these resolutions, which were passed unanimously.

Mr. Martyn voluntarily handed in the following guarantee to be inserted in the Minutes.

"To the President and Council of the National Literary Society. Gentlemen,

"I hereby undertake to hold you harmless and free from any financial liability in connection with the promotion of the Irish Literary Theatre.

(Signed) EDWARD MARTYN." [52]

Another method of arousing interest in the performances was the publication in May of the magazine *Beltaine*, edited by Yeats. It contained a list of the guarantors for the performances; Lionel Johnson's Prologue to *The Countess Cathleen*, which was spoken on the evening of production by Dorothy Paget; Johnson's short essay on the play; George Moore's introduction to *The Heather Field*, reprinted from the published book; a factual account of the rise of Ibsen and Bjornson by C. H. Herford, reprinted from *The Daily Express*; and an article entitled 'The Theatre' by Yeats, which was reprinted from *The Dome*, and later included in *Ideas of Good and Evil*; and a group of unreprinted paragraphs on various topics by Yeats, gathered under the title of "Plans and Methods". After a brief mention of the contemporary drama of Norway and the efforts of the Théâtre Libre in Paris and the Independent Theatre in London, Yeats continued:

The Irish Literary Theatre will attempt to do in Dublin something of what has been done in London and Paris; and, if it has even a small welcome, it will produce, somewhere about the old festival of Beltaine, at the beginning of every spring, a play founded upon an Irish subject. The plays will differ from those produced by associations of men of letters in London and in Paris, because times have changed, and because the intellect of Ireland is romantic and spiritual rather than scientific and analytical, but they will have as little of a commercial ambition. Their writers will appeal to that limited public which gives understanding, and not to that unlimited public which gives wealth; and if they interest those among their audience who keep in their memories the songs of Callanan and Walsh, or old Irish legends, or who love the good books of any country, they will not mind greatly if others are bored.[53]

Then, after mentioning that the Committee of the theatre was considering a production of Denis Florence MacCarthy's translation of Calderon's *St. Patrick's Purgatory* for 1900, and that Fiona Macleod, Standish O'Grady and others had promised plays, he briefly discussed the style of acting and speech in the two plays about to be produced:

In a play like Mr. Martyn's, where everything is subordinate to the central idea, and the dialogues as much like the dialogues of daily life as possible, the slightest exaggeration of detail, or effort to make points where points were not intended, becomes an insincerity. An endeavour has therefore been made to have it acted as simply and quietly as possible. The chief endeavour with Mr. Yeats's play has been to get it spoken with some sense of rhythm.

\* \* \*

The two lyrics, which we print on a later page, are not sung, but spoken, or rather chanted, to music, as the old poems were probably chanted by bards and rhapsodists. Even when the words of a song, sung in the ordinary way, are heard at all, their own proper rhythm and emphasis are lost, or partly lost, in the rhythm and emphasis of the music. A lyric meaning, and its rhythm so become indissoluble in the memory. The speaking of words, whether to music or not, is, however, so

35

perfectly among the lost arts that it will take a long time before our actors, no matter how willing, will be able to forget the ordinary methods of the stage or to perfect a new method.

\*　　\*　　\*

Mr. Johnson, in the interpretative argument which he has written for *The Countess Cathleen*, places the events it describes in the sixteenth century. So Mr. Yeats originally wrote, but he has since written that he tried to suggest throughout the play that period, made out of many periods, in which the events in the folk-tales have happened. The play is not historic, but symbolic, and has as little to do with any definite place and time as an *auto* by Calderon. One should look for the Countess Cathleen and the peasants and the demons not in history, but, as Mr. Johnson has done, in one's own heart; and such costumes and scenery have been selected as will preserve the indefinite.[54]

As the May performances approached, the excitement of those involved in the production increased. James H. Cousins recalled an amusing encounter with Moore just days before the opening performance:

Prior to the unique event, which everyone knew was going to make history, a send-off was given in a reception at which all the brainy world was present, and some of the possibilities, including myself. Before the speeches there was an informal movement in which everybody met everybody else. I noticed a quaint figure of a man dawdling about passing a remark to this one and that. He struck me as particular, though I could not say why. He was notably well-dressed, carried himself with ease, but his pasty face and vague eyes, and particularly his straw-coloured hair that looked as if it had been pitchforked on for the occasion, seemed a contradiction to his air of distinction. I asked an acquaintance who the comedian was, and learned that he was George Moore, the novelist who was more famous than some people thought he ought to be. A few minutes later I was making some notes in a pocket book relative to the occasion. To my surprise the novelist came over

36

to me and remarked on the importance of the occasion. "Only a great poet," he said, "would have brought me from London." The reference, I knew, was to Yeats, and I warmed to the novelist for his generosity to a poet. I pondered the phenomenon of so famous a person wasting an opinion on me — and then had a nasty glimmer of an idea that he had mistaken me for a pressman.[55]

Some newspapers saw the new theatre group's potential for offering an alternative to the imported plays then filling the stages. On the Saturday preceding the opening performance, *The Daily Express*, which criticized Yeats's play as un-Irish, nevertheless welcomed the coming productions:

> The Irish Literary Theatre is making a bold effort at reform in a direction where reform is absolutely necessary, and where, if it can be effected, its results will make for immediate and incalculable good. We do not suppose that there was ever any period when the theatre was a greater national influence than it is today in Great Britain and Ireland, or when that influence was more widely perverted and abused. The evil shows itself in a thousand ways, but may always be traced to one cause — the cause which the Irish Literary Theatre seeks to eliminate by the encouragement of an example which has every moral and spiritual claim upon success. Just two hundred years ago Dr. Jeremy Collier published his scathing attack upon the "Immorality and Profaneness of the English Stage", and under that just condemnation the greatest of an age of great playwrights blushed and were silent. Today the same immorality and profaneness — in shapes just as brutal and far more insidious — are flaunted before the eyes and minds of a dramatic public which has a hundred votaries for every one that laughed at *The Country Wife*, or *The Beaux' Stratagem*. And yet the plays at which Collier launched his indignant satire were at least redeemed by the wit and learning of Congreve and Wycherley and Farquhar. The theatre of today has not even this scant excuse to offer for its universal degradation and immorality. Those who are responsible for the production of our modern plays have to make their appeal to a public which a continuous process of vulgarisation has re-

duced to such a level that it no longer required that its vicious pabulum should be dressed with the sauce of intellect or wit. . . . That *The Countess Cathleen* and *The Heather Field* strike an Irish note and aim at a national idea gives them an intimate claim upon Irish support, but their first claim is that they appeal to the intellect and the spirit, and forsake the old familiar appeal to the senses. Whether they be successful acting plays or not is a question which will be decided next week. Whatever way that question be decided it does not affect the purpose of a movement whose object is to furnish an opportunity of submitting to the test of actual performance, year after year, plays which in the present state of public taste, commercial managers could not afford to put on the stage. It is the duty, as we hope it will be the pleasure, of every Irishman to encourage and promote by every means in his power a movement so necessary, so practical, and in its essence so consonant with the best interests of morality and education.[56]

But on the same day, *The Daily Nation*, which was to lead the attack on *The Countess Cathleen*, printed the following leading article:

As may have been seen by a reference to our advertising columns, *The Countess Cathleen*, an "Irish Literary Drama", by Mr. W. B. Yeats, is to be performed, for the first time, in Dublin, on Monday next, the 8th of May. We accepted the advertisement in ignorance of the nature of the drama. Now that we have read it, we wish to protest in the names of morality and religion, and Irish nationality, against its performance. And we hope very earnestly that . . . those Irish Catholics, who may form a portion of the audience, will so give expression to their disapproval as to effectually discourage any further ventures of a similar kind. . . .

The production of such a play as *The Countess Cathleen*, on the occasion of the inauguration of what was intended to be a distinctively national institution, is nothing short of an outrage. The absolute contempt which has been displayed by the promoters and managers of the Irish Literary Theatre for the discrimination, good taste, and self-respect of the citizens of Dublin, is insulting to the last degree. . . . We trust, as we have already said, that those who are responsible for a gross and scandalous breach of faith with the public of this country, will receive their deserts on Monday night in the practical evidence afforded them that the people of the Catholic capital of Catholic Ireland cannot be subjected to affront with impunity.[57]

Quite clearly, this was incitement to riot.

On Monday, 8 May, at the Antient Concert Rooms, the Irish Literary Theatre gave its first performance of Yeats's *The Countess Cathleen*.[58] No matter how destructive the advance comments had been, they served as free publicity for the performances. As James Cousins recalled,

> The coming performances suddenly became a matter of burning national interest; not, however, because of a realisation of the significance of the birth of Irish drama, but because an Irish critic resident outside Ireland had discovered that an incident in *Countess Cathleen* was "an outrage on Catholic sentiment". The Irish Cardinal banned the play without reading it. Charges in the press and replies by the author did what dignified advertising could not do: the house was filled with partizans of both the critics and the author. The offending incident (a famine-demented peasant in a past era kicking a holy shrine to pieces in revulsion against "God and the Mother of God") had been deleted, but it carried a wake of waves in the text, and as each of these appeared, it was received with a storm of hisses by a group of young men who had been instructed by a morning paper to chase the play off the stage. But an answer to the protests broke from another group of young men who, from the point of view of literature or drama would hardly have noticed the hissed lines, but who began to see in them some hidden excellence that stimulated loud applause. In the duel of hiss and cheer, cheer won. I can give my word as to the victory, for I was one of the victors, and possessed as spoils of conquest a hat with a broken rim through which I had clenched my fingers when waving it in wild applause at nothing in the play but something in the rising spirit of the Arts in Ireland as against the spirit of obscurantism and dishonest censorship. From the point of view of publicity the occasion was a howling success.[59]

39

Joseph Holloway who was, of course, present noted an 'organised claque of about twenty brainless, beardless, idiotic-looking youths [who] did all they knew to interfere with the progress of the play by their meaningless automatic hissing and senseless comments.... Their 'poor spite' was completely frustrated by enthusiastic applause which drowned their empty-headed expressions of dissension.' [60] Seumas O'Sullivan was also there, and years later wrote:

> I was, by chance, in the gallery, and at the fall of the curtain a storm of booing and hissing broke out around the seats in which I and a few enthusiasts were attempting to express our appreciation of the magnificent performance. (I can never forget the exquisite playing and speaking of Florence Farr, who played the part of Aileel, the bard.) But close to me, at the time unknown to me, was a lad who vigorously contributed his share to the applause. It was James Joyce.[61]

T. W. Rolleston in a defence of the demonstration wrote:

> It happens that I was sitting close to the "dozen disorderly boys".... It appeared to me that their expressions of disapproval were not exactly "disorderly".... They expressed their sentiments with vigour, but in a perfectly gentlemanlike manner. They flung no insults at the author or the company; they made no attempt to seriously interfere with the performance, and they applauded as vigorously as anyone, nay, they even led the applause at some of the fine and touching passages in the play.... The impression left on my mind by the whole affair was that a representative Dublin audience had splendidly vindicated, in the teeth of bitter prejudice and hostility, an author's right to a fair hearing for his work, and also that the hostile element in the audience had expressed itself in a manner, which, if one is permitted to be hostile at all, had no trace of malice or stupid violence.[62]

On 9 May *The Freeman's Journal* gave an approving if sententious summation:

> *The Countess Cathleen* has been subjected to a good deal of criticism on moral grounds because of the sentiments to which

40

the evil characters give expression, as if the bad could be otherwise than evil. But there is no confusion of the moral standards in the play, no calling of bad good and of good bad, as has been recently the fashion in several really demoralising plays produced in Dublin. In reality it is a spirit-drama of the "Faust" type, but with a motive far removed from the essentially sensual motive of that much played theme. The presentation of such a play under the conditions described must, of course, make even a greater innovation on the ordinary playgoer's expectations and make success all the more difficult. Themes of the kind have hitherto been presented to the accompaniment of trembling harmonies and Wagnerian discords. To present them in their literary simplicity is to travel very far indeed from the theatrical conventions of the hour. Under the circumstances the promoters of the Irish Literary Theatre must have had their expectations fulfilled last evening. An audience of between four and five hundred assembled to witness the first production of *The Countess Cathleen*. A small knot of less than a dozen disorderly boys, who evidently mistook the whole moral significance of the play, cast ridicule upon themselves by hissing the demons under the impression that they were hissing the poet. But the audience, representative of every section of educated opinion in Dublin, was most enthusiastic, recalling the actors and the author again and again and cheering loudly.[63]

But *The Daily Express* found less to applaud in the play. This hissing was directed against expressions which were 'not, in our opinion, entirely above criticism from certain points of view'. Indeed, not only were the protests defensible, but Yeats's play itself was not dramatically effective — a criticism, incidentally, to be levelled at many of Yeats's plays in the ensuing years.

From the passages we have quoted its great poetic beauty will be seen, but poetic beauty is not the same as dramatic beauty, and we think it can hardly be denied that the problem of presenting an action on the stage in which the sequence of events shall at once satisfy the intellect as being natural and inevitable, and satisfy the imagination as forming an artistic

41

harmony, has not been fully solved. The demons have in them too much or too little power over material things; the Countess is ready to give up her soul for her people, but she never goes to the hut, close to her door, when they are thronging to sell, to entreat them to be mindful of their eternal weal. The personages and events are no doubt intended to be placed in an unreal mystical world, but they pass over the borderland now and then, and are either not real enough or not unreal enough to be fully accepted by the reader's imagination. Defects of this kind will occur to every reader and indicate a certain want of expression in dramatic composition — by far the hardest and also the noblest form of poetry — which will probably be largely remedied in Mr. Yeats's future work. We venture to think, however, as regards that work, that Mr. Yeats would do well to leave the presentation of the Irish peasantry and their religious atmosphere to those who know them intimately. Mr. Yeats is a king in fairyland — in the world of imaginative symbol and spiritual thought — but he does not know the Irish peasant and what he believes and feels, and the Irish peasantry in this play are, and always were, totally incapable of the acts and sayings attributed to them. We do not say that they are too good or too wise or too religious, but merely that their minds are not made that way. The conception that "God and the Mother of God have dropped asleep" or the central conception of the excessive value of a beautiful Countess's soul . . . are ideals absolutely foreign to anything that can be called Irish in character and spiritual outlook. That genuine dramatic faculty is shown in the play is undeniable, but to write a perfectly satisfactory stage drama Mr. Yeats needs training, experience, and knowledge of humanity in the concrete.[64]

The acting, particularly of May Whitty and of Florence Farr, was much admired, but no commentator gives a vivid or even particularly clear impression of how the actors looked, how they sounded, how they moved, or what they did. Apparently the production was not exactly a smoothly professional one, and its defects may have been somewhat glossed over in the generally enthusiastic response which the occasion evoked. Holloway, at any rate, did remark:

Much of the last act was spoiled by a creaky door, and the too liberal use of palpable tin-tray-created thunder claps. The staging was good if unpretentious, and the dresses excellent; and the piece went without a hitch, although the stage room was somewhat scanty.[65]

However, the honest lowbrow from *The Evening Herald* remarked, 'Indeed, the whole performance was weird.'

On 10 May *The Daily Nation* printed the following letter which it had solicited from Cardinal Logue:

> Dear Sir — You invite my opinion on the play of Mr. Yeats, *The Countess Cathleen*. All I know of the play is what I could gather from the extracts in Mr. O'Donnell's pamphlet and your paper. Judging by these extracts, I have no hesitation in saying that an Irish Catholic audience which could patiently sit out such a play must have sadly degenerated, both in religion and patriotism.
>
> As to the opinions said to have been given by Catholic divines, no doubt the authors of these opinions will undertake to justify them; but I should not like the task if it were mine.— I am, dear sir, yours faithfully,
>
> MICHAEL CARDINAL LOGUE[66]

On 11 May the *Independent* printed an outspoken letter from Frederick Ryan, who was in years to come to be an actor, writer and secretary for the Irish National Theatre Society.

> Sir — In view of the "set" which is being made in some quarters on Mr. W. B. Yeats's play, *The Countess Cathleen*, and the unblushing appeals to religious bigotry and intolerance which it has occasioned, it is necessary, I think, for those who still value mental freedom, to protest against the monstrous claim that is thereby set up. With Mr. Yeats's verse or Mr. Yeats's philosophy I am not now concerned. The thesis of his play may be approved or disapproved. But everyone who values intellectual liberty is concerned to claim for Mr. Yeats his right to express his thought. On that ground — whilst one can quite understand Mr. Yeats's difficulties — it is, I think, to be regretted that he should have adopted the line of defence

43

he did on Saturday. It is surely somewhat humiliating that a fine poet, as Mr. Yeats undoubtedly is, who sets himself to a serious and intellectual task, should feel obliged to go, cap in hand, as it were, to "two Catholic divines" before presenting his work to an audience of his countrymen. Let us get out of this stifling atmosphere of restriction and petty, insincere bigotry. Let us claim for Mr. Yeats — if he will not claim it for himself — his full right, in common with every other man's, to the free expression of his thought, even if fifty newspaper theologians denounced him, or a hundred "Catholic divines" howled their anathemas. The Irish Literary Theatre, and the movement with which it is connected, claims to foster intellectual life in Ireland. I would remark that this object would be better attained by taking the boldest and most impregnable position, than by pandering to, or even countenancing the ignorant prejudices of the least enlightened of our people. Surely, we have not got to the stage yet of bowing down before *The Daily Nation*, or taking our views from a prelate whose conception of public conduct is such as to enable him to denounce a work he has not read, on the strength of some distorted extracts. — Yours, etc.,

FREDERICK RYAN[67]

On 12 May the readers of *The Daily Nation* heard again from O'Donnell:

Dear Sir — There can be no doubt about it, there are two versions of the repulsive *Countess Cathleen*. Only in the one for his London public does Mr. W. B. Yeats set his new model Celtic peasant "to kick to pieces" the shrine of the Blessed Virgin. In the version for his Dublin admirers "the young bard" of West Britain has remembered that prudence is a virtue. But we are now entitled to inquire will Mr. W. B. Yeats place his London public also in possession of his cautious resolution? Though small, it should not be deceived by the fond imagination that W. B. Yeats achieved with impunity the glory of Cromwell.

I have also failed to perceive, even in the gurgling gush of the "Dull'un's Journal" and the "Rhodesian Dependent" that another Yeatsite showpiece, "The Slaying of Father John by

44

the Demon Swine", has been preserved to point the way to those moral and intellectual ideals which the Rhodesians tell us are yet in store for Papist Dublin.

I think that there is one matter, however, which can fully console all who strove to dyke back the flood of mawkish nastiness which was being let loose upon the country, and this is the high-minded witness to Irish honour and Irish Faith which, in noble contradistinction to a couple of Catholic reptile journals, was borne by such Protestant organs as *The Daily Express* and *The Irish Times*.

*The Daily Express's* rebuke of Mr. W. B. Yeats's anti-Irish blasphemies is none the less crushing because it strives to spare the silly offender. . . .

*The Irish Times*, while stating the dismal "failure" of the miserable "drama", takes occasion, in reference to Mr. W. B. Yeats's "ideal" of Souls for Gold, to declare with generous pride that the barter of spiritual life for physical advantage is simply abhorrent to "the history of Ireland" and of the entire "Celtic Nation".

Hurrah for the Irish Protestant who remains an Irishman!— I remain, dear sir, yours faithfully,

F. HUGH O'DONNELL[68]

And on 10 May a group of students at the Royal University in Dublin, not including James Joyce, submitted a letter to the editors of various newspapers protesting the performances of *The Countess Cathleen*. It concludes, 'we feel it our duty, in the name and for the honour of Dublin Catholic students of the Royal University, to protest against an art, even a dispassionate art, which offers as a type of our people a loathsome brood of apostates.' [69]

In general, however, the production was regarded as a vindication of Yeats and of the effort, and the production of Martyn's less esoteric *Heather Field* on the following evening was quite unmarred by hissing from the gallery. *The Freeman's Journal* reported:

The success which attended the experiment of establishing an Irish Literary Theatre when its inaugural play, *The Countess Cathleen* was produced on Monday, developed last night into something very nearly approaching a triumph when Mr. Edward Martyn's drama, *The Heather Field*, was put on the

45

boards. The audience was again a distinguished one, but not so large as on the previous occasion. On the other hand, however, there was no hostile element present, a circumstance which gave Mr. Martyn's play a great advantage over Mr. Yeats's, and allowed the story to be followed without interruption from the gradual awakening of interest in it to its tragic and beautiful conclusion. . . . Here . . . is a play that reveals a tragedy of social and domestic life although there is not the remotest suggestion in it from beginning to end of the disordered eroticism which is responsible for so many stage successes in London and Paris during recent years. . . .

No description of this moving and beautiful play can possibly convey any idea of its pathos and power. The drama reads well, but it plays superbly. And it was acted last night with a finish and completeness which no one could have looked for on so limited a stage. The Carden Tyrrell of Mr. Thomas Kingston was an interpretation which satisfied the artistic sense fully, and vividly realised the author's conception. . . . Altogether *The Heather Field* was a remarkable success. From first to last it was punctuated by the warmest applause, and at the end its author was called before the curtain and received with loud and long-continued cheering.[70]

*The Evening Herald* called the play 'A fine wholesome drama', while the *Independent* gushed that, 'It is impossible to speak in moderation of Mr. Edward Martyn's drama, *The Heather Field*, which was produced by the Irish Literary Theatre last night. The power, the beauty, and the excellence of Mr. Martyn's work took everyone by storm. . . .' *The Irish Times*, however, came closer to the evaluation which the play would probably receive today:

Now, so far as the every day play-goer is concerned, *The Heather Field* will scarcely excite anything like the feelings that it would seem to have produced in Mr. Moore; to many it may appeal as a deep analysis of human nature, as an effort to read into life as it exists round about us mystical and exalted readings, but to a man who goes to a play to be amused, instructed, or initiated into the workings of the mainsprings of human conduct, *The Heather Field* is little likely to be of any assistance. . . . Apart altogether from that, *The*

46

*Heather Field* is wearisome because it has no action worthy of the name; its dialogue is stilted; its characters are not very deftly drawn; and its reflection of Irish life is not very convincing. The cold methods of the Norwegian dramatists can never be applied with any truth to even the Irish landlord . . . without parodying the very essences of Irish life.[71]

Max Beerbohm, who had succeeded Bernard Shaw as drama critic of *The Saturday Review*, had attended the performances and also the congratulatory dinner which *The Daily Express* gave for the Literary Theatre on 11 May at the Shelbourne. One feels that he may have been somewhat carried away by the *bonhomie* of the occasion, for he remarked in his *Saturday Review* notice:

> Not long ago this play was published as a book, with a preface by Mr. George Moore, and was more or less vehemently disparaged by critics. Knowing that it was to be produced later in Dublin, and knowing how hard it is to dogmatise about a play till one sees it acted, I confined myself to a very mild disparagement of it. Now that I have seen it acted, I am sorry that I disparaged it at all. It turns out to be a very powerful play, indeed. For the benefit of my colleagues, I may add that it has achieved a really popular success in Dublin — a success which must be almost embarrassing to the founders of a Literary Theatre.[72]

When the play, with substantially the Dublin cast, was given one afternoon performance at Terry's Theatre in London on 6 June, Beerbohm's colleagues drew the following conclusions:

> The actors were not to blame if *The Heather Field* did not altogether please. (*The Echo*)

> Mr. George Moore, having delivered himself of the pronouncement that Mr. Edward Martyn, the author of *The Heather Field*, and Shakespeare are our only two dramatists, there remains little for anyone else to add — except that if Mr. Martyn is in need of an armorial motto, he might choose "Save me from my friends." (*The Daily Mail*)

47

. . . a drama of drainage, wandering wearily around the question of agricultural improvements and the relations of a dreaming and insane Irish proprietor with his tenants and the Land Commission can have no chance of popular success. (*The Daily Telegraph*)

. . . it says a great deal for the acting that *The Heather Field* is endurable on the stage at all. (*The Times*)

. . . very dull and gloomy. (*The Standard*)

No; *The Heather Field* may be "literary drama", but is not "acting drama". (*The Daily Mail*)

\* \* \*

George Moore did not come over to Dublin for the first nights, and so Martyn, with more flamboyance than usual, telegraphed him, 'The sceptre of intelligence has passed from London to Dublin.' [73] Holloway wrote more prosaically in his journal, 'Beyond a doubt, the admirable performance of *The Heather Field* has made the Irish Literary Theatre an unmistakably established fact, and an institution which all Irish people of culture and refinement ought to be justly proud of.' [74]

To celebrate the success of the project, on 11 May 1899, *The Daily Express* gave a dinner at the Shelbourne Hotel for those involved in the productions. George Moore had arrived in Dublin by then, and attended it, as did Yeats, Martyn, Douglas Hyde, John Eglinton, Max Beerbohm, John O'Leary, Standish O'Grady, and others. The opening speech by T. P. Gill, the newspaper's editor, reflects the cordiality of the occasion; he did not deny his newspaper's opposition to Yeats's play, but nevertheless saw great promise in the venture:

They had had an exciting week in Ireland (hear, hear), a week which would be memorable in the literary history of the country (applause). For the first time Ireland, which, goodness knew, had known plenty of excitement from other causes, had been profoundly stirred upon an intellectual question. He regarded the controversy which Mr. Yeats's play had aroused as one of the best signs of the times (applause). It showed that

48

they had reached at last the end of the intellectual stagnation of Ireland (hear, hear), and that, so to speak, the grey matter of Ireland's brain was at last becoming active (hear, hear). . . . In the Irish Literary Theatre movement they had the support of men of different views upon many matters, including, he believed, the theology of "Countess Cathleen" (laughter and applause). They were not required to surrender their freedom of judgment in respect to that production or any production which they hoped would be placed upon the stage from year to year (applause). For his own part, he was free to say that while he was a great admirer of Mr. Yeats's poetry and the wonderful beauty of his *Countess Cathleen*, he . . . did not regard the play as by any means the best of Mr. Yeats's works, as there were, no doubt, some who did, and he would not accept it as a presentation of the life and character of Ireland, if it were offered to them as such (applause). The thoughts of those cowering hinds did not represent the attitude of the Irish peasantry towards the things of their religion (applause). Might he say that he claimed that they should treat with respect the feelings of those who, taking Mr. Yeats's play very literally as a piece of realism, had expressed the strongest dissent upon these points (hear, hear). . . . What should he say of Mr. Martyn? (Applause). He . . . produced a great and original play, and that Ireland had discovered in him a dramatist fitted to take rank among the first in Europe (loud applause). . . . There was now the opportunity for the regular theatrical managers . . . they might do worse than take *The Heather Field* with its company just as it stood, and put it for a week on the stage at the Gaiety or the Royal.

Yeats spoke next, and referred to the controversy raised:

At last, apathy and cynicism, deep besetting sins of their country, were beginning to evaporate (applause), and, like the chairman, he welcomed exceedingly the controversy which had arisen about his play. . . . There were the issues which they should always be fierce upon, but they were the only issues in this country which they were accustomed to treat with entire apathy (applause). His only regret in connection with the whole matter was that Cardinal Logue, who was such a good friend

49

to national movements like that of the Gaelic League . . .
should have been misled about the nature of the play. However, he . . . hoped that if ever Cardinal Logue ever found
leisure to read the play, he would discover how deeply he had
been misled. He [Yeats] had not singled any particular argument that moved him [Logue] to write that letter. He . . .
must therefore simply summarise very shortly what had been
said against his play and answer it. He did not answer it in the
hope of convincing the most ardent of his opponents. He spoke
"not to convert those who did not believe, but to protect those
who did" (laughter). The chief arguments against the play were
three: first that the story was German, secondly that he had
blasphemed in it, and thirdly that he had slandered the
country. A very ingenious antagonist was anxious to prove that
the play was not Celtic, and therefore looked to a country
which by common consent was not Celtic, and pitched upon
Germany. Well, as a matter of fact, a well-known writer told
them that it was an Irish story, and in Mr. Larminie's book,
*West Irish Folk-Tales and Romances*, it was, he believed,
stated that the story was one of those imaginative fables which
go through all countries and belong to no country. The argument that he was a blasphemer was a very simple one. The
utterances of the demons and lost souls had been described as
the beliefs of himself (laughter). The charge that he had
slandered the country was worked out with great ingenuity. It
was said Mr. Yeats had made the peasants thieves and the
women false to their husbands, and it was asked is that Celtic?
Well, he was ready to admit that nobody ever robbed in
Ireland, and that no woman ever false to her husband. That
might be true, but it was perfectly irrelevant, for, after all, it
was nothing against the truth of a thing to say that it never
happened (laughter and applause). His play, of course, was
purely symbolic, and as such it must be regarded. Literature
was the expression of universal truths by the medium of
particular symbols; and those who were working at the
National Literary movement and at all such movements were
simply trying to give to universal truths the expression which
would move most the people about them. In all countries
where suffering had made patriotism a passion they had found
literature turning to that patriotism as to its most powerful

re-echo (applause). On that they must rely if they were to stir
the people of the country profoundly. This was the great sword
that had been put into their hands, and what they had to do
was to spiritualise the patriotism and the drama of this country.
What time had in store for them the future alone would tell;
but it looked as if the writers of this country were seeking for
spiritual things and lifting their voice against that externality,
that worship of power, and the worship of merely external
magnificence which seemed to be spreading over the English-
speaking races (applause).

Martyn, Beerbohm and others spoke very briefly, and then
George Moore expressed his enthusiasm for the revival he now
saw as beginning:

> I feel conscious that I must seem like a man who, having
> deserted his mother for a long time, returns to her with effusion
> when he hears that she has become rich and powerful. . . .
> There have been since the ancient bards, poets of merit, com-
> petent poets, poets whom I do not propose you should ever
> forget or think less of; but Ireland, so it seems to me, has had
> no poet who compares for a moment with the great poet of
> whom it is my honour to speak tonight. It is because that I
> believe that in the author of *The Countess Cathleen*, Ireland
> has discovered her ancient voice, that I have undertaken this
> journey from London, and consented to what I have hitherto
> considered to be the most disagreeable task that could befall
> me — a public speech. I should not have put myself to the
> inconvenience of a public speech for anything in the world,
> except a great poet, that is to say a man of exceptional genius,
> who was born at a moment of great national energy. This was
> the advantage of Shakespeare and Victor Hugo as well as Mr.
> Yeats. The works of Mr. Yeats are not as yet, and probably
> never will be, as voluminous as those of either the French or
> English poet, but I cannot admit that they are less perfect. The
> art of writing a blank verse play is so difficult that none except
> Shakespeare and Mr. Yeats have succeeded in this form. This
> assertion will seem extravagant, but think a moment and you
> will see that it is nearer the truth than you will suppose. We
> must not be afraid of praising Mr. Yeats's poetry too much;

51

we must not hesitate to say that there are lyrics in the collected poems as beautiful as any in the world. We must be courageous in front of the Philistine and insist that the lyric entitled "Innisfree" is unsurpassable. Had the Irish poets who came before Mr. Yeats had the same advantage as Mr. Yeats, they might have written as well. We will give them the benefit of the doubt, and it is only fair to assume that Mr. Kipling, the poet that England is now celebrating, would not have written the most hideous verses ever written in a beautiful language, if he had not lived in a specially hideous moment.[75]

\*　　\*　　\*

The attention given by historians to the Irish Literary Theatre has obscured the fact that work was being done quietly in the provinces by other Irishmen, to further the cause of an Irish drama. For instance, the following letter by Alice Milligan[76] was printed in *The Daily Express* on 21 January, and mentions what must be the first modern production in the Irish language:

Sir — Mr. W. B. Yeats, in his interesting letter of Saturday last on the Irish Literary Theatre,[77] made references to the dramatic entertainments given in connection with the recent Aonach Tir-Conail at Letterkenny, Co. Donegal, and quoted the success of those ventures as encouraging him to believe that plays appealing to the higher intelligence of an audience can attain success.

Having taken part in the production of one of these plays, *The Passing of Conall*,[78] I think that I may be permitted to express an opinion on the subject. Opinion when founded on experience, is always of value, and, *en passant*, let me say that I think *The Daily Express*, which is setting a good example to the Press of Ireland in so many things, might very well set the example in refusing to publish correspondence such as that in Wednesday's paper, over the signature, "A West Briton", on the subject of learning Irish. When an opinion is expressed by a person whose ignorance is palpable, why should it be inflicted on the intelligent reading public in the shape of a letter to the Press? A "West Briton's" assertion that Irish language and literature are extinct is as untrue as that the world is flat, or that two and two make five, and *The Express* editor, knowing this well, might very well act as dictator.

This is apparently a digression from the main subject of my letter, but is not so in fact. Both Mr. Yeates [*sic*], as an Irish literary man, and a "West Briton" will be interested to know that a main feature of the Letterkenny play was the introduction of an act written in Gaelic verse by a living Gaelic poet, and enacted by Gaelic speakers. The experiment was so successful that Dr. Douglas Hyde, Miss Norma Borthwick, and other leading members of the Gaelic League, present at the production, were convinced of the importance of using the stage to promote the revival of the native Irish language as a medium of literature and culture. The next Oireachtas, which will be held in Dublin at the end of May, will likely be the occasion of a dramatic entertainment in which the Irish language alone will be used, and which, at the same time, will be instructive and attractive to those who only understand English and other foreign languages. Ancient Irish legendary literature gives us in the Ossianic dialogues the nearest approach to drama in an ancient native literature. Taking the disputes between Oisin and St. Patrick as a basis, I have sketched for the Gaelic League a dramatic entertainment which has met with approval, though it is not yet formally adopted by any committee.

I have suggested that a few members of the League in Dublin, who have considerable elocutionary power, should impersonate the aged Oisin, Patrick, and his clerics, and that from the old versions of the dialogues some of our poets should condense the most important parts, embodying Oisin's laments for his lost comrades, Fin and the Fianna, a narrative of the elopement of Diarmuid and Grainne, and his own wanderings to Tir-nan-oig. During the narration, Oisin, by magic art, is to summon up for the benefit of the astonished clerics visions of the chief scenes in his heroic youth. These in a series of beautiful tableaux, appearing behind a gauze curtain in an inner stage, will form the chief feature of the entertainment.

In Belfast last May during Feis Ceoil week, we produced such tableaux with undoubted success, our subjects being scenes from the story of Cuchulain and the Flight of Diarmuid and Grainne. In Belfast they were accompanied by an explanatory lecture given by T. O'Neill Russell. A step in advance will be taken in Dublin by introducing a dramatic setting and also by using only the native language.

Our venture will come off most likely a full month after the production of Mr. Yeats's and Mr. Martyn's plays, and the fact that the Gaelic League has theatrical ambitions will only increase public interest in the National Literary Theatre's dramas. We will have much to learn from each other, and perhaps our Gaelic production will lead Mr. Yeats to decide on dramatising or adapting his own Wanderings of Oisin for the Literary Theatre to produce in the first year of the next century.

Very truly,

ALICE L. MILLIGAN[79]

The productions referred to were those given at the Aonach Tir-Conail on 18 November 1898, at Letterkenny, Co. Donegal. During the week's festivities, an operetta, *Finola*, by Brendan J. Rogers and Sister Mary Gertrude, was performed; also presented were two plays on Irish subjects: *The Coming of Conall*, by Sister Mary Gertrude, and acted by students of the Sisters of Loreto Convent, and an anonymous play, possibly by Father Eugene O'Growney, entitled *The Passing of Conall*. The last named was the most important, as it contained one scene in Irish. *The Freeman's Journal* reported on its performance:

Tonight before a crowded audience the first public performance took place of the Irish drama *The Passing of Conall*. The hero, the ancestor of the Clan O'Donnell, is shown in his old age appealing to Saint Caillin of Fermagh to grant him a vision of the scenes of his youth. The play then proceeds, and there are interesting scenes of Irish life in the fourth and fifth centuries. . . . The drama has been written by a celebrated student of Irish history, and a prominent member of the Gaelic League, who desires to have his identity concealed. . . . One scene, that of St. Patrick at Tara, has been translated into Irish by "Padraic" of the New York Gaelic movement — Mr.

54

Patrick O'Byrne, now of Killybegs. His translation is very fine and . . . thoroughly preserves the spirit of the original. . . . The scene was acted both in Irish and English.[80]

The scene of St. Patrick at Tara, with its dialogue in Irish, marked the beginning of Gaelic drama. It was presented several times during the next year; in Belfast on 16 March, with P. T. MacGinley and Alice Milligan in the cast, and again on 3 April 1899 in Derry.

The potential for drama in Irish as a means of encouraging the language revival was immediately apparent. Early in 1899, the journal of the language movement, *Fáinne an Lae*, spoke of the need to encourage productions in Irish, and described the types of plays needed:

> While we sympathise with this effort to create an Irish stage, we may be permitted to regret the utter absence of a Gaelic Theatre. If we are not mistaken, this absence has been readily explained by more than one literary wiseacre as due to the lamentable fact that dramatic composition is not in accord with the peculiarities of the Gaelic language Ráiméis! This argument may be classed with those of the great "Celtic" class, which chiefly consist of incantations in which the words "glamour", "mysticism", and "Renaissance" will be found invaluable.
>
> The reason why we have no Gaelic plays is that political troubles made a Gaelic Stage impossible while the literary class still existed, and in later times the disappearance of almost all education from the country prevented any demand for a Gaelic drama from coming into existence. The only attempts that seem ever to have been made in this direction appear in Father O'Carroll's scenes in the early numbers of *The Gaelic Journal* and the sketch produced at the Feis Adhamhnain in Letterkenny last November. The latter should be warmly applauded as an effort to make the Gaelic Drama a reality, and it was a pity that it was not made known more widely. . . . In several of the branches it ought to be possible to produce a little drama. The only real difficulty we can see is that it does not at all follow that the members who have the greatest ability in musical or dramatic work are able to speak Gaelic or that

55

those who speak Gaelic have any dramatic taste. . . . It is not necessary that such a play should be original, probably it would have to be translated. But it should not be long, for three reasons. First, the difficulty of writing; second, the difficulty of learning and speaking the parts; third and principal, the difficulty of inducing the audience to stand it. But these difficulties would not be as serious in the case of a farce, an historical sketch, or a comedietta. Three, or at most four, characters would be quite enough for such a play, and they should not all be male characters. Melodrama would probably be the safest line of all. Its popularity is perennial, and many a poor play . . . gains greatly by the introduction of a couple of good songs.[81]

The tableaux vivants mentioned above by Miss Milligan relied on delicate and colourful scenes to portray episodes from Irish history and legends. The May 1898 performance in Belfast was the first of these on an Irish subject:

The Feis Ceoil week ended brilliantly with the unique display of tableaux vivants which came off in the Exhibition Hall on Saturday evening [6 May 1898] under the auspices of the local Gaelic League. For some years back this society had held a sort of Feis Ceoil on its own account, and these concerts have been remarkably successful, but this year, as people might be supposed to be sated with music, the Gaelic League struck out on new lines, and we can heartily congratulate all concerned on the success of their undertaking. . . . The proceedings opened by Dr. St. Clair Boyd introducing as orator and exponent of the first series of tableaux, Mr. O'Neill Russell, the well-known Gaelic scholar and litterateur. Mr. Russell, who has made a special study of the ancient tales of the Red Branch era, explained to the audience that they were about to see representations of real historic persons who flourished in Ireland about the beginning of the Christian era. Maeve, Queen of Connacht, having a grudge against Connor MacNessa of Ulster, invaded the Northern province at the head of her army.

Her outposts were attacked by a young champion Cuchullin, who met and slew in single combat all the warriors she sent against him. At last she bribed Ferdia, the friend of Cuchullin, a youth, to challenge him to fight. The curtain rising on the first tableau showed Queen Maeve, stately and fair and fierce, in robes of orange and white, listening to the auguries of a dark-haired prophetess, who, with flashing eyes and warning gestures, foretold the dangers of the war in which she was embarking. The second scene showed the Connaught queen enthroned in her tent interviewing her dauntless enemy, the young Ulster champion, a heroic stalwart youth with flowing golden locks, dressed in deerskins, and armed with shield and spear. The queen's daughter, Finnbarr, a young girl, all in white, shrunk in fear and wonder by the side of her beautiful and stately mother. In the next scene Finnbarr was offered as bride to Ferdia, a dark-curled young warrior. Maeve assumed an attitude of entreaty, and had taken from her robe the royal brooch as an additional bribe to the young man to urge him to the combat. Then the curtain rose on the two friends face to face in battle array, but Cuchullin clasps Ferdia's hand and gazed on him in sorrowful reproach. The combat was then represented in several scenes, which were loudly applauded. The champions displayed the most wonderful powers of standing still as statues in strained and difficult attitudes. At length Ferdia was shown dying in his friend's arms bewailed by Queen Maeve, on whom Cuchullin hurled scornful reproaches. . . .

The second series, on Diarmuid and Grainne, was narrated by P. J. O'Shea. The last series was also narrated by him; the subject was Grace O'Malley (Granuaile):

The historical series of tableaux were completed by a series alluding to Grace O'Malley's visit to Queen Elizabeth. The English Queen, in jewelled majesty, sat in state with attendant courtier and lady, and a better Queen Bess could scarcely be imagined. Granuaile, tall, majestic, severely simple, contrasted excellently with her British Majesty, and the red-haired gallowglass who attended her contrasted as markedly with the courtier and lady in ruffs and velvet. The well-known story of Granuaile at Howth was then shown. The child who personified the stolen heir was as good as the best of the grown-up actors, and evidently entered into the spirit of the play as simply as if engaged in a make-believe game in the nursery at home. The

57

ferocious figure of the gallowglass and the enraged Granuaile were most striking. Dark Rosaleen (Ireland) next appeared, amidst rapturous applause, a perfectly beautiful figure, dark-eyed, sad-faced, with a wreath of roses, and harp twined with flowers. This completed the historical series of pictures, and a complete change in the character of the programme re-awakened the curiosity of the audience.[82]

Their popularity as a form of entertainment is testified to by the 1899 performance of tableaux vivants at the Chief Secretary's Lodge in Dublin, based on Yeats's *Countess Cathleen*. Although Yeats had nothing to do with this performance, it was repeatedly brought up in attacks on Yeats in later years, when he was labelled "Dramatic Entertainer for Dublin Castle".[83]

*     *     *

A literary movement was gaining shape rapidly. By the middle of 1899, Yeats could look with confidence to continued growth of the Irish Literary revival. He spoke at a meeting of the College Historical Society, Trinity College, Dublin, to the proposition: 'That any attempt to further an Irish Literary Movement would result in Provincialism.' *The Daily Express* reported:

> Mr. Yeats, who was very cordially applauded, in the course of his reply, said that one of the things which had certainly given all of those who worked in this literary movement the greatest possible pleasure, had been the way in which it had been discussed by many different representatives of Irish opinion. They had found an interest taken in the movement which went beyond their expectations, and he hoped the University of Dublin would yet delight to keep watch over all that which was distinctive and racial in this country. He did not believe that a literature rising out of racial characteristics was provincial. A peasant dressed in his national costume was not provincial. The small shopkeeper in the country town dressed in the costume of London or Paris was provincial. Cosmopolitanism had never been a creative power, because cosmopolitanism was a mere mirror in which forms and images reflected themselves. It could not create them, and was the very essence of provincialism. If they went down into any part of England, Ireland, or Scotland, and analysed the

things that gave them the impression of provincialism they would find everywhere that they were the cast off fashions, the cast off clothes, the cast off thoughts of some active centre of creative minds. They were, in literature, the opinions which the provincial of Dublin, or of London, or of Edinburgh supposed to be the opinions of London, but which London had cast off many years ago. It was because great cities by their isolation from the tranquil life of the country, and by their great crowds, gradually lost that tranquility in which original ideas grew up, that movements like the Irish literary movement had always been welcomed in centres such as London and Paris. It was a most extraordinary error to suppose, as a speaker had supposed, that the writers of this movement began it because they had been rejected by critical opinion in England. A charge was indeed made against them by extreme Nationalists that they were a little group of writers forced upon this country by English critics. Only the other day he read in an extreme organ of patriotic opinion, that it was all very well so long as Mr. Yeats wrote for English readers and English critics, "but now that he tried to establish an Irish Literary Theatre it was time to crush him" (laughter). Now that he was bringing into this country cosmopolitan ideas, now was the moment to crush him (renewed laughter). London welcomed the radical ideas of other countries. There came to her from the ends of the world spirits full of lofty thoughts and ideals, just as they came to ancient Rome, and London gradually stifled their creative energy, gradually turned their thoughts into commonplace, gradually ground them in her commercial machine. That was not so in the days when the world was happiest in creative energy. That was not so in Italy or in Greece, and he did not think it would be so in the English-speaking world of the future. It was impossible that those nations which spoke for good or for ill, the English tongue would accept perpetually the ideas of one city, which was no longer moved by any high ideal. America had a national literature, and America wrote in English. Ireland would have a national literature which would be written to a very great extent in English. Scotland would probably again begin to express herself in a way personal to herself, and Australia and South Africa and the other English-speaking countries would sooner or later express their

59

personal life in literature. Henrik Ibsen, who was known to all nations, was once one of the leaders of the National movement in Scandinavian literature. That movement, too, had had its extravagances. There could not be a creation of energy in any country without extravagance. In literature, or politics, or art, or anything else, extravagance was merely the shavings from the carpenter's bench. It was an overflow of energy. It was, no doubt, regrettable; no doubt all human errors were regrettable; but extravagance was far better than that apathy, or cynicism, which were deep-besetting sins here in Dublin. Every Irish writer for many years, every Irish person who had taken up any intellectual Irish question whatever, had found his coldest welcome in his own city. He had sometimes found translators in a foreign land before he had found readers at his own door. Sir Samuel Ferguson lived unknown to what was called the educated opinion of this country. Although he was a most original and distinguished poet, he was unknown in his own city. In taking up the work of giving to Irish intellect a sincere expression of itself they were taking up a work, not for Ireland only, but for the world. Every nation had its word to speak. He believed the work of Ireland was to lift up its voice for spirituality, for ideality, for simplicity in the English speaking world. Ireland had a unique history. But they could not touch upon that. Whatever that history might have been, whatever might be said about it, Ireland would have a destiny shaped by that history. Ireland had prepared herself in sorrow and in self-sacrifice for the destiny which self-sacrifice and sorrow gave always to men and nations. The literature of England at the present day was becoming a glorification of material faith and material wealth. He believed that Ireland with its legends, its profound faith, with its simplicity, with its sincerity, would lift up its voice for an empire of the spirit greater than any material empire. The world was like a great organ. Sometimes the hand of destiny was upon one stop, and sometimes upon another, and as the hand moved along the stops, the nations awoke or slept, spoke or were silent. Yesterday the pre-destined hand rested upon the stop we call Spain. To-day Spain is silent. To-morrow the hand may rest upon the stop that we call Ireland, and Ireland become a part of the music of the world. (Applause).[84]

# 1900

The main events in 1900 in the commercial theatre were visits by several famous touring companies. In October, Forbes Robertson appeared at the Gaiety in *The Devil's Disciple*, *Othello*, and *Hamlet*. The Gaiety also saw several visits of the D'Oyly Carte Company, while less memorable groups presented the usual crowd-pleasers, such as *San Toy*, *Jim the Penman*, *The Little Minister*, and, of course, *Charley's Aunt*. On 25 August, Mrs. Patrick Campbell played at the Theatre Royal in Maeterlinck's *Pelléas and Mélisande*. Frank Fay, who was still contributing drama reviews to *The United Irishman*, found some fault with the production — there was too much light on the stage, for instance — but he added, 'Mrs. Patrick Campbell was born to play Mélisande; her acting seemed to be flawless. Her tendency to chant, instead of speaking her words, became perfectly charming when the lines to be spoken are those of a poet like M. Maeterlinck.' [1] But a week later, reviewing Mrs. Campbell's production of Rostand's *Les Romanesques*, translated into English as *The Fantasticks*, Fay cited the disgrace of the Dublin audience for laughing at one of the most beautiful speeches in the play. However beautiful the play may have been, the Dublin audience was clearly not yet converted to poetic drama.

\*     \*     \*

The provincial audience was treated to nothing quite so esoteric as *Pelléas and Mélisande*. Obscure professional companies, 'fit-up' companies, made the rounds of the 'smalls' in Ireland, presenting what had been, and was to be, their staple fare for years — the tried and true melodrama, the broad comedy, and even the occasional classic. These plays were presented in village halls under the most primitive conditions, and something of this rugged gypsy life may be seen in the reminiscences of Val Vousden:

> I was engaged to play "utility" parts with a dramatic company, which rejoiced in the sub-title of: "The Only Real Company Touring!" . . . I forbear to mention the name of the village where I was going to join this combination. I landed at the little railway station. It was quite dark; it looked as if no

61

one had been travelling on that train but the engine men, the guard and myself. The lonely porter informed me that the village was about two-and-a-half miles away. There was no possible chance of a lift and therefore there was nothing for it but to 'pad the hoof'.

It was a cold, miserable, October evening of rain. Not ordinary rain. It spat hurtfully in my face. . . .

At last I arrived in the one-street village. There were no street lamps. The only light I could see was the glare from a shop window. To that shop I made my way. . . .

I knocked on the hard counter. No answer. . . . Becoming impatient I kicked the counter. Then a half-ginger, half-grey-haired man with filthy whiskers and a "wounded" spectacles on the end of his nose burst out of a little door at the end of the shop. Waving a newspaper at me he roared:

"I tould ye people afore, there is no lodgin's here, an' I don't know of any lodgin's ayther, an' even if I did, I wouldn't tell ye. So be off to hell outa this or I'll set the bloody dog at ye!"

Well, he recognised I was an actor anyhow! . . .

The drama that evening was *East Lynne*. The Manager asked me if I could manage to study, roughly, the part of Lord Mount Severn. In those days veteran roles were played by the youngsters and the romantic juveniles by toothless old men! However, I managed to pull through despite the fact that I was wearing brown spats over socks and shoes that were not properly dried. The village people thoroughly "enjoyed" themselves, for they wept all through the play.

I recollect a little accident that evening. When Madame Vine threw herself across the dead body of the boy, calling out "Dead! Dead! and never called me mother!" the bed unfortunately collapsed. . . .

I joined another company and reached the proud position of "Star Leading Man". I may not have received a very big salary although I must admit that occasionally it was fabulous — very much so. The scene is laid in Ballystar (let us call it). When we arrived the "Heavyman" — that is the gentleman who played the villain roles — and myself dropped into a tiny public-house near the station. We called for refreshments and were about to enquire about the appreciation of the drama in Ballystar, when the young lady behind the counter became very embarrassed on hearing her mother call out from the kitchen: "Mary! Mary! Take the butther off the counter, the actors have arrived!"

Well, in Ballystar there was only one place in which we could perform, and that was up on a big loft, over stables. I used to dress in one of the stables with the light of a candle stuck on a nail in the wall. There was a horse there, and as he munched his hay he would turn around occasionally to watch me making-up. The animal often became very restless when we were playing a drama that required shots to be fired.

I used to wonder what effect our baritone had on him. In the variety portion of the programme this terrible man would insist on singing. Unfortunately, he was a relation of the Manager's wife; he was the only blot on our fair reputation. Audiences, on the whole, were very patient; but there were some places where they laughed him off the stage. But it was useless. He *would* sing. A few bars from him of *The Heart Bowed Down* would upset the most congenial atmosphere that ever any group of performers could ask for.

He did not confine himself to baritone songs either. I remember one evening in County Galway when he was finishing, in his usual crude manner, the song *When Other Lips*:

> "Then you'll remember,
> You'll remember me!"

a man from the back of the hall shouted: "Yerra, we'll never forget ye!"

It was announced in Ballystar that by special request we would stage Wilson Barrett's famous play, *The Sign of the Cross*, on Thursday evening. We had not played this very popular drama for a long time, as the wardrobe essential for its production had become very shabby. For instance, the white Roman toga I used to wear became so dilapidated that we had to throw it out on the dust-heap. A toga had to be procured by hook or by crook for Marcus Superbus, the Roman Tribune, by Thursday evening.

Now, a toga is not picked up for the asking in a place like Ballystar, and the funds available for new wardrobe were very scarce indeed. Something had to be done. I had a brain-wave. The place where I was lodging was "wondrous neat and clean", especially the bed linen. I had my toga — the white sheets! . . .

I ascended the ladder leading from the stable to the hayloft, where our two-feet-high stage was erected. The loft was packed to suffocation. In the well-known scene when Marcus points to the arena of the lions, "Mercia, come to the light beyond," an unforgettable thing occurred. The "lions" were roaring in the arena, waiting to devour the Christians. I suppose I must give credit where credit is due: our baritone used to do this excellently. Now, whether the *faux pas* was due to my emotional acting or a slight laxity on the part of Nero when he was pinning me up, I do not know. The folds of the toga fell down anyway. . . .

Suddenly there was an outbrust of laughter from the audience which froze me stiff, and my final humiliation came when I discovered that the young lady who was playing Mercia was doubled up with hilarity too! The landlady, you see, was evidently a very economical soul and had converted flour bags into bed linen, so that in full view of the audience was displayed in blue print the trade mark of a well-known Irish flour mill.[2]

\*     \*     \*

An inevitable part of the repertoire of the provincial touring company in Ireland was the patriotic melodrama, such as *The Colleen Bawn* or *The Siege of Limerick*. In its own way, the Irish Literary Theatre also became increasingly patriotic in 1900. Moore and Martyn and even sometimes Yeats discussed the theatre in terms of its relation to the national well-being. In fact, they seemed to be discussing the future of the Irish language, or the pernicious influence of Trinity College, or the imminent Dublin visit of Queen Victoria, more than they were discussing dramatic theories and aesthetic ideals.

This sense of belonging to a great national resurgence was reflected not only in the statements of the theatre's leaders, but also in the generally uncritical enthusiasm with which the plays were received by the press and the public. There was no repetition of a *Countess Cathleen* imbroglio; there was no hint this year of a division between art and patriotism. Indeed, Martyn suggested that English drama was contemptible because England was deca-

64

dent, and that Irish drama was admirable because Ireland was high-minded and nobly pure. In 1900, there was practically no one to disagree.

In *The Dome* for January, Yeats wrote a high-minded essay on 'The Irish Literary Theatre', in which he speculated that a 'strong imaginative energy' and 'a genius greater than their own' had somehow descended upon the Irish writer. 'Scandinavia,' he wrote, 'is, as it seems, passing from her moments of miracle; and some of us think that Ireland is passing to hers.' [3] In another essay, 'Plans and Methods', which appeared in this year's issue of *Beltaine*, Yeats wrote that Martyn's new play, *Maeve* — and indeed Moore's new play, *The Bending of the Bough*—both symbolised 'Ireland's choice between English materialism and her own natural idealism. . . .' [4] It was a chief function of the theatre 'to bring Ireland from under the ruins' of commercialism and materialism.

George Moore's contribution to *Beltaine* was an article called 'Is the Theatre a Place of Amusement?' In it, he made a distinction between amusement and pleasure:

> People seek amusement, not pleasure, in a theatre. To obtain pleasure in a theatre, a man must rouse himself out of the lethargy of real life; his intelligence must awake, and the power to rouse oneself from the lethargy of real life is becoming rarer in the playgoer and more distasteful to him. . . . The playgoer wants to be amused, not pleased; he wants distraction — the distraction of scenery, dresses, limelight, artificial birds singing in painted bowers. In Mr. Tree's production of the *Midsummer Night's Dream* an artificial rabbit hops across the stage, and the greatest city in the world is amused. . . .
>
> Art is evocation, not realisation; therefore scenery should be strictly limited, if not abolished altogether; dresses and furniture as much as scenery beset the imagination and prevent the spectator from union with the conception of the poet. But all reformation must proceed gradually. . . . So I have allowed a little inoffensive scenery to encumber the stage during the performance of my play. . . . To hunt four days a week in Leicestershire costs about £1,000 a year, and pheasant-shooting is not less expensive. To give every spring such original plays as the Irish Literary Theatre contemplates giving, and another week in the autumn of great plays by Ibsen, Maeterlinck, and

65

Tolstoi, would not cost five hundred a year, and might cost nothing, for they might even pay their expenses. And the performance of great dramatic masterpieces of European renown, and plays dealing with our national life, history, and legend, would be, I think, of inestimable advantage. These performances would make Dublin an intellectual centre, which London is not, and would stimulate the national genius as nothing else would — far more, it is my belief, than a university or a picture gallery.

The theatre is the noblest form of art until it becomes a commercial enterprise, then it becomes the ante-room of the supper club, and is perhaps the lowest. There is probably nothing in life so low as a musical comedy, for in the musical comedy the meaning of life is expressed in eating, drinking, betting, and making presents to women; nor does the morality of these pieces gain by the constant use of the word marriage.[5]

Edward Martyn contributed to *Beltaine* an article called 'A Comparison between Irish and English Theatrical Audiences', in which he attacked contemporary English character, English literature and English theatre. It is with the theatre especially, he wrote, that:

. . . decadence irrevocable and complete has set in. It is no use saying that Shakespeare's plays draw because they have been turned into variety shows, where scenery and dresses are in greater prominence than the poetry of Shakespeare. Present him as he should be presented, without all this pantomime, and then see how he would fare with English audiences, whose taste is for nothing but empty parade, where the stage is degraded to a booth for the foolish exhibition of women, or for the enacting of scenes purposely photographing the manners of the society rakes and strumpets of the day. This is the condition to which English literature and English drama have fallen. The situation reminds us of what Rome was at the turning-point of her supremacy and empire. Then her literature and taste began to disappear. The plays of Terence gave place to the brutish decadence of the arena, just as the great drama of England has given place to brutish and imbecile parade. . . .

But turning to Ireland what do we see? Instead of a vast

cosmopolitanism and vulgarity, there is an idealism founded upon the ancient genius of the land. There is, in fact, now a great intellectual awakening in Ireland, and, as is the case with all such awakenings, a curiosity and appreciation for the best. This has come about naturally of itself, in spite of the efforts of certain persons and institutions whose aim seems to be to create in Ireland a sort of shabby England. Some have sought to introduce the shoddy literature and drama, others the decadent profligacy of morals so much in vogue in English society. Their labours have borne no fruit. Ireland is virgin soil, yielding endless aspiration to the artist; and her people, uncontaminated by false ideals, are ready to receive the new art.[6]

Alice Milligan contributed a short essay in which she summarized the Dermot and Grania story as background for her own play, *The Last Feast of the Fianna*. She concluded by remarking, 'I understand that Mr. W. B. Yeats has explained my little play as having some spiritual and mystical meaning. . . .' Here, Yeats appended his own footnote:

> The emotion which a work of art awakens in an onlooker has commonly little to do with the deliberate purpose of its maker, and must vary with every onlooker. Every artist who has any imagination builds better than he knows. Miss Milligan's little play delighted me because it has made, in a very simple way and through the vehicle of Gaelic persons, that contrast between immortal beauty and the ignominy and mortality of life, which is the central theme of ancient art.[7]

Miss Milligan continued:

> . . . but to tell the truth I simply wrote it on thinking out this problem. How did Oisin endure to live in the house with Grania as a stepmother after all that had happened? We know, as a matter of fact, that he was allured away to the Land of Youth by a fairy woman, Niamh of the golden locks. I have set these facts side by side, and evolved from them a dramatic situation.[8]

Finally, Lady Gregory, looking back at the previous year's accomplishments, expressed pride in the success of the Irish Literary Theatre:

It is not for any of us, who have been concerned in the project from its beginning, to speak of the merits of these plays. *The Countess Cathleen*, now in its third edition, has so often been reviewed as a poem that it does not need any new criticism. *The Heather Field* was given, after its success in Dublin, at a matinee at the Strand Theatre in London, by Mr. Thomas Kingston. It has now been translated into German, and is to be produced, with Mr. Martyn's permission, at Berlin, at Vienna, at Breslau, and at Dresden. In America it is to be produced by Mr. Metzler at New York, Boston, Washington and Philadelphia.[9]

*        *        *

Despite Lady Gregory's recitation of successes, the preparations for the second season had not been entirely placid. For Edward Martyn at least, the new season had been a source of considerable anguish.

George Moore claimed he had helped 'dear Edward' in the construction of *The Heather Field*. 'Not a line of the play was actually written by Moore, but he had shown Martyn the way throughout,' writes Moore's biographer.[10] Moore was to have a great deal more to do with his friend's next play, *The Tale of a Town*. Some time in 1899, Martyn had sent Moore the finished script, and this was Moore's reaction:

> The first half-dozen pages pleased me, and then Edward's mind, which can never think clearly, revealed itself in an entanglement; "Which will be easily removed," I said, picking up the second act. But the second act did not please me as much as the first, and I laid it down, saying: "Muddle, muddle, muddle." In the third act Edward seemed to fall into gross farcical situations, and I took up the fourth act sadly. It and the fifth dissipated every hope, and I lay back in my chair in a state of coma, unable to drag myself to the writing table. But getting there at last, I wrote — after complimenting him about a certain improvement in the dialogue — that the play seemed to me very inferior to *The Heather Field* and to *Maeve*.

68

"But plainer speaking is necessary. It may well be inferior to *The Heather Field* and to *Maeve*, and yet be worthy of the Irish Literary Theatre."

So I wrote: "There is not one act in the five you have sent me which, in my opinion, could interest any possible audience — Irish, English, or Esquimaux." [11]

In the summer, Moore and Martyn made an expedition to Bayreuth, but Moore was unable to get his friend to work on the play. In the autumn, Moore was staying with Martyn in Tullyra Castle, and Yeats was at nearby Coole Park with Lady Gregory. Under their joint pressure, Martyn made some revisions in the script, but Yeats's reaction was, 'No, no; it's entirely impossible. We couldn't have such a play performed.' [12] Moore agreed, but phrased it more kindly:

"If there were time, you might alter it yourself. You see, the time is short — only two months"; and I watched Edward. For a long time he said nothing, but sat like a man striving with himself, and I pitied him, knowing how much of his life was in his play.

"I give you the play," he said, starting to his feet. "Do with it as you like; turn it inside out, upside down. I'll make you a present of it!"

"But, Edward, if you don't wish me to alter your play —"

"Ireland has always been divided, and I've preached unity. Now I'm going to practise it. I give you the play."

"But what do you mean by giving us the play?" Yeats said.

"Do with it what you like. I'm not going to break up the Irish Literary Theatre. Do with my play what you like"; and he rushed away. [13]

Moore and Yeats then began to collaborate on the revision. According to Moore, 'The only fault I found with Yeats in this collaboration was the weariness into which he sank suddenly, saying that after a couple of hours he felt a little faint, and would require half an hour's rest.' [14] Apparently most of the revision was done by Moore. As he wrote to his brother:

I am afraid Martyn suffered a good deal. He says I spoil[ed] his play but that is an illusion. I recast the play, but not enough. I should have written a new play on the subject. . . . Then Edward said he could not sign it, and he refused to let it be played anonymously so I had to sign it.[15]

*     *     *

In the week of 19 February, the Irish Literary Theatre opened its second season at the Gaiety Theatre, with Edward Martyn's *Maeve,* Alice Milligan's *The Last Feast of the Fianna,* and the Moore-cum-Yeats-after-Martyn *The Bending of the Bough.* The variety of the offerings reflected the emphases of the developing group: two plays based on Irish mythology, both consciously or even self-consciously poetic and mystical; and one play of contemporary social relevance, realistic in manner and subject. All three plays were clearly nationalistic, at least in their implications, and the press and public were almost unanimously enthusiastic in their praise. The Martyn and Milligan plays were performed on Monday night, and *The Freeman's Journal* reported:

> No one who was present last night in the Gaiety Theatre could fail to note the extraordinary contrast between the audience which assembled there to judge the merits of *The Last Feast of the Fianna* and *Maeve* . . . and that which, twelve months ago, attended at the Antient Concert Rooms to witness the presentation of *The Countess Cathleen* and *The Heather Field.* On the former occasion the Irish Literary Theatre stood on its trial, and the verdict was extremely uncertain. To tell the truth, the Dublin public was not prepared for symbolic plays. Even those who believed in the genius of Mr. Yeats and the dramatic instinct of Mr. Martyn, were dubious as to the great and gallant experiment that was being made. The cynics had a good look in, indeed, and during the year they seemed to have quite disposed of the enthusiasts. Yet the enthusiasts, nothing daunted, have turned up again, and stronger than ever. Stronger than ever: that is why we must note the great contrast between the position of the Irish Literary Theatre last year and this year. In 1899 the plays were produced in the Antient Concert Rooms before small

70

audiences, very largely composed of the men and women who believe in the future of the Irish literary movement; last night *Maeve* and *The Last Feast of the Fianna* were produced before one of the best houses ever seen in the Gaiety Theatre, composed of all classes of the community, from the highest to the lowest. Every portion of the theatre was well filled, from the gods to the pit, and, so far as we could see, there were only two boxes empty. . . .

Certainly, nothing could have been more promising than the way in which the Gaiety audience took the two plays that were presented to them last night. To ordinary theatre-goers, accustomed to witness the obvious dramas of to-day, one would have thought that a picture of the Court of Fionn MacCumhal would have been a very tiresome affair. It must be said, too, that Mr. T. Bryant Edwin quite failed, except in outward appearance, to realise that great Celtic hero. Yet, Miss Milligan's little drama — simply a paraphrase from the old Gaelic story of Diarmuid and Grania — were [sic] followed with breathless interest. . . .

Mr. Martyn's psychological drama *Maeve* followed. Mr. Martyn's *The Heather Field* of last year puzzled the crowd, but Mr. Martyn is incorrigible, and insists on puzzling the crowd still. In making this remark we, of course, only refer to the crowd that flocks to the theatre to see, say, *Charley's Aunt*. . . . We have seen nothing so wonderful in an Irish theatre for many years as the way in which the audience in the Gaiety last night followed the allegory in Mr. Martyn's play.[16]

*The Daily Express* gave more space in its review to *The Last Feast of the Fianna* than to *Maeve*. Miss Milligan's play, looking back to the Ossian and Patrick dialogues, seemed a more proper way to create a national drama than Martyn's Ibsenism. Of *The Last Feast*, the paper wrote:

. . . it has a charm, particularly for Irish people, which makes up for its deficiencies in dramatic intensity. If it has no other merits, it reproduces, at all events, in a vivid manner the main characteristics of the heroic age of Ireland. It refreshes us with a pleasant breath of poetry, for Miss Milligan's is a poet's

71

touch, and there is sufficient novelty and charm in her work to arrest the attention of her audience. It was curious to see a crowd of spectators, accustomed to the highly-spiced vulgarities of the modern theatre, applauding with genuine relish a poetical thought or a musical passage.[17]

Dorothy Hammond was admired, as was Fanny Morris, but T. Bryant Edwin's Fionn 'scarcely brought out with sufficient impressiveness the nobility of the hero'.

*Maeve* was thought to need pruning, but, 'It was admirably acted . . . [and] was enthusiastically received. Its symbolic meaning was easily understood by the audience, and perverted by the gallery into a political attack upon England.' Dorothy Hammond was again particularly admired, and the only actor who was criticized was J. Herbert Walter whose Hugh Fitzwalter 'was a little too much of the conventional Englishman'.[18]

*The Irish Daily Independent* also devoted much more space to *The Last Feast of the Fianna* than to *Maeve*, even though the first play lasted only twenty minutes:

The scene was beautifully staged, presenting the King and Queen and Court, comprising a fine grouping of cup-bearers and bondswomen, all richly attired in ancient Gaelic costume.[19] The play then proceeds, the dialogue being of a declamatory order, couched in that very descriptive style of prose poetry such as runs through the Ossianic translations or inventions. The text is of an impressive and rhythmical style, but not altogether innocent of crudities. But the whole colouring of the piece is vivid, and is calculated to work upon the imagination of listeners. Some very beautiful music — ancient Irish airs supplied by the Gaelic League and orchestrated by Mrs. C. Milligan-Fox, sister of the authoress of the play — was contributed in the form of a double-string quartet with fine effect. . . .

The piece was received with great enthusiasm. Miss Milligan was called before the curtain, and had to bow her acknowledgement. Next followed Mr. Edward Martyn's two-act drama, *Maeve*. The piece is a psychological drama, which is delightfully fanciful and fairy-like. It is much richer in imaginative lore than *The Heather Field*. . . .[20]

72

The one dissenting note in this chorus of praise was *The Irish Times*:

The declared object of the Irish Literary Theatre is worthy of the most intense respect and admiration; that the dry-rot which has eaten into the English drama should be ended everybody will agree, but if, in place of vivacity and a relief from care and the seriousness of modern life, we are offered insipidity, dullness, the very condemnation of wit, of vigour, of liveliness — if, in fact, everything that can relieve man from the stress and struggle of this intense workaday world of ours, is banished from the only place where nowadays one can get the slightest reprieve from the commonplace and the oppressive, then give us back, by all means, the musical comedy, the inane farce imported from France, and spoiled in the importation, give us something which means nothing in place of that which is supposed to mean everything, but which requires a bore at your elbow to explain it and its hidden and incomprehensible mysteries. These remarks are entirely intended as a comment upon the impressions produced last night by Mr. Edward Martyn's play, and they are not intended in any unfriendly or unsympathetic sense. Why he should have marred a fine psychological novel — and we don't like the adjective, although we use it — by endeavouring to adapt it to the stage, of which, apparently, the author knows absolutely nothing, is perfectly mysterious. *Maeve*, the play, is absurd and ridiculous, because it is not a play, because it is written in direct contravention of the very essentials of the stage, because it appeals, not as a play should appeal — to the eye, to the ear direct, to the emotions direct — but because it appeals solely to the mind. Fine, logical, consistent argument against human nature it certainly is, but it is not, as a play should be, a reflex of human nature, and therefore Mr. Martyn's impressive work as a play is a complete and unadulterated failure. The man in the stalls it makes yawn. . . . As a play, *Maeve's* best quality is its shortness, and we leave it with this remark, that we hope to read it yet, expanded, developed, as Mr. Martyn can expand and develop it, and without any recollections of the attempt to put it in action on the boards of the theatre. Miss Milligan's one-act piece, *The Last Feast of the Fianna*, really

73

assumed the form of a full-dress recitation of a pleasing and nicely written poem. It has no pretence to be a play, although anyone who has read the story of Grania and of Fionn and the rest of them knows well enough that the cycle in which they move is rich beyond almost any similar period in dramatic materials. Miss Milligan, however, has caught far more intensely the imaginative and poetic features of the subject than its immense human interest, and the result is a series of very pretty animated pictures, which should have for their setting an Arctic winter in place of the warm atmosphere of Ireland. Both Miss Milligan and Mr. Martyn have apparently to learn this — that the mere mention of a few Irish names does not and cannot make an Irish drama, for they failed in precisely the same way to make an interesting stage piece in that both of them are more concerned with the words they make their people speak than the reason why they speak them. Miss Milligan's little effort is interesting in its way, but has no claim for the slightest toleration on the stage. Mr. Martyn's work, on the other hand, defective as it is for the purposes of the theatre, is entitled to the greatest respect on the part of every man who values thought as against mere verbiage. . . . The impersonation of the Fairy Woman in the first piece by Miss Hammond and of Maeve O'Heynes by the same actress in Mr. Martyn's piece should stamp her as a poetic artiste of the very first rank. Never had an actress a more difficult hand of cards to play, and never assuredly did an artiste come more creditably through an ordeal. The only thing that would incline us to alter our idea of the value of the two pieces would be this — that while Miss Hammond was on the stage she held the attention of the audience spell-bound, and gave to two absolutely impossible characters a touch of genuine interest which must have been a complete surprise to the authors themselves. Her speaking of the description of the "Land of the Ever Young", in Miss Milligan's poem, was as beautiful a piece of elocutionary work as anyone could desire, and throughout the second piece she sustained a herculean task with little less than genius. . . . The other artiste who made a fine impression was Miss Agnes B. Cahill, who appeared as Finola O'Heynes, and who demonstrated most conclusively that she has mastered to a very perfect degree the art of byplay which is almost altogether neglected on the English stage at present. . . . The pieces were well staged, and the other roles were sustained as well as they could be sustained by any set of players. The theatre was well filled, and the plays were well received.[21]

On the next evening, 20 February, *The Bending of the Bough* was produced, and, despite, undoubtedly, some misgivings about the author of *Parnell and his Island*, the play was so warmly received that it replaced the other two pieces as the Saturday night production. Its first-night audience was smaller than that on Monday, but its topical satire appealed to the reviewers. As *The Freeman's Journal* wrote:

> The play is, in fact, a powerful, biting, and unsparing political sabre directed against the influences that have destroyed the Irish gentry's sense of patriotism and reduced them to the position of social dependents upon an alien society and country. The veil of imagination is but of the tiniest, and the plot is a history in brief of the Financial Relations agitation in its genteel stage. A critic described it as the "rise, fall and extinction" of Lord Castletown. And though that is too pointed an identification, the dramatist has analysed and laid bare the petty causes and sordid interests that have always lain between the Irish landlord and leadership among his own people.[22]

If the well-disposed *Independent* had been somewhat terse in its approval of *Maeve*, it was able to wax fulsome over *The Bending of the Bough*, 'George Moore's Brilliant Play':

> The Irish Literary Theatre achieved a far-reaching triumph last night when it produced at the Gaiety Geo. Moore's much-anticipated play, *The Bending of the Bough*. The production is beyond doubt the most remarkable drama which has been given to the nation for many years. It satirises in brilliant, biting lashes of irony the relations existing between the Celtic race and its Saxon oppressors, the agitation of the one to shake off the yoke of the other, retarded as victory has been from time to time by the fawning submission of time-serving weak-

75

lings amidst the class in subjection, to the flattery or bribes of the "predominant partner". The story, which only requires the most superficial reading between the lines to bring out the international allegory which it embodies, seems simple and commonplace enough. . . . The powerful significance of the play in the light of current politics should draw big houses to the succeeding performances. Many of the people in the balcony laughed heartily at the countless epigrammatic sayings in the course of the piece, in blissful ignorance that some of these expressions were keenly satirising their very selves. . . .[23]

*The Daily Express* gave *The Bending of the Bough* a thoughtfully approving review, although it regretted that 'Contemporary issues are presented under so very thin a disguise, and form . . . the very groundwork of the plot of Mr. Moore's play. These issues become antiquated and pass away, and when they do so what will remain of the interest of *The Bending of the Bough?*' More specifically, the paper remarked:

It will be seen that the play makes two appeals — a broad appeal to the popular feeling on the Financial Relations question, with which Mr. Moore ingeniously associates all the current feelings about the preservation of the Gaelic language, the cultivation of Irish literature, and similar topics, and a more subtle appeal to the sense of tragedy in the frustration of ideal aims and the abandonment of a spiritual mission. The audience, which was not so large as that of Monday night, but which numbered among it nearly every man and woman of intellectual instruction in Dublin, was undoubtedly delighted with the performance and followed the development of the plot with the keenest sympathy. The first scene, showing a meeting of the Corporation, in which Jasper Dean, à la Mark Antony, fires an indifferent and hesitating body with his own passion and conviction by a fine effort of oratory, formed an admirable introduction to the play, and left the audience pleased and expectant. When the humour and satire of the scenes in which the two maiden aunts of Jasper try to dissuade him from courses so shocking to "respectable" people told with excellent effect, and every polished sentence created a ripple of merriment. . . . The least successful scene was un-

76

doubtedly that at the close of the play, in which, after the popular tumult following on Jasper's desertion, the dishevelled corporators seek refuge in his house. The language and action of this part of the play are somewhat out of gear with the situation — men with torn garments and bleeding heads do not discuss affairs in their reflective fashion. This, however, is the only episode in which there has been any failure in dramatic realisation. The character of Kirwan, the man who is quietly and steadfastly faithful to his star, though he knows that he can never lead his fellows along the path he has chosen, and sees even those he has inspired fall away from their mission, is very finely conceived and drawn by the author, and was played impassively by Mr. William Devereux, although one felt sometimes a little annoyed by his close resemblance in manner and appearance to Mr. George Alexander. The part of Jasper Dean was taken by Mr. Percy Lyndal, who rendered successfully, though not without a little staginess, the character of a young enthusiast. . . . Valentine Foley, the clever and volatile journalist, who takes the impression of every mind which addresses him sympathetically, was rendered with great success by Mr. Eugene Mayeur, though we do not see why his costume should suggest that of a sportsman so much more than that of an editor. . . . The minor parts were mostly pretty well filled, but the make-up of the Mayor of Northhaven left a great deal to be desired.[24]

Joseph Holloway was less enthusiastic. He recognized *The Bending of the Bough* as a brilliant political satire, but remarked quite accurately that 'as an acting drama I feel sure little more will be heard of it.' Although the actors were from the English professional stage, they seemed in this instance to have adopted an acting style which was later characteristic of the Irish players. Holloway notes: 'The acting was for the most part good, though perhaps too slow, but I noticed one peculiarity — in the chief performers that of gazing vacantly out into the audience and seldom addressing each other; in fact, so strongly marked is this peculiarity indulged in by players . . . that I have christened it the "Irish Literary Theatre stare".'[25] Contemporary stage practice may have condoned an inanimate, dreamlike manner in Maeterlinck and some of Shakespeare, but the practice of facing the audience rather

77

than each other in Moore's realistic play undoubtedly foreshadows the style of acting later identified with the Abbey Theatre. That this style should appear before the Fays took charge of the acting would seem to indicate the importance of Yeats in encouraging such a style. Later in the year, when Mrs. Campbell's company performed Maeterlinck's *Pelléas and Mélisande*, Holloway noted the similarity to Yeats's 'weird, static, mystic suggestiveness'. *The Irish Times* was even more distinctly unimpressed:

> A very interesting event took place last night at the Gaiety — namely the production of *The Bending of the Bough*, by Mr. George Moore, under the aegis of the Irish Literary Theatre. There is no one more entitled to respectful consideration than George Moore, but that the author of *Esther Waters* should have signed his name to this production requires some explanation. We who have read his works, and who have acknowledged him one of the greatest English novelists of the generation, placed on our trial as in a sense we are, will say that this is not George Moore's work, and does not represent his art. Having sat for three long weary hours in the Gaiety Theatre, if the writer were asked to tell the story of the play we would be compelled to sit silent. Story none, dialogue dull, action weak—that is the play which an audience was asked to assist in last night. Where does George Moore come in . . . in the wretched attempt to adapt Ibsen's insipid municipal drama, *An Enemy of the People*, to the Dublin stage? George Moore, whose books, however much we may dislike and disagree with them, never had anything to do with the lifeless and contemptible blocks which form the *dramatis personae* of this piece — never had anything to do with the limping plot which in this instance is supposed to constitute an action. Action, plot, dialogue, literature — where can they be found? One might as well ask where George Moore is to be found. Ask anyone who had never before heard of the so-called play, and who was in the theatre last night, to tell the story — story there is none, plot there is none. Of dull, dry, insipid, unnatural, wretchedly commonplace conversation there is an immensity — where is George Moore? The fact is that this *Bending of the Bough*, or whatever else it is called, is not — cannot be — Mr. George Moore's. . . . To approach

the occasion in the language of convention, a fairly well-filled house received the play with a fair degree of favouritism; but so far as the writer is concerned, he cannot give any reason why the piece should be tolerated. . . . How is it that men writing for an Irish audience should think that Ibsen and his methods are the right thing? Against such an idea we most strenuously protest.[26]

Whoever the *Times* reviewer was, he seems certainly to have had more than an inkling that the play was not precisely Moore's.[27]

\*     \*     \*

Despite the persuasive strictures of *The Irish Times,* the more general view of the literary theatre was that expressed in a leading article in *The Irish Daily Independent*:

The measure of a country's greatness is the merit of its art. Now, literature, being the highest form of art, and drama the most exalted form of literature, it follows that no country can be truly great which cannot boast great drama and good literature. . . . And though no Shakespeare has yet arisen to give Ireland drama which takes admiration captive, there is hope that out of the new literary movement there may come dramatic seed which, like the small grain in the parable, shall grow until it spring into the greatest tree in the forest of pure literature. For, in the Ireland of today are many of the circumstances that attended the grand literary revivals of which history tells. Our land had passed, and even now is passing, through a period of unrest. Men's minds are agitated; mighty questions force themselves upon us; and from out of the turmoil and the conflict there come thoughts, and yearnings, and desires, which struggle to take shape in literature, just as the agitation which preceded and closed in the day of Shakespeare bore its fruit in thought which took enduring shape in poetry and prose and drama such as England has not known before or since the vast Elizabethan age.[28]

Despite the rhetorical gush, the statement had considerable truth.

\*     \*     \*

To celebrate the success of the performances, the National Literary Society gave a luncheon on 22 February at the Gresham Hotel for the members of the Irish Literary Theatre. After the luncheon there were, inevitably, speeches:

Dr. Douglas Hyde, in proposing "The Health of the Irish Literary Theatre", said that theatre had now been with them for two years, and if he were to say that it was justified by its works, he should be according it a very small meed of praise: not only had it been justified of its works, but it had been more than justified (hear, hear). It had been at once a performance and a promise; a performance, which he was sure, had come up to their expectations; and a promise that the Irish national genius, working in future upon untrammelled lines, and deliberately trying to cut itself off from English influences, which had for so many years been the bane and ruination of Irish art, would be a credit to the island which gave it birth (applause). The aim and object of the Irish Literary Theatre was to embody and perpetuate Irish feeling, genius, and modes of thought. The Irish Literary Theatre was one, an important one, but still only one of the many agencies which were at this present moment at work in trying to create a new Ireland, proceeding upon national lines. By national, he meant something absolutely uncontentious, non-political, and non-sectarian (hear, hear). The first play they had the pleasure of seeing, *The Last Feast of the Fianna*, (applause), was really only a first representation of the theme at which Irish writers and Gaelic speakers had been working for 1,200 years, and he was convinced that if the play had been played in Irish before an Irish-speaking audience it would come as something perfectly natural to them (applause). Then, again, Mr. Martyn's *Maeve* exemplified another feature of the nationality of which he was speaking. In that play the writer represented the eternal illimitable passion of Irish memory, Irish regret, Irish idealism, struggling with, and vanquishing, the more or less complacent self-satisfaction of English prosperity and Anglo-Saxon smugness (applause). And with what words should he characterise the genius which had passed before their eyes in a couple of brief hours, the very essence of those so heterogeneous discordant elements of Irish life, which so many Irishmen with impotent despair in their hearts had been watching, fuming, and raging round them during the last few years (hear, hear). He believed nobody who entered the theatre and heard that play, and the closing words as the curtain fell, could have left the theatre as he entered it (hear, hear). Amongst the many agencies which were working towards the re-creation of a distinctly national genius, the Gaelic League was not the least (applause). Within the last week or two the managers of 800 schools had petitioned that the children under their charge should be brought up as Irish speakers: and he might mention in connection with that, that the speech delivered last week by the foremost man upon the Board of National Education in Ireland (applause) had been one of the most momentous facts which he could remember in Irish life since he came of age, because it simply meant a reversal of ascendancy movement in Ireland (applause).

The toast was drunk with enthusiasm.

Mr. George Moore, who was warmly received, replied: —
I feel that I must apologize for appearing before you with an MS of my speech in my hand. The sight of an MS in the country where oratory flourishes everywhere, in all ranks of society, and in all conditions of intellect, must appear anomalous and absurd. But I am an exception among my gifted countrymen. I have not inherited any gift of improvisation, and the present is certainly no time for experiment, for, I believe, I have matter of importance to lay before you, and it will be less labour for you to give the extra attention which the condensation of the written phrase demands than to reduce to order the painful jumble of words and ideas, mixed with painful hesitations, which is the public speech of everyone except the born orator. Of the plays which were performed this week I do not intend to speak, and of the plays which the Irish Literary Theatre hopes to produce next year, I only propose to say that a play by Mr. Yeats and myself, entitled *Grania and Dermuid*, [sic] will probably be produced (hear, hear). A more suitable subject than the most popular of our epic stories would hardly be found for a play for the Irish Literary Theatre, and I may say that it would be difficult to name any poet that Ireland has yet produced more truly elected by his individual and racial genius to interpret the old legend,

81

than the distinguished poet whose contemporary and colla-
borateur I have the honour to be (hear, hear). But even if this
play should prove to be that dramatic telling of the great
story which Ireland has been waiting for these many years, it
will not, in my opinion, be the essential point of next year's
festival, for next year we have decided to give a play in our
own language, the language which to our great disgrace we do
not understand (applause). Alas, there will be fewer in the
theatre who will understand the Irish text than a Latin or
Greek one: so the play will be performed for the sake of the
example it will set. The performance of plays in our language
is part and parcel of the idea which led up to the founding of
the Irish Literary Theatre. The Irish Literary Theatre has
been founded to create a new centre for Irish enthusiasm, a
new outlet for the national spirit and energy. This is the first
object of the Irish Literary Theatre (hear, hear). I may say
it is its only object, for if we achieve this we achieve every
object: all other objects are co-relative; for all plays that
represent national spirit and energy are literature, and they are
literature because they perforce put on the stage grief, suffering,
pity and passion, rather than some passing phase of social life
or some external invention which may be used as a pretext for
scenery, dresses, and limelight. And to emphasise this position,
to make it clear to everyone, we are of the opinion that we
should give a play in Irish (hear, hear). I would not be understood to mean that the Irish play to be given next year is to
stand as a mere sign for our project; it will do this, it is true,
but it will do a little more than this — it will serve as a flag to
lead to the restoration of our language as the literary and
political language of this country. But before I speak of the
necessity of the restoration of our language, I will tell you
about the play that we have decided to produce. The play is
not one originally written in the Irish language: it is a translation of a play written in the English language, and for this
choice I am responsible. Lady Gregory, Mr. Martyn, Mr.
Yeats, and myself — here I must break off for a moment to
say that Lady Gregory will be the one amongst us who will be
able to follow the Irish text (applause). Lady Gregory, Mr.
Yeats, and Mr. Martyn were all equally agreed as to the necessity for producing a play in our original language, but I am

responsible for the decision to produce a translation rather than an original play in Irish. In my opinion an original play in Irish would be too hazardous an adventure; the art of writing for the stage is not easily acquired — the number of Irish writers is limited, and to produce a bad play written in Irish would be a misfortune. Moreover, I think our first Irish play has to rest on a solid literary foundation so that it may be possessed of a second life apart from its first life, which is necessarily transitory. I wish to present those who read our language with a piece of solid literature, and for this end my choice fell on a play at once simple and literary — *The Land of Heart's Desire* — by Mr. W. B. Yeats (applause). Mr. Yeats was at first averse to the translation of the play. I never grasped his reasons, but this was perhaps my fault, for I was overborne with the desire to obtain his consent, and he has given his consent. Dr. Douglas Hyde, whose Irish scholarship has passed beyond question, has been pleased to promise to translate the play for us. More on this point I need not say. Mr. Yeats will make what further explanations may be necessary, and I will hasten to the essential subject — the subject on which I have come to speak to you — the necessity of the revival of the language if Ireland is to preserve her individuality among nations. . . .

After speaking long and enthusiastically upon the Irish language, Moore concluded with a point that amused people somewhat at his expense:

Many of us here are too old or have not the leisure to learn a new language. I am amongst these. I am too old, and have not the leisure to learn Irish (laughter and "no, no"). In my youth Irish was still spoken everywhere; but then the gentry took pride in not understanding their own language. It was our misfortune that such false fashion should have prevailed and kept us in ignorance of our language, but it will be our fault if our children do not learn their own language. I have no children, but I shall at once arrange that my brother's children shall learn Irish (laughter). I have written to my sister-in-law telling her that I will undertake this essential part of her children's education. I will arrange that they have a nurse straight from Aran (laughter), for I am convinced that it profits a man nothing if he knows all the languages of the world and knows not his own (applause).

Mr. Martyn also responded, and thanked the company very sincerely for the kind way in which they had always received whatever work he had put before them. This year he was very proud to be associated with Miss Milligan, who had produced a beautiful little work — in fact, of its kind, a perfect work of art (applause).

Mr. W. B. Yeats, in proposing the toast of "The Irish Literary Society", said the vital question of the moment was the Irish language. The whole fate of the language might be this very week hanging in the balance. A new educational system was about to be introduced for Ireland. It might depend upon the action of their representative in Parliament whether that system was one that would preserve the Irish language throughout the country or one that would stifle it. Mr. Starkie's speech was certainly admirable (applause). It was, perhaps, the most sympathetic and intelligent speech which any official had made in Ireland upon any question for many years. But they had seen false dawns and deceptive lights so that no one could be quite sure. He thought that all Irishmen should insist upon their representatives in Parliament opposing any denationalising system of education; if any such denationalising system was introduced into Parliament they would require their Parliamentary representatives to use obstruction, insult, and every old weapon with which they had met the stranger in the past. And the present was a good moment for meeting the stranger and forcing from him that which they needed (applause). In the National Literary Society people of all politics had met together resolved upon preserving the distinctive soul of this country. It was only their misfortune that the Society had had to work in the English tongue. It was well that every man should know his enemy, and Mr. Moore had helped them in his most powerful play, that whirlwind of passion, *The Bending of the Bough*. The Society was not provincial. Trinity College was provincial (applause). That was why, for all these past years it had produced not one creative mind, it had not produced one man who possessed a really distinguished command of the English language (cries of "Ferguson" and

"Hyde"). He meant in recent years. Without any fear that his prophecy would be proved false he would venture to say that in ten years more of the intellect of this country would be with them, in Trinity College all the ablest of the students would be with them; in ten years those who were now against them would feel the shadows gathering about them (applause).[29]

*   *   *

Frank and Willie Fay were also busy. They continued actively with the W. G. Fay Comedy Combination, giving many performances from their simple repertoire, plays such as *The Irish Tutor* and *That Rascal Pat*. In 1900, W. G. Fay worked with Maud Gonne's Daughters of Erin, in directing the first public performance of Father Dinneen's play in Irish, *An Tobar Draoidheachta* (*The Magic Well*). Then on 24 and 25 October, the brothers presented *Robert Emmet*, a play by an American writer, Robert Pilgrim. W. G. Fay directed the production and painted the scenery. The cast was made up of the Dramatic Society of St. Theresa's Total Abstinence and Temperance Association, and the performance was given in their hall in Clarendon Street, the same one used two years later by Fay's company for the first performance of Æ's *Deirdre* and Yeats's *Kathleen ni Houlihan*. The single newspaper review, that in *The United Irishman*, praises the company for its industry and verve, but says little about the play itself.[30]

The Daughters of Erin were planning to continue their own experiments in patriotic drama, and on 30 December Maud Gonne wrote to Alice Milligan: 'Before leaving Ireland I write to ask if you will really help the Inghinidhe na hEireann with the Gaelic tableaux we talked of when I and Miss Killeen were in Belfast. Without your help we feel very much afraid of trying them as none of us have had much experience in tableaux.'[31] On the same day, Maud Gonne's chief helper, Máire T. Quinn, wrote Miss Milligan more specifically:

Dear Miss Milligan,
   Miss Gonne has asked me to write you with reference to the Gaelic Tableaux, which we are so anxious to have in Dublin.

85

We were so pleased to hear from Miss Killeen that you were interested in the project and had so kindly promised to give us the benefit of your experience and assistance in carrying them out.

. . . St. Patrick's Day falls on a Sunday and we believe we shall make a pile of money as people have no place to go on such a night, besides the entertainment will be very appropriate as we shall have Gaelic Hymns, sacred songs, with tableaux of St. Patrick and St. Brigid. I give you herewith a rough sketch of what we would like to have, and shall be so grateful if you will kindly give me any hints and suggestions you have as to the best way of grouping, music and songs appropriate etc. . . . This is what we would like — or something similar — make any suggestions that occur to you for which we shall be grateful:

1. St. Brigid.
2. St. Brigid and her maidens.
3. St. Patrick asleep. Shepherd boy.
4. St. Patrick preaching at Tara.
5. The conversion of King Laoghaire's Court.
6. Maev. and her Chariot.
7. Ditto.
8. Children of Lir.
9. Ditto.
10. Ditto.
11. (Suggest one please.)
12. St. Patrick and St. Brigid conversing.[32]

\*     \*     \*

The new Irish drama at the end of 1900 was not only bolstered by the support of the nationalist societies and the popular press. Some further support came from an unlikely source when the Roman Catholic Archbishop of Dublin, Dr. Walsh, in a dedication address of a church, referred scathingly to the imported British drama of the commercial stage:

86

Now my reason for speaking here to-day of this necessarily unpleasant and painful subject is that I wish to convey to Mr. Martyn, publicly, and in the presence of so many of the representatives of the Press, what I have long since said to him in conversation, namely, that in my opinion, the only real hope we can have to seeing our city and country rid of that prolific source of corruption that is now freely open in our midst, lies in the success of the movement, in which he is deeply interested, and in which he has from the beginning taken a foremost part. He knows what I refer to. I am firmly convinced that the evil will never be really checked so long as Dublin is left dependent for its theatrical representations, as it now is, upon the weekly visits of roving companies of players, with their imported plays, — plays, the evil suggestiveness of which, I understand, is intensified at times by a variety of devices that would not be tolerated even in London, but are freely indulged in by some of those actors when they are playing in what are known as "the provinces", our city of Dublin being, of course, included in that term. . . . The remedy is to be looked for in the success of the movement, in which Mr. Martyn and others associated with him are engaged, for the establishment of a genuinely Irish National Theatre in Dublin (applause). No other can fulfil the promise of that name, unless it is one no self-respecting Irishman, no self-respecting Irish lady, who goes to the theatre at all, need be ashamed or afraid to go to (applause).[33]

The troubles of 1899 seemed entirely resolved, and for the moment at least the Literary Theatre had the vocal elements of Dublin solidly behind it.

# 1901

Other than the Irish Literary Theatre's performances at the Gaiety, most of the important dramatic events of 1901 were at the Theatre Royal. A visit, in the week of 11 February, of Henry Irving and Ellen Terry, gave Dubliners a chance to see the more popular Irving showpieces, such as *The Merchant of Venice*, *The Bells*, and *The Lyons Mail*. On 12 June, Madame Réjane played *Sappho* at the Royal, and on other nights Hervieu's *La Course du Flambeau* and Becque's *La Parisienne*. On 4 July, Mrs. Patrick Campbell opened a three-night engagement with Echegaray's *Mariana*. Her company contained Gerald du Maurier and George Arliss. Beerbohm Tree and his company opened on 19 August in *Twelfth Night*, and late in October Forbes Robertson appeared in *Othello* and other plays.

\*     \*     \*

Maud Gonne's patriotic woman's organization, Inghinidhe na h-Eireann, or The Daughters of Erin, was quite active during the year, staging both tableaux vivants and plays. In a matinee and two evening performances on 8, 9, and 10 April, they staged at the Antient Concert Rooms three different programmes of tableaux. The tableaux were varied by musical interludes, recitations, character sketches, and an Irish Ceilidh — 'a representation of an Irish country home where all the neighbours gather together in convivial meeting' and which 'affords excellent opportunities for the country folk to display their skill in music, singing and dancing. . . .' The press generally reported that the programmes were received enthusiastically, but one may suspect that some of the enthusiasm was patriotic. A non-Gaelic Leaguer like Holloway took a more sombre view of the proceedings:

> In attending the final performance of the series of Gaelic tableaux vivants organised by the members of the "Daughters of Erin" Society held in the Antient Concert Rooms I had quite a new experience in the entertainment line, and I must say that some take their pleasure very sadly if they *enjoyed* the fare provided by the organisers of this "Irish" night. Is there

not something enlivening in the whole range of Irish song and story? And if so why not introduce a little of it into the "Irish" entertainments that are springing up on all sides, and not give one the impression they are "waking" someone or some thing. The ill-lighted hall and the melancholy dirge-like airs selected for interpretation by the chorus during the tableaux were eminently calculated to put one in the blues after a short time and the air of ill management, such as unnecessary delays, excessive and continuous noise behind the curtains, and the constant coming in and going out of the performers and their friends into the lobby of the hall between whiles, added to the discomfort of the ordinary amusement seeker. Were it not for the real excellence of an occasional solo and the novelty of the Irish "ceilidh", gloom would have overwhelmed me. . . . Can't one be cheerful and Irish at the same time?[2]

In the week of 26 August, the Daughters of Erin added the production of plays to their Irish nights, and *The Freeman's Journal* remarked in its review of the first night's performance:

A truly Irish night's entertainment was inaugurated last night in the Antient Concert Rooms, amid salvos of "arís", the full-throated and more resonant Gaelic equivalent of the encore, when it became necessary to recall an amateur actor, a singer, or an authoress who essayed the interpretation of one of her own creations. From the rise of the curtain till its fall, the dominant idea is clearly, encouragingly Irish, and it is the old tongue that often responds to the warm breath of Gaelic, that in moments of acute enjoyment or admiration sweeps from the audience stagewards. . . . There were songs and dances, tableaux vivants, and a specially written play. . . . Miss Milligan, whose true insight into the feeling of the moment, went back to splendid '98, must have been strongly tempted to betray strict historical perspective to an inclination to introduce Kitchener's last proclamation. If it were not for the fact that they are hanging rebels for the wearing of the Vierkleur, the casual critic might be betrayed into the error of speaking of this workmanlike little play as "of the conventional Irish drama type". It is true we have heard the whole story before— the hunted rebel, in whose breast the hot love of country

90

burns, the loving home heart, and the true peasant soul. . . .

The Harp That Once is prettily staged. There is a want of action, it is true, and the scene of the harp air ought to be taken in hand very seriously, but there is no reason why on Wednesday night the full effect should not be given to a very clever bit of stage work from the strictly histrionic standpoint.[3]

What we seem to have here is a gentle review of a conventional play which was rather amateurishly staged. The following evening saw the first production of another Milligan play, *The Deliverance of Red Hugh*, and of P. T. MacGinley's *Eilis agus an Bhean Deirce* (*Eilish and the Beggarwoman*), which was performed in Irish and for the first time in Dublin. The *Independent* reported:

The admirable entertainment on purely Irish lines which was arranged by the *Inghinidhe na hEireann* was continued last evening in the Antient Concert Rooms. The attendance was far short of what the merits of the performances should have called forth. The programme was of a particularly attractive character, and was strongly calculated to appeal to the national sentiments of the audience. One of the principal features was the production by Mr. W. G. Fay, for the first time on any stage, of a dramatic incident in two scenes by Miss A. L. Milligan, entitled *The Deliverance of Red Hugh*. The piece is strong in dramatic interest. It represents the captivity of Red Hugh and his comrades, the defiance which the young Irish chieftain offers to his jailers, and the ultimate escape of The O'Donnell and the two O'Neills through the friendly offices of one of the guards, who, being Irish on his mother's side, is won over to the cause of the prisoners, and assists them to make their way out of durance. . . . The performance of a one-act play in Irish by P. T. MacGinley, entitled *Eilis agus an Bhean Deirce* was very acceptable. The piece was constructed in clever style, and the parts were effectively filled.[4]

MacGinley's play was a simple one-act comedy, in which a woman is tricked by her son into giving her belongings to a tinker woman. According to the *Freeman*, it 'kept the audience in roars of laughter'.[5]

\*      \*      \*

91

Again, the theatrical event of the year was the appearance of the Irish Literary Theatre. Edward Martyn, piqued by Yeats's and George Moore's revision of *The Tale of a Town*, had withdrawn his financial support, but the previous ventures had been sufficiently successful to interest the manager of the Gaiety Theatre, and so Yeats and Moore approached the English actor-manager F. R. Benson who had frequently played in Dublin and whose name was a box-office attraction.

Although George Moore was in many ways an excellent replacement for Martyn, his name was to prove something of a drawback. Patriots had not forgotten his early critical volume *Parnell and his Island*, and his reputation for a sort of vague Godlessness and immorality were important factors in the generally critical reception of *Diarmuid and Grania*, the play upon which he collaborated with Yeats and which was the new season's chief attraction.

The story of the Yeats-Moore collaboration on *Diarmuid and Grania* is a famous one, and is most fully discussed in Moore's *Ave*, with what veracity the delighted reader may himself judge. According to Moore, Yeats's idea of play construction was to have their first act horizontal, their second perpendicular, and their third circular — whatever those terms may mean. It was finally decided that Moore would have the last word on construction and that Yeats would have the last word on style. A pure and appropriate style was to be evolved by Moore writing the original draft in French, by Lady Gregory translating that into English, by Tadhg O'Donoghue translating the English into Irish, by Lady Gregory translating the Irish back into English, and by Yeats, after this purifying process, putting 'style upon it'. Moore did actually go to France to begin the writing. 'It is impossible,' he said, 'to write this play in French in Galway. A French atmosphere is necessary....' [6] About four pages of what he managed to write in, as he called it, 'my French of Stratford atte Bowe', he printed in *Ave*.

Both men, of course, were prolific writers and in different ways both were business-like craftsmen. So a play emerged. Nevertheless, they were an ill-matched team, and their next attempt at collaboration was, no doubt fortunately, abortive.

The season's second play was a short piece in Irish by Douglas Hyde, *Casadh an tSugáin* or *The Twisting of the Rope*. This short piece, performed after the long play, was acted by Irish-speaking amateurs; and, even if we discount that enthusiasm generated by patriotism, it seems to have been a most engaging and lively production. Although a chorus of criticism from both patriots and intellectuals greeted *Diarmuid and Grania*, there was nothing but praise for *The Twisting of the Rope*.

Reports of the rehearsals of Hyde's play vary somewhat, but George Moore certainly regarded himself as responsible for its production. He was at this time extremely enthusiastic about promoting the Irish language, and he quotes in *Salve* the following interchange with Yeats:

> "You had better go over to Birmingham and see if you can't get another woman to play the part."
>
> "But our play doesn't matter, Yeats; what matters is *The Twisting of the Rope*. We either want to make Irish the language of Ireland, or we don't; and if we do, nothing else matters. Hyde is excellent in his part, and if I can get the rest straightened out, and if the play be well received, the Irish language will at least have gotten its chance."
>
> Yeats did not take so exaggerated a view of the performance of Hyde's play as I did.[7]

In a letter quoted elsewhere in this chapter, Moore implies his disappointment with the production of *Diarmuid and Grania*, and suggests that this semi-failure was the price that he had to pay for his attention to the Hyde rehearsals.

Also in *Salve*, Moore writes that he desired the Irish actors in Hyde's play to learn their parts during rehearsal. 'And for three weeks I followed the Irish play in a translation made by Hyde himself teaching everyone his or her part, throwing all my energy into the production, giving it as much attention as the most conscientious *régisseur* ever gave to a play at the *Français*.'[8] The following letter of Moore's bears out this claim and indeed suggests that the accounts in *Hail and Farewell* are more trustworthy than has been thought:

Dear Hyde,

I am sending a proof of the play to Miss O'Kennedy. I have written begging of her not to learn it by heart and I hope you will not learn your part until you have rehearsed the play and know the positions and the business. Much better begin by reading the play and trying to act the positions. In this way the actor instinctively suits his reading to the reading adopted by the actress. In acting we must take into account the limitations of the people we are acting with. There will be plenty of time to rehearse the play but your presence in Dublin will help us. You will be able to help me to keep up the correspondence in the Press. I wish you would send a short letter to the Truly Nationals, better still to *The Irish Times*. Yes, write to *The Times*. I forced that paper to publish an apology; it libelled me, inadvertently, it is true, but I seized on the occasion to demand an apology, and I was very stern for a newspaper is like a dog, no use until it has been thrashed. *The Times* will now publish all we please to send it.

Always yours,<br>George Moore

Did you see the correspondence about the music for *Diarmuid and Grania*. If not see yesterday's *Freeman* and today's.[9]

The other claimant for the direction of the Hyde play is Willie Fay. It was during the rehearsals of *Diarmuid and Grania* that Moore first met the Fays, but of Willie he only remarked that, 'the enthusiasm which *The Twisting of the Rope* had evoked brought Willie Fay to my house one evening, to ask me if I would use my influence with the Gaelic League to send himself and his brother out, with a little stock company, to play an equal number of plays in English and Irish.' In his own memoirs, W. G. Fay has a different story:

Mr. Moore had intended to produce this play [*The Twisting of the Rope*] himself, but he found his experience in dealing with professional actors in London of little use in coaching the Gaelic-speaking amateurs supplied by the League. Indeed it was, if anything, a hindrance, and so he finally sent for me to know if I would take over the job, which I was very glad to do. My knowledge of Gaelic was not extensive [in *Salve* Moore quotes Fay as saying that neither he nor his brother had any Gaelic at all], but my experience of producing amateurs was, and, with Dr. Hyde to help me, I knew I could manage. I got all the actors to speak their lines in English first while I gave the business and the positions. When they had got these right we turned the play back into Gaelic and in this way put it together bit by bit. It was all a valuable experience for me because it proved that, given the good-will of the actors, I could get the same acting value out of the play whether it was spoken in English or Gaelic.[10]

In a letter written in 1904 to Joseph Holloway, Frank Fay remarked, 'By the way, I don't know whether you know that only for the brother, *The Twisting of the Rope* could not have been given. He rehearsed and produced it at the Gaiety.'[11]

In later years particularly, the Fays tended to be understandably belligerent in claiming credit for their early efforts, but it is probably unfair to deny Moore any significant part in the rehearsal of the play. At any rate, it is quite impossible at this date to untangle who did what, and the best that can be said is that the production of Hyde's play was lively and effective, and enjoyed by all who saw it.

The rehearsals of *Diarmuid and Grania* did not go too smoothly either. Moore visited the Bensons in Brighton in August, and it was apparently with Benson that the much deplored idea of bringing a sheep onstage originated. As Moore wrote to Yeats:

He is very much taken with the idea of sheep-shearing. He says he will carry in a sheep. [In Act 2 there was a stage direction, "Enter Diarmuid and a shepherd carrying fleeces."] I told him a sheep is a difficult animal to carry, but he says there will be no difficulty for him. The stage will show fleeces hung about, there will be branding irons and crooks. . . . I cannot tell you how pleased I am; I walk about the streets thinking of the fleeces and the sheep."[12]

Later, when the Benson company had come over to Dublin, the sheep had shrunk to a kid, and Yeats wrote to Lady Gregory:

Yesterday we were rehearsing at the Gaiety. The kid Benson is to carry in his arms was wandering in and out among the stage properties. I was saying to myself, "Here we are, a lot of intelligent people who might have been doing some sort of decent work that leaves the soul free; yet here we are, going through all sorts of trouble and annoyance for a mob that knows neither literature nor art. I might have been away, away in the country, in Italy perhaps, writing poems for my equals and my betters. The kid is the only sensible creature on the stage. He knows his business and keeps to it." At that very moment one of the actors called out, "Look at the kid, eating the property ivy!" [13]

Nobody was entirely happy with the casting, and the actors, many of whom later became well known, had some difficulty with the pronunciation of the names. As J. C. Trewin sums up various testimonies:

At rehearsal W. G. Fay discovered that they were pronouncing Diarmuid in three or four different ways, and calling Grania Grawniar or Grainyah. Matheson Lang said that, though Yeats was very particular about pronunciation, nobody could manage the name of Caoelte. The company called it "Kaoltay"; Yeats said it ought to be "Wheelsher". That night Harcourt Williams was addressed successively as "Wheelchair", "Cold-tea", and "Quilty", to the horror of patriots. But patriots hated the play.[14]

\*     \*     \*

Shortly before the performances in the Gaiety, the theatre again published its magazine, although the name was changed from *Beltaine*. As Yeats explained, 'I have called this little collection of writings *Samhain*, the old name for the beginning of winter, because our plays this year are in October, and because our Theatre is coming to an end in its present shape.' [15] The issue contained some introductory paragraphs by Yeats, called 'Windlestraws', on a variety of subjects; a short essay by Moore called 'The Irish Literary Theatre'; an even shorter essay by Martyn called 'A Plea for a National Theatre in Ireland'; a retelling of 'The Legend of Diarmuid and Grania' by Lady Gregory and signed with her initials; the text in Irish of Hyde's *Casadh an tSugáin*, and an unsigned translation into English of the play, by Lady Gregory.

Yeats's 'Windlestraws' has been several times reprinted, save for one short paragraph and occasional single sentences, and so we will

96

not reprint it again here. The most important point that he made, however, was that the Irish Literary Theatre in its present form was coming to an end. He also discussed with not complete accuracy several Gaelic plays the writing of which the Literary Theatre inspired, among them were P. T. MacGinley's *Eilis agus an Bhean Deirce,* Father Peter O'Leary's *Tadg Saor,* and Father Dinneen's *Creadeamh agus Gorta;* he gently criticized Miss Lefanu's play for its imitation of old models; he summarized several schemes which had been proposed for the continuation of the theatrical movement; and he briefly referred to the probable criticisms which this year's performance would arouse.

> We do not think there is anything in either play to offend anybody, but we make no promises. We thought our plays inoffensive last year and the year before, but we were accused the one year of sedition, and the other of heresy. We await the next accusation with a cheerful curiosity.[16]

The last sentence he did not include when he republished these remarks.

George Moore's essay was a capsule review of the past two years of the Literary Theatre, and is particularly interesting for his comments upon the faults of previous productions.

> It is now nearly three years since Mr. Yeats and Mr. Martyn explained to me their project of The Irish Literary Theatre. I imagine that they were moved by a disinterested love of Ireland; by a desire to create a sort of rallying point for the many literary enthusiasms and aspirations they saw beginning in Ireland. I was moved to join them because I had come to know the hopelessness of all artistic effort in England. I discovered the English decadence before I discovered my conscience; at that time I merely despaired of any new literary movement ever rising in England. I saw nothing about me but intellectual decay and moral degradation, so I said: "Well, my friends, let us try." I knew Mr. Edward Martyn's play, *The Heather Field,* and his *Maive,* [sic], and I knew Mr. Yeats's *Countess Cathleen;* "these," I said, "will do for a start, but what have we got to follow them?" They answered. "You will write us a play, and somebody else will write after you. One must not look too far ahead."

And then began the most disagreeable part of the adventure: excursions to theatrical clubs in the Strand and in the streets leading from the Strand; the long drives to ladies who lived in flats in picturesque neighbourhoods, and arranging for these men and women to come to Dublin. I took upon myself the greater part of these petty annoyances — Mr. Martyn taking upon himself, perhaps, the greatest annoyance, distributing of tickets, and keeping the accounts. I think that this kind of theatrical management must be very like the endeavour of kind-hearted ladies to bring some fifty and odd children into the country for a holiday. In both, there is a great deal of "Has Johnny lost his cap" and "Will Jimmy arrive in time?"

During the rehearsal, I often asked myself why I had consented to waste my time in this fashion; the reason was hidden from me; even now I know, only through faith, that I acted rightly and that if the collecting of the actors and the rehearsals of the plays had proved ten times more troublesome, it would still have been worth the trouble. And this, for some reason that is still hidden from me, and not altogether because *The Heather Field* had been admitted to be the most thoughtful of modern prose plays written in English, the best constructed, the most endurable to a thoughtful audience. It was played in a hall, on a platform amid ludicrous scenery. But, being a prose play, it did not suffer so much from want of space as *The Countess Cathleen*, and it was the better acted play, for it is always easier to find actors who can act plays of modern life than it is to find actors who can speak verse and embody vast sentiments. For the adequate representation of such a play, something like a gulf should separate the actors from the audience, and there should be a large, deep stage full of vague shadows. Green landscapes are not required in Rembrandt's portraits, and I have often wondered why they are used as a background for actors. The more elaborate the scenery, the worse it is for the purpose of the poet and the actor; and new scenery, harsh as a newly-painted signboard, like that amid which *The Countess Cathleen* was played, is the worst scenery of all. *The Countess Cathleen* met with every disadvantage. Here is a list which must not, however, be considered exhaustive: — First, the author's theory that verse should be chanted[17] and not spoken; second, the low platform insufficiently separated from the audience; third, a set of actors and actresses unaccustomed to speak verse; fourth, harsh, ridiculous scenery; fifth, absurd costumes.

The theories of the author regarding the speaking of verse I hold to be mistaken; I do not think they are capable of realization even by trained actors and actresses, but the attempt of our "poor mummers of a timeworn spring", was, indeed, lamentable. Many times I prayed during the last act that the curtain might come down at once. Nevertheless, the performance of *The Countess Cathleen* was not in vain. The beauty of the play was so intense that it was seen through the ridiculous representation as the outline of a Greek statue through the earth it is being dug out of. *The Countess Cathleen* awakened in all who saw it a sense of beauty. I think a sense of beauty once awakened is immortal. I do not think anyone who ponders over a piece of antique sculpture, shall we say a broken bas-relief from Pompeii, ever forgets that keen sense of beauty which arises in his heart, and the imperfect and broken representations of *The Countess Cathleen* awakened in me just such a sense of beauty as I have experienced in dim museums, looking at some worn and broken bas-relief.

The performances of our plays were so successful that the managers of the Gaiety Theatre asked us to produce our next plays in their theatre, and so confident were they of the ultimate success of our enterprise that they offered us their theatre on the same terms they gave to an ordinary troop of mummers. It is more difficult for me to speak of the second performances than of the first, because I undertook to re-write Mr. Martyn's play, *A Tale of a Town*, a play which the Irish Literary Theatre did not think advisable to produce. The public will soon have an opportunity of judging our judgment, for Mr. Martyn has decided to publish the original text of his play. So much of the character of his play was lost in my rewriting that the two plays have very little in common, except the names of the personages and the number of acts. The comedy, entitled, *The Bending of the Bough*, was written in two months, and two months are really not sufficient time to write a five act comedy in; and, at Mr. Martyn's request, my name alone was put on the title page. Mr. Martyn's *Maive* [sic] did not gain by representation, it was inadequately acted, and the idea of the play is clearer in the printed text than it was on the stage. But all who saw the play will remember it; it will flash across their minds, and will become more and more realizable with time.

This year *Diarmuid and Grania* will be given, and though it is longer by two acts than Dr. Hyde's play, it is not so important, for the three act play is written in English, and the one act play is written in Irish. Dr. Hyde's play will be the first Irish play produced in a Dublin theatre: I thought till the other day that it would be the first Irish play produced in Dublin, but now I hear that the organization called *Inghean* [*sic*] *na h-Eireann* has produced at the Antient Concert Rooms (it was in this room that *The Countess Cathleen* and *The Heather Field* were performed), a play in Irish. In a way it would have pleased our vanity to have been the first in Dublin with an Irish play, but this would have been a base vanity, and unworthy of a Gaelic Leaguer. There has been no more disinterested movement than the Gaelic League. It has worked for the sake of the language without hope of reward or praise; and if I were asked why I put my faith in the movement I would answer that to believe that a movement distinguished by so much self sacrifice could fail, would be like believing in the failure of goodness itself.

Since we began our work plays have been written, some in Irish and some in English, and we shall be forgiven if we take a little credit for having helped to awaken intellectual life in Ireland. Many will think I am guilty of exaggeration when I say that The Irish Literary Theatre has done more to awaken intellectual life in Ireland than Trinity College. The Irish Literary Theatre is the centre of a literary movement, and our three years have shown that an endowed theatre may be of more intellectual service to a community than a university or a public library.[13]

In his short article, Edward Martyn noted that, 'There are many movements now for the encouragement of Irish manufacture in all its branches and for preventing the scandalous outpouring of Irish money into the pockets of Englishmen and other foreigners.' After mentioning particularly a scheme for the establishment of a school to teach the making of stained glass, he then argued, 'Is it not time that our dramatic art also should be placed on a national basis?'

100

Are we so degenerate that we cannot meet this demand also by a supply of national art? The first requisite is to provide a stock company of native artists because the foreign strollers are too wedded to the debased art of England to fall in with the change. This can only be done by instituting a school for the training of actors and actresses, a most important branch of which should be devoted to teaching them to act plays in the Irish language. Now it is quite legal and feasible to obtain a grant from the Department of Technical Instruction for this purpose which is the same in principle as the teaching of stained glass manufacture. It is a home industry in the best sense, and means a vast economic saving to the country, besides being a most refining educational influence. . . .

With a company of artists such as I have described we might put before the people of Ireland native works, also translations of the dramatic masterworks of all lands, for it is only by accustoming a public to the highest art that it can be led to appreciate art, and that dramatists may be inspired to work in the great art tradition.[19]

* * *

In the issue of *The All-Ireland Review* which appeared just two days before the performances, Standish O'Grady[20] launched the first attack on *Diarmuid and Grania*.

This story is only one out of thousands of stories about the great, noble, and generous Finn — the greatest, the noblest, and perhaps the most typical Irishman that ever lived — the one story, I say, out of them all in which the fame of the hero and prophet is sullied, and his character aspersed.

And, speaking for myself, I am not one little bit obliged to Mr. Yeats or to Mr. Moore for writing and exhibiting an Irish drama founded upon an utterly untrue chapter of pretended Irish history, written in the decadence of heroic and romantic Irish literature. Needless to say, I shall not go to see their drama.[21]

A rather chilling omen.

* * *

101

The plays were first produced on Monday evening, 21 October 1901, at the Gaiety Theatre, Dublin. They were originally scheduled to play on Monday, Tuesday and Wednesday evenings, and there was also a matinee on Wednesday of *Diarmuid and Grania* alone, since the actors in Hyde's play were unable to arrange to be away from their jobs in the afternoons. Although F. R. Benson later remarked that the Irish plays were not as well attended as the Shakespearian production, *King Lear*, which was to be given by the Benson company on the other days, they were at any rate sufficiently popular for it to be announced later in the week that they would also be performed on Friday evening.

Generally, the response of the audience seems to have been one of enthusiastic good will. There was some boredom with *Diarmuid and Grania*, and the appearance of F. R. Benson with a kid in his arms drew laughter from the galleries. Nevertheless, the intermissions were filled with the singing of patriotic songs, Yeats was greeted with wild applause when he took his curtain call,[22] and he and Maud Gonne were greeted when they left the theatre by fervid patriots who wanted to unhitch the horse from the carriage and pull it themselves through the streets.

\* \* \*

On Tuesday, *The Freeman's Journal* gave the productions a two-column review, remarking in part:

> The success of the performance of the Irish Literary Theatre last night at the Gaiety Theatre argues well for the possibility of the institution becoming a permanent one in Dublin. That this success was owing in a great measure to a new departure — the presentation of a play in Irish by Dr. Douglas Hyde — was obvious. Every Gaelic Leaguer, every student of O'Growney, everyone interested in the old tongue who could elbow his way into the theatre was there last night, and the enthusiasm was tremendous. But the fact that the play in English, *Diarmuid and Grania*, was given by a company already well known and popular in Dublin must also have helped not a little to fill the theatre. Of Dr. Douglas Hyde's charming little one-act play, *Casadh an tSugáin, The Twisting of the Rope*, which was presented after *Diarmuid and Grania*, there is

102

nothing to be said but praise. It is a perfect little genre picture, which, in the completeness of detail and deft precision of light and shade, irresistibly reminds one of an interior painted by one of the masters of the Dutch school. . . .

Of the acting of this little piece, considering the fact that all the parts were filled by amateurs, it is almost impossible to speak too highly. Dr. Douglas Hyde himself, who played Hanrahan, is a born actor. His eloquent tenderness to Una threw into strong relief the fierce savagery and scorching contempt with which he turned on Sheamus and his friends when they attempted to interrupt him, and his soft, weird crooning of his passionate verses was inimitable. . . .

If the Irish play of Dr. Hyde is the most satisfying and successful effort of the Irish Literary Theatre, the play of *Diarmuid and Grania* by Mr. W. B. Yeats and Mr. George Moore is the most ambitious it has done. . . . In the hands of Mr. Yeats and Mr. Moore the story has undergone considerable modification. Many of the minor incidents have been omitted and the strings of the drama have been tightened. The effect of this selection and pruning has been, from the purely dramatic point of view, excellent. It has brought out the essential points of the story, and given it an intensity and a coherence it would otherwise have lacked. But in thus weaving anew the threads of this old tale of love and vengeance the authors have spun from their loom a new fabric. They have twisted the threads into a more intricate pattern; and while the new Diarmuid and Grania are vastly more interesting personages, considered from the point of view of human emotion, than they were in the old tale, they have, perhaps, lost a little of the simplicity, the inevitableness, the elemental character which seems to belong to these figures of a mythical age, and have become characters which it is easy to fancy in modern garments. So far has the process been carried out that Grania recalls recent heroines of the novel and the stage. . . .

Mrs. Benson's Grania was an excellent imitation of the manner of Mrs. Patrick Campbell. Mr. Benson, as Diarmuid, played in the cultivated and intelligent manner which had always characterised his performances. Mr. Frank Rodney was a capable Fionn, and Mr. Alfred Brydon a dignified and effective King Cormac. Miss Lucy Franklein played carefully as Laban, but was hardly weird enough to be convincing. Much praise is due to Mr. Arthur Whitby for his admirable impersonation of Conan the Bald, a character-study which relieved the overwhelming tragedy of the play.[23]

*   *   *

*The Irish Times* gave a generally affirmative review also:

> To Mr. Yeats's poetic inspiration was added Mr. Moore's gift of construction, of welding varied elements into a dramatic whole, so that the play was an admirable example of fine workmanship. . . . Dr. Hyde's play went very brightly. His own acting carried it off with great verve, and it evidently delighted the audience. The costumes were most appropriate, but we have our doubts about the *fichu* being worn in Munster farmhouses a hundred years ago.[24]

*The Irish Daily Independent and Nation* was kind, but sounds as if it were praising the intention more than the deed:

> In *Diarmuid and Grania* Messrs. Moore and Yeats have produced a piece of considerable power to charm. Its dialogue is of a high order. It is couched in a lofty and cultured key, with many strong poetical passages, and a great deal of matter that will capture the imagination. . . . The play is one that would probably read better than it lends itself to staging. Still it is actable to a greater extent, perhaps, than any other piece hitherto played by the Irish Literary Theatre, excepting *The Bending of the Bough*.
>
> The staging of the piece is very handsome, the scene on the wooded slopes of Ben Bulben being very picturesque. But the lighting was too aggressive, while in the cottage scene the changes of atmosphere out of doors were rather in the nature of a phenomenon.[25]

The writer who signed himself 'M.A.M.' in *The Evening Herald* found much to criticize, and, as he did not allow himself to fall into hysterical condemnations, he sounded very persuasive:

104

To be perfectly frank, this work of Messrs. Yeats and Moore is a bit of a disappointment. It is very dreary at times, there is a wearisome repetition of sentiment in long dialogues and irritating speeches, and a startling absence of any Celtic atmosphere. Lay the action in Sussex, Wessex, or Kent, call the men Cedric and such names, dress the parts for the period, and who would suggest that there was a trace of the work of Celtic revivalists in the entire three acts? . . . The stage version lands one in a world of metaphysical meanderings, whose Grania argues as if she took out her M.A. degree in Boston, and then Diarmuid replies with rocks of thought as if he were a deep student of Herbert Spencer.

There is too much of Grania in the play. One gets tired of her whims and graces, her whining and monotonous low-toned talks. In the second act one feels it is a great pity she has no children. A cradle in the corner and something in it would occupy her mind, and prevent her falling into dozes before the fire, vainly regretting in a timid, feminine way like a woman whose dressmaker has disappointed her on the night of the ball.

The sentiments, despite the old-time suggestions of fourteenth-century baronial halls, sound very modern. In fact, in Mrs. Benson's hands, Grania is an embryo Mrs. Tanqueray, B.C., and every moment one expects her to confide to the audience some passages in her past that would raise her in the interest of all ladies present to the level of the second Mrs. Tanqueray herself.

One of the most grating drawbacks in this piece is the absence of mobility in the Knights of Tara and all connected with that establishment. One hears nothing but muttered doubts of one another's honour; every man accuses the other of pledge-breaking, drunkenness, lying, or something else. King Cormac himself is a mild precursor of Polonius, who has his eye on every one of them; and the minor knights and others in suits of pre-Christian pyjamas raise titters when they should draw tears. . . .

As to the players, they did all right. As stated, Mrs. Benson plays a long, weary, dreary part, and succeeds in losing the sympathy of the audience. This may not be her fault. Grania is unlovable, uninteresting. In the second act it would be mightily proper if Diarmuid took a rod and beat her. But maybe such methods of restoring reason to wives and others, as the modern bastinado was unknown to the Knights of the Red Branch. It was a serious slip in domestic arrangements to so neglect them. . . The scenery is appropriate, if the first set — a dingy stock scene — be excepted.[26]

\*     \*     \*

Frank Fay treated the productions at length in two articles. His general view was one of approval for the plays and of criticism for the acting. Of *Diarmuid and Grania*, he said:

> . . . Mr. Yeats and Mr. Moore have given us a fine play, and, as I venture to think, a beautiful one, though perhaps the characters are not drawn on the heroic scale in which they appear to one's mind's eye.
>
> Mr. Standish O'Grady, who repudiates the legend as 'an utterly untrue chapter of pretended Irish history, written in the decadence of heroic and romantic Irish literature", will certainly be wise if he abstains, as he said he will, from going to see it. But it is good enough for me, and I venture to think most people will be delighted with it. I cannot say that I am displeased that the authors have humanised the heroic and made Diarmuid a man and Grania a woman of flesh and blood like ourselves; our hearts go out to them more readily than if they were merely beautiful statues. It may be doubtful whether two authors of such opposite literary temperaments as Mr. W. B. Yeats and Mr. George Moore benefit by collaboration, but I do not feel that *Diarmuid and Grania* has suffered thereby.

He also felt that, 'the greatest triumph of the authors lies in their having written in English a play in which English actors are intolerable. . . . Truly *Diarmuid and Grania* must be even a finer play than I think it, to have survived the vulgar acting it received.' [27]

In a later column, Fay elaborated his attack:

> . . . I cannot help thinking that much of the disappointment I have heard expressed about the play is really the result of the execrable — I can use no milder word — acting it received at

the hands of Mr. Benson and his company. . . . I am a great admirer of Mr. Rodney, Mr. Benson's leading man, and to see his superb acting I have long endured Mr. Benson's elaborately bad acting in Shakespeare's and other plays. . . . All the plays produced by the Irish Literary Theatre have called for one quality which, except in Mr. Rodney's case, is not cultivated by the Benson company, I mean beauty of speech. In *Diarmuid and Grania* I am bound to say I did not find Mr. Rodney's delivery beautiful; moreover, he was, like the others, impossible, because he was an Englishman; but he did not, in such acting as he was able to give, reduce *Diarmuid and Grania* to the level of *The Corsican Brothers*, as the others did. That Mr. Benson should bring a lamb or a kid or whatever the animal was, on the stage did not astonish me (nothing that he could do would astonish me), but I think the authors might, at the rehearsals, have insisted on his not doing so. . . . I now see that such acting as *Diarmuid and Grania* received was worse than useless. It was as much as I could do to sit out the acting on the occasion of my second visit, and I only did so in order to once more enjoy *Casadh an t-Sugáin*, which I did, and thoroughly.[28]

Of course, Fay was not an unprejudiced critic. He was campaigning in *The United Irishman* for Yeats and his friends to turn to some group of Irish actors, such as the group led by his brother and himself, to act out the Irish plays. Yet, he was not so uncritical as to allow the Irish-speaking amateurs in Douglas Hyde's play to escape without an admonition:

Dr. Hyde was in great form, and his humour got over the footlights in a wonderful way for a novice; he was irresistible, and the little piece went very well. I say this to encourage all concerned, and I mean it; but I would have them understand that if they want to go on acting plays in Irish, or in English either, they must be prepared to face a lot of hard work, and to remember that an artist is never done learning. And let them take great care to be distinct in their speech; an audience will do a great deal of the acting itself if it only hears the words, and will forgive much to the actors.[29]

The costumes drew some criticism:

> The designing of the costumes for *Diarmuid and Grania*, as
> well as the archaeological researches necessary for the mount-
> ing of the play, was undertaken by Mr. Benson's secretary,
> who went to a good deal of trouble in consulting illuminated
> manuscripts and other sources of information in order to
> ensure the accuracy of the aesthetic details. It may be doubted,
> however, whether the appearance of the warriors in the first
> act is really very reminiscent of Fionn and his Fianna as they
> entered the Banquet Hall at Tara. As usual, the attempt at
> realistic production has not been a success, and Fionn's striped
> trews, the material and colouring of which is so obviously and
> aggressively modern, can hardly be said to be convincing. Had
> a more subdued and suggestive method been employed both
> with regard to costumes and scenery — had a little more been
> left to the imagination of the audience — the effect would
> have been infinitely better.[30]

James H. Cousins wrote the following caustic 'First Night
Impression' of *Diarmuid and Grania*:

> In the first act of *Diarmuid and Grania* the actors fall asleep;
> in the last act the audience do. This is an example of sustained
> sympathetic affection seldom known, and a specimen of that
> 'dramatic unity' for which Pater contended, and which could
> have delighted his heart. So successfully indeed was the atmos-
> phere of the play transferred to the auditorium that many of
> the auditors in their dreams — as they indulged in forty winks
> while waiting for something to happen — confused the burial
> of Diarmuid with that of Moore — Sir John, I mean, for the
> other one is not dead yet, unfortunately, as a dramatist, though
> a rude person might say a nasty thing just here —, and "not a
> drum was heard, not a funeral note," of Dr. Elgar's music.
> My most vivid recollection of the second act is of an aged
> King half blindly groping about a spinning-wheel, and mut-
> tering: "There is no more flax on the distaff." I quite believed
> him; and the authors need not have written a further act to
> prove it.

There was a gentleman in the third act who saw the wind. It was during a dreadful storm in which the lightning flashed like a demented cinematograph, and the thunder was banged out of a drum in such a way as to suggest the "Twelfth" suddenly gone drunk before the right time. Quoth he: "I have never seen such a wind as this before." But he has nothing to do with the case. It is the boar I am thinking of, the mysterious boar which haunted the play. This boar never once showed his unhallowed snout, but his influence was felt right through. There was a hunting of this boar, and the audience were informed in advance what to look for in the way of a denouement. While they were leaning back in their seats waiting for the end to drag itself along, "Ah," said one of the actors, "I see someone coming through the woods. It is Conan the Bald, and they are pushing him along." Then from the pit stalls there came a voice, laden with the perfume of chocolate drops, and it sweetly said, "Please ask them to push the play along also."

Now this Conan the Bald was the "villain" of the piece in a way: its evil genius: its comedy relief: a bare-browed, bare-legged scoundrel who took huge delight in prophesying evil. He was in at the beginning, the middle, and the end: in fact the play was Conan — and bald.

"The fools are laughing at us," said Diarmuid to Grania. It was the truest word he ever spoke.[31]

Years later in his autobiography, Cousins vividly described the excitement of the first night:

> . . . *Diarmuid and Grania* was announced as under the joint authorship of W. B. Yeats and George Moore. The partnership was regarded by certain of Yeats's admirers as a descent into Hades. But some consolation for the degradation of a spiritual poet to the companionship of a literary scavenger, as Moore was then considered, was attempted to be found in the hope that the fall of Yeats might bring about the redemption of Moore. Moments of poetry elicited the whispered exclamation, "Ah! that's Willie." Other phrases were attributed to "dirty George". But it came out, as a disturbing rumour, that the

typical poetical Yeatsian patches were by Moore, and the typical Moorish splashes of realism were by Yeats. Be this as it may, some interchange of quality was apparent in the succeeding independent works of the collaborators. . . . The play passed on to an applauded conclusion; but there were stirrings of discontent in the minds of many at the end of the first act. At the end of the second act the discontent was vocal among the auditors. The old bardic tale, with its picturesqueness and chivalry, was evidently undergoing a reversion of the process of bowdlerisation; it was being vulgarised into a mere story of a young man breaking faith with his host and abducting his wife. In addition to this disqualification in the view then prevailing in Ireland, the play disclosed the defects, so contrary to the Irish temperament, of being dull and slow. There were calls for the authors at the final curtain. Yeats, being the less garrulous but more explanatory of the duad when opportunity offered, came before the curtain, and spoke of the efforts of the promoters of the Irish Literary Theatre to break down the "vulgarity" of the English commercial theatre. Some of the audience took this as a subtle joke, and laughed. But Yeats was deadly serious.[32]

Within days considerable opposition arose to *Diarmuid and Grania*, and even the originally sympathetic *Freeman's Journal* joined the attack:

*Diarmuid and Grania* continues to draw large audiences to the Gaiety Theatre. Gossip has it that the play is not given by Mr. Benson's company in the form in which it left the hands of its authors, and that some passages of doubtful propriety were excluded by the actors. How far this may be true we do not know. If it is true it is credible to Mr. Benson's judgment, and the pity of it is that he did not carry his objections a little further. There is in particular one general proposition concerning women which, however archaic in form, is an unmistakable echo of the Paris boulevards. It comes with a shock on the audience, and is an offence which even the most audacious of latter-day problem playwriters would shrink. It will not bear quotation in a newspaper. It degrades the character of Grania and its disappearance would help the play. Unhappily, however, Grania as presented at the Gaiety is own sister to Evelyn Innes, and the play would have to be written all over again (by someone else) to alter that impression.[33]

Attacked from the right by the popular press, the theatre also came under attack from the left. Standish O'Grady had already before the production expressed his misgivings about dramatizing the legendary stories. In late October, the theatre was attacked by James Joyce. Joyce, then a student at University College, had attended the performances of the Irish Literary Theatre in 1899 and 1900. Well read in continental literature and influenced by Ibsen and Hauptmann, he had begun to write a play which possibly he hoped the Irish Theatre would produce. According to Joyce's biographer, Richard Ellmann, the announcement of the third year's programme seemed to the young Joyce offensively parochial, and so he published a short essay called 'The Day of the Rabblement', in which he wrote:

> The Irish Literary Theatre gave out that it was the champion of progress, and proclaimed war against commercialism and vulgarity. It had partly made good its word and was expelling the old devil, when after the first encounter it surrendered to the popular will. . . . The Irish Literary Theatre must now be considered the property of the rabblement of the most belated race in Europe.[34]

Joyce's remarks on Yeats, Martyn, and Moore were phrased in a tone of brash superciliousness that must have seemed, coming from one of his experience and years, both insolent and absurd. Nevertheless, what he said was not without justice. Although complimenting *The Wind Among the Reeds* and *The Adoration of the Magi* highly, he thought it 'unsafe at present to say of Mr. Yeats that he has or has not genius'. He thought that Martyn and Moore were 'not writers of much originality':

> Mr. Martyn, disabled as he is by an incorrigible style, has none of the fierce, hysterical power of Strindberg, whom he suggests at times; and with him one is conscious of a lack of breadth and distinction which outweighs the nobility of certain pas-

111

sages. Mr. Moore, however, has wonderful mimetic ability, and some years ago his books might have entitled him to the place of honour among English novelists. But though *Vain Fortune* (perhaps one should add some of *Esther Waters*) is fine, original work, Mr. Moore is really struggling in the backwash of that tide which has advanced from Flaubert through Jakobsen to D'Annunzio: for two entire eras lie between *Madame Bovary* and *Il Fuoco*. It is plain from *Celibates* and the later novels that Mr. Moore is beginning to draw upon his literary account, and the quest of a new impulse may explain his recent startling conversion. Converts are in the movement now, and Mr. Moore and his island have been fitly admired. But however frankly Mr. Moore may misquote Pater and Turgenieff to defend himself, his new impulse has no kind of relation to the future of art.[35]

In 1901, these judgments sounded harshly intolerant to the point of stupidity; now, despite their ardour they do not seem unsound. He concluded with a familiar Joycean theme:

If an artist courts the favour of the multitude he cannot escape the contagion of its fetishism and deliberate self-deception, and if he joins in a popular movement he does so at his own risk. Therefore, the Irish Literary Theatre by its surrender to the trolls has cut itself adrift from the line of advancement. Until he has freed himself from the mean influences about him — sodden enthusiasm and clever insinuation and every flattering influence of vanity and low ambition — no man is an artist at all.[36]

Frank Fay, feeling that Joyce had made 'some grossly unjust assertions' and had a adopted 'a rather superior attitude', replied:

One would be glad to know in what way the Irish Literary Theatre has pandered to popularity. Is it by producing a play in Irish? I ask this because Mr. Joyce speaks of 'sodden enthusiasm and clever insinuation and every flattering influence of vanity and low ambition". But I have yet to learn that either the Irish Literary Theatre or the Irish Language movement is popular. Surely they both represent the fight of the minority against the "damned compact majority". Mr. Joyce sneers at Mr. Yeats, Mr. George Moore and Mr. Martyn; but sneering at these gentlemen has become so common that one wonders why Mr. Joyce should fall so low. Lastly, Mr. Joyce accuses the Irish Literary Theatre of not keeping its promise to produce European masterpieces. If he will read *Samhain* he will see that the Irish Literary Theatre still hopes to do that. That it has not done so, is mainly a matter of money. Those who write and talk so glibly about what the Irish Literary Theatre ought to do and ought not to do are people who have no idea of the difficulties such an institution has to contend with.[37]

*     *     *

A thoughtful analysis, unbiased by patriotism, of this year's production was written in *The Fortnightly Review* by the politician and literary man Stephen Gwynn:

> ... *Diarmuid and Grania* could not be mounted without a good deal of costly stage machinery, so that, taking all in all, Mr. Benson took a considerable risk, and conferred a service on the people in Ireland who care for literature which one may hope will not be forgotten. I do not think *Diarmuid and Grania* an admirable production. I do not think it was irreproachably acted. But I do think that to have it acted at all promoted that keen quickening of intellectual interest which is the soul of education. Archbishop Walsh, at all events, speaking for his Church, adopted this point of view when he commended the work of the Irish Literary Theatre as an attempt to counteract the demoralising and vulgarising effect of the theatrical performances which England exports to Dublin.
>
> The trouble was that when the play came to be produced, it did not seem altogether adequate as an antidote. People said, and not without reason, that Mr. Moore and Mr. Yeats had gone to Irish legend to find in epic tradition the plot of an average French novel. ... All this is not to deny the play is well constructed, that it is picturesque, that it has passages of great beauty. Mr. Yeats and Mr. Moore have established their reputations long ago. But the elements are incongruous, and I can conceive of nothing more unfortunate for both men than further collaborations of this kind.[38]

Gwynn also gave a useful picture of the audience's reaction to Hyde's play:

How much they understood is a matter of which I have heard divergence of opinion, and some people told me that I did not allow for the cleverness of my countrymen when they were making believe to understand. I can only say that I have seen Japanese plays performed with the perfection of art to an intelligent audience who knew the outline of the story, and the response was very different. I have seen even French plays played by great artists to an ordinary theatre-going public, and the applause was apt to hang fire. Here the words were caught up almost before they were out of the speaker's mouth; and I heard from behind me shouts in Irish of encouragement to the performers in the dance. I never was in an audience so amusing to be among; there was magnetism in the air. In the entractes, a man up in the gallery with a fine voice, sang song after song in Irish, the gallery joining in the chorus, and an attentive house applauding at the end. One began to realise what the Gaelic League was doing — and one felt a good deal out in the cold because one had to rely on the translation.

However, with the help of that translation — admirably written by Lady Gregory, one of the chiefs of the enterprise — — I made out pretty well; and indeed, one would have been stupid to fail, for Dr. Hyde, though he did not know how to walk the stage, had a command of expression with face and voice that very few actors could rival.[39]

For the play itself, he had high praise:

. . . it is not a big thing. But it is the real thing. It is Irish, and it is literature. The fun is on the top, and the poetry is on the top; but underneath lies a humour that is not superficial, a pathos that moves us in defiance of reason. . . . If one can be any judge from the sense given in a translation and the ear's perception of the verbal melody, it could stand comparison with a *proverbe* of Musset's or (more appositely) with Théodore de Banville's *Gringoire*. And it will probably be played many times for many years in many parts of Ireland. A national theatre that begins with this has at least something in its repertory.[40]

\*    \*    \*

*Diarmuid and Grania* was the first of the theatre's plays to use music in any integral fashion. As Percy M. Young wrote in his study of Edward Elgar:

During the summer [of 1901] George Moore wrote, asking if Elgar would write a horn tune to be played during *Grania and Diarmid* [*sic*], a joint work with W. B. Yeats, which was to be performed under Benson's direction at the Gaiety Theatre in Dublin. Moore, having heard and liked Elgar's music at Leeds, wrote out of the blue. In the end, as the result of a cordial correspondence, Elgar composed not only the requested horn motiv but some incidental music, a song and a Funeral March. When Elgar sought permission from Yeats to publish a song from the play he received this letter — one of Yeats's rare utterances on the subject of music.

Monday, March 23 [1903]
18, Woburn Buildings, Euston Road

Dear Sir:
Yes certainly. With great pleasure. I must give myself the pleasure of letting you [know how] wonderful, in its heroic melancholy, I thought your Grania music. I wish you could set other words of mine and better work than those verses, written in twenty minutes but you are welcome to them.
Yrs. sincerely,
W. B. YEATS

Excuse this scrawl I am very busy as I am off to Dublin to look after the rehearsal of a play of mine.[41]

This was Elgar's first music for the stage, and Young goes on to say that

. . . it won George Moore's high regard. "Elgar," he said, "must have seen the primeval forest as he wrote, and the tribe moving among the falling leaves — oak leaves, hazel leaves, for the world began with oak and hazel." In fact Elgar achieves all this with a juxtaposition of A major and A minor tonality divided among the horns, and with a single phrase delivered by the clarinet. The Funeral March has outlived its first purpose and is now in the general repertoire of funerary pieces. It is a rich obsequy, fit for the heroic Celtic theme which Yeats and Moore celebrated, and given the proper dignity of antiquity by being cast in a modal atmosphere. The Aeolian mode turns up — as it does sometimes in Mendelssohn — as though it belonged to the age and had not been imported by special licence. There is, too, a magniloquent trio in this march, wherein may be heard the distant tread of the first symphony. Here Elgar shows how two parts may sound like ten. . . . But the gem of the collection is the song "There are seven that pull the thread", in which Elgar unusually refers to the idiom of folk-music. This delicate evocation — with the thread pulled through by violins and violas, and sun-in-water reflected in snatches of clarinet, with a whimsical and recurrent phrase in the upper strings (related to a passage in the second symphony) and an occasional harp chord to give the wash of elusive and Irish clouds — is Elgar's most perfect song. It bears comparison with Schubert.[42]

Of the Funeral March, John F. Porte writes:

The solemn procession has a mixture of wistfulness and melancholy, quite unlike the massiveness, gloom, or frenzy of traditional funeral marches. Elgar has caught a mood of rather touching resignation, not without dignity; this may be an outer indication of his freedom from neurotic tendencies, his spiritual philosophy being unable to regard Death in the light of tragedy or fatalism. It is external writing, however, and therefore has no close relationship with the composer's inner feeling. . . .[43]

And W. H. Reed remarks:

The funeral march is of great beauty and well merits the designation Elgar so frequently used: *Nobilmente.* There is nothing grim or morbid about it and it has a quiet dignity of expression no mere words could possibly utter. Elgar also conjures up a feeling of wistfulness in the listener's mood, much as he does in the flowing theme in the *Introduction and Allegro* for strings or in some of the quieter portions of the symphonies. The theme of the funeral march is simple and rhythmically striking.[44]

\*     \*     \*

F. R. Benson writing in 1930 remarked that

> The music was very beautiful, and the play full of poetic thought. I do not quite know to what extent my wife and I were good in the title-rôles, or whether the play was not sufficiently dramatic for the virile Dublin audience; but it failed to attract as much as Shakespeare, though it certainly aroused a great deal of interest, and gave much pleasure to the performers, and the public who witnessed it. I suppose the veracious chronicler will have to write it down as only a qualified success.[45]

Benson also described Yeats's curtain speech.

> The enthusiastic poet, W. B. Yeats, in front of the curtain at the end of the first night's performance, seized the opportunity to indulge in invective against English actors, English companies and all their works. His eloquent periods were abruptly cut short by Mrs. Benson grasping his coat-tails and dragging him back on to the stage. Three-parts Irish herself, she volubly protested that we were an English company, that at his invitation we had crossed the stormy St. George's Channel, and had done our best, according to our capacity, for his play. We could not possibly allow him to step forward on our stage and insult us and our nation. Of course he saw that he had made a mistake, and, like the Irish gentleman he is, reappeared with chastened brow to qualify his remarks and make the *amende honorable*.[46]

*     *     *

Yeats's remarks in *Samhain*, to the effect that the Irish Literary Theatre had now completed its allotted span, evoked considerable speculation about what kind of movement should succeed it. One of the most interesting comments came from Frederick Ryan, writing under the pseudonym of 'Irial', in an article called 'Has the Irish National Theatre Failed?'. Ryan's suggestions were apparently close to what Yeats himself was beginning to think, and they were also prophetic, for the movement which arose out of the Irish Literary Theatre developed closely along these lines. Ryan was to become the first secretary of the Irish National Theatre Society, one of its actors, and the author of *The Laying of the Foundations*, one of its early plays.

117

It is not with any disrespect to the work which has been done by the Irish Literary Theatre that I say it seems like a flash in the pan, a nine-days' wonder, which is praised and abused—especially abused — on all sides, and then forgotten.

The fault seems to me to have been that the whole scheme was far too ambitiously conceived. There is not a public here capable of supporting at such a level such a theatre and on such a scale as the experiments have indicated. . . .

Moreover, beyond possibly supplying models to young writers, the Irish Literary Theatre so far has merely been the vehicle by which literary men of already assured status and who already possessed the ear of the world, were able to have their plays produced which in any case would have secured a reading public owing to their authors' names. . . . In short, the fact remains that beyond, perhaps, *The Last Feast of the Fianna*, the Irish Literary Theatre during its three years has not really brought to the surface any young writer hitherto unknown.

Now it seems to me that with the amount of money which must have been spent on these performances, a permanent institution run on much simpler lines, and going much deeper down, might have been founded. It would easily be possible to purchase or build a small hall or theatre capable of seating five or six hundred persons, neatly, though not lavishly equipped. In this, which should become a popular theatre, there would be an opportunity for producing, on a simple and inexpensive scale, the work of young authors. . . . The National Theatre must be virile with the strength of the life around us. It may now breathe the atmosphere of the demigods, and anon the atmosphere of the cottage and the market-place. If one might venture such a criticism, I would say that the Irish Literary Theatre has shown too strong a partiality for the mystical and the semi-supernatural. That kind of drama has its place, but the National Theatre should be limited by no literary preferences and should let the Irish drama form itself under the influence of natural inclination.[47]

Despite his difficulties with Yeats, George Moore was unwilling to sever his connection with the theatrical movement, and on 13 November *The Freeman's Journal* printed the following interview with him:

The future, if any, of the Irish Literary Theatre has been the subject of much speculation, and of varied prophecy. Whether the experiment of three years holds out sufficient hope to warrant an attempt to establish a permanent theatre; what should be the aims of such a theatre; how to establish it, and how to carry it on are questions discussed with interest by many people. No name has been more prominent in the recent history of the Irish Literary Theatre movement than that of Mr. George Moore. The fact that he is something of a storm-centre for criticism lends additional interest to his views. An interview with Mr. Moore could not fail to be entertaining reading, so we have interviewed Mr. Moore. He is no longer a mere visitor to Dublin, occupying a room in a hotel or a "pied-a-terre". He has come over to Ireland for good — for what good time will show us — and is a ratepaying resident with a house in Ely Place. The interview is, as will be seen, somewhat one-sided, the interviewer confining his attention to eliciting Mr. Moore's opinions, and giving them as closely as possible in his own words.

INTERVIEWER  In *Samhain* Mr. Yeats said that the Irish Literary Theatre has completed its term of three years. If I remember rightly he says that he may be writing an epitaph. Is that a likely contingency?

MR. MOORE  I hope not, for the Irish Literary Theatre is the outward sign of the awakening of intellectual life in Ireland. What Mr. Yeats meant was that the three years during which we undertook to carry on the Theatre whether we succeeded or failed have come to an end. Our success with "Grania" has made the future more safe. We hope to be able to carry on the Theatre. We shall try to carry it on until the nation is ripe for a National Theatre.

INTERVIEWER  What are your plans for the immediate future?

MR. MOORE  We decided this year to produce a play by Dr. Douglas Hyde, with Hyde in the principal part, and for next year we are trying to get a play by a priest to produce in our next session. I have written to Father O'Leary for leave to produce his play if possible. He has given me leave, but the play is in several scenes, and will have to be reconstructed, I think.

119

INTERVIEWER   Will Father O'Leary alter his play for you?

MR. MOORE   That I cannot say. I shall have to write to him on the subject.

INTERVIEWER   There is Father Dinneen; I hear that he has nearly completed a new play?

MR. MOORE   So I have heard.

INTERVIEWER   And is your mind set upon a play by a priest?

MR. MOORE   If Ireland is to have a National Theatre it must be frequented by all classes — by all who believe in Irish nationality. We want to bring the priests into the Theatre.

INTERVIEWER   But there is a rule forbidding . . .

MR. MOORE   Yes, and that rule I want rescinded. The theatre needs purification. I want to redeem it from the counting houses and the various immorality that the counting-house brings in its train. The Archbishop has spoken against the detestable musical comedies, but his words lose force, for he is speaking from hearsay.

INTERVIEWER   Am I to understand that you are seeking to establish a censorship?

MR. MOORE   Yes; a censorship, and I think I can have no better censor than the Church. I am glad the Irish Literary Theatre has decided to have a play by a priest next year, for I want a censorship. There is no law forbidding a priest to write a play, though he is forbidden to attend the performance of a play.

INTERVIEWER   And the anomaly created by the performance of a priest's play will, you think, result in the rescinding of the established rule?

MR. MOORE   I hope so. And with the rescinding of the rule the censorship will come.

INTERVIEWER   But I should have supposed that a censorship would be resented by you — that you would think it likely to interfere, shall I say, with what you call "the pursuit of art for art's sake".

MR. MOORE   I do not contemplate writing anything the Church
will condemn. I am sure Mr. Yeats and Mr. Martyn do not.
I do not know what the Committee of the Literary Theatre
think about it, but I am convinced that a censorship is necessary. The admirable Middle Ages prove that. I am willing, so
far as I am concerned, to submit the National Theatre, should
it be established, to the censorship of the Church. I plead that
in the interests of art the Church may undertake this task.
The intelligent censorship of the Church will free the stage
from the unintelligent and ignorant censorship of the public,
the censorship of those without personal convictions, and of
those whose ideas are the conventions and the gossip of the
little coterie they frequent. It is from that censorship that I
wish to rid the stage, nor is this a new idea of mine. So long as
ten years ago I wrote an article defending the London censorship against Mr. Archer, who attacked it. The London censorship is a lay censorship, and a lay censorship is almost futility;
but the ecclesiastical censorship would be an ideal state of
things. It would confer upon art the limitations which art
enjoyed in the Middle Ages. I do not approve of the publication
of letters in the papers regarding the morality of the stage.
I do not believe in these pretences of opinion, for they are not
opinions — they are the prejudices of the moment, the gossip
of the neighbours. Not one man in a thousand is capable of
forming an independent opinion regarding the morality of a
work of art. The ordinary man has no time to think on such
subjects, and his spasmodic letter of protest does no good. It
only attracts people's attention to the consideration of subjects
which it would be much better for them not to consider at all.
I have noticed that when these letters appear the writers
generally protest against plain speech. So long as the conventions and the gossip of Brixton and Rathmines are respected
the stage indulges in the most shockingly degrading spectacles.
But the moment the dramatist ventures to break the conventions and to disregard the idiom of respectable circles the
morality of the play is called into question. It matters not
how noble and how faithful the treatment may be. The
dramatic critics are not any better than the public. Do they not
all think that Mr. Pinero has been influenced by Ibsen? As
well might you talk of the influence that Michelangelo

exercises upon the pavement artist. Now, ecclesiastical censorship would redeem us from all this. Ecclesiastical censorship would put limitations upon art, and art has never suffered from limitations. Art suffers from indefinite licence. Above all ecclesiastical censorship would free us from the intolerable censorship of public opinion regarding morals.

INTERVIEWER   You do not apparently anticipate any quarrel between you and the priest about what is right and wrong in art?

MR. MOORE   One quarrels with a fool about art, one never quarrels with an intelligent man about it, whether he is priest or lay man. If any difference of opinion should arise regarding a phrase I should never consider it a hardship to make a sacrifice for someone's convictions. I prefer to make a sacrifice for the sake of someone's convictions than to make a sacrifice for the sake of someone's prejudices or someone's pocket.

INTERVIEWER   Nobody doubts that the cleansing of the stage and the raising of public taste are necessary to the establishment of a National Theatre.

MR. MOORE   Yes; the stage must be redeemed from the counting house. Money is the original vice, and it is the placing of the theatre on what is called a commercial basis that has brought about the licence and the vulgarity of the musical comedy. Every year the theatre makes an appeal to the desire of amusement, every year the theatre is moved further out of ideas and more into scenery and stockings. If Shakespeare is presented, scenery and dresses and songs and dances make atonement for the ideas. Some time ago, I think about a month ago, you published a long letter on the subject of a National Theatre. Your correspondent at first seemed to me better informed than the usual correspondent is, but the value of his letter was discounted by his suggestion that a National Theatre might be run "on commercial lines". He spoke of five thousand pounds subscribed, and instanced a theatre in Berlin, and his letter vexed me much, for it was an example of the almost hopeless obtuseness we have to deal with. If this matter is to be discussed we must begin by agreeing that a National Theatre is quite a different thing from a brewery, and cannot be expected to pay dividends any more than a National Library or a National Gallery, or Trinity College. The moment a theatre is expected to pay dividends there is nothing for the manager to do except to look out for a musical comedy like *The Shop Girl*, or *The Runaway Girl*, or *Kitty Grey*, or for a farcical comedy like *Charley's Aunt* and to run it as long as it will run in town, and to send out companies to gather up all that money that can be gathered in the villages. If the question of the National Theatre is to be discussed, let all those who discuss it be agreed regarding one thing, that a National Theatre gives people an interest in the town in which they live, and that it is an educational and ennobling influence, and far more necessary, more far-reaching in its effects than a picture gallery, or even a library. Although the National Theatre will not pay dividends upon the money subscribed, any more than Shamrock II., a National Theatre would be of enormous pecuniary value to Dublin. Some months ago I raised this question in your columns; I pointed out that we poor Dubliners, overtaxed, exhausted by unjust financial burdens as we are, are not only foolish to buy goods that the foreigners import into this country, but foolish enough to pay, perhaps, £150,000 a year to English companies for our amusements. The National Theatre would be supported by the priests, and would gradually bring about the ruin of these travelling companies who take, at least — think of it — £150,000 a year out of Ireland; and a National Theatre would not only stop this leakage, but it would give employment to a number of young people with talent for acting, for scene-painting, for writing and for music. I have been criticised lately for accepting the most beautiful music from an English musician. I was told I should have paid an Irishman to write the music for me. When Dublin has decided to stop this fearful leak of £150,000 a year, and to amuse itself, instead of importing amusements, it will have the right to tell me that (if I should be with the management of the National Theatre) I must employ more native talent, actors, scene-painters, and musicians. No one will be more willing to comply with this demand than I shall be; no one will recognize its justice more completely. The present moment is opportune for such a Theatre. The National language is being revived. Dr. Hyde's play was an enormous success; it delighted everyone;

123

and, as I am being very much criticised at this moment, I will take this opportunity of saying that I knew how to make sacrifices for the language. I remained in Dublin to rehearse Dr. Hyde's play, instead of going to Birmingham to rehearse Mr. Yeats's and my own. I was determined that at all costs Dr. Hyde's play should be well performed. Everything has to be paid for, and I can say with truth that it was I who paid for the admirable performance of the Irish play. But to return to the matter in hand—the establishment of a National Theatre. The plays performed there would be performed under the direct censorship of the Church. They would consist of selections from the masterpieces of the world, some Russian, some Flemish, some Scandinavian, some French masterpieces, but the central idea of the Theatre would be the restoration of the Irish language. A short Irish play would be given constantly, perhaps every night. I daresay some enthusiasts would wish the whole of the performance to be in Irish, and would denounce the Theatre because it was not. I am afraid these people would cause me many a sigh, and not a little irritation, but these enthusiasts would be useful, and though they sometimes prove a little trying, we would not be without them.

INTERVIEWER   Now, Mr. Moore, will you tell me how you propose to get money for this National Theatre?

MR. MOORE   It would be an easier thing for me to tell you first about how much it would cost. I think I could manage to do a great deal if the Theatre were given to us rent free, rates, gas, and policing paid for us, and a subscription of a thousand a year. Sir Thomas Lipton spent a quarter of a million of money trying to do something which is already forgotten, building a vessel which no one would live in, a sort of toy boat which is now up for sale. For this sum of money he could have given London an endowed theatre equal to the Comédie Française; for much less he could give Dublin a National Theatre, and a National Theatre would secure to a man much more permanent and more vital immortality than a museum or a picture gallery, or I may say anything else in the world.

INTERVIEWER   Then your hope, Mr. Moore, is in the millionaire?

124

MR. MOORE   I cannot say that it is. Money is vice, and he who has got money does not see far; his sight is short. A University would not reach as many as a theatre, whose concern was with ideas, whose ambition was to present life from a high, noble, intellectual point of view. I am afraid it will take some time for the Corporation to see that a theatre of the kind I have indicated would be of great moral, intellectual, and pecuniary benefit to Dublin. But one never knows from what side help may come. I do not think I have got anything more to say on this question.

INTERVIEWER   But you have not told me, Mr. Moore, what are your plans for the next performance to be given by the Irish Literary Theatre.

MR. MOORE   Mr. Martyn has written a new play, *The Enchanted Sea*, I think that this should be performed. I saw him last night on the subject, and I told him that we were all agreed that this play should be performed. I proposed to him the revival of *The Heather Field*, because this play when originally acted in the Antient Concert Rooms was a very great success. I think the revival of the play would prove more successful. I think every one would like to see it again. I should like to see *Heather Field* performed for three nights and *The Enchanted Sea* for three nights, and I should like to see *The Heather Field* preceded or followed by a play in Irish by Father O'Leary, and I should like to see *The Enchanted Sea* preceded or followed by a play by Father Dinneen. I am now awaiting Mr. Martyn's answer.[48]

On the same day the paper published a leading article which attempted to refute a number of Moore's points. It seemed that no matter what rigorously patriotic or moral stance Moore might adopt, he could never quite hope to quell the suspicions which his previous writings and reputation had aroused in his countrymen. In this instance, the paper remarked, 'Mr. George Moore . . . has been trained in that realistic school that aims professedly at painting life as it is, but concentrates itself only upon one side of life and upon the morbid element even there.' On the next day, *The Freeman's Journal*, for instance, printed an attack on *Diarmuid and Grania* from a priest who had apparently not even seen the production.

125

The Irish Literary Theatre Company, if I may so call it, has been in existence for some years, and has, I understand, produced some good results. But their labours this year do not seem to have in them much of the spirit of reform or of regeneration, judging by the selection of such a sensual and immoral legend as *Diarmuid and Grania* for dramatic representation. . . . If rumour speaks truly, it was just as grossly represented as it dare be.

Now, it occurs to me that if the selection of that legend, and the manner of its dramatic presentation, represents the bent of mind of some of the gentlemen connected with the Irish Literary Theatre, the sooner the healthy-minded amongst them repudiate these gentlemen the better.

The general public can have no confidence in gentlemen capable of such a production as the play *Diarmuid and Grania*. It may be said that they profess themselves willing and anxious to improve. My answer is: Sudden conversions are rare, and certainly some term of probation is necessary before the public can be led to believe that they are safe guides in such matters.

The transition from a foetid atmosphere to the pure ethereal blue of the heavens is not to be made in a week or in a month. The evil odour will cling. . . .[49]

On the same day Moore, still gamely fighting, replied to the previous day's leading article.

Dear Sir — I am sorry you do not agree with me about the necessity for an endowed theatre. Germany and France think that these institutions are necessary in modern conditions, and France and Germany are certainly the highest civilisations in Europe.

In none of the subsidised theatres of France and Germany can such a play as *Sweet Nell of Old Drury* be performed, and I do think, and will always think, that the unintellectual drama is injurious to a nation, that it is, in fact, an immorality.

The Church has always been considered sufficient guide in matters of faith and morals. I am willing to accept the censorship of the Archbishop; I believe that a play passed by him stands in need of no further censorship; and I am sorry that

what looks at first sight like an enthusiasm for private judgment
makes you prefer that of the papas and mamas.

Truly yours,

GEORGE MOORE.[50]

On the next day, Yeats disassociated himself from Moore's pro-
posals, and in effect publicly disassociated himself from Moore.

Dear Sir — A phrase in a letter which you publish to-day
makes it desirable that I should define the attitude of the Irish
Literary Theatre and my own attitude towards the proposed
censorship. Mr. Moore makes his proposal on his own authority. The Irish Literary Theatre gives no opinion. When Mr.
Moore told me his plan I said that I had no belief in its
practicability, but would gladly see it discussed. We cannot
have too much discussion about ideas in Ireland. The discussion over the theology of *The Countess Cathleen* and over the
politics of *The Bending of the Bough* and over the morality of
*Diarmuid and Grania,* set the public mind thinking of matters
it seldom thinks of in Ireland, and I hope the Irish Literary
Theatre will remain a wise disturber of the peace. But if any
literary association I belong to asked for a clerical censorship
I would certainly cease to belong to it. I believe that literature
is the principal voice of the conscience, and that it is its duty
age after age to affirm its morality against the special moral-
ities of clergymen and churches, and of kings and parliaments
and peoples. But I do not expect this opinion to be the opinion
of the majority of any country for generations, and it may
always be the opinion of a very small minority. If Mr. Moore
should establish a national theatre with an ecclesiastic for a
censor, and ask me to join the management I shall refuse, but
I shall watch the adventure with the most friendly eyes. I have
no doubt that a wise ecclesiastic, if his courage equalled his
wisdom, would be a better censor than the mob, but I think
it better to fight the mob alone than to seek for a support one
could only get by what would seem to me a compromise of
principle.

A word now upon another matter. You suggest in your
review of Mr. Martyn's plays that certain changes made by

127

Mr. George Moore in his adaptation of *The Tale of a Town* for the Irish Literary Theatre, were made for political reasons. This is not the case. Every change made was made for literary and dramatic reasons alone.

W. B. YEATS[51]

On the next day, Moore wrote again:

Dear Sir — You misinterpret my ideas, no doubt unconsciously, regarding the proposed change in the censorship of the stage.

If there is to be a National Theatre, I believe a personal censorship is a necessity. I do not believe the ordinary man and woman to be capable of giving a valid opinion regarding the moral worth of a play. The ordinary man and woman are capable of being emotionally moved by a play, and that is enough, but they are not capable of any critical appreciation of the play. The ordinary man and woman are not articulate, and when they strive for utterance they lose themselves in devious nonsense. Nor is it the business of the ordinary man and woman to consider questions that are in the main theological questions, and I do not think that it is desirable, in the interests of morality or of art, that they should allow their minds to dwell upon such matters. It would be better to choose someone to think for them, and the Archbishop, or the priest he might appoint as his reader, would prove a sufficient censorship. I think the morality of plays that have passed this censorship should not be challenged.

In your remarks on the proposed ecclesiastical censorship you have forgotten that the censorship of the stage has been for many years in the hands of the papas and mammas, and you have forgotten that their moral sense has failed to redeem the stage from the musical comedies against which his Grace has so often spoken. Your continued belief in the discrimination of papas and mammas seems a little strange. To be quite candid with you, I do not understand your position, and I should like to know if you are for or against the proposed change in the censorship.

Very truly yours,

GEORGE MOORE.[52]

The newspaper had the last word:

> . . . Mr. Moore and Mr. Yeats wrote for the Irish Literary Theatre, and produced at the Gaiety Theatre a play called *Diarmuid and Grania*. That play shocked and irritated a number of people. Some of them wrote to the papers to express their irritation. The play, apart from all considerations as to the prudence of choosing such a subject, contained certain passages so audacious in the freedom of their speech that they provoked what we believe to be natural and just indignation. . . . If the control of the Irish Literary Theatre remains as at present, we are satisfied that many papas and mammas will not risk going to its performance. An ecclesiastical censorship would re-assure them. But as to the probability of such a censorship we are not sanguine. Mr. Yeats — one of the principal figures of the Literary Theatre — will have nothing to do with it; and we believe the ecclesiastical authorities are no more anxious to revise the plays of Messrs. Moore, Yeats, and colleagues than Mr. Yeats is to see them so revised.[53]

\*　　\*　　\*

After the production at the Gaiety, George Moore attempted to interest the Gaelic League in subsidizing provincial tours of the Fays and their company in Gaelic drama. Nothing came of this attempt, and the Fays were soon involved with Yeats. This year, then, marked Moore's last strong connection with the Irish theatre. His own attempts at playwriting, both alone and in collaboration, suggest that the Irish drama lost no master dramatist; and certainly the evidence also suggests that Moore, despite his own confident opinion of his powers, as a director was far from being an incipient Antoine or Stanislavsky.

Although his connection with the Irish drama was, largely at the instigation of Yeats, severed, his services to modern Irish literature were not over. It seems an improbable enthusiasm for him, but we are inclined to credit his statements about the Irish language. He did, after all, go on to write the superb stories in *The Untilled Field* originally as works to be translated into Irish. These stories, together with his novel *The Lake*, may be plausibly taken as the distinguished beginnings of modern Irish prose fiction; and the magnificently witty *Hail and Farewell* was to begin a tradition of highly original memoir-writing which has so far given us some of the most interesting and individual work of W. B. Yeats, Oliver Gogarty, Seán O'Casey, Micheál MacLiammóir, Denis Johnston, Frank O'Connor, Seán O'Faolain, and Austin Clarke.

Max Beerbohm gave a prophetic estimate of Moore when he wrote in 1900:

> It may be that the Irish Literary Theatre marks the beginning of a great dramatic literature in Ireland, and that in England there will be no more great plays. Personally, I have great hopes of the Irish Literary Theatre; but I do not, on the other hand, despair of drama in England. I do not agree with Mr. Moore that Art cannot return to a nation. . . . However, my aim is not to refute Mr. Moore's interesting theories but to assure myself and my readers that Mr. Moore is not lost to us for ever. His, as I have said, is a mind violently exclusive, and present disgust of London is amply explained by the impending production in Dublin. But even if the Keltic Renascence prove to be the most important movement ever made in Art it will not long enchain him. His blazing passions burn themselves out rapidly, and the white-hot core gapes for other fuel. At heart he is a dilettante, though he differs from most of his kind in that his taste is concentrated always on one thing, but nothing can hold him long. That he was born in Ireland does not imply any probability that he will stay there. For the moment, he is fulfilled of patriotism, but only because the kind of Art in which he is immersed happens to have sprung from his native soil. A few weeks hence, if I hear that he has appeared in Edinburgh and declared that to be the only place to live in, I shall not be surprised. And I know that the prodigal will come back, at last, to London, the city which has harboured him through most years of his maturity. I hope I shall go to see his play in Dublin, for I suspect that it will be his only contribution to Irish Art. Already, even in his article, I find signs that his allegiance is straying.[54]

The modern Irish drama would not have been significantly impoverished if George Moore had not come to Dublin, but its first years certainly would have been less gay and less lively.

# Appendix I: Anglo Irish Drama, *a checklist to* 1901

This list attempts to give the date of first publication, the date of first production, and the original cast of the significant plays of the Irish Dramatic Revival in its first years. It includes, as will subsequent lists in later volumes, only the most significant plays written in the Irish language, such as those of Douglas Hyde or P. T. MacGinley. It does not include new plays written in the Boucicaultian manner, such as those by J. W. Whitbread, for they owed little or nothing to the new movement in literature. It does not include plays written by Irishmen but basically English in inspiration, such as those by Dr. John Todhunter. It does not, for the most part, include plays which lack any tincture of literary or theatrical or historical merit. It does, however, include a handful of plays written before 1899, which belong to the spirit of the Dramatic Revival.

The plays are listed chronologically by date of first production. When plays were not produced or when the production date remains uncertain, they are listed by the date of their first publication. The cast lists, whenever possible, are based upon the original programmes, rather than upon the sometimes variant cast lists to be found in the books of some published plays. Often, neither programme nor published book was available, and in such cases the cast lists have been formed by a comparison of available newspaper accounts.

Usually, any currently available reprint of a play is also listed.

## 1894

**W. B. YEATS**

*The Land of Heart's Desire*
First produced: 29 March 1894,
at the Avenue Theatre, London.

CAST

| | |
|---|---|
| Maurteen Bruin | James Welch |
| Shawn Bruin | A. E. W. Mason |
| Father Hart | G. R. Foss |
| Bridget Bruin | Winifred Fraser |
| A Faery Child | Dorothy Paget |

Directed by Florence Farr
First published: London: T. Fisher
Unwin, 1894; Chicago: Stone &
Kimball, 1894; all of Yeats's plays
are reprinted in *The Variorum
Edition of the Plays of W. B.
Yeats*, ed. Russell K. Alspach
(New York: Macmillan, 1966).

## 1898

**ALICE L. MILLIGAN**

*The Green upon the Cape*,
a Play in One Act.
No record of production.
First published: *The Shan Van
Vocht* (Belfast), (4 April 1898).

**ANON.**
(Probably Fr. Eugene O'Growney)
*The Passing of Conall*
First produced: 18 November 1898,
at the Aonach Tirconaill, Letterkenny. Most of the play was
performed in English, but one
scene was played in Irish.

CAST

| | |
|---|---|
| Conall Gulban | Mr. Craig |
| St. Caillin | Mr. Oram |
| Felimidh | Master McKinney |
| King Dathi | Mr. Larkin |
| King Laere | Mr. Taylor |
| Conall Gulban (youth) | Dr. Martin |
| Eoghan | Mr. B. McFadden |
| Doghra (Irish Druid) | Mr. McCully |
| Crudo (British Druid) | Mr. Craig |
| Ferdach | Mr. O'Callaghan |
| Malathna | Master Paulson |
| Duffash | Mr. Mulhern |
| Britto | Mr. O'Donnell |

| | |
|---|---|
| Gallo | Mr. McCaul |
| Firmus | Mr. Magner |
| St. Patrick | Mr. Canning |
| Chief Huntsman | Mr. McDermott |
| Ethan | Miss Diver |
| Mor | Miss Harkin |
| Emer | Miss Blake |
| Soldiers, Huntsmen, Attendants | |

CAST
of the Scene played in Irish

| | |
|---|---|
| St. Patrick | Mr. Bonnar |
| King Laoghaire | Mr. Oram |

First published: The scene in Irish
appeared in *The Freeman's Journal*
(19 November 1898), and an
English translation, probably by
Patrick O'Byrne, appeared in *The
Freeman's Journal* (21 November
1898). The entire play has not
been published.

## 1899

**W. B. YEATS**

*The Countess Cathleen*,
a Tableaux Version
First produced: January 1899, at
the Chief Secretary's Lodge, The
Phoenix Park, Dublin.

CAST

| | |
|---|---|
| Shemus Rua | Mr. V. Grace |
| Two Demons | Mr. Coffey |
| | Mr. Rolleston |
| Máire | Miss Penn |
| Teig | Miss Ruth Balfour |
| Countess Cathleen | |
| | Countess of Fingall |
| Oona | Miss Harriet Stokes |
| Ladies of Cathleen's Court | |
| | Miss Armstrong |
| | Miss Porter |
| Aleel | Mr. Ward Jackson |
| A Harper | Mr. Dickinson |
| Steward of the Castle | |
| | Sir David Harrel |
| A Peasant Girl | Miss Harrel |
| Two Angels | Miss Lily Stokes |
| | Miss Angel Stokes |
| Cherubs | Miss N. and Miss M. |

Balfour, Miss Enid Foster,
and The Hon. Sybil Cadogan
Music Arranged and Conducted
by Dr. Culwick

132

## W. B. YEATS

*The Countess Cathleen,*
a Miracle Play in Four Acts
First produced: 8 May 1899, by
the Irish Literary Theatre, at the
Antient Concert Rooms, Dublin.

CAST

First Demon    Marcus St. John
Second Demon    Trevor Lowe
Shemus Rua, a Peasant
     Valentine Grace
Teig Rua, his Son
     Master Charles Sefton
Maire Rua, his Wife
     Madame San Carolo
Aleel, a Bard    Florence Farr
Oona, Cathleen's Nurse
     Anna Mather
Herdsman    Claude Holmes
Gardener    Jack Wilcox
First Peasant    Franklin Walford
Sheogue    Dorothy Paget
Peasant Woman    M. Kelly
Servant    F. E. Wilkinson
The Countess Cathleen
     May Whitty
Directed by Florence Farr
First published: *The Countess
Kathleen and Various Legends and
Lyrics.* London: T. Fisher Unwin,
1892; Boston: Roberts Bros., 1892;
reprinted in *The Variorum Plays.*


## EDWARD MARTYN

*The Heather Field,*
a Play in Three Acts.
First produced: 9 May 1899, by
the Irish Literary Theatre, at the
Antient Concert Rooms, Dublin.

CAST

Barry Ussher, a Landowner,
Student, Philosopher, etc.
     Trevor Lowe
Lord Shrule, a Neighbouring
   Landowner    Marcus St. John
Lady Shrule, Lilian, his Wife
     Anna Mather
Carden Tyrrell    Thomas Kingston
Mrs. Grace Tyrrell, born
Desmond, his Wife    May Whitty
Kit, their Son, Nine Years Old
     Master Charles Sefton
Miles Tyrrell, Scholar of

Trinity College, Dublin, and
Brother of Carden    Jack Wilcox
Doctor Dowling    Claude Holmes
Doctor Roche    F. E. Wilkinson

First published: *The Heather Field
and Maeve,* intro. by George
Moore. London: Duckworth, 1899.
A slightly revised edition of *The
Heather Field* was published se-
parately by Duckworth in 1917.
The current standard edition of the
play was published as Volume I
in the Irish Drama Series of De
Paul University, Chicago, 1966.


## 1900

## EDWARD MARTYN

*Maeve,* a Psychological Drama
in Two Acts.
First produced: 19 February 1900,
by the Irish Literary Theatre, at
the Gaiety Theatre, Dublin.

CAST

The O'Heynes, Colman O'Heynes,
   Prince of Burren    Blake Adams
Maeve O'Heynes (his Daughter)
     Dorothy Hammond
Finola O'Heynes (his Daughter)
     Agnes B. Cahill
Hugh Fitz Walter, a Young
   Englishman    J. Herbert Beaumont
Peg Inerney, a Vagrant
     Mona Robin
Music Composed and Conducted
   by Vincent O'Brien
First published: *The Heather Field
and Maeve,* intro. by George
Moore. London: Duckworth, 1899;
reprinted separately by Duckworth
in 1917; re-printed with Alice Mil-
ligan's *The Last Feast of the
Fianna* in Volume II of the Irish
Drama Series of De Paul Univer-
sity, Chicago, 1967.


## ALICE L. MILLIGAN

*The Last Feast of the Fianna,*
a Dramatic Legend in One Act.
First produced: 19 February 1900
by the Irish Literary Theatre, at
the Gaiety Theatre, Dublin.

Fionn Mac Cumhal
                  T. Bryant Edwin
Oisin          Franklin Walford
Caoilte Mac Ronan
                  John F. Denton
Grania, wife of Fionn
                  Fanny Morris
Niamh, a Fairy Princess
                  Dorothy Hammond
Special Music by
          Mrs. C. Milligan Fox
First published: In *The Daily Express* (23 September 1899, and 30 September 1899); first separate publication, London: David Nutt, 1900; reprinted with Edward Martyn's *Maeve* in Volume II of the Irish Drama Series of De Paul University, Chicago, 1967.


GEORGE MOORE
(AND EDWARD MARTYN)
*The Bending of the Bough*, a Comedy in Five Acts.
First produced: 20 February 1900 by the Irish Literary Theatre, at the Gaiety Theatre, Dublin.

CAST
Joseph Trench, the Mayor
                  Alex Austin
Aldermen of the Corporation:
Jasper Dean      Percy Lyndal
Daniel Lawrence   W. W. West
Thomas Ferguson
                  John F. Denton
Valentine Folay   Eugene Mayeur
Ralf Kirwan   William Devereaux
James Pollock   T. Bryant Edwin
Michael Leech   W. F. Rotheram
John Cloran, the Town-Clerk
                  J. H. Beaumont
George Hardman, Lord Mayor
  of Southaven      Blake Adams
Miss Millicent Fell, his Niece,
  Engaged to marry Alderman
  Dean          Agnes B. Cahill
Miss Caroline Dean, Maiden
  Aunt of Alderman Dean
                  Mona Robin
Miss Arabella Dean, Maiden
  Aunt of Alderman Dean
                  Annie Hill

Mrs. Pollock, Wife and First
  Cousin of Alderman Pollock,
  Sister of Alderman Pollock,
  and Cousin of the Deans
                  Fanny Morris
Mrs. Leech, Wife and First
  Cousin of Alderman Leech,
  Sister of Alderman Pollock,
  and Cousin of the Deans
                  Dorothy Hammond
Macnee, Caretaker of the
  Town Hall     Franklin Walford
A Waiter at the Hotel
                  William P. Kelly
  Directed by George Moore
First published: London: T. Fisher Unwin, 1900; a slightly different version was also published in the same year, Chicago: Herbert S. Stone, 1900; the two versions are collated in the edition edited by William J. Feeney, and published as Volume III of the Irish Drama Series of De Paul University, Chicago, 1969.


ALICE L. MILLIGAN
*Oisin in Tír-Nan-Oig*, a Legendary Play in Verse in One Act, Part Two of a Trilogy of which *The Last Feast of the Fianna* is Part One.
No record of production.
First published: In *The Daily Express* (7 October 1899, and 14 October 1899); reprinted in *Sinn Féin* (23 January 1909).


ALICE L. MILLIGAN
*Oisin and Padraic*, a Legendary Play in Verse in One Act, Part Three of the above-mentioned Trilogy.
No record of production.
First published: In *The Daily Express* (4 November 1899, and 11 November 1899); reprinted in *Sinn Féin* (20 February 1909).

## 1901

### P. T. MAC FHIONNLAOICH (P. T. MacGINLEY)

*Eilis agus an Bhean Déirce,*
a Comedy in Irish in One Act.
The date of first production is uncertain. The first production in Dublin, and probably the second production of the play, was on 27 August 1901, by the Daughters of Erin at the Antient Concert Rooms.

CAST

(Of the revival on 31 October 1901. Probably the same as the original cast.)

| | |
|---|---|
| Eilis | Máire T. Ní Cuinn (Máire T. Quinn) |
| Concubar, a mac | Proinsias Mac Siubhlaig (Frank Walker) |
| Meadba, bean déirce | Máire Ní Perols |

Directed by W. G. and F. J. Fay
First published: In *Miondrámanna.* Baile Atha Cliath: Connradh na Gaedhilge, 1902; a translation by Mrs. Sheila O'Rourke and Father Patrick Corkell appears in *Lost Plays of the Irish Renaissance,* eds. Robert Hogan and James Kilroy (Dixon, California: Proscenium Press, 1970), pp. 17-21.

### ALICE L. MILLIGAN

*The Harp That Once,*
a Play in Two Acts.
First produced: 26 August 1901, for the Daughters of Erin, by the Ormonde Dramatic Society, at the Antient Concert Rooms, Dublin.

CAST

| | |
|---|---|
| Denis Lynch, a Fugitive Patriot | J. Dudley Digges |
| Captain Coverdale, Hussar, in Command of a Company | E. O'Higgins |
| Lieutenant Farmer, Officer of Hussars | Brian Callender |
| Nancy Kelly, Lady O'Brien's Housekeeper | Alice L. Milligan |

| | |
|---|---|
| Polly | Miss J. Meagher |
| Lady Selina O'Brien | Sara Allgood |
| Mabel, her Stepdaughter | Máire T. Quinn |

Directed by W. G. and F. J. Fay
No record of publication.

### ALICE L. MILLIGAN

*The Deliverance of Red Hugh*
a Dramatic Incident in Two Scenes.
First produced: 27 August 1901, for the Daughters of Erin, by the Ormonde Dramatic Society, at the Antient Concert Rooms, Dublin.

CAST

| | |
|---|---|
| Red Hugh O'Donnell | J. Dudley Digges |
| Art O'Neill | Patrick Bradley |
| Henry O'Neill | Michael J. Quinn |
| The Governor of Dublin Castle | Peter White |
| An Officer | P. J. Kelly |
| Pierce | Thomas S. Cuffe |
| Martin | F. J. Fay |

Directed by W. G. Fay
First published: In 'St. Patrick's Day Double Number' of *The Weekly Freeman* (13 March 1902), both in English and in Irish.

### JOSEPH P. COLLUMB (PADRAIC COLUM)

*The Children of Lir,*
a Poetic Tragedy in One Act.
No record of production.
First published: In *Irish Weekly Independent and Nation* (14 September 1901), reprinted in *The Journal of Irish Literature,* Vol. II, No. 1, (January 1973).

### GEORGE MOORE AND W. B. YEATS

*Diarmuid and Grania*
a Play in Three Acts.
First produced: 21 October 1901, by F. R. Benson's Company, for the Irish Literary Theatre, at the Gaiety Theatre, Dublin.

135

King Cormac      Alfred Brydone
Finn MacCoole      Frank Rodney
Diarmuid      F. R. Benson
His Chief Men:
Goll      Charles Bibby
Usheen      Henry Ainley
Caoilte      E. Harcourt Williams
Spearmen:
Fergus      G. Wallace Johnstone
Fathna      Walter Hampden
Griffan      Stuart Edgar
Niall, a Head Servant
      Matheson Lang
Conan the Bald, One of the
Fianna      Arthur Whitby
An Old Man      H. O. Nicholson
A Shepherd      Mr. Owen
A Boy      Ella Tarrant
A Young Man      Jean Mackinlay
Grania, the King's Daughter
      Mrs. F. R. Benson
Laban, an Old Druidess
      Lucy Franklein
Directed by F. R. Benson
Special Music Written by
Dr. Edward Elgar
First published: In *The Dublin
Magazine* (April-June 1951); re-
printed in *The Variorum Plays.*


DOUGLAS HYDE

(from a Scenario by Lady Gregory)
*Casadh an tSugáin*, a Comedy in
One Act, translated by Lady Gre-
gory as *The Twisting of the Rope.*
First produced: 21 October 1901,

by the Keating Branch of the
Gaelic League, for the Irish Liter-
ary Theatre, at the Gaiety Theatre,
Dublin.

CAST

Hanrahan, a Wandering Poet
      Douglas Hyde
Sheamus O'Heran, Engaged to
Oona      Tadhg O'Donoghue
Maurya, the Woman of the
House      Eibhlin O'Donovan
Sheela, a Neighbour
      Frances Sullivan
Oona, Maurya's Daughter
      Miss O'Kennedy
Neighbours and a Piper
(In the 31 October 1904 revival,
Eamonn Ceannt played the Piper.)

Directed by George Moore
with W. G. Fay

First published: In *Samhain*
(October 1901); first book publi-
cation, in English, in *Poets and
Dreamers: Studies and Transla-
tions from the Irish* by Lady Gre-
gory (Dublin: Hodges, Figgis &
Co. Ltd., and London: John Mur-
ray, 1903); first separate publica-
tion, in Irish and Engish (Baile
Atha Cliath; An Cló-Cumann,
1905); and there have been two
recent reprints of *Poets and
Dreamers* — one by the Kennikat
Press (Port Washington, New
York, 1967), and one in the Coole
Edition of Lady Gregory's Works
(Gerrards Cross: Colin Smythe
Ltd., 1971).

136

# Appendix II

In *The Freeman's Journal* for 20 November 1898, was printed the following scene which had been played at the Aonach Tir Conaill in Letterkenny, and which was apparently the first dramatic representation in the Irish language.

CONALL GULBAN
Roibh-Rádh

Tógamuid teampall mar is cóir dúinn é
In onóir Adhamhnáin, patrún Dún na nGall;
Ardóchamaoid a n-diú, le congnamh Dé
Sean-chlú, Tír-Chonaill — is dílis dúmu gach ball,
Gach cnoc, gach crois, gach cailseán as gach coill
'O Aileach árd na Righ go gleann dubh Coluimchill'
Is iomdha ollamh, oide, laoch 'gus naomh
For beó i gcuimhne linn i mbaile 'gus i dtír,
Acht cia d'fhág ainm in a dhiaigh ariamh
Ar stair na h-Eireann chomh pésdomeamhail a's fíor
Le Conall Gulban, sinnsear saor ár gclann,
Thug cliú d'ár dtír 'gus do gach duine ann?
Is fada Conall ins an gcill 'na luidhe
Faoi 'n gcréafóig throim 'sta athrughadh mor
Ar fhear 's ar nós 'gus ar gach uile ní
O mhair a riaghail san tír, acht fós tá glór
'Gus blas na Gaeilge in gach béal go binn
Mar chluinfidh sibh anois ag éisteacht linn,
Ar sun na míle bliadhain agus níos mó
Tiocfaidh Conall Gulban rómhaibh anocht,
I gculaidh 'gus i mbéas na n-aois fadó
'Gus guidhim-se bhur gcarthannacht d'ár n-imirt bhoicht!


AMHARC VI — TEAMHAIR

Tigeann Pádraic isteach le fear iomchaire na croise.

PÁDRAIC  Beannacht Dé air a bhfuil annso! Dhuit-se, a Rígh,
         Agus d'Eirinn uile faoi do riaghail,
         Bheirim beannacht agus teachtaireacht mhór
         O'm Mhaighistir mhaith, mo Thirgeanna agus mo Rígh.

LAOGHAIRE  Is teachdaire 'gus ní sagart thú, mar sin.
           Cia h-é do Rígh; cad í an teachdaireacht
           Bheireann tú chugainn?

CRÚDO      Labhrann sé i gcosamhlachdaibh.
           Is sé a Rígh an Dia adhrann sé.

PÁDRAIC    Tá sóisgéal liom a líonas suas gach aoin
           Le síothcháin agus sólas thig ó neamh amháin.
           Is sé mo Rígh mo Dhia, árd-Rígh na bhflaitheas;
           Is sé Rígh na Ríghtheadh, agus Flaith na bhfláith.
           Ní coimh thigheach an guth so daoibh go léir;
           Acht ina seachránacht do chaill na Gaedhil
           A n-eólas air; acht tá a ghuth ós árd
           Ag mothughadh maithe in bhúr measg go fóill.
           O'n aimsir úd do labhair mo Dhia libh
           Tré béalaibh móráin fáidh, 'gus chuir sé síos
           A mhac ó neamh — sin é an t-Iosa Chríost
           Fá-n mian liom cáint a dhéanamh libh anocht —
           An Críosd a chomhnuigh linn; an Críosd a d'éag
           Ionnus go mbéidheadh sinn béo; a's tr' éis a bháis
           Go sdiúirfeadh Seisean slán go flaitheas Dé
           Na daoine lean a theagasg 'gus a riaghail.
           Sin é an fáth a dtáinic mé anocht
           Le cúireadh dhílis daoibh, a chlann na nGaedheal,
           A theacht air ais faoi dhlighthibh fíora Dé.

LAOGHAIRE  An bhfaca tú na fáidhe móra so?
           An bhfaca tú an Críost-se ar do chan tú?
           Nó bhfuil aon chinnteacht agat ar a gcúmhacht?

PÁDRAIC    An bhfaca tú, a Rígh Cormac maith MacAirt,
           A riaghlaigh seal i dTeamhair móir na Midhe?
           Ar aithin tú Mac Neasa mhair 'na Rígh
           I gCúige Uladh céadta bliadhain ó shoin?
           An bhfaca tusa Ailp na mullach mbán
           A Chonnaire bás Rígh Dhathí chrodha chaoin?

LAOGHAIRE  Ní fhacamar na righte so ariamh,
           Nó Ailp an tsneachda, acht bheir fiadhnaisídhe
           'Gus sgríbhinnidhe ró-fhior a gcunntais dúinn
           Gur mhair a leitheid ann.

PÁDRAIC                    Eist liom, a Rígh,
           Tá'n sneachda bán ar mhullach mhaol na h-Ailp
           Ag féachaint síos ar thalaimh ghlais Iodáilte
           'Nna susdheann cathair chlúdhamhail na Róimh!
           Fá'n am 'n ar chómhnuigh Conchobar caomh Mac Nessa
           'Na rígh le neart in Uladh dubh na mbeann,
           Do tháinic iomad fiadhnaise go dtí 'n Róimh
           A chómhnuigh seal le Críost 'gus chonnairc siad
           A chúmhacht 'gus a bhás, a árdughadh suas ar Neamh;
           'Gus chonghaigh siad go cúramach 'na gceann

138

An stair a bhaineas leis an am fadó —
Is focla fiadhnais' as gach sgríbhinn díobh
Tá againne a ndiú; is dearbhadh iad
Ar rúnaibh Dé innseochaidh mé anois
Do Dhraoithibh Eireann tá annso i láthair
Má's mian leó fios an fhirinn fhághail.

CRÚDO Ní'l sé in do chumas, a ghear aindia
Na neithe uile so do dhearbhadh dhúinn.
Chuirfeá ar gcúl go deó an t-adhradh mór
A bhéirimuid do ghealach, gréin, a's réalt.
'Smar mhalairt, mhúinfeá dhúinn do chreideamh úr.
Seadh, sheas mé 'stigh i gcroidhe na Róimhe féin
'Gus chualidhe mé ó sheanmóntaidhe do Chríost
Go bhfuil aon Dia agaibh, agus triúr in aon —
Ní féidir do na neithibh sin a bheith.

PÁDRAIC Tá 'n chrian, an ghealach a's gach réalt 'san spéir
A lasadh suas an t-slíghe go flaitheas árd;
Is sian an coiscéim buin ná staidhridh óir
A ritheas suas go cathaoir Ríoghda Dé;
Mar theachdaire lionnireach insan spéir atáid
A labhras linn an soisgéal go ó'n Rígh.
Ma thigeann, a Mhaolaithne eachlach ríoghamhail
Go geataidh móra Theamhrach, a' bhfaghann sé
An t-urraim 'gus an t-onóir gheabhas Rígh?

MAOLAITHNE Ní gheibheann sé acht onóir teach daire —
[B'eas oaóis an Tach rígh píos mó thabhairt dó.

PÁDRAIC Is é as ondhi do Rígh na bhflaitheas]*
Urraim Dé a thabhairt do lonnradh neimhe;
Oir ní'l 'san ghréin 'sna réaltaibh nó 'san rae
Acht néithe beaga bheireann cunntas dúinn
Ar chúmhacht agus ghlóir móir an Té
A riaghlaigheas iad-san in a slíghe gach lá.
Tráchtann an Draoi fá rúnaibh chreidimh Chríosd,
Acht tabhradh seisean míniughadh dúinn ar dtús
Ar thairngearachd no nDraoitheadh dúbhairt go mbéidheadh
Lámh bhuaidheach ag an Ghaedheal 'san am the la teacht
I dtírchibh bhfad i gcéin. Cá bhfuil no buadha so?
Cia h-iad na Draoithe? Cá h-as a dtáinic siad?
Ní'l freagra agaibh-se, acht éistidh liom:
Ní'l leis an gclaidheamh nó 'n lann nó tréanas lámh
A bhainfeas clann na h-Eireann cúmhacht mhór
Acht geóbhaidh siad a réim faoi bhrat na croise,
'Gá iomchar leó ó thráighibh loma?
Go sléibhtibh Appinin, le congnadh Dé —
Le congnadh Dé i n-aon, 'gus aon i dtrí.

*Two illegible lines. The material within brackets is a guess.

139

CRÚDO        Aon Dia fíor, acht triúr Dé in aon! —
             Cé'n inntinn fir a thuigeas cáint mar shin?
             Ní féidir leis a leithid so a beith.

PÁDRAIC      An measann tú gur thuig aon fhear ariamh
             Mar déanann Nádúir mhór a h-obair féin?
             Acht fós tá 'n obair déanta léi gach lá.
             Fosglann sí gach dhuille 'gus gach bláth,
             Cad mar is féidir leis an phóirín bheag
             Bhrígh freimhe, croinne, craoibhe bheith 'na lár?
             Féach an tseamróg so do fhásas faoi do chois
             Tá réidh le freagra ar do cheist anois.
             Ní'l ar an tseamróig sin acht duille amháin
             Acht ins an duille sin tá triúr go beacht.
             'Gus ní'l aon áit 'san dtír nach bhfásann sí.
             Mar sin béidh creideamh fíor na Trionóide.
             Ar bun gan mhoill ar fud na h-Inse Fáil
             'Gus béarfaidh class na h-Eireann onóir mhór
             Do'n t-seomróig ghil, óir sé an glas a bhéadheas
             'Na dhath ar bhrat a gcineadh sin go bráth,
             Is cuma c'áit 'san domhan a gcasfar iad.
             A phrionnsaidh 'sa a mhná uaisle tá annso,
             Ma's mian libh fírinne an chreidimh fhághail
             A thug mé in bhur measg, tar liom go léir,
             Oir ar an léana mín úd thios anois
             Tá 'n pobal mór a fanacht ar an sgéal
             A líonfas a n-anámaibh le grása Dé.

EITHNE       A Phádraic, rachfamaoid le h-éisteacht leat.

DUBTHACH     Leanfamaoid;

EOGAN                      Eisteochamaoid.

MOR                                     Creid-fimid.

CRÚDO        A rígh, a rígh! seachain an sagart-se,
             'S ná leig tú féin go síorruidhe in a chómhair!

             (*Exeunt omnes acht na Draoithe agus Laoghaire.*)

IAR-RADH

CONALL       An aisling a bhí orm nó 'n bhfaca mé
             An t-am 'na raibh mé óg a'r lásoin luath?
             Dar liom go raibh me 'rís i seilg fiadh,

                              140

'S ar siubhal le Dathí thar an t-sáile mór?
Gur sheas mé rís i dTeamhair lá's Pádraic ann
Ag faghail an bhaisdidh naomhtha ó n-a láimh
Ag Eas Aoidh Ruaidh. An aisling a bhí ann,
Ta sgaptha 'nois mar chéo?

CAILLÍN                          Má b'aisling í
Níor imthigh sí gan sólas. Nach cuimhneach
Leat geall Phádraic?

CONALL                          Is sé an geall so
Bheir sólas do mo chroidhe. Tá mo mhuintir
'Gus mo cháirde lá fada ins an uaigh
Acht tá a gclass-san beó n'ar measg go fóill
I ngleanntaigh dubha doracha Tír Chonaill
Shíos ar mhaighibh míne Loch Súlidhe,
Air fud na Rosann 'gus i sean-Ghaoth Dóbhair.
Mar bheidheadh in aisling chím an t-am a' teacht,
Na m-béidh an chrois go h-árd ar iomad cill
O mhullach Eargail go spincthibh Sléibhe Liag,
Is iomdha naomh ar laoch de chineál Chonaill
A dhíonfas ballaidh beannuighthe Dhúin na nGall.
'San am le theacht; fad, fada romhainn
Chidhim teampoil ghlórmhar ag á thógbhail suas
I Leitir Cheannainn a' cur i n-úmhail do'n t-saoghal
Go bhfuil clann cródha Chonaill cuimhneach ar a nDia.
Slán leis an am tá thart, slán libh, mo ghaol,
Tá 'g éirigh suas arís ós cómhair mo shúil!
Tá mise réidh anois le dul o'n t-saoghal,
Tá 'n ola déighionnach 'gus an uaigh ag fuireacht.
Tá Dia cúmachtach agus Pádraic mór
Le cloinn Thír-Chonaill 'lig a coimhéad mar is cóir.

Críoch.

Under the title of 'The Tara Scene in English', the following partial
translation appeared in *The Freeman's Journal* of 21 November:

(*A solemn chant of the Church is heard, suggesting the Hymn of St. Patrick
or of a Litany.*) *Enter St. Patrick with Crossbearer and Attendants. Duffach
alone rises to greet him; the others remain as before.*

PATRICK    A blessing on all here! To thee, O King,
And to all Erin under thy command
I bring a greeting and a solemn message
From Him I serve, my Monarch and my King.

141

LAERE    Thou art a herald, then, and not a priest!
         Who is thy monarch, and what embassy
         Bring'st thou to us?

DOGHRA   The stranger speaks in figures.
         His monarch is the God whom he adores.

CRUDO    His coming heralds strife and war and death!

PATRICK  My message is of peace and bliss to all,
         Of Happiness that Heaven alone can give.
         My monarch is my God, the King of Heaven,
         He is the King of Kings, the Lord of lords;
         Nor is this voice a stranger to your hearts;
         In ages past your fathers heard his words,
         But in the distant wanderings of the Gael
         You have forgot his name; His voice
         Still moves your hearts to virtue, pity, justice.
         Now God has spoken since your fathers' time
         Through many mighty prophets, and has sent
         His Son from Heaven — Christ — Whose holy name
         I now proclaim to you, Who lived and died
         That we might learn to live, and after life
         To bring to Heaven on high, the good who trust
         His name and power. Hither I now come
         To summon back the children of the Gael
         To hear the voice of God and learn His law.

LAERE    Hast thou thyself beheld these mighty prophets
         Or Christ thou speakest of, or known their power?

PATRICK  Hast thou, O King, seen Cormac, son of Art,
         Who lived and ruled in Tara? Hast thou known
         MacNessa, King of Ulster? Hast thou seen
         Those Alpine hills that saw King Dathi die?

LAERE    We have not known these kings, nor have we seen
         The snowy Alps, but witnesses of credit
         And records duly kept give full assurance
         As eye or ear can give.

PATRICK  Hear then, O Kings:
         The snowy summits of the Alps look down
         On Italy, and point to distant Rome;
         When Conor son of Nessa ruled in Ulster
         There came to Rome the very witnesses
         Who lived with Christ and saw this godly power,
         His death and His return unto Heaven;
         Who held, besides, the records of the past.

142

These records and the words of witnesses
Transmitted to our times are firm proof
Of all the truths which I will now unfold
Unless your Druids fear to hear the truth.

CRUDO Thou canst not, impious stranger, prove those things
Thou wouldst forbid the worship which we pay
To sun and moon and sacred stars of heaven;
Thou wouldst, instead, teach us thy mysteries,
For I have stood in mighty Rome itself
And heard from Christian teachers that thy God
Is one and also three — three Gods — not one —
Impossible for mind to understand.

PATRICK The sun and moon and shining stars above
But point the way unto the highest heavens;
They are the footstool of the lofty throne
Of God invisible; they, like brilliant heralds,
Speak to us of the King and hear this message.
Say, thou, Malathna, if a royal herald
Doth come to Tara's gates, does he receive
The honour of a King?

MALATHNA The honours of a herald are his due.
To give him more dishonours every king.

PATRICK And 'tis dishonour to the King of Heaven
To honour as a god the brilliant lights
Announcing but the glory and the power
Of Him who rules and moves them in their paths.
The Druid speaks of Christian mysteries,
But let him first explain the prophecy
of Druids' oracles, by heaven permitted,
Foretelling future triumphs of the Gael
Beyond the seas. Where are the promised triumphs?
Whence and when came the Druids?
You cannot tell. Then listen; Erin's sons
Shall conquer not by war nor sword nor spear,
But by this sacred standard of the cross
Which they shall bear from bleak Iona's strand
To distant Appenine and by the power
Of God, one only God, but one in Three.

CRUDO 'One God, but three in One.' What earthly mind
Can comprehend such things? They cannot be!

PATRICK What mind can comprehend how nature works?
But still she works, unfolding leaf and flower;
How can a little seed contain the essence

143

Of root and trunk and branch, and leaf and flower;
Behold this shamrock growing at our feet
Ready to give an answer to thy question,
For three in one and one in three, its leaves
Extend o'er all the land. So shall the faith
In triune God extend through Inisfail,
And Erin's sons the shamrock shall exalt
And take its very colour for its banners
Where'er their footsteps lead throughout the earth.
Princes and royal ladies here assembled.
If you would learn the truth I come to teach
Come with me, for upon the plain beneath
The people wait to hear the joyous words
Their souls do hunger for.

CRUDO *to*    Beware, O King,
LAERE    And go not with the stranger priest.

ETHNA    Patrick, we come.

DUFFACH    We follow thee (Eoghan) to hear thee (Mor) and to believe.

(*Exit Patrick and attendants followed by everyone except the Druids, who keep back Laere.*)

# Notes

## 1899

1  Edmund Curtis, *A History of Ireland* (London: Methuen & Co. Ltd., 1950), p. 388.

2  Æ, 'The Dramatic Treatment of Heroic Literature', in *Samhain: An Occasional Review Edited by W. B. Yeats* (Dublin: Sealy Bryers & Walker; London: T. Fisher Unwin, 1902), p. 11.

3  *Ibid.*, p. 12.

4  Ernest A. Boyd, *Ireland's Literary Renaissance* (Dublin & London: Maunsel & Co. Ltd., 1916), pp. 94-95.

5  Colman's verses were spoken by Mr. Farren on 19 January 1821, at the opening of the Theatre Royal. They were printed in *The Dublin Evening Post* for 21 January 1821, and they were reprinted in a four-page pamphlet issued by the theatre of its re-opening on 13 December 1897. A copy of the pamphlet is to be found in the National Library of Ireland.

6  Hamilton's address is printed on pp. 1-2 of the pamphlet mentioned above.

7  Frank J. Fay, 'Irish Drama at the Theatre Royal', *The United Irishman* (8 July 1899); reprinted in *Towards a National Theatre: The Dramatic Criticism of Frank J. Fay*, ed. Robert Hogan (Dublin: The Dolmen Press, 1970), p. 18.

8  Frank J. Fay, 'Irish Drama at the Theatre Royal', *The United Irishman* (29 July 1899); reprinted in *Towards a National Theatre*, p. 20.

9  After an earlier appearance in the provinces, *Charley's Aunt* was presented in London in December, 1892, and had an initial run of four years. *The Oxford Companion to the Theatre* (3rd edition) remarks that the play 'has figured in the repertory of almost every amateur and provincial theatre, as well as being played all over the world in English and in innumerable translations. At one time it was running simultaneously in 48 theatres in 22 languages, among them Afrikaans, Chinese, Esperanto, Gaelic, Russian, and Zulu.' In the most recent revival we have seen of the play in Dublin, by Illsley and McCabe at the Olympia, it opened on St. Stephen's Day in 1962, and played for a month to crowded houses, in a theatre with a capacity of about 1500.

10  Bernard Shaw, *Our Theatres in the Nineties*, Vol. II (London: Constable & Co. Ltd., 1932), p. 172.

11  Fagan was born in 1873 in Belfast, and was at various times in his career an actor, a playwright, and a distinguished producer. His acting

career began in 1895 with the Benson Company, and he played from 1897 to 1899 with Tree. *The Rebels* was followed by — to mention only his most successful pieces — *The Prayer of the Sword* of 1904 in five acts and prose and verse, *The Earth* of 1913, *Doctor O'Toole* of 1917, his Pepysian comedy *And So To Bed* of 1926, and *The Improper Duchess* of 1931. He also wrote successful dramatizations of *Treasure Island* and of Hawthorne's *Wonder Tales*. As a producer, he was notable for forming the Oxford Playhouse in 1923 and becoming a director of the Festival Theatre, Cambridge, in 1929. His more notable London productions included Brieux's *Damaged Goods* in 1917, various Shakespeare productions, *The Government Inspector* in 1920, *The Cherry Orchard* in 1925, and *The Spook Sonata* in 1927. He managed the Irish Players and produced many of their plays. Among the Irish plays he brought to London were O'Casey's *Juno and the Paycock* and *The Plough and the Stars*, Lennox Robinson's *The Whiteheaded Boy*, and George Shiels's *Professor Tim*.

12  Joseph Holloway, *Impressions of a Dublin Playgoer* (24 September 1895). This is a vast manuscript journal housed in the National Library of Ireland. It covers a period of about fifty-six years, from the late 1880's to the early 1940's, and is approximately 25,000,000 words long. A selection of the years from 1899 to 1926 has been edited by Robert Hogan and Michael J. O'Neill and published under the title of *Joseph Holloway's Abbey Theatre* (Carbondale: Southern Illinois University Press, 1967). See also a further selection, from 1926 until Holloway's death: *Joseph Holloway's Irish Theatre, 1926-1931* (Dixon, California: Proscenium Press, 1968); 1932-1937 (1969); and 1938-1944 (1970).

13  *Ibid.*, 15 September 1896.

14  *Ibid.*, 6 October 1896.

15  *Ibid.*, 4 May 1897.

16  *Ibid.*, 29 June 1897.

17  *Ibid.*, 9 November 1897.

18  Holloway actually wrote 'unsensible', which is no doubt also apt, but probably not what he intended.

19  *Ibid.*, 21 December 1897.

20  *Ibid.*, 3 August 1898.

21  *Ibid.*, 9 August 1898.

22  *Ibid.*, 3 November 1898.

23  Frank J. Fay, ' "Wolfe Tone" at the Queen's Theatre', *The United Irishman*, (26 August 1899), p. 5.

146

24　Frank J. Fay, ' "The Irishman" at the Queen's Theatre', *The United Irishman*, (9 September 1899), p. 5.

25　Frank J. Fay, ' "The Green Bushes" at the Queen's Theatre', *The United Irishman*, (16 September 1899), p. 5.

26　Holloway, *Impressions*, 13 August 1895.

27　*Ibid.*, 7 September 1898.

28　From the programme of 15 November 1897, contained in a small bound volume of Olympia Theatre Programmes, 1896-1946, housed in the National Library of Ireland.

29　Frank J. Fay, 'Irish Drama at the Theatre Royal', *The United Irishman*, (8 July 1899), p. 1.

30　W. G. Fay and Catherine Carswell, *The Fays of the Abbey Theatre*, (New York: Harcourt, Brace & Co., 1935), p. 71.

31　Nevertheless, the group did get plenty of practice. W. A. Henderson gives what is probably not a complete list of the group's activities in 1899. On 2 January they played at the Coffee Palace in Townsend Street; on 3 and 4 January at the Textonion Bazaar; on 21 January at the Dalkey People's Concerts; on 6 February at the Coffee Palace; on 17 March at the Workmen's Club in York Street, when Frank Fay gave some readings; on 1 May at the Coffee Palace, when they presented *Round the Corner*; on 2 and 3 May at St. Teresa's Hall; on 13 May at the Town Hall in Dalkey; on 16 October at the Coffee Palace; on 25 and 26 October at St. Teresa's Hall, when they presented four different plays; on 19 October at the Rathmines Town Hall; on 8 December at Adelaide Road Presbyterian Church, when Frank Fay gave a reading; on 18 December at the Coffee Palace, when they gave two plays and Dudley Digges gave a recitation. Henderson Ms. 1729, National Library of Ireland.

32　Holloway, *Impressions*, 3 December 1897.

33　George Fitzmaurice, 'Maeve's Grand Lover', *The Irish Weekly Independent and Nation* (17 November 1900), p. 6.

34　Mary Costello, 'A Daughter to Marry', *The Lady of the House*, (Christmas, 1900), pp. 49-50, 53-54.

35　George Moore, *Hail and Farewell : Ave* (London: William Heinemann, 1911), p. 43.

36　W. B. Yeats, 'I Became an Author', *The Listener* (4 August 1938), p. 217.

37　Joseph Hone, *W. B. Yeats, 1865-1939* (London: The Macmillan Co., 1960), p. 107.

38　Alan Wade, ed., *The Letters of W. B. Yeats* (London: Rupert Hart-Davis, 1954), p. 231.

147

39  Lady Gregory, *Our Irish Theatre* (London & New York: G. P. Putnam's Sons, 1913), pp. 8-9.

40  Denis Gwynn, *Edward Martyn and the Irish Revival* (London: Jonathan Cape, 1930), pp. 125-127.

41  Letter of Æ (George W. Russell) to Edward Martyn, quoted in Gwynn, pp. 127-128.

42  From an unsigned review in *The Theatre* (1 April 1893), p. 215.

43  J. T. Grein, *The New World of the Theatre, 1923-1924* (London: Martin Hopkinson & Co., 1924), p. 27.

44  Clifford Bax, ed., *Florence Farr, Bernard Shaw, W. B. Yeats, Letters* (New York: Dodd, Mead & Co.), pp. 21-22.

45  *Ibid.*, p. 23.

46  Moore, *Ave*, p. 91.

47  Wade, *The Letters of W. B. Yeats*, p. 317.

48  Hone, *W. B. Yeats*, p. 169.

49  F. Hugh O'Donnell, *Souls for Gold* (London: Nassau Press, 1899).

50  W. B. Yeats, 'The Irish Literary Theatre', *The Freeman's Journal*, (12 January 1899), p. 5.

51  See letter of W. B. Yeats to Fiona MacLeod (William Sharp), early in 1897, inviting her to submit a play: in Elizabeth Sharp, *William Sharp (Fiona MacLeod)* (London: William Heinemann, 1910), pp. 280-282; reprinted in Yeats's *Letters*, pp. 279-280.

52  Probably W. A. Henderson who was for years the secretary of the National Literary Society, contained in Henderson Ms. 1729, N.L.I.

53  W. B. Yeats, 'Plans and Methods', *Beltaine* (May 1899), pp. 6-9.

54  *Ibid.*

55  James H. and Margaret E. Cousins, *We Two Together* (Madras: Ganesh & Co. Ltd., 1950), p. 56. There is a discrepancy between this report and Moore's account in *Ave* that he was not in Ireland at this time.

56  Editorial, *The Daily Express* (13 May 1899), p. 4.

57  Editorial, *The Daily Nation* (6 May 1899), p. 4.

58  During the week of 8 May, the Irish Literary Theatre had the following competition from the commercial theatres. At the Gaiety, Mr. Herbert Sleath's Company from the Strand Theatre, London, was presenting 'the immensely successful American Farce' *What Happened to Jones* and an unnamed Comedietta. At the Theatre Royal, Mr. C. J. Abud's

148

Company from the Court Theatre, London, was holding the boards with *The Highwayman, Faithful James,* and *A Pantomime Rehearsal.* At the Queen's, Mr. Rollo Balmain's Company was appearing in 'the latest London Dramatic Success', *The Man in the Iron Mask.* The Empire Palace, 'Dublin's Premiere Amusement Palace', was presenting its usual 'Stupendous Attractions' and 'Sparkling Programme'. The feature artiste was Mlle. De Dio in 'She' or the Fire of Life, in which the audience was promised a 'Grand Transition of Youth and Beauty to a realisation of Charred Remains!' This spectacle, presumably suggested by Rider Haggard's novel, contained 'dazzling Electrical Effects' and was alleged to be 'one of the most expensive and Grandest Scenes Ever Witnessed in Dublin'. Among the 'Hosts of Stars' also on the Programme were the Robinson-Baker Trio, who were American scientific trick jumpers; Minnie Cunningham, 'Dublin's Little Idol'; Mr. Leo Dryden, 'Most Legitimate Vocal Actor on the Stage'; Manning and Prevost, comic acrobats; and Tennyson and O'Gorman, 'Leading Irish Comedians . . . (From all Principal London Halls)'. Among the 'Stupendous Attractions' at the Lyric Theatre of Varieties were Captain Devereaux's Company of Canine Comedians, and Les Karsy's Miraculous Myriophone ('The Marvellous Piece of Mechanism Breathes the Very Soul of Music, Specially Engaged for the Great Paris Exhibition of 1900, Now Shown for the first time in Ireland, a Magnificent Treat for the Lover of Music').

59  Cousins, *We Two Together,* p. 57.

60  Robert Hogan and Michael J. O'Neill, eds., *Joseph Holloway's Abbey Theatre* (Carbondale: Southern Illinois University Press, 1967), p. 6.

61  Seumas O'Sullivan, *The Rose and Bottle and Other Essays* (Dublin: The Talbot Press, 1946), pp. 119-120.

62  T. W. Rolleston, Letter, *The Freeman's Journal* (10 May 1899), p. 6.

63  'The Irish Literary Theatre', *The Freeman's Journal* (9 May 1899), p. 5.

64  'The Literary Theatre', *The Daily Express* (9 May 1899) p. 5.

65  Hogan and O'Neill, *Holloway's Abbey Theatre,* p. 7.

66  Michael Cardinal Logue, Letter to Editor, *The Daily Nation* (10 May 1899), p. 5.

67  Frederick Ryan, Letter to Editor, *The Irish Daily Independent* (11 May 1899), p. 3.

68  F. Hugh O'Donnell, 'Bowdlerizing the Countess', *The Daily Nation* (12 May 1899), p. 5.

69  Letter to Editor, *The Daily Nation* (10 May 1899), p. 5.

70  'The Irish Literary Theatre', *The Freeman's Journal* (10 May 1899), p. 5.

71 'The Irish Literary Theatre', *The Irish Times* (10 May 1899), p. 5.

72 Max Beerbohm, 'In Dublin', *The Saturday Review* (13 May 1899), pp. 587-588.

73 Moore, *Ave.*, pp. 94-95.

74 Hogan and O'Neill, *Holloway's Abbey Theatre*, p. 9.

75 'Irish Literary Theatre: Dinner at the Shelbourne Hotel', *The Daily Express* (12 May 1899), pp. 5-6.

76 Alice Milligan (14 September 1865 - 13 April 1953) was throughout her life a student of Irish language and culture. In Belfast she edited the *Shan Van Vocht* and later *The Northern Patriot*, both journals advocating the revival of Irish art and writing and Ireland's separation from England. She wrote several volumes of poetry, as well as a number of plays on Irish history and mythology, the best known of which is *The Last Feast of the Fianna*, produced by the Irish Literary Theatre in 1900. For a charming short reminiscence of her in her old age, see Benedict Kiely's article 'The Whores on the Half-doors' in *Conor Cruise O'Brien Introduces Ireland*, ed. Owen Dudley Edwards (London: Andre Deutsch, 1969), pp. 150-151.

77 'About six weeks ago an anonymous play in four acts about an old Irish story and a musical play with words by a nun, were acted in Letterkenny before enthusiastic audiences.' W. B. Yeats, 'The Irish Literary Theatre', *The Daily Express* (14 January 1899), p. 3. Most of this article was printed in a revised form as 'Plans and Methods', *Beltaine* (May 1899), pp. 6-9.

78 The Irish interlude of this play is printed in Appendix II, with its English translation.

79 Alice Milligan, Letter to Editor, *The Daily Express* (21 January 1899), p. 3.

80 'Imtheacht Conaill', *The Freeman's Journal* (19 November 1899), p. 6.

81 'A Gaelic Theatre', *Fainne an Lae* (4 February 1899), pp. 37-38.

82 'The Gaelic League Festival', *The Irish News and Belfast Morning News* (8 May 1898), p. 6.

83 'Tableaux Vivants at the Chief Secretary's Lodge', *The Daily Express* (26 January 1899), p. 5.
Yesterday evening and on Tuesday evening the Chief Secretary for Ireland and Lady Betty Balfour entertained a limited number of guests with a number of tableaux vivants based on Mr. W. B. Yeats's poetical play, *Countess Cathleen*. The salient points in the tragedy of the noble-hearted Countess were admirably condensed into a series of nine tableaux, commencing with the temptation and fall of Shemus Rua, and ending with a beautiful picture of Cathleen 'passing to the floor in

peace'. The various parts were taken by ladies and gentlemen who were in thorough sympathy with the Celtic inspiration of the poet, and the scenes were simply, yet richly staged. Historical accuracy was observed with regard to the dresses and ornaments, some of which were modelled on actual Celtic specimens preserved in our National Museum. Between, and sometimes during the tableaux the audience was delighted with old Irish songs and instrumental music. None who heard it last night will easily forget the splendidly sorrowful notes of the Celtic 'goll' or 'caoine', which was sung during the passing of the Countess. The striking success of the entertainment was proved by the fact that, although the silent art of the tableau is not the best medium for conveying the influence of a subtle literary atmosphere, last night's pictures were wonderfully effective in interpreting to the spectators something of that impalpable glamour which permeates the best work of Mr. Yeats and his school. To Lady Betty Balfour herself, the daughter and grand-daughter of poets, the prestige of this difficult literary accomplishment is very largely due.

84  'Trinity College and the Literary Theatre', *The Daily Express* (1 June 1899), p. 5.

# 1900

1  F. J. Fay, 'Pelléas et Mélisande at the Theatre Royal', *The United Irishman* (1 September 1900); reprinted in *Towards a National Theatre,* p. 44.

2  Val Vousden, *Val Vousden's Caravan* (Dublin: Cahill & Co. Ltd., 1941), pp. 13-16.

3  W. B. Yeats, 'The Irish Literary Theatre, 1900'. *Beltaine* (1900), pp. 22-24; reprinted from *The Dome* of January 1900.

4  W. B. Yeats, 'Plans and Methods', *Beltaine* (1900), pp. 3-6.

5  George Moore, 'Is the Theatre a Place of Amusement?', *ibid.,* pp. 7-10.

6  Edward Martyn, 'A comparison between Irish and English Theatrical Audiences', *ibid.,* p. 12.

7  Yeats, *ibid.,* p. 21.

8  Alice Milligan, 'The Last Feast of the Fianna', *ibid.,* pp. 20-21.

9  Lady Gregory, 'Last Year', *ibid.,* pp. 25-26.

10  Joseph Hone, *The Life of George Moore* (London: Victor Gollancz Ltd., 1936), p. 220.

11  Moore, *Ave,* pp. 166-167.

12  *Ibid.,* p. 278.

13  *Ibid.,* p. 284.

14  *Ibid.,* p. 285.

15  Hone, *Moore,* pp. 221-222.

16  'The Irish Literary Theatre', *The Freeman's Journal* (20 February 1900), p. 5.

17  'Irish Literary Theatre', *The Daily Express* (20 February 1900), p. 5.

18  *Ibid.*

19  The 'By the Way' column in *The Freeman's Journal* noted on 21 March 1907, that in this original production of *The Last Feast of the Fianna,* John O'Leary, Yeats's friend and the old Fenian leader, 'favoured the authoress by appearing amongst the band of warriors feasting at the banquet board. His appearance in the robes of a warrior of the ancient Fianna was particularly striking and appropriate, and, as this may have been his only appearance on the stage, it is pleasing to know that a photograph of him was taken as a memento of the occasion.' (p. 8)

In an article, 'Staging and Costume in Irish Drama', published in the 30 March 1904 issue of *Ireland's Own*, Alice Milligan noted that Grania in this production 'wore a rose-coloured sateen robe, dark-blue serge mantle, golden veil and ornaments'. She also remarked that the character of Niamh on this occasion 'wore a pale-green clinging robe, with silver lustre scarf and girdle, strings of pearl and iridescent shells, and a veil of filmy chiffon, clasped with a silver fillet'. And finally she remarked: 'I am here bound to confess as a dreadful warning to others that at *The Last Feast of the Fianna* in the Gaiety Theatre I forgot to arrange the bill of fare. There was not a scrap of food of any sort on the board in consequence.' (pp. 6-7)

20  'Irish Literary Theatre', *The Irish Daily Independent* (20 February 1900), p. 6.

21  'The Irish Literary Theatre', *The Irish Times* (20 February 1900), p. 6.

22  'The Irish Literary Theatre', *The Freeman's Journal* (21 February 1900), p. 5.

23  'Irish Literary Theatre', *The Irish Daily Independent* (21 February 1900), p. 5.

24  'Irish Literary Theatre', *The Daily Express* (21 February 1900), p. 5.

25  Holloway, *Impressions*, 20 February 1900, Ms. 1798, N.L.I.

26  'The Irish Literary Theatre', *The Irish Times* (21 February, 1900), p. 6.

27  James Cousins in *We Two Together* wrote: 'There were rumours that its authorship was either a composite affair or a plagiarism; and some confirmation of one or other of the rumours appeared to be found later when Mr. Martyn published *The Tale of a Town*. Both plays, it was whispered, were pilfered from Æ who told the original story to both Moore and Martyn.' (pp. 57-58)

28  'The Irish Literary Theatre', *The Irish Daily Independent* (22 February 1900), p. 4.

29  'The Irish Literary Theatre', *The Freeman's Journal* (23 February 1900), p. 6.

30  'Robert Emmet', *The United Irishman* (17 November 1900), p. 7.

31  Letters to Alice L. Milligan, Ms. 5048, National Library of Ireland.

32  *Ibid.*

33  'Dedication of St. Margaret's', *The Freeman's Journal* (26 November 1900), p. 5.

# 1901

1  'Inghinidhe na hEireann, Gaelic Tableaux Vivants', *The Freeman's Journal* (10 April 1901), p. 5.

2  Holloway, Impressions, 10 April 1901. Ms. 1799, N.L.I.

3  'Inghinidhe na hEireann, A Successful Entertainment', *The Freeman's Journal* (26 August 1901), p. 6. Miss Milligan's play was referred to by Dudley Digges as *'The Harp That Once* (and only once, thank God)'. Quoted in Fay and Carswell, p. 68.

4  'Gaelic Tableaux', *The Irish Daily Independent and Nation* (28 August 1901), p. 5.

5  P. T. MacGinley was an enthusiastic Gaelic Leaguer who at this time wrote three short plays which were published under the auspices of the Gaelic League. *Eilis agus an Bhean Deirce* has been translated into English and published under the title of *Lizzie and the Tinker*, in the collection *Lost Plays of the Irish Renaissance*, eds. Hogan and Kilroy (Dixon, California: Proscenium Press, 1970).

6  George Moore, *Ave*, p. 354.

7  George Moore, *Salve* (London: William Heinemann, 1912), p. 107.

8  *Ibid.*, p. 106.

9  Letter of George Moore to Douglas Hyde, written on 17 September 1901, in the possession of Robert Hogan. The correspondence referred to was prompted by a *Freeman's Journal* interview with George Moore on the question of why Elgar, rather than an Irish composer, was chosen. Summarized by the *Freeman*, his answer was: 'Because George Moore does not know any Irish musician who can write for orchestra except one in Paris, who is not available.' 'The Irish Literary Theatre', *The Freeman's Journal* (13 September 1901), p. 3.

10  Fay and Carswell, pp. 114-115.

11  Quoted in Hogan and O'Neill, *Holloway's Abbey Theatre*, p. 34.

12  Quoted in J. C. Trewin, *Benson and the Bensonians* (London: Barrie and Rockliff, 1960), p. 129.

13  Quoted in Lady Gregory, *Our Irish Theatre*, pp. 28-29.

14  Trewin, pp. 130-131.

15  W. B. Yeats, 'Windlestraws', *Samhain* (1901), p. 10. *Beltaine* was the old name for May, beginning of summer. It and Samhain were the two great feasts of the Celtic year. This passage is also to be found in *Explorations* (London, 1962), p. 84.

16  *Ibid.*, p. 9.

17  Footnote by W. B. Yeats: 'I do not want dramatic blank verse to be chanted, as people understand that word, but I do not want actors to speak as prose what I have taken much trouble to write as verse. Lyrical verse is another matter, and that I hope to hear spoken to musical notes in some theatre some day.'

18  George Moore, 'The Irish Literary Theatre', *Samhain* (1901), pp. 11-13.

19  Edward Martyn, 'A Plea for a National Theatre in Ireland', *Samhain* (1901), pp. 14-15.

20  Standish James O'Grady (1846-1928) was at this time the editor of the *All-Ireland Review*. In addition to his work mentioned in the chapter '1899', his trilogy, composed of *The Coming of Cuchulain, The Gates of the North* and *The Fall of Cuchulain*, gave also a fictionalized version of Celtic legends. See Hugh Art O'Grady's *Standish James O'Grady: The Man and the Writer* (Dublin and Cork: The Talbot Press Ltd., 1929), and Phillip L. Marcus, *Standish O'Grady* (Lewisburg: Bucknell University Press, 1970).

21  Standish O'Grady, 'The Story of Diarmid and Grania', *All-Ireland Review* (19 October 1901), p. 244.

22  George Moore was not, Yeats announced from the stage, in the house. However, in *Salve*, Moore writes that, although he had originally intended not to go, Frank Fay persuaded him to.

23  'The Irish Literary Theatre', *The Freeman's Journal* (22 October 1901), p. 4.

24  'Gaiety Theatre: The Irish Literary Theatre', *The Irish Times* (22 October 1901), p. 4.

25  'The Irish Theatre', *The Irish Daily Independent and Nation* (22 October 1901), p. 5.

26  M.A.M., 'Too Much Grania', *The Evening Herald* (22 October 1901), p. 2.

27  Frank J. Fay, 'The Irish Literary Theatre', *The United Irishman* (26 October 1901), p. 2; reprinted in *Towards a National Theatre*, p. 73.

28  Frank J. Fay, 'The Irish Literary Theatre', *The United Irishman* (2 November 1901), p. 2; reprinted in *Towards a National Theatre*, pp. 77-78.

29  *Ibid.*

30  'By the Way', *The Freeman's Journal* (24 October 1901), p. 4.

31  A typed article attributed to Cousins by W. A. Henderson, and contained in Henderson Ms. 1729, N.L.I.

32  Cousins, *We Two Together*, pp. 62-63.

155

33 'By the Way', *The Freeman's Journal* (24 October 1901), p. 4.

34 James Joyce, 'The Day of the Rabblement', *The Critical Writings of James Joyce,* eds. Ellsworth Mason and Richard Ellmann (London: Faber and Faber, 1959), p. 70.

35 *Ibid.,* p. 71.

36 *Ibid.,* pp. 71-72.

37 Frank J. Fay, 'The Irish Literary Theatre', *The United Irishman* (2 November 1901), p. 2; reprinted in *Towards a National Theatre,* p. 79.

38 Stephen Gwynn, 'The Irish Literary Theatre and its Affinities', *The Fortnightly Review* (1901), pp. 1055-58.

39 *Ibid.,* pp. 1058-59.

40 *Ibid.,* p. 1062.

41 Percy M. Young, *Elgar* (London: Collins, 1955), pp. 96-97.

42 *Ibid.,* p. 355.

43 John F. Porte, *Elgar and his Music* (London: Sir Isaac Pitman and Sons Ltd., 1933), pp. 86-87.

44 W. H. Reed, *Elgar* (London: J. M. Dent & Sons, Ltd., 1949), p. 64.

45 F. R. Benson, *My Memoirs* (London: Ernest Benn Ltd., 1930), p. 311.

46 *Ibid.*

47 'Irial' [Fred Ryan], 'Has the Irish National Theatre Failed?' *The United Irishman* (9 November 1901), p. 3.

48 'The Irish Literary Theatre, Interview with Mr. George Moore', *The Freeman's Journal* (13 November 1901), p. 5.

49 'Sacerdos', letter in *The Freeman's Journal* (14 November 1901), p. 4.

50 George Moore, letter to Editor in *The Freeman's Journal* (14 November 1901), p. 4.

51 W. B. Yeats, letter to Editor in *The Freeman's Journal* (15 November 1901), p. 4. Reprinted in Yeats's *Letters,* pp. 356-357.

52 George Moore, letter in *The Freeman's Journal* (16 November 1901), p. 5.

53 *Ibid.*

54 Max Beerbohm, *Around Theatres* (London: Rupert Hart-Davis, 1952), pp. 60-61.

# Index

157

Herford, C. H., 34.
Hill-Mitchelson, E. and Charles H. Longdon, 16.
*His Last Legs* (W. B. Bernard), 22.
*History of Ireland : Cuculain and His Contemporaries* (S. O'Grady), 8.
*History of Ireland : The Heroic Period* (S. O'Grady), 8-9.
Holloway, Joseph, 95, 146n. Quoted 14-17, 19, 22, 34, 40, 43, 48, 77-78, 89-90.
Hone, Joseph, Quoted 25, 31, 68.
Horniman, A. E. F., 24.
*The Hostage* (B. Behan), 17.
Hugo, Victor, 51.
*Humanity* (C. Locksley), 16-17.
Hyde, Douglas, 9, 48, 53, 80, 83, 85, 92-95, 96, 100, 102-104, 107, 114, 119, 123-124.

Ibsen, Henrik, 28, 65, 111, 121.
*Ideas of Good and Evil* (W. B. Yeats), 34.
*Il Fuoco* (G. D'Annunzio), 112.
Independent Theatre, 27-28, 34.
*The Irish Daily Independent*, 43. Quoted 46, 72, 75-76, 79, 91, 104.
*An Irish Gentleman* (D. C. Murray), 11.
Irish Language, 52-53, 81, 82-84, 90-91, 92-95, 102-104, 107, 112, 129.
Irish Literary Society of London, 9.
'The Irish Literary Theatre' (W. B. Yeats), 65.
*The Irishman* (J. W. Whitbread), 18.
Irish National Theatre Society, 21, 43, 117.
*The Irish News* and *Belfast Morning News*, Quoted 56-58.
*The Irish Times*, 45, 79, 94. Quoted 46-47, 73-75, 78-79, 104.
*The Irish Tutor* (R. Butler), 22, 85.
Irving, Henry, 89.
*The Island of Statues* (W. B. Yeats), 24.

Jacobsen, Jens Peter, 112.
*Jeannie Deans* (C. H. Hazlewood), 12.
*Jim, The Penman* (C. L. Young), 61.
Johnson, Lionel, 34, 36.
Johnston, Denis, 130.
Jones, Henry Arthur, 13.
Joyce, James, 40, 45, 111, 113. Quoted 111-112.
*Juno and the Paycock* (S. O'Casey), 17.

*Kathleen ni Houlihan* (W. B. Yeats), 85.
Kavanagh, Rose, 9.
Kickham, Charles J., 8.
*King Lear* (Shakespeare), 102.
*The King of Friday's Men* (M. J. Molloy), 17.
Kingston, Thomas, 46, 68.
Kipling, Rudyard, 52.
*Kitty Grey*, 123.

*The Lady of the House*, 23.
*The Lady of the Lake*, 12.
*The Lady of Lyons* (E. Bulwer-Lytton), 11.
*The Lake* (G. Moore), 129.
*The Land of Heart's Desire* (W. B. Yeats), 9, 24, 28, 83, 132.
Lang, Matheson, 96.

Larminie, William, 50.
*The Last Feast of the Fianna* (A. Milligan), 67, 70-74, 80, 118, 133-134.
Lawson, John, 16-17.
*The Laying of the Foundations* (F. Ryan), 117.
Lecky, W. E. H., 26.
*The Lily of Killarney* (J. Oxenford and D. Boucicault), 11.
*The Limerick Boy* (J. Pilgrim), 22.
*Literary History of Ireland* (D. Hyde), 9.
*The Little Minister* (J. M. Barrie), 11, 61.
*Little Miss Nobody* (H. Graham), 11.
*Little Red Riding Hood*, 14.
Lipton, Sir Thomas, 124.
Locksley, Charles, 16-17.
*The Love Songs of Connacht* (D. Hyde), 9.
Logue, Michael Cardinal, 31, 39, 49-50. Quoted 43.
Lyndal, Percy, 77.
*The Lyons Mail* (*Courier of Lyons*) (C. Reade), 89.

MacCarthy, Denis Florence, 35.
MacGinley, P. T., 55, 154n.
Mackay, Charles, 21.
'MacLeod, Fiona' (see William Sharp).
MacLiammóir, Micheál, 130.
*Madame Bovary* (G. Flaubert), 112.
Maeterlinck, Maurice, 65, 77.
*Maeve* (E. Martyn), 65, 68-69, 70-74, 80, 97, 99, 133.
*Magda* (L. N. Parker), 11.
Magee, W. K. (see John Eglinton).
*The Man of Forty* (Walter Firth), 10.
Mangan, James Clarence, 8.
Moody Manners Opera Company, 11.
*The Manoeuvres* (H. A. Jones), 13.
*Mariana* (Echegaray), 89.
Martyn, Edward, 24, 25-28, 30, 31, 33, 45-51, 54, 64-65, 82, 84, 87, 92, 96, 99, 111, 121, 125, 127-128. Quoted 66-67, 68-74, 100-101.
Matthews, E. C., 11-12.
Mayeur, Eugene, 77.
*The Merchant of Venice* (Shakespeare), 89.
*Midsummer Night's Dream* (Shakespeare), 65.
Miller, Kennedy, 19.
Milligan, Alice, 55, 56, 84, 85, 90-91, 150n, 152-153n. Quoted 52-54, 67.
Milligan-Fox, C., 72.
Molloy, M. J., 17.
Mollison, William, 12.
Moore, George, 27-28, 30, 33, 34, 36-37, 47, 48, 64, 75-79, 81, 84, 92, 95-96, 101, 102-118, 125-130. Quoted 24, 29-30, 51-52, 65-66, 68-70, 93-94, 95, 97-100, 115, 118-125, 126-127, 128.
Morrell, H. H., 10.
Morris, Fanny, 72.
*Mosada* (W. B. Yeats), 24.
Mouillot, Frederick, 10.
Murray, David Christie, 11.
Murray, Thomas E., 13.
Musset, Alfred de, 114.

National Literary Society, 9, 33, 80-85.
Nerney, Tom, 12.

New Theatre Royal, 9-12.
*The New World* (F. Darcy), 15.
*The Notorious Mrs. Ebbsmith* (A. W. Pinero), 11.

O'Byrne, Patrick, 54-55.
O'Casey, Sean, 17, 30, 130.
O'Connor, Frank, 130.
O'Donnell, F. Hugh, 31-33, 43. Quoted 31-33, 44-45.
O'Donoghue, Tadhg, 92.
O'Faolain, Sean, 130.
O'Grady, Standish, 8-9, 33, 35, 48, 106, 111, 155n. Quoted 101.
O'Growney, Fr. Eugene, 54.
O'Heynes, Maeve, 74.
*Oisin and Padraic* (A. Milligan), 134.
*Oisin in Tri-Nan-Oig* (A. Milligan), 134.
O'Kennedy, Miss, 93.
Oldham, Edith, 34.
O'Leary, John, 25, 48, 152n.
O'Leary, Fr. P., 119-120, 125.
Olympia Theatre, 20-21.
*The Only Way* (F. Wills), 11.
*On Shannon's Shore* (F. Cooke), 18-19.
*One of the Bravest*, 14.
O'Shea, C. J., 57.
O'Sullivan, Seumas, Quoted, 40
*Othello* (Shakespeare), 61,89.
*Our Irish Visitors*, 13.

*Paddy Miles* (J. Pilgrim), 22.
Paget, Dorothy, 34.
*La Parisienne* (Henri Becque), 89.
Parnell, C. S., 8, 31.
*The Passing of Conall* (E. O'Growney), 52, 54, 132.
*Pelléas and Mélisande* (M. Maeterlinck), 61, 78.
Pettitt, Henry and Sir Augustus Harris, 11.
Pinero, Arthur Wing, 13, 21.
'Plans and Methods' (W. B. Yeats), 34, 65.
*The Playboy of the Western World* (J. M. Synge), 17, 30.
*The Plough and the Stars* (S. O'Casey), 30.
*Poems and Ballads of Young Ireland*, 9.
Porte, John F. Quoted, 116.
*Les Précieuses Ridicules* (Moliere), 13.
*The Prodigal Daughter* (H. Pettitt and A. Harris), 11.

Queen's Royal Theatre, 14-20.
Quinn, Maire. Quoted, 85-86.

Reade, Charles, 14.
*The Rebels* (J. B. Fagan), 13-14.
Reed, W. H. Quoted, 116.
Rehan, Ada, 12.
Réjane, [Madame], 89.
*Robert Emmet* (R. Pilgrim), 85.
Robertson, Forbes, 61, 89.
Robinson, Lennox, Quoted, 8.
*Rob Roy MacGregor* (I. Pocock), 12.

162